JOHN KEATS'S
DREAM OF TRUTH

JOHN KEATS'S
DREAM OF TRUTH

By

JOHN JONES
Fellow of Merton College, Oxford

" The Imagination may be compared to
Adam's dream – he awoke and found it truth."

BARNES & NOBLE, Inc.
NEW YORK
PUBLISHERS & BOOKSELLERS SINCE 1873

PUBLISHED IN GREAT BRITAIN BY
Chatto & Windus Ltd.
42 William IV Street
London, W.C.2
*
First published in the United States of America, 1969
by Barnes & Noble, Inc.

SBN 389-01002-2

For
MY MOTHER

CONTENTS

I: THE FEEL I HAVE

1 First 1
2 Teignmouth and Around 2
3 Feel, Sex and *Isabella* 11
4 Negative Capability and again *Isabella* 16
5 The Merely Sensuous Man 32
6 Feel and Know 41

II: THE ABSTRACT IDEA

1 The Choice of a Word 69
2 *Hyperion* 74
3 *The Fall of Hyperion* 91

III: SNAILHORN PERCEPTION

1 To See as a God Sees 105
2 Sensation, Imagination, Intellect, Beauty, Truth, Pleasure 113
3 The 1817 Poems 122
4 *Endymion* 127

IV: HAVENS OF INTENSENESS

1 Natural Sculpture 150
2 Imagination Again 164
3 To Ripen or to Wither? 173
4 The Chief Intensity 189

V: THE LABYRINTHIAN PATH

1 Space, Time and the Odes 214
2 *The Eve of St. Agnes* and *Lamia* 232
3 *To Autumn* Revisited 260

POSTSCRIPT ON ROMANTIC FEELING 270-295

INDEX OF PERSONS 297

INDEX OF KEATS'S POEMS 301

I: THE FEEL I HAVE

1 First

THERE is a moment in *The Eve of St. Agnes* when Porphyro has hidden himself in Madeline's bedroom and she has undressed and got into bed:

> *Stol'n to this paradise, and so entranced,*
> *Porphyro gazed upon her empty dress,*
> *And listen'd to her breathing, if it chanced*
> *To wake into a slumberous tenderness. . . .*[1]

Inside a story of the flimsiest wish-fulfilling fantasy, convincing things happen. The "paradise" seems, and by itself is, nothing at all. But the absent body, somehow so creaturely, strikes like a sharp familiar pain through "her empty dress". Sex, we say; Keats and sex. And then the next two lines enfold sex in a larger, domestic yet sublime apprehension of the girl's breathing caught up into the living rhythm of sleep. The truth of that gentle paradox "wake" is Keats's mark. But truth to what? The moment is truly observed, and it is true to the dream of love, to our shyest thoughts about those we want to be near and to sleep with. We say sex at our peril. The effect is finally so ample and so tender. And there the word itself is, "slumberous tenderness". At once other tender Keatsian moments crowd forward, like the *Nightingale Ode's* "tender is the night", inevitable where it belongs and suddenly crass when Scott Fitzgerald makes the title of a novel out of it.

Our subject, then, is the dreaming man and the realist. The erotic poet whose sex dilates into fire and food and shelter and animal closeness, very personal and primitive, a sensual humanism. The poet wielding a vocabulary most potent when most idiosyncratic. I confess a superstitious awe of tenderness. More—and perhaps worse—than that, every section-heading of this book is a phrase from three consecutive sentences of a single letter he wrote: as if I thought his words, even in casual prose, might sometimes be enchanted. And in fact that is what I do think.

---

[1] Stanza XXVIII. All quotations are from H. W. Garrod's *Poetical Works of John Keats* (Oxford English Texts), second edition, 1958. I quote Keats's letters from *The Letters of John Keats*, ed. H. E. Rollins, 1958, with minor corrections to make reading easier.

2 *Teignmouth and Around*

The Spring of 1818 found Keats at Teignmouth on the South Devon coast. He was twenty-two, with his first volume of poems already published and the long verse romance *Endymion* finished and in the press. His own affairs had not taken him West and South, but the health of his younger brother Tom which demanded the mildest climate they could afford. While in truth Tom was dying, slowly, of consumption, his strength seemed up and down from week to week and even from day to day; so they hoped for the best, and when reason for hope was hard to find they tried to live in the present.

Down in Devon it rained and rained, as it can, and the brothers sat in their lodging and joked about the new scenes and names and faces. John had plenty of time for letter-writing. To one friend he gave the news "Atkins the Coachman, Bartlet the Surgeon, Simmons the Barber, and the Girls over the Bonnet shop say we shall now have a Month of seasonable Weather—warm, witty, and full of invention";[1] and to another, generalising in that vein of unforced worldliness, a strange thing in so young a man: "The Hedges by this time are beginning to leaf—Cats are becoming more vociferous—young Ladies that wear Watches are always looking at them—Women about forty five think the Season very backward".[2]

This was also the period in which he wrote some of the best remembered of all his letters—no valid division can be made into serious and trivial—beginning near the brink of his departure from London with the one to his publisher, John Taylor, in which he expounds his personal "axioms": of which the first is that "Poetry should surprise by a fine excess and not by Singularity", and the last and even more famous "That if Poetry comes not as naturally as the Leaves to a tree it had better not come at all".[3] Then on arrival at Teignmouth, in reply to his parson friend Bailey, a new curate anxious about his sermon: "You know my ideas about Religion. I do not think myself more in the right than other people, and that nothing in this world is proveable. . . . Now my dear fellow I must once for all tell you I have not one Idea of the truth of any of my speculations"[4]—thus betraying a scepticism which we recognise at once as first cousin to his

---

[1] *Letters*, vol. I, p. 246.   [2] *Ibid.*, p. 265.
[3] *Ibid.*, p. 238.   [4] *Ibid.*, p. 242.

worldliness, warmed by the same mature secular charity. Then to James Rice, his cheerful and witty drinking companion, but also a man cursed with ill health: "What a happy thing it would be if we could settle our thoughts, make our minds up on any matter in five Minutes and remain content—that is to build a sort of mental Cottage of feelings quiet and pleasant—to have a sort of Philosophical Back Garden, and cheerful holiday-keeping front one— but Alas! this can never be."[1] Then to John Hamilton Reynolds, another friend of near his own age, with the much-quoted affirmation, "I have not the slightest feel of humility towards the Public—or to any thing in existence—but the eternal Being, the Principle of Beauty,—and the Memory of great Men".[2] And finally on May the third, the last letter before the journey back to London and perhaps the finest in the Teignmouth canon, his meditation—again to Reynolds—on "this Chamber of Maiden Thought" and the other stages of what he calls "a simile of human life as far as I now perceive it".[3]

All these passages have been pored over. So has the one which I am particularly concerned with. It forms part of yet another of the Devonshire letters, and is Keats's reaction to news received from Benjamin Robert Haydon the painter that he has got his picture "Christ's Entry into Jerusalem" into a condition "better than I have ever had it yet—and in a good state to compleat it".[4] Keats replies:

I am nearer myself to hear your Christ is being tinted into immortality —Believe me Haydon your picture is a part of myself—I have ever been too sensible of the labyrinthian path to eminence in Art (judging from Poetry) ever to think I understood the emphasis of Painting. The innumerable compositions and decompositions which take place between the intellect and its thousand materials before it arrives at that trembling delicate and snail-horn perception of Beauty—I know not your many havens of intenseness—nor ever can know them—but for this I hope nought you achieve is lost upon me: for when a Schoolboy the abstract Idea I had of an heroic painting—was what I cannot describe I saw it somewhat sideways large prominent round and colour'd with magnificence—somewhat like the feel I have of Anthony and Cleopatra. Or of Alcibiades, leaning on his Crimson Couch in his Galley, his broad shoulders imperceptibly heaving with the Sea.[5]

Keats on Beauty; Keats on Poetry and Painting in a state of creative jostle. It is easy to understand the attention this passage has received. But my choice falls on five apparently unrelated

[1] *Ibid.*, p. 254.   [2] *Ibid.*, p. 266.   [3] *Ibid.*, p. 275.
[4] *Ibid.*, p. 258.   [5] *Ibid.*, p. 264.

details: "the labyrinthian path", "snail-horn perception", "havens of intenseness", "the abstract Idea", "the feel I have". The first three phrases are rather impressive; the others, especially the last, seem no more than odd. To anybody running an eye over this quintet, the inclusion let alone the preferring of the last will bear a perverse stamp.

Nevertheless "the feel I have" matters most because it bestows coherence on the whole group. All five come to make sense in the shadow of "feel". They resonate. They cease to be phrases and become the flavour of Keats, so definite a flavour that we may speak of their tight internal logic—without suggesting that an aesthetic theorist or some other kind of intellectual creature lies hidden in the letter to Haydon. The point, the general truth about Keats's letters, is that the self-confirming sensibility of the major poet who wrote them permeates their detail in unsuspected ways.

To begin then with that unpromising "feel", whose strangeness is at first sight so very mild that all interest seems to be concentrated in the cross-reference between poetry and painting,[1] while Keats's choice of this noun rather than the more usual "feeling" is a preference one wouldn't trouble to remark. The failure to take note is an unwitting admission that we stand passively in his shadow, and that we stand in it (so to speak) in a double sense: at once under his uniqueness and under his shared Romanticism. "Feel", we shall see, is Keats's word. "Feeling" is a Romantic word. Indeed I call feeling with its cognate verb *the* Romantic word,[2] but a word which has become so dulled and degraded that we need all the historical imagination we can muster in order to appreciate the fresh and challenging aspect it once had, and its sharp cutting edge in those battles of ideas which raged across Europe from the middle of the eighteenth century. When Ronald Knox chided the liberal theologians with their mealy-mouthed compromising of dogma and creed, who corrected "I believe" to "One does feel",[3] he indicated a vastly ramified process of enfeeblement in which theology is no more deeply implicated than politics or literature or metaphysics. In any twentieth-century context, the man who begins a sentence with "I do feel" can be convicted of mental free-wheeling. He may be playing for time. Perhaps he has nothing to say anyhow. His reader or listener folds his hands and waits for the show to start. But it was not

[1] "Anthony and Cleopatra" is of course Shakespeare's play. The description of Alcibiades rests on Plutarch.
[2] This belief is elaborated in my *Postscript on Romantic Feeling*.
[3] *Absolute and A Bit of Hell*.

always like that. The Wordsworthian solitary who had come to a pitch of Christian understanding in which he could claim to *"feel his faith"*,[1] was intended to mark a personal crisis of the greatest urgency (Wordsworth is a writer unlavish with his italics), and also a decisive victory for the process of natural education championed in *The Prelude* and elsewhere: a process in which "feeling comes in aid / Of feeling"[2] until, at the furthest reach of the egotistical sublime, "We feel that we are greater than we know".[3] And similarly with Coleridge—although here the crisis, while comparably important, is one of defeat and imaginative disaster—when he offers the following account of his troubles in the *Dejection Ode*:

> *I see them all so excellently fair,*
> *I see, not feel how beautiful they are.*

And with Shelley when he tells us the dead Adonais "is a presence to be felt"[4]—though when he adds "and known" the old issue of his mental slackness revives. And with Byron when he says

> *I live not in myself, but I become*
> *Portion of that around me; and to me*
> *High mountains are a feeling . . .*[5]

sounding the modish note which makes my point most neatly.

It would be easy but idle to multiply examples of crisis-occurrences of "feeling" and "to feel". They abound throughout Romantic Europe, and may be referred simultaneously and with equal force to Romanticism's historical origins and its theoretic *raison d'être*. If we seek, as some have sought, for a founding father of the movement, and want to know why Rousseau has much the strongest, though of course not an absolute, claim to that title, we must look first to the word "feeling" for our answer. Then if we ask why the thing called Romanticism should have happened at all, and decide that those authorities are broadly right who speak of a revolt against dryness and abstraction and rules, against the rationality of the age of reason, once again our most effective means of plotting the course of that revolt (or rather that series of revolts) is a close, patient, phenomenological study of the fortunes of feeling, *sentiment, Gefühl.*

---

[1] *The Excursion*, I, 226. [2] *The Prelude*, XII, 269.
[3] *The River Duddon*, Sonnet XXXIV.
[4] Stanza XLII. Compare with the *Dejection Ode* Shelley's *Defence of Poetry* where he argues that poetry "compels us to *feel* what we *perceive*".
[5] *Childe Harold's Pilgrimage*, III, lxxii.

5

An examination of the kind proposed would reveal, inevitably and soon, a formidable wealth of contrast. At the same time it would establish that fundamental accord which is denied by one party and upheld by the other in the contemporary debate over the usefulness of the term Romanticism. In an influential essay[1] the late A. O. Lovejoy argued that so many mutually opposed—not just different—things have to be included under the single heading Romanticism that we should acknowledge the concept to be worthless and abandon it forthwith. The stark nominalism of this view has provoked response, most notably from Professor René Wellek who set about demonstrating[2] a sufficient pan-European coherence in aims and achievements to justify our continuing to use the singular form of the word. But on both sides, and in the subsequent literature of this debate, there has been a lack of concern for the Romantic work done by feeling which strikes me, no doubt naturally, as astonishing and culpable.

Wellek, for example, deployed his evidence under the heads Nature, Imagination, Symbol, Myth. My Feeling is not among his four, let alone supreme. And yet the neglected word would prove more effective than any of Wellek's cherished ones in establishing the kind of underlying unity he and others of his persuasion are interested in. Limiting ourselves (since our subject is Keats) to Wordsworth's Wanderer and Coleridge's desponding self, we may observe a whole range of obvious surface differences contained within feeling's scope. The differences stem in one way or another from the contrasted situations of religious optimism and aesthetic pessimism. The unifying force I would ascribe to a certain straddling function which is always discernible in Romantic feeling. Coleridge and the Wanderer both postulate a condition of affective knowing, of heart-certainty; the one has to report failure, the other claims success, in the quintessentially Romantic exercise of preserving one's balance in the concept-lighted world of reason while securing a foothold in the trackless dark of the emotions. And the straddling word for this straddling deed is feeling. I do not know a single Romantic artist or *philosophe*, anywhere in Europe, who scruples to work it hard. Nor, by the same token

---

[1] "On the Discrimination of Romanticisms", *Proceedings of the Modern Language Association*, XXIX (1924); reprinted in his book *Essays in the History of Ideas*, 1948. Lovejoy offered another statement of his views in "The Meaning of Romanticism for the Historian of Ideas" (*Journal of History of Ideas*, II, 1941).

[2] In "The Concept of Romanticism in Literary History" published in *Comparative Literature*, I, 1949. See also his "Romanticism Re-examined" in *Romanticism Reconsidered*, ed. Northrop Frye, 1963.

(since the ambitious posture which feeling denotes is manifestly vulnerable), a single serious critic of the movement who does not attack the straddling effort itself, arguing that feeling—though he may not name the word—is either a pretentious synonym for emotion or an evasive and cowardly one for knowledge.

We have here a means of measuring the triumphs of Romanticism and analysing its failures, and noting its latterday debasement in Knox's perfectly representative "one does feel" where the hostile alternative must be pressed home: this is either a tarting up of emotional commitment to religion or it is a craven device to avoid affirming belief unambiguously. The cap fits, and we cannot avoid wearing it by maintaining, truly, that "one does feel" belongs nowadays with those inert and mindless locutions which scarcely emerge into consciousness. But to admit that much does not diminish Romanticism; it merely recognises that the tide of the great revolution still flows under us, carrying us along with the rubbish and dirty froth of its latest stages. Against which continuing thrust, the anti-Romantic or positively neo-classical sallies of the twentieth century have raised only a faint counter-ripple.

As I observed just now, it is because our assumptions remain so dominantly Romantic, and because the heart of Romanticism is feeling, that we have to use our historical imagination over Keats's "the feel I have". Just as it calls for conscious effort to appreciate what the Romantic invocation of feeling amounted to, so, when we speak of having the feel of a motor-car or a social situation or a sonata, such expressions are lodged deep in the tissue of our everyday linguistic habits, and we do not immediately see we are walking on private ground. Not that Keats was the first man to say "the feel I have", any more than the European Romantics invented feeling in any manageable, scientific sense of 'invent'. In his case as in theirs, what matters is the impressing of a literary *persona* upon a usage, the difference being that the *persona* stamped on feeling is generic, it is the diversified unity of Romanticism itself, while the figure we see on the other is Keats's own.

His features may be traced in one of the earliest and worst poems to survive. Sir Gondibert, a character in the feeble Spenserian fiction *Calidore*,

> *has doff'd his shining steel,*
> *Gladdening in the free and airy feel*
> *Of a light mantle—*[1]

[1] L. 138.

an example of the kind of thing that falls complacently on a twentieth-century ear (for we all talk about the airy feel of light clothing) but which struck contemporaries as tiresome to the point of freakishness and licence. We have a record of one educated, sober contemporary expressing himself forcibly about feel. Richard Woodhouse was a devoted admirer of Keats's work, and for that reason the evidence of his opinion is more valuable than the strictures of the reviewers in *Blackwood's* and the *Quarterly*, who were trying to find fault. He also knew Keats's writing better than anybody else, having studied it and transcribed much of it—some of it several times over. Woodhouse says:

I plead guilty, even before I am accused, of an utter abhorrance of the word "feel" for feeling (substantively). But Keats seems fond of it and will ingraft it "in aeternum" on our language. Be it so.[1]

His words suggest gloomy resignation, and no doubt he managed to maintain that attitude in the face of such occurrences as Gondibert's "airy feel" or Endymion's "deadly feel of solitude".[2] But there was one "feel", the occasion of the present statement, which proved too much for him; he had to turn poet and redraft the final stanza of the lyric "In a drear-nighted December":

> *Ah! would 'twere so with many*
> *A gentle girl and boy!*
> *But were there ever any*
> *Writh'd not at passed joy?*
> *The feel of not to feel it,*
> *When there is none to heal it,*
> *Nor numbed sense to steel it,*
> *Was never said in rhyme.*

Some will sympathise with Woodhouse in his inability to swallow "the feel of not to feel it". And certainly everyone will respect him for not foisting his own version on Keats when he transcribed the poem, a thing he did no less than three times. This honesty, altogether characteristic of him, seems to have been lacking in the person who, in 1829 with Keats eight years dead, provided a pair of literary periodicals (the *Gem* and the *Literary Gazette*) with a version of the lyric in which the offending line is replaced by "To know the change and feel it". A desire not to print the only version we can be sure Keats wrote has been evident throughout, and is with us still. In 1939 was published H. W. Garrod's definitive edition of the poems. There Garrod printed "To know the change and

[1] *The Keats Circle* (1948), ed. H. E. Rollins, vol. I, p. 64.
[2] *Endymion*, II, 284

feel it", in the teeth not merely of the three Woodhouse transcripts but of Keats's autograph—the only one then known. On his side was nothing that could be ascribed with any confidence to the poet, or even dated from his lifetime.[1] Nineteen years later, in 1958, came the second edition of Garrod's book. In the meantime another autograph had been discovered,[2] and this confirmed "the feel of not to feel it" while recording in its margin, in a hand which is certainly not Keats's, the favoured *Gazette* version. Nevertheless Garrod persisted in his earlier course.

I mention this not in order to pick holes in Garrod's admirable work, but to dramatise the fate of 'feel'. Was Woodhouse's initial complaint a matter of taste in words and nothing more, and is the contemporary question a loftier but still restricted problem of textual scholarship? Woodhouse appears not to have entertained the thought that this perverse preference of Keats's might be worth going into. Nor, probably, did it occur to Garrod, or the other editors who over the years have printed the *Gazette* version, that their decision threatened them with wider repercussions, critical and interpretative.

The contention that Keats did not just happen to prefer 'feel' takes us back to the little batch of Teignmouth letters. He was telling the painter Haydon about his feel of Shakespeare's *Antony and Cleopatra*, and of Alcibiades lying in his galley as Plutarch describes him. He was also denying he had "the slightest feel of humility towards the Public". Then there was the letter he wrote Reynolds that wet Spring, on the morning after the one to Haydon:

Devonshire continues rainy. As the drops beat against the window, they give me the same sensation as a quart of cold water offered to revive a half drowned devil—No feel of the clouds dropping fatness; but as if the roots of the Earth were rotten cold and drench'd.[3]

And another, earlier complaint about the Teignmouth weather:

This devonshire is like Lydia Languish, very entertaining when at smiles, but cursedly subject to sympathetic moisture. You have the

---

[1] Two transcripts give "To know the change and feel it". The first (Garrod's "Hampstead transcript") is probably copied from the *Literary Gazette*. If so, it has no authority. The other appears in a volume compiled in 1828 by two members of the Keats circle, J. C. Stephens and Isabella Jane Towers. The *Gazette* and the *Gem*, which printed independently of each other, must, one admits, have got their copy from somewhere. Garrod asks (lvii): "For if Keats himself did not write the *Gazette* version, who did?" The answer is, we don't know.

[2] By Mr Alvin Whitley, who announced his find in the *Harvard Library Bulletin* (1951).

[3] *Letters*, vol. I, p. 267.

sensation of walking under one great Lamplighter: and you can't go on the other side of the ladder to keep your frock clean, and cosset your superstition.[1]

And finally, in yet another letter:

We are here still enveloped in clouds—I lay awake last night listening to the Rain with a sense of being drown'd and rotted like a grain of wheat.[2]

This sampling has already presented us with the feel of light clothes, of solitude, humility, a Shakespeare play, Alcibiades, and continuing wet weather. Moreover the last three letters break out of the shell of language into another state where sensibility remains committed to feel but is no longer tethered to the word. In the first, 'feel' and 'sensation' are found together. In the second 'sensation' has taken over. In the third we have moved on to 'sense'. But the single unremitting focus of all three is feel.

Keatsian feel is obviously catholic in the range of feeling-situations which it embraces; there can be no question of it identifying some refined or specialised application of the broad term 'feeling'. Now the width of feel goes hand in hand with a kind of stuntedness, and I mean to lay great stress on this particular coupling because it is the width that places Keats at the heart of the Romantic movement and the stuntedness that isolates him utterly. Romantic feeling-situations are everywhere in Keats, but they are subject to a process of guillotining which effects in the one stroke a physical truncation of the word feeling and a delimitation of his genius. The most direct road to his originality lies through the question, what does his feel mean? This provokes the answer that it bears the universal Romantic stamp of heart-certainty, but stands alone in being a heart-certainty about nothing beyond itself. When Keats talks about the feel of solitude or of Shakespeare, he conveys to us no insights into those promising subjects; all truth is contained in, and all attention bent upon, the feel he has of them. His imaginative energy is driven back upon itself, and his talent fulfilled and exhausted in a very special self-guaranteeing exercise.

Romantic feeling, in contrast, drags a 'what' or 'how' or 'why' in its train. The Wanderer's affirmative feeling directs us to the 'what' of his religious belief, and Coleridge's failure of feeling to the 'how' of "how beautiful" the natural appearances are which he sees and describes. The essential characteristic of Romantic feeling is its open-endedness, and the true justification for calling it *the* Romantic word is that we find it to be *the* perspective along which

---

[1] *Letters*, vol. I, p. 245.   [2] *Ibid.*, p. 273.

we look when we read the European Romantic writers; and indeed it easily happens that we become so dominated by this body of great literature as to forget that feeling is our perspective of the moment and take it for the very light we see by, at all times, everywhere. Hence, I suspect, the failure of well-informed men like Lovejoy and Wellek to attend to it. For reading the famous lines

> *I have felt*
> *A presence which disturbs me with the joy*
> *Of elevated thoughts*

is like looking through a perfectly clean window at an absorbing spectacle. That spectacle may be called either the mystical experience of *Tintern Abbey* or the Wordsworthian 'what' which his generic Romantic feeling brings in its train. We have eyes only for the 'what', the experience, and we tend to lose all awareness of the frame "I have felt" within which the experience takes place. This is the reason for calling Romantic feeling open-ended, and the force of the contrast with Keats's end-stopped feel. Nor must we let grammar and syntax deceive us. Wordsworth's "I felt and nothing else"[1] is nevertheless open-ended, while the end-stopping of Keats's

> *Do gently murder half my soul, and I*
> *Shall feel the other half so utterly!*[2]

is not affected by the fact that the verb has an object.

3 Feel, Sex and 'Isabella'

Keats's blatant eroticism has often been remarked, and I would simply add that end-stopped feel lies at the root of the trouble—in so far as it is a trouble. For his weakness is from the outset entangled with his strength. In his later and better work it soon becomes clear, I think, that the erotic phenomenon is only part of a much bigger question of the potent, disconcerting[3] directness and credibility his end-stopping wins for him. But early on, in the 1817 volume and *Endymion*, the feeling and fondling and tasting, all difficult to escape from, very often appear hopelessly servile to sex.

---

[1] *The Prelude* (1805), XI, 238.   [2] *Endymion*, IV, 309.
[3] The word *disconcerting* is used very effectively by Mr John Bayley in "Keats and Reality" (Proceedings of the British Academy, 1962). This is one of my large debts to his essay.

Sometimes there is no more to be said, the appearance is the joyless reality. Sometimes, without taking the sex away, Keats removes the boring constriction; his reader is left with a nameless sensual pungency, a strong smell which asserts itself not primarily because he can be an effective erotic poet when he likes (as he unquestionably can) but because he is always, potentially, our great English exponent of the larger thing.

The importance of this priority can scarcely be exaggerated. To take some bearings from a very early poem, mild and unsexual:

> *Lo! I must tell a tale of chivalry;*
> *For while I must, the lance points slantingly*
> *Athwart the morning air: some lady sweet,*
> *Who cannot feel for cold her tender feet,*
> *From the worn top of some old battlement*
> *Hails it with tears, her stout defender sent:*
> *And from her own pure self no joy dissembling,*
> *Wraps round her ample robe with happy trembling.*[1]

None of this is good, but it is obviously Keats; while not literature it is *quelque chose*, and the explanation rests in the gratuitous yet characterful feel-situations of the cold feet and the robe wrapped round. Run a pen through the fourth and the last lines and the whole thing lapses into nonentity. Then, any suburban Regency Petrarch, any admirer of Leigh Hunt, might have perpetrated it. And the Keatsian imprint of those two lines is feel.

Still within the 1817 volume, but moving closer to sex:

> *Soon they awoke clear eyed: not burnt with thirsting,*
> *Nor with hot fingers, nor with temples bursting:*
> *And springing up, they met the wond'ring sight*
> *Of their dear friends, nigh foolish with delight;*
> *Who feel their arms, and breasts, and kiss and stare,*
> *And on their placid foreheads part the hair.*[2]

Closer to sex because, of course, of the feeling of arms and breasts and the kissing. Nevertheless the passage is dominated by a logic other than sex's, not merely through the obvious succession of parching, heat and bursting in the middle, but also the eyes and foreheads at either end of the series. Keats's draft of the first line, reading "Nor heated Eyes", supplies the private hint that his poetry transforms the eye from an organ of outward sense to one of inner touch-and-taste, active and passive, feeler and felt. Eyes are there to be kissed in Keats ("kist each other's tremulous eyes"),[3] to

---

[1] "Specimen of an Induction to a Poem", 11.
[2] "I stood tip-toe", 225   [3] *Ibid.*, 146.

be "shut softly up alive",[1] to contain "a dewy luxury",[2] to be "breathed upon"[3] and "rain'd violets upon".[4] "We put our eyes into a pillowy cleft"[5]—we do no sustained ordinary seeing with our eyes in his universe, apart from the deliberate exception of *Lamia*. Whence derives the sheer oddness of the invocation "Oh ye! who have your eye-balls vexed and tired" in the sonnet on the sea, and also the tiny but unmistakable gesture in the "Song of Four Fairies":

> *Sprite of Fire, I follow thee*
> *Wheresoever it may be,*
> *To the torrid spouts and fountains,*
> *Underneath earth-quaked mountains;*
> *Or, at thy supreme desire,*
> *Touch the very pulse of fire*
> *With my bare unlidded eyes.*

As with eyes, so with foreheads: from the tiresome reiterations of the 1817 volume ("He bares his forehead to the cool blue sky",[6] "With forehead to the soothing breezes bare"),[7] through some weird occurrences, again not good but characterful, in which the forehead is endowed with a kind of sensitiveness foreign to its ordinary self but proper to an organ of feel ("Holding his forehead, to keep off the burr / Of smothering fancies"),[8] through open in-dulgencies of feel like "more near against the marble cold / He had touch'd his forehead"[9] and masked ones like "with forehead 'gainst the window-pane",[10] to the famous things in mature Keats: "Nor suffer thy pale forehead to be kiss'd" in *Melancholy*, and "A burning forehead and a parching tongue" in the *Grecian Urn*.

Obviously one can't be expected to read all this into the un-adorned eyes and foreheads of that "I stood tip-toe" passage from 1817; I only mean to suggest that the logic of feel has an embryonic completeness which would otherwise go unsuspected. Even so, enough lies on the surface for us to judge the relative emphasis of feel and sex. In an age of popularised Freud, the fashionable argument would be—and in various Keatsian contexts often has been—that his presenting a passage like this in the form of a re-union of "dear friends" is an unconscious bluff; that its real sub-stance is self-indulgent erotic daydream; that the feeling and kiss-ing give him away. Convinced that this assessment is exactly wrong, I would reply that the erotic suggestion of the feeling and

---

[1] *Endymion*, IV, 104. [2] *Ibid.*, II, 676. [3] *Lamia.*, I, 124.
[4] *Endymion*, II, 427. [5] *Isabella*, XLI. [6] *Calidore*, 6.
[7] *To My Brother George*, 56. [8] *Endymion*, II, 138.
[9] *Ibid.*, II, 265. [10] *Eve of St. Mark*, 49.

kissing is a faintly comical misjudgment on the young poet's part, arising from the fact that his narrative has been pulled into the orbit of feel. The show of sex in his work is often a side-effect of the plausibility which stamps the end-stopping process; and precisely this plausibility gives its touch of character to the present passage. For "on their placid foreheads part the hair" really is an extraordinary idea. Who but Keats? The size, stillness, the naïve *sexless* dignity of those foreheads are a step on the road to the intensely personal classicism of the gods and goddesses in *Hyperion*. And indeed it is easy to reproduce the unintended comedy, as well as the touch of character—the thing that exclaims "Keats!"—by isolating lines and phrases in his latest, most carefully finished work—

> *She press'd her fair large forehead to the earth—*[1]

just as it is easy, early and late, to show the erotic imagination wide awake and active.

But still, what chiefly deserves notice is the concentration of sexual power in the vocabulary of feel, in contrast with the inertia of the rest. Only the verb has any life in this 1817 couplet:

> *Small good to one who had by Mulla's stream*
> *Fondled the maidens with the breasts of cream;*[2]

and in the notorious cry, "Those lips, O slippery blisses",[3] it would be hard to devise a paler abstraction than "blisses" or a feel-adjective of sharper bite than "slippery". I believe his language always works like this where, against the main tenor, feel is the servant of sex rather than sex a planet, and a great one, revolving round feel's sun.

To remark an aura of helpless sleep-walking innocence to Keats's feel is not to impute some sort of guilt to his sex, but simply to subordinate sex as one lays the hand of criticism on his power to achieve effects of broad generosity and disinterest—and to do this against apparently hopeless odds. The most striking example, though by no means his best work, is a revolting story taken from Boccaccio, *Isabella*. And *Isabella* has the further interest that it was written immediately after the immature *Endymion* and before the later things which found their way, most of them, into the book of poems published in 1820.

The girl Isabella has a lover who is tricked away from her by his enemies and murdered and secretly buried. She sets out with her old nurse, finds the grave, digs down to the body and cuts off the

---

[1] *Fall of Hyperion*, I, 379.   [2] *To Charles Cowden Clarke*, 33.
[3] *Endymion*, II, 758.

head which she takes home and hides in the bottom of a garden-
pot; and she

> cover'd it with mould, and o'er it set
>
> Sweet basil—[1]

hoping thus to have the head by her always, and cherish it un-
disturbed. The centre of horror is the exhuming of the corpse:

> Soon she turn'd up a soiled glove, whereon
> Her silk had play'd in purple phantasies,
> She kiss'd it with a lip more chill than stone,
> And put it to her bosom, where it dries
> And freezes utterly unto the bone
> Those dainties made to still an infant's cries:
> Then 'gan she work again; nor stay'd her care,
> But to throw back at times her veiling hair.
>
> That old nurse stood beside her wondering,
> Until her heart felt pity to the core
> At sight of such a dismal labouring,
> And so she kneeled, with her locks all hoar,
> And put her lean hands to the horrid thing:
> Three hours they labour'd at this travail sore;
> At last they felt the kernel of the grave,
> And Isabella did not stamp and rave.[2]

And while no two stanzas can show how this unpleasant story is
tamed by art and sometimes rendered very beautiful, the couple
in front of us do force upon the judgment a decisive alternative. In
fact it is impossible to start reading the poem at any point without
quickly having to decide whether the object under contemplation
is the work of a sick erotic fancy, or something very like such a
work on the surface and very different underneath. In our stanzas
the alternative voices itself as a choice between taking the
kissing of the glove as a rather obscene necrophiliac key to the
whole or as a link in the chain of feel which extends from the initial
insistence on temperature, through the touching action of "put"
with its verbal and physical repetition in the next stanza, to the
even bolder duplication of "felt" in its symmetrical balancing of
inward feel towards the heart's "core" and outward feel towards
the grave's "kernel". Altogether an interesting test case. "At last
they felt the kernel of the grave" is a blazing inspiration, plain
enough, but it is not easy to say why. The verbal sumptuousness,
the standard Keats, of "Her silk had play'd in purple phantasies"
looks small beside it. One runs one's eye back and notes the

---

[1] Stanza LII.   [2] XLVII and XLVIII.

emotional ground-swell building up under the commonplace little "felt". The point I made a moment ago about the vital feel-situation and the dead (sexual) remainder, is illustrated by the freezing and especially the drying touch in contrast with the almost unbelievable vulgar fatuity of "Those dainties made to still an infant's cries"—though the turn towards family and home is an omen of greatness. It might be argued that "dries" is a forced move; Keats needs a rhyme for "phantasies", the word he relishes. The moral, however, is not that "dries" should be dismissed as outlandish, but that the emergency which sends Keats out looking for a rhyme is the one which drives him into the heart of his instinctive self-certainty, to cling there. Such saving moments of crisis will be met with again; and the dominating feel-effect of temperature will also reappear, but shorn of its present crudity, in the "bitter chill" of *St. Agnes*, the sharp April air and "immatur'd green vallies cold" of *St. Mark*, the opposed cool and fever of the *Nightingale Ode*, and the hanging warmth of *Autumn*—just as *Autumn* will bring together the "core" and "kernel" of the second stanza and fulfil their latent consummatory impulse, their inclining towards ripeness and completion which has helped to establish our obscure but very ample satisfaction in "At last they felt the kernel of the grave".

4 Negative Capability and again 'Isabella'

I want to isolate, from our two stanzas of *Isabella*, the picture of the heroine throwing back her hair as she digs. So far I have confined the discussion of end-stopped feel more or less within the limits which vocabulary dictates. Temperature was a slight extension beyond the overt "feel I have". And now Isabella introduces Keats's human beings—the feel he has of other people.

He coined his own name for it: Negative Capability. The phrase only appears once, and to understand what he meant by it we have to assemble four passages from four different letters.

Brown & Dilke walked with me & back from the Christmas pantomime. I had not a dispute but a disquisition with Dilke, on various subjects; several things dovetailed in my mind, & at once it struck me, what quality went to form a Man of Achievement especially in Literature & which Shakespeare possessed so enormously—I mean *Negative Capability*, that is when man is capable of being in uncertainties, Mysteries, doubts, without any irritable reaching after fact & reason—

Coleridge, for instance, would let go by a fine isolated verisimilitude caught from the Penetralium of mystery, from being incapable of remaining content with half knowledge.[1]

As to the poetical Character itself (I mean that sort of which, if I am anything, I am a Member; that sort distinguished from the Words-worthian or egotistical sublime; which is a thing per se and stands alone) it is not itself—it has no self—it is every thing and nothing—It has no character—it enjoys light and shade; it lives in gusto, be it foul or fair, high or low, rich or poor, mean or elevated—It has as much delight in conceiving an Iago as an Imogen. What shocks the virtuous philosopher, delights the camelion Poet. It does no harm from its relish of the dark side any more than from its taste for the bright one; because they both end in speculation. A Poet is the most unpoetical of any thing in existence; because he has no Identity—he is continually in-forming and filling some other Body. The Sun, the Moon, the Sea and Men and Women who are creatures of impulse are poetical and have about them an unchangeable attribute—the poet has none; no identity —he is certainly the most unpoetical of all God's Creatures. If then he has no self, and if I am a Poet, where is the Wonder that I should say I would write no more? Might I not at that very instant have been cogitating on the Characters of Saturn and Ops? It is a wretched thing to confess; but is a very fact that not one word I ever utter can be taken for granted as an opinion growing out of my identical nature—how can it, when I have no nature? When I am in a room with People, if I ever am free from speculating on creations of my own brain, then not myself goes home to myself: but the identity of every one in the room begins so to press upon me that I am in a very little time annihilated— not only among Men; it would be the same in a Nursery of children: I know not whether I make myself wholly understood: I hope enough so to let you see that no dependence is to be placed on what I said that day.[2]

In passing however I must say one thing that has pressed upon me lately and encreased my Humility and capability of submission, and that is this truth—Men of Genius are great as certain ethereal Chemicals operating on the Mass of neutral intellect—but they have not any individuality, any determined Character.[3]

Now the first political duty a Man ought to have a mind to is the happiness of his friends. I wrote Brown a comment on the subject, wherein I explained what I thought of Dilke's Character. Which resolved itself into this conclusion. That Dilke was a Man who cannot

[1] *Letters*, vol. I, p. 193.
[2] *Ibid.*, p. 386. Near the middle, "informing" is an emendation proposed by George Beaumont (*Times Literary Supplement*, 27 February and 1 May, 1930). The text reads "in for". And "so to press", near the end, is J. C. Maxwell's sug-gestion (*Notes and Queries*, 17 May, 1947). Here the text has "to to press".
[3] *Ibid.*, p. 184.

THE FEEL I HAVE

feel he has a personal identity unless he has made up his Mind about
every thing. . . . Dilke will never come at a truth as long as he lives;
because he is always trying at it.[1]

So the story of Negative Capability opens and closes with Keats's
Hampstead neighbour Charles Wentworth Dilke, who had once
earned his living (like Dickens's father) as a clerk in the Navy Pay
Office; and the story is haunted throughout by Shakespeare, who
appears *in propria persona* in the first passage, under the guise of Iago
and Imogen in the second, among the unnamed "Men of Genius"
in the third, and by implicit contrast with poor Dilke in his inability to "come at a truth" in the last. The parallel between Coleridge discontented with half-knowledge and Dilke needing to make
up his mind about everything is obvious. Indeed I suspect that
from the outset, the real contrast, as Keats listened to Dilke airing
his views on the way to the pantomime and back, was between his
companion of the moment and the Shakespearean type; and that
Keats's regard for a very good friend caused him to take Coleridge
instead—the garrulous and prematurely aged Coleridge who was
once to walk with Keats "at his alderman-after-dinner pace for
near two miles I suppose. In those two miles he broached a thousand things. . . . I heard his voice as he came towards me—I heard
it as he moved away—I had heard it all the interval—if it may be
called so".[2]

Anyhow, "Dilke's Character"[3] had to wait nearly two years
after the Negative Capability letter for its exposition. And whatever may have been Keats's opinions and intentions as between
Dilke and Coleridge, he has left these four scattered statements
which together make adequate sense. The reference to Wordsworth, the single great exception, remains beautifully mysterious
and urgent with possibilities; but we have an unambiguous outline
of the norm of poetic genius which Keats calls Negative Capability, and within which—quite clearly and firmly for all his
modest tact—he places himself.

Various imaginative writers have said that the way to make
your characters live is to respect their freedom.[4] Keats's "negative"
poet, flanked by the images of the cameleon and the chemical sub-

---

[1] *Letters*, vol. II, p. 213.   [2] *Ibid.*, p. 88.
[3] Dilke had a distinguished career as a literary and political journalist, and
could not be called a prosaic man. His wife was very good fun. Keats records
fighting a battle with her with celery stalks (*Letters*, vol. II, p. 30).
[4] Henry James most memorably, to my mind, in his essay on Balzac and his
characters: "It was by loving them—as the terms of his subject and the nuggets
of his mine—that he knew them; it was not by knowing them that he loved."

stance, is his version of this widely affirmed truth. Like the others, he recognises that the thing you must leave alone and admire in its separate existence—the thing you must love—is also the thing you are in the throes of making. His "conceiving an Iago" grasps the nettle firmly. This reasserts the built-in paradox of Negative Capability, as it silently confronts the rest of the world's Positive Incapacity.

Keats's version is nevertheless a very singular one. We tend to talk about writers 'getting inside' their creation as if this were a single talent which they shared and whose working were roughly the same in each of them. But, of course, a moment's thought opens up a gulf between the drama and the novel. The physicalities of theatre that rush forward to serve Shakespeare when he does something as simple as make Macbeth look down at his hands and say "This is a sorry sight", can in no circumstances be made available to the novelist. Whereas Tolstoy, on his side, inhabits a perfectly non-dramatic universe when his author's voice informs us that the music running through Petya Rostov's head before he rode forward to his death was a fugue, the same voice adding that Petya did not in fact know that this was the name for it. Or Tolstoy's unhurried account of Dolly at Anna's house experiencing, beneath her very keen embarrassment at her shabby clothes and dull ways, an uncondemning knowledge of her own life's rightness. These are examples of the highest art; and Nicholas's fugue a particularly neat and triumphant demonstration of the artist's power, if only he is great enough, to lay down the law for a character without destroying that character's freedom for a reader. Naturalism is neither here nor there. A convincing impossibility makes better art, as Aristotle said, than a possibility we can't believe in; and sophistication finds it hard to add anything useful to the simple man's simple statement that he believes in Macbeth and Dolly and Nicholas.

All belief does not taste the same, though, and my theme is the distinguishable conviction that attends Keats's end-stopped feel. In the context of his achievements in Negative Capability (as opposed to his theorising, which is also highly individual), this conviction emerges with Isabella when

> 'gan she work again; nor stay'd her care,
> But to throw back at times her veiling hair.

We are not given what she thought about at this moment of crisis but what she felt, and what she felt was the impeding and obscuring curtain of hair in her eyes as she bent forward over her task. It would also be true to say that Tolstoy gives us what Dolly felt as she bent forward over *her* task of deciding what to wear; but we cannot begin to discuss that rich freight of meaning without running an eye before and after, along the imagined, historical curve of her sensibility. Thus we involve ourselves in a shorthand appraisal of Dolly's private destiny. Dolly and Macbeth (for the gap between dramatic and novelistic creation has a bridge across it) live by convincing development towards credible ends. But Isabella enjoys no temporal reality at all, which means that we, reading, can grasp no scheme of ends, no natural teleology, to credit her with. Keats's creative act is a closed circuit, exhausting itself in a single apprehension of the blinding feel of hair. This is the imaginative stroke we are praising when we call his picture convincing or realistic or what we will.

Then if end-stopping is the essence of Negative Capability, how does Keats sustain his human beings once he 'gets inside' them? What becomes of that consciousness which we know and test and in effect define by its seemless continuity—a continuity at the heart of old achievements and new departures, of the nineteenth-century novel and of Proust and Joyce? What of truth to self? Leisurely novelistic truth or the foreshortened truth of Shakespeare's poetry? Or truth to the self that lies beneath a surface of contraries, as in Lawrence and Ibsen and Dostoevski?

The disappointing answer is that we must admit a very crucial sense in which there are no human beings in Keats's poetry. Some quaint wording in the second Negative Capability passage merits attention at this point, for it is his way of talking about 'getting inside' his creation. He says that the poet is continually "filling some other Body". Now "body" has a strangely non-committal ring, and we see why when he proceeds to sweep in the sun and moon and sea together with men and women. Naturally that is not a complete list. Richard Woodhouse made some notes on Negative Capability, stating:

He has affirmed that he can conceive of a billiard ball that it may have a sense of delight from its own roundness, smoothness and very volubility, and the rapidity of its motion.[1]

In short, Keats could have filled that body.

Anchoring Negative Capability to a billiard ball may seem frivolous, and so may wondering what he could have made of it

---

[1] *The Keats Circle*, ed. H. E. Rollins, vol. I, p. 59. Woodhouse thought this record interesting enough to repeat it in slightly different terms (*The Keats Circle*, vol. I, p. 275).

poetically: the delicious feel of the cloth, the cue's touch, the clack against its brothers, the kiss of the cushion, the deep snuggling repose of the pocket "more secret than a nest of nightingales";[1] and the thing itself

> *Full, and round like globes that rise*
> *From the censer to the skies*
> *Through sunny air—*[2]

or "globed" simply like the peonies of *Melancholy* and the human brain—the physical object—of his *Fall of Hyperion*.

But consider "my globed brain".[3] Compare it with those tender foreheads, and the human eye "shut softly up alive", and the goddess's ear, "thine own soft-conched ear" of *Psyche*. And surely it will be agreed that some of his poetry is snatched out of a love-affair with the ludicrous. His remark about the billiard ball is and is not a joke. Negative Capability, the power to fill other bodies, reveals him invading countless privacies, imagining sheer inner-nesses of feel so powerfully as to turn an eye into some secure little housed animal, and an ear into a soft-shelled, warm-blooded crustacean of his secret fancy. Always the nub of the matter is end-stopped feel operating with a catholicity grand enough to contain human beings, but to contain them on terms which we would not elsewhere think of as humanly tolerable. People can only enter the Keatsian kingdom of feel by conforming to a rule of mindless in-troversion. Because they do enter his kingdom, my attributing of mindlessness to them must be taken as provisional: much more of this later. As we read we do not exactly fail to respect their humanity; we come to grasp them in their removed sensual totality —as we might observe, without derogation, that someone who habitually eats alone has ceased to address his food like the rest of us. The spectrum of Negative Capability has the billiard ball at one end and human beings at the other, and in the middle such plant-animal existences as the metamorphosed brain and eye and ear. His imagination draws the two wings in upon the centre. Even in his letters we can see the human condition being assimilated to something more centralised and Keatsian-poetic:

The greater part of men make their way with the same instinctiveness, the same unwandering eye from their purposes, the same animal eagerness as the hawk. The hawk wants a mate, so does the man—look at them both, they set about it and procure one in the same manner. They want both a nest and both set about one in the same manner—

---

[1] *Sleep and Poetry*, 8.   [2] "Hadst thou liv'd", 21.
[3] *Fall of Hyperion*, I, 245.

they get their food in the same manner. The noble animal Man for his amusement smokes his pipe—the Hawk balances about the clouds—that is the only difference of their leisures. This it is that makes the amusement of life—to a speculative mind. I go among the fields and catch a glimpse of a stoat or a fieldmouse peeping out of the withered grass—the creature hath a purpose and its eyes are bright with it. I go amongst the buildings of a city and I see a man hurrying along—to what? The creature has a purpose and his eyes are bright with it.[1]

The man and his pipe are absolutely toneless; but Keats could have done something with the situation of the balancing hawk, and with that self-possessed animal microcosm of bright eye, warm fur and tiny heart-beat. Above all, he could have commanded the purposive instinct, like Isabella's, the girl absorbed in her digging. When we come to the famous description of the old woman being carried in her sedan chair in Ireland, we do not need his likening of the sedan to a dog kennel and its occupant to an ape to make us conscious of the same gravitational tug towards Negative Capability's centre:

Imagine the worst dog kennel you ever saw placed upon two poles from a mouldy fencing. In such a wretched thing sat a squalid old woman, squat like an ape half starved from a scarcity of biscuit in its passage from Madagascar to the Cape—with a pipe in her mouth and looking out with a round-eyed skinny-lidded inanity—with a sort of horizontal idiotic movement of her head—squat and lean she sat and puff'd out the smoke while two ragged tattered girls carried her along. What a thing would be a history of her life and sensations.[2]

I have seen this last passage quoted in support of the belief that the world has lost a novelist through Keats's devotion to verse. But even in the Noah's Ark of the novel, his history of the old woman's sensations would appear very strange. It would be a timeless and an eventless history, a heap of feel-pebbles. We should find ourselves contemplating that hushed introversion already noted in Isabella as she digs and sweeps her hair aside and goes on digging. The pipe-smoking Irishwoman, for all her age and feebleness, would prove just as resolute a morsel of unqualified life as the bright-eyed fieldmouse and the active Isabella; and like them she would lack the specifically human differentiation which flows from memory and foreboding and the whole machinery of circumspection. Life strikes us as invincible in Keats, but consciousness as radically unmental and discontinuous; with the result that the human self he projects bears a superficial resemblance to the people of a writer like Pirandello who is deliberately (as well as creatively)

[1] *Letters*, vol. II, p. 79.   [2] *Ibid.*, vol. I, p. 321.

adumbrating a doctrine of multiple selfhood, or like Beckett, spokesman of the pointless, laying his axe at the root of our ordinary waking expectations. Such comparisons are without serious interest because Keats is not deliberate, he has no doctrine, no Dilkelike settled opinion; only a centripetal urge drawing his people inward upon the Negative Capability norm, thus distinguishing them from other people's people and endowing them with their very special kind of vitality.

To be vital is to be lifelike, the common reader reasonably supposes. In Isabella's case, the blind absorption with which she digs rings true; anyone in her shoes might strike an onlooker like that, although it takes a nudge from Keats to make us see it. Such ringing true may seem to support a broader claim to vitality than the one I have been advancing by way of Negative Capability. But in fact we are talking about the same thing all the time. For when we acknowledge some human truth in Keats's people, we catch ourselves exclaiming in the same breath, how like the utter privacy of some feeling animal or plant. We meet the two lovers in the opening stanza:

> *They could not sit at meals but feel how well*
> *It soothed each to be the other by—*

like two birds on a branch. But also how human and true to life. And how inevitably Keatsian in the enclosure of that "feel". Lorenzo

> *might not in house, field, or garden stir*
> *But her full shape would all his seeing fill;*

reaffirming that the eye in Keats is an organ of ripe inclusive sensation which has not much to do with other men's seeing. This love of Lorenzo's manifests itself through heart and blood:

> *all day*
> *His heart beat awfully against his side;*
> *And to his heart he inwardly did pray*
> *For power to speak; but still the ruddy tide*
> *Stifled his voice,*

and his love's eloquence is that of the dumb but sensitive forehead, poised on the verge of absurdity:

> *So once more he had wak'd and anguished*
> *A dreary night of love and misery,*
> *If Isabel's quick eye had not been wed*
> *To every symbol on his forehead high;*
> *She saw it waxing very pale and dead,*
> *And straight all flush'd;*

23

and its consummation, heralded by the classic temperature-contrast, perfects the savouring feel with which "her full shape" has already pleasured his eye:

> *"Love! thou art leading me from wintry cold,*
> *"Lady! thou leadest me to summer clime,*
> *"And I must taste the blossoms that unfold*
> *"In its ripe warmth this gracious morning time."*
> *So said, his erewhile timid lips grew bold,*
> *And poesied with hers in dewy rhyme:*
> *Great bliss was with them, and great happiness*
> *Grew, like a lusty flower in June's caress.*

Very like a flower, Polonius might echo.

And thus Keats sensualises the "happiness" of his love story. And in the next stanza the flower both disappears as an invoked presence and is brought nearer in imagination by the substitution of the "fragrance" of love's flower smell for the two-tier metaphor of "taste the blossoms"; while the feel of mingled scents which is the lovers' meeting now stands opposed to the very different but equally joyous feel-situation of their parting:

> *Parting they seem'd to tread upon the air,*
> *Twin roses by the zephyr blown apart*
> *Only to meet again more close, and share*
> *The inward fragrance of each other's heart.*

When he devised "tread upon the air" this feel-idea was not the tired commonplace it has since become. The flowers of *Isabella*, on the other hand, are immemorial; so their originality is in danger of being missed for a different reason. They have changed their role again in the stanza immediately following, and now constitute the passive environment of love:

> *All close they met, all eves, before the dusk*
> *Had taken from the stars its pleasant veil,*
> *Close in a bower of hyacinth and musk,*
> *Unknown of any,*

whereupon Keats brings his narrative to an emphatic halt[1] by suddenly standing back from the lovers in order to see them in the light of their ultimate sad fate, a fate we "pleasure in" to read; and asking "Were they unhappy then?"

The answer marks his full close. And in the final couplet the flowers of *Isabella* have shifted yet again, without relinquishing

---

[1] Before introducing the murderers—"With her two brothers this fair lady dwelt"—and their plot against Lorenzo.

their centrality. Indeed they now embrace both love's environment and its fulfilment, hinting also a tragic aftermath. The stanza closes on a clinching paradox, a bitter-sweet oxymoron of poison in ripeness, death in life, eminently tastable and scentable and therefore a feel-paradox. *Isabella's* flowers have almost become the poem.

> *But, for the general award of love,*
> *The little sweet doth kill much bitterness;*
> *Though Dido silent is in under-grove,*
> *And Isabella's was a great distress,*
> *Though young Lorenzo in warm Indian clove*
> *Was not embalm'd, this truth is not the less—*
> *Even bees, the little almsmen of spring-bowers,*
> *Know there is richest juice in poison-flowers.*

All within thirteen stanzas. They opened with Love and now end with Death, two enormous themes which are effectively carried by the verse, but carried upon an astonishingly slender—not fragile—basis of imaginative creation. Love finds its poetic voice in the bare little circumstance

> *They could not sit at meals but feel how well*
> *It soothed each to be the other by;*

and Death is bounded by the denial to Lorenzo, in his makeshift grave, of the posthumous pleasure of "warm Indian clove". But those meals and that clove—another hard-pressed rhyme of genius—are enough. They conjure an immediate dilation of sympathetic vision, as if we had walked through a gate into the widest of summer meadows. End-stopped feel is the name of that narrow gate, while Keats himself describes one of the fine prospects which meet the eye when we step through it as the exercise of Negative Capability. What he calls "filling other Bodies" involves him, as we have just seen, with the dead no less memorably than with the living; and with the unborn too in another *Fairy's Song*:

> *Shed no tear—O shed no tear!*
> *The flower will bloom another year.*
> *Weep no more! O! weep no more!*
> *Young buds sleep in the root's white core.*

Here the last line reveals the urge towards climax,

> *the birth, life, death*
> *Of unseen flowers in heavy peacefulness;*[1]

---

[1] *Endymion*, I, 234.

the impulse behind the ode *To Autumn*. Keatsian climax stands opposed to Shelley's cyclical account of nature and the seasons;[1] just as Keatsian feel repels the whole mental texture of Shelley. Undoubtedly,

> *when feeble dreams*
> *Visit the hidden buds, or dreamless sleep*
> *Holds every future leaf and flower*[2]

is very beautiful; but Shelley's buds are dormant consciousness, and Keats's embryonic ripeness.

That line also takes us back to Keats lying awake in his Teignmouth lodgings, listening to the rain "with a sense of being drown'd and rotted like a grain of wheat". And the fact is, his power to apprehend remote existences in their secret, intense life makes it difficult to set a limit to the potentialities of Negative Capability—which was the point of mentioning the billiard ball. At the same time a narrative poem like *Isabella* demands of him an extreme instinctive agility in avoiding the intractable, because the truth to life of its human portraiture has to wait upon the negative-capable talent. Human beings are admitted, I said, into his kingdom, but not on their own terms. When the poem is going well, its nimble creator bounds safely from firm spot to firm spot like Conan Doyle's villain chasing butterflies through Grimpen Mire. Disaster overtakes him when his negative-capable gift and the human tale he has to tell fail to coincide. Isabella digging and brushing the hair out of her eyes is like a busy animal and like a real human being—and this is good. "And Isabella did not stamp and rave" is not like an animal or a human being—and this is puerile. Reality ebbs away as soon as the poem's action escapes from its net of feel-situations. We are then left with a comic strip without the pictures.

When Keats suddenly asks a big question like "Were they unhappy then?" we have a very curious sense of panic. The story and Negative Capability are threatening to come apart, and we are afraid of being stranded. The same thing happens with the happiness of the lovers. "Pleasure" is the crucial word. Isabella lies bereft and reaches out for the lost feel of her murdered lover.

> *She weeps alone for pleasures not to be;*
> *Sorely she wept until the night came on,*
> *And then, instead of love, O misery!*
> *She brooded o'er the luxury alone:*

[1] Thus the cyclical thought in Keats, "the flower will bloom another year", is always totally undistinguished.

[2] *Mont Blanc*, 88.

His image in the dusk she seem'd to see,
And to the silence made a gentle moan,
Spreading her perfect arms upon the air,
And on her couch low murmuring "Where? O where?"[1]

Her "pleasures" expose an interesting disunity within the girl herself: between Isabella wondering what has happened to her lover ("O where?") and Isabella upset about her missing sweets of love. The first reflects the ordinary high-mindedness of civilised convention in literature and life; the second, even if we try to avoid taking those pleasures in a narrowly erotic sense, strikes oddly gross. The disunity cannot, I think, be justified, but it may be explained. Keats, like many other writers, is put into difficulties by the poverty of our language of sensation; but what is an occasional problem for them has become omnipresent and cardinal for him. In the first place it is easier to talk about the look of things than about their physical feel, and Keats's focus upon touch and a highly idiosyncratic innerness of contact means that he approaches sensation the hardest way. But beyond all that it needs to be re-affirmed that end-stopped feel is more than a favourite indulgence; it is the true characterisation of his talent, so there can be no question of his finding alternative and easier routes to his goal of saying what he has to say.

The key to Isabella's "pleasures" is, then, linguistic poverty. Not so much local and specific poverty, for we have already noticed, at a quick preliminary glance, how temperature-contrasts and two-tier metaphors like "taste the blossoms" work to render the feel of feel—and more will follow. There is plenty to consider. At the generalising level, however, the scene becomes much more bare. What can one say in broad approval of a sensation except that it is pleasant? That, in a nutshell, is Keats's problem. It dwarfs the descriptive task. And one important consequence of his struggle to solve it is the semantic enlargement of the word pleasure. He, on his side, wants to ennoble and solemnise pleasure, but without compromising its primordial hedonistic simplicity; while we on ours judge the maturity of his work more than we realise by our ability to take Keatsian pleasure seriously. Melancholy, in the ode which bears her name, is found "aching Pleasure nigh"; and few of us doubt that Keats intends pleasure—"Joy's grape"—to work hard for him in the little universe of the poem; and so, like Humpty Dumpty, he pays it extra. Whereas Isabella's "pleasures" arouse a blank initial response, rather as when some common word

---

[1] Stanza XXX.

is given an unexplained private twist in casual talk. Or in a letter like the one Keats wrote his publisher, John Taylor, about a passage in *Endymion*:

The whole thing must I think have appeared to you, who are a consequitive Man, as a thing almost of mere words—but I assure you that when I wrote it, it was a regular stepping of the Imagination towards a Truth. My having written that Argument will perhaps be of the greatest service to me of any thing I ever did. It set before me at once the gradations of Happiness even like a kind of Pleasure Thermometer —and is my first Step towards the chief Attempt in the Drama—the playing of different Natures with Joy and Sorrow.[1]

The "argument" he refers to here begins with the question "Wherein lies happiness?" and leads to the "crown" of life on earth which is "love and friendship", and finally reposes in "love immortal". A high and earnest affair, therefore, to which the word pleasure appears comically inadequate. This situation, in a letter written a month or two before he began *Isabella*, neatly anticipates the poem at the point where it presents the heroine's missed pleasures as if they measured up to her lost lover. In both cases the fault is Keats's in that he has not yet learnt—a year or so before he wrote the ode *On Melancholy*—how to pay pleasure extra. But it is also ours to the extent of our lazy assumption that what is unlofty for others is so for him. Even in the letter to Taylor we have our warning that all is not what it seems to be; the creative pressure of his thumb is discernible on that home-made "Pleasure Thermometer"—simply through the appeal to temperature. Soon afterwards, when he comes to write *Isabella*, story and people are enmeshed in the net of feel. Temperature is a single strand among many, the chief of which—those flowers which are not there primarily to be looked at—I have tried to unravel for closer study. Together these strands bind us to the poem; they are the grip which we call the poem's enchantment while it holds, and Keats's absurd unevenness when it is broken. In the stanza immediately before the "pleasures not to be", the poet addresses his heroine

> *Poor Girl! put on thy stifling widow's weed,*
> *And 'scape at once from Hope's accursed bands;*

and leaves us wondering who but Keats would take the oppressive feel of black mourning clothes as the thing to put his finger on. Play our old trick of running a line through "stifling" and writing "sombre" (say) instead; and the preposterous badness of the lines

---

[1] *Letters*, vol. I, p. 218.

becomes inescapable. Replace "stifling" and the former hesitation of judgment returns with it: not good exactly, but characterful. Keats's "stifling" is pure projected feel, pure filling of other bodies in the exercise of Negative Capability.

His doing this again and again determines how we receive Isabella. It cannot redeem her "pleasures" from the poverty I complained of, but it causes us to see her with believing eyes—see her at that point where the human girl (as Mr Chadband would call her) and the naked feeling life (provoking our "How like an animal!") intersect and catch fire with a certainty which is Keats's alone.

In this respect too, *Isabella* is an immature poem. When, later, we turn to the heroine of *St. Agnes* we shall find an overpowering conviction in the birdlike timid creature ("trembling in her soft and chilly nest") who looks up at Porphyro, her lover come to her, with "blue affrayed eyes wide open"; and he reads the fear in her face and for a moment all the sex drains out of his love, and "upon his knees he sank, pale as smooth-sculptured stone". We are moved by the deep truth of it, and recognise that beside Madeline Isabella deserves to be called decorative. But she does share with Madeline the fundamental characteristic of a body which has been negative-capably filled, and that is the status of pure object. All other people are objects for ourselves, of course, but they are also potential subjects; we are aware of them as other minds capable of turning us, today's observers, into tomorrow's observed. Keats's human beings are peculiar in their lack of all presence as potential subjects, which is perhaps the most cogent reason for imputing a defining, if provisional, mindlessness to them.

I have just mentioned Madeline settling in her nest. Keats says she is "like ring-dove fray'd"; her voice is stifled as Lorenzo's was and her heart's painful eloquence suggests "a tongueless nightingale". All that is easy to remark. But the decisive stroke is those wide-open blue eyes with fear and bland regard in them, but no mind, as others conceive mind, behind. The unnamed mistress in *Melancholy* has, unlike Madeline, no animal imagery to support her:

> *Or if thy mistress some rich anger shows,*
> *Emprison her soft hand, and let her rave,*
> *And feed deep, deep upon her peerless eyes.*

Nor does she need it, for our sense of pure object is already absolute. There is no human reciprocity lurking within the situation as Keats imagines it. The mistress cannot answer back—her raving could never be thought of thus—and she cannot even stare back except as a leopard might stare as one gazed into the shallow mystery of its beautiful eyes. Keats's invitation to emprison and feed deep exactly touches the nerve of his originality in characterisation. He brings to mind with a shock of contrast the Jamesian ideal, the common ideal, of authorly love for the fictions which were carved out of one's own side and which one's will sustains, but which are free inhabitants of the books they live in.

This love, their gift of freedom, cannot be withheld entirely by a writer who has talent. Mr P. G. Wodehouse's autobiography describes his method of composing a ten-thousand-word 'scenario' before he begins a novel, so that he shall have something of substance—of more authority than an ordinary synopsis—to refer to when his characters threaten to get out of hand. He waves the scenario in their faces; and "I say to them 'No larks' ". Thus he denies them freedom by a conscious effort, in the interest of his own tight comic mode. And thus he excludes himself from the Jamesian norm. Now Keats also looks as if he is going to exclude himself; but this is only because of the way he sharpens yet further the already keen paradox of the writer giving freedom to the thing which exists only at his pleasure. For while even an Emily Brontë or a Dostoevski—even writers in whose books everyone dances to the tune of a single very evident and persuasive vision—appears to move off sooner or later and let his characters get on with it, Keats makes no such pretence but remains on top of his always. And yet they too are free. The impudence of "emprison" and "feed deep" is unconstraining. Here, as in the letter about the apelike old woman in her dog-kennel sedan, his superiority is complete, and completely without condescension.

The fine flower of Negative Capability blooms, retiringly, in such appraisals as "her peerless eyes". Compare his classical commendation of Isabella's "perfect arms". How near, and yet how far, this coolness is from the routine of male complacency. How framed, how perfected, our comprehension of the object on the couch with arms stretched out. And how rich, in consequence, the physicalities of this poetry. They form the secure repository of its value, and leave the reader to make what he can of the fact that *Isabella* transmutes the beastliness of Boccaccio's story not by spiritualising it, nor by cunning selection, but by squeezing the last sensuous drop out of each phase in turn; and this is true equally of direct touch, taste, smell, and of the negative-capable projection of feel. The stanza in which Isabella dotes upon Lorenzo's severed head, foul with "smeared loam":

She calm'd its wild hair with a golden comb,
And all around each eye's sepulchral cell
Pointed each fringed lash[1]

presents the exhilarating spectacle of a very young poet daring to be himself.[2] And the later one in which the decomposing head nourishes the basil plant growing above it, takes us much further again:

And so she ever fed it with thin tears,
Whence thick, and green, and beautiful it grew,
So that it smelt more balmy than its peers
Of basil-tufts in Florence; for it drew
Nurture besides, and life, from human fears,
From the fast mouldering head there shut from view. . . .[3]

It declares life's total dependence upon death in a sudden knife-flash premonition of the greatest of all his poems, the ode *To Autumn*. This "nurture" of *Isabella* points to the entirely unwitty confluence of opposites in the ode, where it is made obvious that life and death are inexplicable apart, and no more in need of explanation, together, than a fine autumn day—or a healthy plant. The characteristically bold repose upon smell leaves nothing to be explained; but it is also true that we are in the grip of a wonder of nature as we enjoy the sweetness drawn by the basil-tuft from Lorenzo's "fast mouldering head".

These were the thoughts prompting my initial claim for *Isabella*, that it is often open and generous and even grand, where everything would seem to point towards an obsessive narrowness. The emphasis of Keats's treatment is not, despite appearances, perverse; he conceives Isabella kissing Lorenzo's exhumed head, and combing its hair and pointing its eyelashes, not in order to show what he can achieve in the teeth of decorum and good sense, but because his gift happens to be thus. And his gift is a large one, and marvellously sane. I laboured the subordination of sex to end-stopped feel (which includes Negative Capability) in an attempt to give his imagination elbowroom; and it only remains to say that the attempt was made as much for sex's sake as for feel's. I mean that the picture of Lorenzo and Isabella sitting at table and sensing their comfort for each other is as memorable as it surely is because it affirms sex's underground connection, even in the young and emotionally frantic, with a whole complex of tender instincts reaching back and back towards a wellbeing in which silence and a shared meal and a loved presence merge in the profoundest dreamlike peace.

[1] LI.   [2] In fact these details are not in Boccaccio.   [3] LIV.

5 *The Merely Sensuous Man*

Keats's readers have mostly thought of him as a sensuous, not an intellectual poet, and it follows that there is an element of commonplace in what has been said so far. This genial coincidence, as Coleridge termed his thefts from Schelling, is not something to try and wriggle out of; partly because Dr Johnson spoke the truth when he said that the common reader is nearly always right, given generations of time to make his mind up; and partly because the stuff of an agreed and central conviction about a major writer is not easily exhausted. Everybody—except a few moralising professional critics—believes that Shakespeare's imagination is distinguished first by its magnanimity; but the obvious is hard to deal with adequately when it appears in this form. Again it scarcely admitted doubt that Wordsworth was a philosophical poet until Matthew Arnold, playing a rather cheap forensic trick with the word philosophy (for nobody had supposed—and Arnold knew they hadn't—that Wordsworth was a philosopher in the same sense as Kant or even Coleridge), made this view appear ridiculous. And yet the effort to prove Arnold wrong and the Victorian common reader right who detected in his poetry the same "worn pressure of thought" which Hazlitt saw in his face, need not be futile.

Arnold has also been at work on Keats. As to the love letters:

We have the tone, or rather the entire want of tone, the abandonment of all reticence and all dignity, of the merely sensuous man. . . . The sensuous man speaks in it, and the sensuous man of the badly bred and badly trained sort.[1]

But what about the sensuous poet? Arnold quotes

Light feet, dark violet eyes, and parted hair;
Soft dimpled hands, white neck, and creamy breast,

from a very early and bad sonnet in the 1817 volume, and then advances the general proposition that "a merely sensuous man cannot either by promise or by performance be a very great poet".

My concern is with the diminishing, even the denaturing, of Keats threatened by this concept of the merely sensuous man. What is the force of "merely"? Arnold himself pointed to the

[1] *Essays in Criticism*, Second Series.

"soft dimpled hands" and the love letters. He started a game which can be continued indefinitely. Nothing comes easier than the laying of early verse like the dimpled hands, or not so early verse like

> *taste these juicy pears,*
> *Sent me by sad Vertumnus, when his fears*
> *Were high about Pomona: here is cream,*
> *Deepening to richness from a snowy gleam;*
> *Sweeter than that Nurse Amalthea skimm'd*
> *For the boy Jupiter: and here, undimm'd*
> *By any touch, a bunch of blooming plums*
> *Ready to melt between an infant's gums:*[1]

side by side with passages from his letters in praise of claret and

pear-tasting — plum-judging — apricot-nibbling — peach-scrunching — nectarine-sucking and melon-carving. I have also a great feeling for antiquated cherries full of sugar cracks—and a white currant tree kept for company.[2]

But the exercise can never be very profitable, simply because our fascination and our wish to think about Keats do not arise from the sensuous correspondence of these two with each other but from the larger bond uniting both of them with the feasts of *St. Agnes* and *Lamia* and *The Fall of Hyperion*, with the ripe fruits of *Autumn* and the wine of the *Nightingale*. Indeed the closest verbal parallel of the whole lot is between, "and, please heaven, a little claret-wine cool out of a cellar a mile deep"[3] from a letter to his young sister and

> *O, for a draught of vintage! that hath been*
> *Cool'd a long age in the deep-delved earth,*

in the *Nightingale*. Where is the merely sensuous man here, I wonder?

Arnold's argument runs as follows: Keats is guilty of much merely sensuous writing; a merely sensuous man cannot be a great poet; Keats is a great poet, so there must be more to him than mere sensuousness; there is—when we look we find "flint and iron in him", we find "character". Now whereas Arnold's documentation of sensuousness is ample, that of the *poetical* virtue of flint and iron is almost non-existent. He quotes from a number of letters, from a piece of occasional journalism about the actor Kean, he mentions the prose Preface to *Endymion*—all illustrating the

---

[1] *Endymion*, II, 444. [2] *Letters*, vol. II, p. 149.
[3] *Ibid.*, p. 56.

courage and resolution of the man. Turning at last to the poetry, he says:

In his own poetry, too, Keats felt that place must be found for "the ardours rather than the pleasures of song" although he was aware that he was not yet ripe for it—

> *But my flag is not unfurl'd*
> *On the Admiral-staff, and to philosophise*
> *I dare not yet.*

This Keatsian immaturity Arnold later rephrases as an unreadiness for "moral interpretation" and "the architectonics of poetry". But, he adds, such qualities are not called for in the "shorter things" where Keats can display his "natural magic", expressing himself with "rounded perfection and felicity of loveliness". One would, I think, be justified in supposing that Arnold means to re-affirm (but now in favourable terms) the merely sensuous man, were it not for the accompanying assertion that Keats's passion for the beautiful "is not a passion of the sensuous or sentimental man, is not a passion of the sensuous or sentimental poet. It is an intellectual and spiritual passion". Once again a barrage of quotation from the letters supports his proposition, and once again his argument based on the verse is negligible. But, of course, Arnold has already said that the poet Keats was not ripe for philosophising, moral interpretation and the rest; so it is hard to imagine what kind of argument he might resort to.

The very considerable merit of Arnold's essay is, in fact, curiously dependent on its analytic feebleness. Therein lies much of its interest for students of Keats. For had Arnold allowed himself to be discomposed by its inner contradictions and those slurred transitions between mere sensuousness, flint and iron, intellectual and spiritual passion, he might never have summoned the nerve finally and calmly to settle on the poet's natural magic. That conclusion is right as far as it goes, and so is his persistent nagging thought for Keats's sensuousness. The common reader has endorsed both. But he has not bothered to ask whether this particular sensuousness was of the 'mere' kind or not; and for that reason his coupling of a singular temperament and a singular magical way with words is even more unreflective than Arnold's, and more true. He accepts the continuity of the momentous things with the stuff which Arnold justly dismissed (though the snobbery of those thrusts as "the literary circles of Hampstead" is not attractive).

How the vulgar and trivial underwent sea-change into patrician splendour, is not for the common reader to say.

It remains easy to be unafraid of the sensuous Keats so long as you are not trying to express yourself formally about him. And likewise with the hyper-sensitive Keats deriving from Shelley,[1] popularised by Severn's sentimental posthumous portraits, and growing in strength through the Nineteenth Century. Hazlitt, almost incredibly, coined "little western flower" to depict Keats in the clutch of the reviewers. The tale was taken up by the Pre-Raphaelites, and became more shrill and dogmatic as it was elaborated by the Keatsians of the Aesthetic Movement. The flower had to be shielded from the common air; in the second half of the century we may trace a progressive withdrawal from actuality, beginning with the frequent implication that his poetry is somehow or other too good for life, and ending in Oscar Wilde's "Priest of Beauty", where the divorce is not merely open and defiant but a sufficient reason for establishing Keats as one of art's great heroes.

Obviously, he was a very sensitive man. Only when you set about maintaining, simultaneously, the fineness of his perceptions and the vicious wrongheadedness of Wilde's "Priest of Beauty" view does the strenuous critical task begin. You agree that Keats is full of palates and fingertips. Also that these are a sensitive apex or apogee. And then you have to unfold the huge latent significance of the fact that all men possess palates and fingertips.

Therefore the sensuous and hyper-sensitive Keatses are to be thought of as hazards not because they are false but because they are partially true. They are daunting in their partial truth, and rather than risk shipwreck on them the main tradition of commentary has, in recent time, set sail in the opposite direction. That is why Arnold's fumbled antithesis of sensuousness and flint-and-iron, and later of sensuous and intellectual passion, was worth pausing over; it contains so much of the subsequent story in embryo. While Arnold was saved to some extent by that deep literary instinct of his for equivocation at moments of crisis, others have been very seriously troubled by the notion that some decisive choice has to be made between sense and intellect, pleasure and morality. They include Keats himself.

Discussion of his sensuousness begins in 1818 with Richard Woodhouse's complaint about "the feel of not to feel it" from the lyric "In a drear-nighted December". The poem is quotably short.

The "delicate and fragile" genius of the Preface to *Adonais*.

I

In a drear-nighted December,
Too happy, happy tree,
Thy branches ne'er remember
Their green felicity:
The north cannot undo them,
With a sleety whistle through them;
Nor frozen thawings glue them
From budding at the prime.

II

In a drear-nighted December,
Too happy, happy brook,
Thy bubblings ne'er remember
Apollo's summer look;
But with a sweet forgetting,
They stay their crystal fretting,
Never, never petting
About the frozen time.

III

Ah! would 'twere so with many
A gentle girl and boy!
But were there ever any
Writh'd not at passed joy?
The feel of not to feel it
When there is none to heal it,
Nor the numbed sense to steel it,
Was never said in rhyme.

Stating a case against the reading "To know the change and feel it", I said there was more at stake than a disagreement between specialists, and went on to consider end-stopping generally. These wider repercussions are neatly indicated, and within the little poem itself, by Arnold's antithesis of sensuous and intellectual passion. We have to decide between the "feel" of one version and the "know" of the other. A strong light falls on the line under dispute, because it has the important job of declaring what exactly it is that "Was never said in rhyme". Keats did not lack ordinary intelligence. He was aware that knowing a change—loss of youth, love, talents, faith—and responding to it feelingly has very often been said in rhyme; this is perhaps the commonest of all lyric themes. Nor should we be quick to assume that the clinching assertion of the poem's final line is a conscious fraud, and that in so far as he means anything he is only saying that knowing and feeling 'the change' has never been expressed perfectly, or well enough; so really his poem is pretty silly.

On the contrary, the presumption must be that his punch-line intention behind "was never said in rhyme" is genuine. Good intentions do not make good poems, but they do suffice to guarantee the honest force of that "never" and its direct, unequivocal reference to the line under dispute. Quite simply, he must be taken to mean what he says; and once we do so we see that the strongest reason (textual considerations apart) for preferring "the feel of not to feel it" is its intrinsic sound sense. Keats, as I say, was not a fool. His "feel of not to feel" is not a clumsy alternative to the memory of vanished feeling. He has taken the reflection out of remembrance, and has put his finger on that bereft self-enfolded state, the pressure of something missing, definite yet featureless, precise but unutterable, perfectly known and conceptually void. We all recognise the experience, it is a feel we all have. This is, and is worthily, what "was never said in rhyme".

An artist seldom troubles to remark that a thing has not been done unless that particular possibility enters, however vaguely, within his own aspiration. Moreover it is a sign of greatness in an artist that he should want to do what he alone can do, his ambition springing from insight into the exact whereabouts of his originality. In this lyric Keats has hit on a persuasive means of presenting his feel as the closed circuit which it quintessentially is. The negative form (yet positive too, since the feel of *not* to feel is just as much a Keatsian entity as any other feel) scarcely admits of misinterpretation. That is why it troubles people. The only way to force open its closed circuit is to rewrite the line—which is what has happened.

By substituting "know" for "feel" somebody reintroduced reflective mind into Keats's memory and threw his whole poem out of true. It now revolves round a fatuous contrast between us unlucky men who have intelligence and can remember our lost joy, and trees and streams which have no intelligence and cannot. What Keats wrote was a quirky, half-successful comment on the logic of feel. The poem's root contrast, by no means fatuous, was between the feel of present pain and the feel of absent pleasure. The first belongs to the tree and stream in the grip of winter wind and frost, the second to us. With agreeable wit Keats has allowed himself the mental words "remember" and "forgetting" in the first two stanzas, where there is no danger he will be misunderstood. We cannot fail to see that remembering and forgetting is a mere politeness, a poet's courtesy towards his trees and streams. We devalue them accordingly, and in doing this lay ourselves open to the calculated shock of his third and 'human' stanza where the mental words, so far from appearing in full literal force as seems inevitable, are witheld completely and feel dominates.

The same reversal is pursued through the stream's quasi-mental "fretting" and "petting", in contrast with the mindless automatism of the human "writh'd". The preposition in the line "writh'd not at passed joy" also merits attention. Woodhouse appends a note to one of his transcripts of the poem: "*Of* in Miss R.'s copy in Keats's handwriting." One of our two surviving autographs also reads "of" instead of "at", and I wish it were possible to look at the other (the location of which is now not known) to ensure that this unobtrusive variant has not been overlooked there. In any case, we know that Keats wrote "writh'd not of passed joy" at least twice. It is an extraordinary and un-English phrase, but not without its rationale. It is determined by the overall pattern of the human but mind-free third stanza. The snag with "at", Keats's instinct will have told him, is that it undoes the work of "writh'd". On its own "writh'd" conveys an impression of epileptic helplessness, but when "*at* passed joy" is joined to it the mental taint "in contemplation of" begins to infiltrate. Replace "at" by "of" and the automatism is sustained throughout the line. This is the same "of" as in "sick of the palsy" or "of over-eating".

So Keats hesitated. He may well have judged the "of" version intolerably freakish. However "at" does not improve matters much in this direction, while working harm in another. In fairness we should recall that he made no move to publish the poem. It is one of those characterful, instructive semi-failures, and among the things wrong with it, that "writh'd" line provides another illustration of the hair's breadth which separates some ridiculous from some fine effects. It is bad in the same way as

> *And Isabella did not stamp and rave.*

The badness of these two seems to have parted company at a very late creative stage from the excellence of Isabella brushing her hair aside like a horse troubled with flies, and even from the supreme excellence of Madeline:

> *She danc'd along with vague, regardless eyes,*[1]

in whom Keats's sense of the human object grows perfect. The automatism, the witholding of mind's rule, which made the writh-

---

[1] Stanza VIII.

ing and stamping absurd, becomes the very thing we catch our breath at now.

Mental words are not absent, of course, from *The Eve of St. Agnes*; with a poem of any length it is scarcely conceivable that they should be. But whereas the "Drear-nighted December" lyric confines them to the stream and tree, thus forcing upon us a diplomatic valuation, *St. Agnes* disperses them through a network of physical facts—through limb and feature—so eloquently that we lose all desire to weld them together in their conventional unity and to bend them back upon a single latent seat of consciousness. It is Madeline's eyes which are "vague", not her mind:

> *She danc'd along with vague, regardless eyes,*
> *Anxious her lips, her breathing quick and short:*

and her lips which are "anxious". And her breath expectant. Later on her "affrayed eyes" look up at Porphyro standing beside her bed, and her fear is truly within, not behind them—just as his response to what he reads there is in his own "piteous eye", and just as the self-surrender of his passion resides, indeed his entire state resides, in the "unnerved" condition of his arm when

> *his warm, unnerved arm*
> Sank in her pillow.[1]

For he has the same dispelled mentality as she. Which is to say he commands a comparable physical power to haunt us with, a persuasion removing him, as it does her, from other poets' human beings and Keats's own unhappy world of stamping and writhing. In so far as the separation remains a fine one, the reason must be sought in the delicacy of the problem which Keats's genius dictated to him: to render character at a point of intersection with a wider non-human life. The success of Madeline leaves us saying how memorably girlish she is, and also how birdlike. And this double reaction is our firmest possible assurance of the poem's stature. It sets us (for example) wondering why our attitude to the heroine of this romance is fundamentally protective, why, for all the thing's blazing sensual conviction, its sex moves us less than a certain unspiritual tenderness; and when we begin in that vein, we are not likely to underestimate it.

As for Arnold's "merely sensuous man", one might as well say that Porphyro's "warm, unnerved arm" is just an arm. To ask "what if not merely and just?" is to begin the hard work—but with the vital encouragement of knowing the work is there to be

[1] Stanza XXXII.

39

done. Whereas Arnold's "spiritual and intellectual passion" touches the strange authority of that arm nowhere. We only have to recall other dispersed, autonomous organs, like the eye "shut softly up alive" and the "soft-conched ear", to be certain the truth is somewhere else.

Arnold's "spiritual and intellectual passion" is corrupting as well as irrelevant, because of the lofty talk it encourages. In the "Bright star!" sonnet,

> *Pillow'd upon my fair love's ripening breast,*
> *To feel for ever its soft fall and swell* . . .

Keats really does want to feel for ever, and an Arnoldian high-mindedness about love can only take us out of reach of the poem. It also cuts off "Bright star!" from the sharp raw pungency of early Keats:

> *Play with their fingers, touch their shoulders white*
> *Into a pretty shrinking with a bite*
> *As hard as lips can make it:*[1]

where the thing to note is the collusion of direct end-stopping with the projected feel of "shrinking", so tart on the imagination's palate; and where, having remarked that, we should be saying, with an eye on "Bright star!" and many another, that Keats learns how to tame this faculty but never deserts it. At the end of his writing life, knocked off balance by jealous love and probably by unsuspected sickness, he loses control again:

> *Let none profane my Holy See of love,*
> *Or with a rude hand break*
> *The sacramental cake:*
> *Let none else touch the just new-budded flower;*[2]

falling back into the unworked eroticism of 1817. But when we consider the general collapse which has occurred here—the repulsive religious rhetoric which *St. Agnes* had managed with such tact —the potential strength of "touch" reasserts itself.

This is what matters, and what Arnold's spiritual and intellectual talk threatens to betray. He is tempting us to follow the man who rewrote "the feel of not to feel it" and force open feel's closed circuit. Not that some people need much tempting. After all, one has to find something to say. And so true lovers of Keats deceive themselves into praising his vision of "pure imaginative forms"

---

[1] *Sleep and Poetry*, 108.   [2] *Ode to Fanny*.

and a "purely ideal world".[1] Then no wonder those books get written about the neo-Platonic allegory of *Endymion*, the Wordsworthian-Christian-Evolutionary humanism of *Hyperion*, the Philosophy of Beauty.

6 *Feel and Know*

Keats too sometimes found himself contemplating the apparent narrowness and suffocation of feel, and asking "Can this be all?"

When confidence ebbed, he did one of two things. He either tried to believe he would outgrow feel one day and become a different sort of poet, or he transcendentalised feel itself into a would-be higher significance. Each of these manoeuvres is instanced, separately, by a single long passage of verse. Both are early, as one would expect: *Sleep and Poetry* from the 1817 volume, and the Pleasure Thermometer argument from the first book of *Endymion*.

The 1817 poem was the outcome of a sleepless night spent on Leigh Hunt's sofa, after a party which broke up so late that Keats decided not to walk home to his lodgings. This situation is referred to in the final lines:

> *The very sense of where I was might well*
> *Keep Sleep aloof: but more than that there came*
> *Thought after thought to nourish up the flame*
> *Within my breast; so that the morning light*
> *Surprised me even from a sleepless night;*
> *And up I rose refresh'd, and glad, and gay,*
> *Resolving to begin that very day*
> *These lines; and howsoever they be done,*
> *I leave them as a father does his son.*

When B. R. Haydon read *Sleep and Poetry* he called it "a flash of lightning that will sound men from their occupations, and keep them trembling for the crash of thunder that *will* follow".[2] The better judgment (as this specimen indicates) would be that it includes some of the feeblest couplet-writing in the whole body of his work. Its overall construction, too, is extremely slack, so that it

---

[1] These phrases are H. W. Garrod's (*Keats*, pp. 56, 58), though the thesis of his book is that "only as he sustains the earnest sensuosity to which nature dedicated him does his genius thrive" (p. 32). I detect Arnold's legacy here.

[2] *Letters*, vol. I, p. 125.

becomes difficult to trace the sequence of "thought after thought" which he refers to. The poem begins at least as badly as it ends:

> *What is more gentle than a wind in summer?*
> *What is more soothing than the pretty hummer*
> *That stays one moment in an open flower,*
> *And buzzes cheerily from bower to bower?*

The answer to these embarrassing questions ("the pretty hummer" epitomises his very worst strain) is given in the further question: "What but thee, Sleep? Soft closer of our eyes!" And with that exclamation we catch a glimpse of the familiar Keatsian eye, the palpable yet secret organ, the object of Sleep's addresses in the famous sonnet, Sleep the "soft embalmer" whom he imagines

> *Shutting with careful fingers and benign,*
> *Our gloom-pleas'd eyes. . . .*

But only a glimpse, because his main concern is to press onward to yet another question:

> *But what is higher beyond thought than thee?*

And to yet another answer:

> *O Poesy! for thee I hold my pen*
> *That am not yet a glorious denizen*
> *Of thy wide heaven—Should I rather kneel*
> *Upon some mountain-top until I feel*
> *A glowing splendour round about me hung,*
> *And echo back the voice of thine own tongue?*
> *O Poesy! for thee I grasp my pen*
> *That am not yet a glorious denizen*
> *Of thy wide heaven; yet, to my ardent prayer,*
> *Yield from thy sanctuary some clear air,*
> *Smoothed for intoxication by the breath*
> *Of flowering bays, that I may die a death*
> *Of luxury, and my young spirit follow*
> *The morning sun-beams to the great Apollo*
> *Like a fresh sacrifice; or, if I can bear*
> *The o'erwhelming sweets, 'twill bring to me the fair*
> *Visions of all places:*

which brings him to the heart of his poem.

The proposal to wait for inspiration "until I feel" seems ordinary enough, but that is because its immediate coupling is with the undistinguished "glowing splendour". As the passage unfolds, the idiosyncrasy of "until I feel" begins to emerge. He does not fall on his knees in search of insight; his prayer to the Spirit of Poetry is for "some clear air" to breathe, smell, taste, get drunk on—in short to have the utter feel of, Keatswise. How this will enable him to write poetry does not appear. Nor should we expect it to, since feel's nature requires it to be indulged for its own sake.

At the same time the passage does enable us to understand something of the significance, for Keats, of indulging feel for its own sake. We meet here, for the first time, an overall pattern in which the end-stopping phenomenon contains both the experience and the experiencing man in a rhythm of climactic intensification. The climax of the feeling poet is of course his death: "that I may die a death / Of luxury", as he says here. This prefaces the much more renowned expression of the urge towards double climax in the *Nightingale Ode*:

> *To cease upon the midnight with no pain,*
> *While thou art pouring forth thy soul abroad*
> *In such an ecstacy!*

It informs the attempt at a clinching stroke in the last five words of the "Bright star!" sonnet:

> *And so live ever—or else swoon to death.*

And it puts in our hand a key to the gnomic conclusion of another much-discussed sonnet, "Why did I laugh tonight?":

> *Verse, Fame and Beauty are intense indeed,*
> *But Death intenser—Death is Life's high meed.*

Enough for the present that intensity serves an ideal of ripe completion, coupling experience and experiencer in a recognisable rhythm, imparting dramatic momentum to Keats's feel, but doing so—a crucial point—without violating its end-stopped character. So far from violating, intensity sets the seal. *Sleep and Poetry* thrusts us forward expectantly through "smoothed for intoxication", as if towards a world beyond intoxication; but in fact we are heading for the full close of "a death of luxury".

To deny that death means the end in *Sleep and Poetry* is to make nonsense of the clear-cut alternative which Keats presents at "or, if I can bear / The o'erwhelming sweets". For now he is envisaging what will happen if he succeeds in staving off the climactic intensity of luxurious death and comes out the other side of his feel-ordeal without dying of it. And in fact the passage expressly opposes the "visions" of the second alternative to the forward but completely self-enfolded movement of "until I feel" in the first.

It matters that we should accept the alternatives for what

43

they are, and not assume some muddled continuity threading them together. With the thought of possible "visions" to come, Keats, like Matthew Arnold, contemplates the breaking open of feel's closed circuit. Fortunately (again like Arnold) his instinct proves stronger in the long run than his analytics; for the second alternative is voiced by pseudo-Keats, by the daunted critic, by the anti-poet within. The prayer to the Spirit of Poetry dies with the death of luxury and the completion of the first alternative. Thereafter he abandons prayer for statement: " 'twill bring to me . . ."—or rather, he abandons prayer for wish disguised as statement. In his prayer he could not and did not attempt to expound the connection between the feel-process and his creative gift; but he knew in his heart that the link existed and simply pictured himself a sacrifice on the altar of feel, to the god of Poetry. In his statement, all this instinctive certainty has melted; the wish for visions becomes father to the thought of how they are to arise and be related to the business of composition:

> or, if I can bear
> The o'erwhelming sweets, 'twill bring to me the fair
> Visions of all places: a bowery nook
> Will be elysium—an eternal book
> Whence I may copy many a lovely saying
> About the leaves, and flowers—about the playing
> Of nymphs in woods, and fountains; and the shade
> Keeping a silence round a sleeping maid;
> And many a verse from so strange influence
> That we must ever wonder how, and whence
> It came. Also imaginings will hover
> Round my fire-side, and haply there discover
> Vistas of solemn beauty, where I'd wander
> In happy silence, like the clear Meander
> Through its lone vales; and where I found a spot
> Of awfuller shade, or an enchanted grot,
> Or a green hill o'erspread with chequered dress
> Of flowers, and fearful from its loveliness,
> Write on my tablets all that was permitted,
> All that was for our human senses fitted.
> Then the events of this wide world I'd seize
> Like a strong giant, and my spirit teaze
> Till at its shoulders it should proudly see
> Wings to find out an immortality.

The silence about language and literature, so complete in the prayer for "some clear air", is now broken with a vengeance, in a shower of "book", "copy", "lovely saying", "many a verse", "write on my tablets". Notice also the swing back to the initial wish for visions at "vistas of solemn beauty"; and the gathering up of the second alternative in the expansive gesture—surprisingly sudden—of the last four lines.

Thus Arnold's antithesis of the sensuous man and the man of spiritual and intellectual passion is phrased by Keats himself in terms of feel and vision. Feel is what it is, simple as faith, and he presents it unqualified and unexpounded. Vision he needs to justify. Vision sets him thinking in two directions, that of literature and that of life. Hence the oscillation of the second alternative between a perfectly shielded domain of the "lovely saying" and an open one accessible to "the events of this wide world", so that the poet may "seize" them. Later criticism has gratefully accepted vision, by way of the literature/life duality. And this is natural enough, since any poet might be expected to discuss the medium he works in, and since the magniloquence of those last four lines sounds like the declared ambition of a *great* poet. Whereas the first alternative offers no handholds. There is, on the surface, no literature and no life, only feel.

Sleep and Poetry goes on to restate these alternatives. They remain distinct, but are now conceived as successive phases within a programme of the poet's life. Keats exclaims:

> *O for ten years that I may overwhelm*
> *Myself in poesy;*

and goes on to describe the country of luxurious, climactic feel; of feeding, tasting, touching:

> *First the realm I'll pass*
> *Of Flora, and old Pan: sleep in the grass,*
> *Feed upon apples red, and strawberries,*
> *And choose each pleasure that my fancy sees;*
> *Catch the white-handed nymphs in shady places,*
> *To woo sweet kisses from averted faces,—*
> *Play with their fingers, touch their shoulders white . . .*

The division between feel and vision is marked by a double paragraph and the question

> *And can I ever bid these joys farewell?*

(corresponding to "or, if I can bear" in the earlier passage) which brings him at once into the country opposite:

> *Yes, I must pass them for a nobler life,*
> *Where I may find the agonies, the strife*
> *Of human hearts: for lo! I see. . . .*

45

And once again the parallel with the earlier passage is obvious, only here the order of presentation has been reversed. The grandiose assertion now comes first ("the agonies, the strife / Of human hearts" are, of course, "events of this wide world"), and vision follows.

I chop off the quotation at "I see" in order to suggest a further resemblance between Arnold's criticism and Keats's self-assessment. Arnold postulated an intellectual and spiritual talent, but was restrained by his sharp nose from making anything considerable of it. His essay doubles back on itself, in praise of the poet's "natural magic". What was in danger of becoming a study of meanings reposes finally in "the fascinating felicity of Keats, his perfection of loveliness". In opposing vision to feel Keats makes a similar gesture, and when vision is coupled with seizing the world's events and finding human suffering, a similar threat of meditative, philosophic treatment has materialised. The object of his "I see" turns out to be the best-known thing in *Sleep and Poetry*, the charioteer with his air-borne car and horses:

> *I see afar*
> *O'er-sailing the blue cragginess, a car*
> *And steeds with streamy manes—the charioteer*
> *Looks out upon the winds with glorious fear:*

and it may fairly be asked what bearing he has on human agonies. Indeed Keats seems to be wondering the same thing; his attitude is inquisitive and he betrays no knowledge of what is frightening the charioteer, nor of what he is looking at and listening to:

> *Most awfully intent*
> *The driver of those steeds is forward bent,*
> *And seems to listen: O that I might know*
> *All that he writes with such a hurrying glow.*

Nor of what he is writing about. "All that he writes" has come completely out of the blue, with no mention of a pen in his hand or of any material to write on. By occupying his charioteer thus strangely—and dangerously, since he is busy driving—Keats falls into the same violent and irrational oscillation between life and literature as in the earlier passage. The tell-tale pattern reappears in which a wished-for vision (the wish implicit in "Yes, I must pass them") splits down the middle into a grand motion towards real life and a constrained fuss about language.

As the poem stumbles on, the difficulty of relating the charioteer to the world of our actual pains and stresses increases, until we

46

come out the other side of uncertainty with the realisation that they are not related at all. The poet's own deeper conviction is precisely this. For after another double paragraph at "glow", he proceeds:

> The visions all are fled—the car is fled
> Into the light of heaven, and in their stead
> A sense of real things comes doubly strong,
> And, like a muddy stream, would bear along
> My soul to nothingness: but I will strive
> Against all doubtings, and will keep alive
> The thought of that same chariot, and the strange
> Journey it went.

So far from providing him with the means to find and seize life's sad actualities, his vision is acknowledged to be a structure which "a sense of real things" will supplant. In this surrender to the world we all live in, the pathos of the enterprise stands revealed. But the collapse of his career's projected second phase, as of the earlier second alternative, is also the vindication of his true scope. A Keatsian grappling with "events" proves to be only a threat after all. *Sleep and Poetry*, like Matthew Arnold's essay, doubles back on itself; its final appeal to "the thought" of the vanished charioteer is not a reposing of trust in something that will interpret life, "the agonies, the strife", "real things". That appeal commits Keats to a picture, a very special kind of picture, a frozen moment, a representation of locked energy, a stasis: "most awfully intent . . . forward bent . . . seems to listen". The charioteer's intent listening is not a significant listening *for* anything; its purpose is entirely fulfilled in the picture of kinetic arrest which it helps to sustain. The question, what is the charioteer listening for? what is he writing about? has no substance inside the universe of Keats's poetry. It is a critical ghost. And in seeing the pointlessness of asking it we solve the problem of Keatsian meaning. Unlike Shelley in almost every other way, he displays first-cousinship whenever and however we consider what his good verse means. While Shelley makes tunes ("Life of Life! thy lips enkindle"), Keats makes pictures. The fixity of these pictures ranges from the kinetic arrest observable in our charioteer to the hopeless leaden repose of Saturn at the beginning of *Hyperion*; and we shall see that a very serious function of Keats's classical mythology is to provide him with raw material for picture-making. His pictures, like his deaths and other intensities, will have room to themselves later. Just now the charioteer confronts us with his emphatic part in *Sleep and Poetry*. He defies his creator, exemplifying D. H. Lawrence's

47

dictum "Never trust the artist, trust the tale". His self-sufficient refusal to traffic in the world's events is something all Keats's pictures share, and when we say the charioteer is not listening *for* anything we are acknowledging his special autonomy and at the same time adding a further chapter to the story of end-stopped feel.

Thus *Sleep and Poetry's* prognostication that Keats will one day outgrow feel is made to refute itself. He declares he needs "vision" to grapple with actuality, but the object of "I see afar" is the charioteer who proceeds to close the circuit once more. Keats never again attempts this simple opposing of feel and vision, either by way of present alternatives or successive phases.

But once, in the Pleasure Thermometer of *Endymion*, he tries to make a higher thing of feel itself. That he took the venture seriously is shown by the letter he wrote about it to his publisher.[1] The Thermometer reads as follows:

> *Wherein lies happiness? In that which becks*
> *Our ready minds to fellowship divine,*
> *A fellowship with essence; till we shine,*
> *Full alchemiz'd, and free of space. Behold*
> *The clear religion of heaven! Fold*
> *A rose leaf round thy finger's taperness,*
> *And soothe thy lips: hist, when the airy stress*
> *Of music's kiss impregnates the free winds,*
> *And with a sympathetic touch unbinds*
> *Eolian magic from their lucid wombs:*
> *Then old songs waken from encloudéd tombs;*
> *Old ditties sigh. . . .*
> *Feel we these things?—that moment have we stept*
> *Into a sort of oneness, and our state*
> *Is like a floating spirit's. But there are*
> *Richer entanglements, enthralments far*
> *More self-destroying, leading, by degrees,*
> *To the chief intensity: the crown of these*
> *Is made of love and friendship, and sits high*
> *Upon the forehead of humanity.*
> *All its more ponderous and bulky worth*
> *Is friendship, whence there ever issues forth*
> *A steady splendour; but at the tip-top,*
> *There hangs by unseen film, an orbed drop*
> *Of light, and that is love: its influence,*
> *Thrown in our eyes, genders a novel sense,*
> *At which we start and fret; till in the end,*
> *Melting into its radiance, we blend,*

[1] Page 28, above.

Mingle, and so become a part of it,—
Nor with aught else can our souls interknit
So wingedly: when we combine therewith,
Life's self is nourish'd by its proper pith,
And we are nurtured like a pelican brood.
Aye, so delicious is the unsating food,
That men, who might have tower'd in the van
Of all the congregated world, to fan
And winnow from the coming step of time
All chaff of custom, wipe away all slime
Left by men-slugs and human serpentry,
Have been content to let occasion die,
Whilst they did sleep in love's elysium.
And, truly, I would rather be struck dumb,
Than speak against this ardent listlessness:
For I have ever thought that it might bless
The world with benefits unknowingly;
As does the nightingale, upperched high,
And cloister'd among cool and bunched leaves—
She sings but to her love, nor e'er conceives
How tiptoe Night holds back her dark-grey hood.
Just so may love, although 'tis understood
The mere commingling of passionate breath,
Produce more than our searching witnesseth:
What I know not: but who, of men, can tell
That flowers would bloom, or that green fruit would swell
To melting pulp, that fish would have bright mail,
The earth its dower of river, wood, and vale,
The meadows runnels, runnels pebble-stones,
The seed its harvest, or the lute its tones,
Tones ravishment, or ravishment its sweet,
If human souls did never kiss and greet?[1]

This rigamarole is the "argument" of his letter to John Taylor. More instructive than the term argument is the thermometer-word which he also uses, "gradations". The first notch or gradation is plain to see—to feel rather. It is the rose-leaf. Contrast that leaf, which is the undergoing of the Pleasure Thermometer's first stage, with the perfectly inane "that which" (one might call it the prose "Truth" mentioned in the letter) "becks / Our ready minds to fellowship divine". The feel of the leaf is real—as Keats would say—but the minds and the divine fellowship are just words, received words, civilities. And this contrast characterises the whole thermometer, for the writing retains traces of individuality wherever it is anchored in the poet's sensual hunger, and ceases to be in

---

[1] I, 777.

any way remarkable when it falls back on the conventions of spiritual talk. He tries, certainly, to appropriate "fellowship divine" to his personal use by tendering the gloss "fellowship with essence"; but although one perceives immediately that "essence" is not a received word, it remains obscure and incapable of rescuing the passage single-handed.

The muddle and enfeeblement are largely his own fault, as they were in *Sleep and Poetry*, though in any case commentators are quick to suppose he is embarking on an account, familiarly Christian or Neo-platonic, of the soul's ascent to God; and they are glad to have their expectations fostered by his failure to keep clear of a ready-made vocabulary of spiritual progress. Therefore "essence" has not made its impact. It ought to carry a warning notice: "If you want to take me for a word of soul and spirit, remember that Keats could only imagine the soul as an organ of, and Heaven a place of, intensified feel". Then we should see it for what it is—one of the four genuine gradations of the Pleasure Thermometer. These are: feel itself (the rose-leaf), the intensifying of feel towards "the chief intensity", the double climax implicit in the cross-reference between end-stopped experience and "self-destroying" experiencer, the heaven of "fellowship with essence" where feel has been successfully intensified and held for ever. He described this heaven to his clergyman friend Bailey in November 1817 during the last days of the writing of *Endymion*, when the whole poem was much in his thoughts. The letter is a meditation on the very question with which our passage opens: "Wherein lies happiness?"

Can it be that even the greatest Philosopher ever arrived at his goal without putting aside numerous objections? However it may be, O for a Life of Sensations rather than of Thoughts! It is "a Vision in the form of Youth", a Shadow of reality to come—and this consideration has further convinced me for it has come as auxiliary to another favorite Speculation of mine, that we shall enjoy ourselves hereafter by having what we call happiness on Earth repeated in a finer tone and so repeated.[1]

We cannot use "repeated in a finer tone" to interpret "a fellowship with essence", or insist on the *intensifying* force of "finer", without presuming to know Keats better than he knew himself. But that, surely, is a proper boldness where we seek to comprehend both the self-certainty of the poet of feel and the self-doubt of the

---

[1] *Letters*, vol. I, p. 185.

man who hesitated between the "Truth" to which "Thoughts" may direct us and that other haven at the end of the road of "Sensations". Some such awareness of alternatives is inevitable in a sane human being who must share the world with other people, whether he wants to or not; everybody has his own version of the thought/feeling dichotomy, and these are hardly ever interesting. We note a poet's version because there is a vital sense in which he inhabits his own world as well as dealing in the common mental categories of what is called, sometimes obtusely, real life.

In Keats's letter to Bailey the poet makes his presence known in the unabashed *naïveté* of a heaven where the feel of earthly pleasure is repeated, comes again—only more so, more intensely. In the letter to his publisher, the poet appears in the image which characterises the whole passage of verse under discussion: that of the Pleasure Thermometer. For a thermometer embraces both feel's repetition and its intensification, each gradation reaffirming the single sensual fact of heat—only more so. In *Endymion* itself the poet can be found in the four fixities which I have named; and it is his voice which frames the crucial question

Feel we these things?

To which we have to return a yes-and-no answer, because the man has been tampering with the poet's work, weakening and confusing it.

The thermometer is the simple truth stated by the confident poet; but the doubting man uses the word "Argument", and as soon as we leave the firm ground of the rose-leaf's feel, trouble starts. This argument is the converse of the "Drear-nighted December" lyric; instead of the feel of not to feel, it attempts to demonstrate the essential (hence "essence") feel of feel. Both undertakings carry a built-in guarantee of failure in that they must violate what they set out to vindicate, abjuring the principle of the closed circuit and so managing the Keatsian object as to make its meaning outrun its feel. Moreover *Endymion* labours under a second crushing burden, which is the false spirituality I remarked at the outset. Thus it reflects the hesitation so evident in the letter to Bailey, between essential feel and bodiless, feel-less truth. Struggling with the feel of feel, it possesses a kind of prose honesty; yielding to soul and spirit, it does not; but it is bad poetry throughout.

The badness, when Keats is pursuing his pseudo-spiritual ideal, is the featureless badness of those "ready minds" and "fellowship divine", leading (as if to make a complete job of the denial of his

51

own talent) to the thought of ourselves shining "free of space". Keats's memorable verse reaches futurity bound hand and foot to space; its imaginative servitude to space is its strength and its very distinction. One cannot relate freedom of this pleasure-thermometer sort to anything of his that has lasted—nor desire for this freedom. Hence the lack of character. We are left yawing aimlessly between an almost cretinous ineptitude ("lucid wombs") and involuntary pastiche. The idea of freedom from space draws him into an alien Shelleyan universe of "a sort of oneness" where "our state / Is like a floating spirit's", with the impression of Shelley hardening still further at

> Melting into its radiance, we blend,
> Mingle, and so become a part of it. . . .

The nightingale "upperched high" begins a backward journey into eighteenth-century Spenser (Keats's commonest juvenile mode), and with

> How tiptoe Night holds back her dark-grey hood

the tonal borrowing goes further back again, to Shakespeare. That line could pass as an overspill from *Romeo and Juliet*,[1] if something were done about "dark-grey".

Where the thermometer's argument holds honestly to feel, the badness of the verse strikes quite different. The pastiche disappears, and the ineptitude (of which there is plenty) does not leave us gazing at an unKeatsian linguistic crust, and gazing without concern for what lies beneath because instinctively satisfied there is nothing; but wondering, instead, what our own poet is trying to say. Sometimes the prose honesty is just prose. "Genders a novel sense" states the sad fate of Keats writing *about* the feel of feel. Sometimes the struggle to communicate is shown by a portentously clumsy involution like the one in the lines following the Shelleyan "radiance". For, grotesque as the association of "pelican brood" with "delicious" and "unsating food" undoubtedly is, the effort which promoted it cannot be entirely dismissed. The legendary pelican feeds its young with its own blood, of course, and I think it likely that Keats took his hint from *King Lear's* "pelican

[1] Perhaps the idea of night's hood, and the word, reached him through Juliet's appeal to "love-performing night" to "spread thy close curtain" and "hood my unmann'd blood" (III, ii). Again, night on tiptoe may have begun in Juliet's bedroom, three scenes later, with "jocund day / Stands tiptoe". Such Shakespearian farragos are common in bad Keats.

daughters".[1] Disaster strikes when the pelican's grim behaviour turns into a gastronomic treat. But the good meal and the young pelicans both have honest work to do. The food must be delicious because the thermometer is one of pleasure, and it must be unsating for the upward movement through the gradations of the thermometer to continue unchecked. The pelican, on the other hand, must live off its parent to reinforce the end-stopped effect of the line

Life's self is nourish'd by its proper pith,

which marks the decisive stroke of truth in the argument as a whole. "Proper" bears the ancient and central sense of "belonging to itself", and by thus bringing "life's self" back upon its own track, Keats once more closes the circuit of feel which his spiritual talk has been jeopardising—and continues to jeopardise. Our final impression is of the inane "human souls" being cancelled, without being redeemed, by the personal appeal to ripeness and quasi-orgasm—the latter only sketchily indicated in "the lute its tones, / Tones ravishment, or ravishment its sweet". These are agencies of intensification. One does not care a rap for the human souls, but the swelling fruit, the melting pulp, the harvest, are a slightly different matter because of their buried reference to the *Autumn Ode* and other great verse; and because they are true to the nature of the Pleasure Thermometer: the same again, only more so.

This honest badness, unlike the other sort, is always illuminating. It shows Keats running his head into an aesthetic noose, but doing so under a very suggestive compulsion, not at random or light-heartedly. The association of the cannibal pelican and the good meal is plainly suicidal, and no doubt it wouldn't take long to devise a happier presentation of life's self-enfolding rhythm. But the fact is, sensuousness and the grammar of the thermometer have him in their grip and force him on, beyond the neutral feeding-on-itself idea, towards an entirely typical reliance on the palate, that busiest of all feel's organs in his poetry. And so the enticing food is no more an accident here, and no more a decorative ploy, than it was in *Sleep and Poetry* where he described the feel-realm of Flora and Pan by "feed upon apples red, and strawberries"; or than it will be when he boldly introduces "spiced dainties" into Madeline's bedroom in *St. Agnes*, there to combine imagined taste with

---

[1] The probability is strengthened by "these pelican duns" in a letter of June 1817 (*Letters*, vol. I, p. 148). Although *Endymion's* progress cannot be followed in detail at this period, the letter and the Pleasure Thermometer are likely to be close to each other.

Keats enjoyed spinning oblique jokes out of *Lear*: for example, "unpoeted I write" (*Letters*, vol. II, p. 173) out of "unbonneted he runs" (III, i).

touch ("jellies soother than the creamy curd") and scent and
temperature ("filling the chilly room with perfume light") in a
prodigious riot of sensation.

Because the food in *Endymion* is not shallow-rooted like "fellowship divine" and "human souls", it holds the attention long
enough for us to note the force of "proper". Likewise of "pith" in
the same line. Life's "proper pith" provides a much-needed
comment on "fellowship with essence", deflecting us from false
spiritualities. We come to recognise that the pithy view of Keatsian
essence is always the right one. Thus in the next book of *Endymion*,
after dream-union with his goddess, the hero addresses her:

> "*O known Unknown! from whom my being sips*
> *Such darling essence, wherefore may I not*
> *Be ever in these arms?*"[1]

And when he wakes and finds her gone, he meditates alone:

> *Now I have tasted her sweet soul to the core*
> *All other depths are shallow; essences,*
> *Once spiritual, are like muddy lees,*
> *Meant but to fertilize my earthly root,*
> *And make my branches lift a golden fruit*
> *Into the bloom of heaven:*[2]

and now the pattern is complete. These two further essences, no
less than the pleasure-thermometer one, are tethered to feel, are
referred to the palate ("sips", "tasted"), denote a heaven of enjoyed sensuous intensities (compare "core" and "pith"), and leave
us facing a blank contradiction between ugly prose honesty
("fertilize" echoes "nourish'd") and emptiness. Here there is even
less doubt how the conflict should be resolved. When the tasted
"soul" stands next to the sipped essence, it lacks the meanest rag
to hide its pretention with. Nor can one miss the hollow and vulgar
commendation of "spiritual"—like "transcendent" in the betraying line

> *And gave the steel a shining quite transcendent,*[3]

like 'fabulous' in the mid-1960s. Such usages may reflect his
skimped education. Certainly—and more important—we see as
we go on, ranging from these inert heavens in early Keats to "the
sacramental cake" which Fanny Brawne has become in a very late
poem, that the only way he can save his religious imagination
from nullity is by dedicating it to some other value.

[1] II, 739.   [2] *Ibid.*, 904.   [3] *Calidore*, 133.

All this boils down to a search for the poet we admire. To say that "the clear religion of heaven" is put to flight by the pelican and life's "proper pith" is not quite to conclude there is no religion in his poetry. But about the pretence of being "free of space", we can be blunt. Ascending the thermometer towards "the chief intensity", when, "at the tip-top", his reader expects a revelation, Keats gives him a picture:

> at the tip-top,
> There hangs by unseen film, an orbed drop
> Of light,—

a picture, moreover, distinguished by a very singular hanging arrest. Its Keatsian stasis (in relation to the revelation which never comes) neatly parallels that of the intent and listening charioteer in *Sleep and Poetry* who frustrated the hope of a visionary statement *about* "the agonies, the strife / Of human hearts". Just this picture-making instinct refutes Keats's talk of freedom from space. Once inside his poetry we do not want to be, cannot imagine being, "free of space". We want to cup the hands of imagination round that "orbed" form, as we do round his "globed peonies" and, indeed, round the "cool and bunched leaves" which start out momentarily in the thermometer from the tissue of pastiche enveloping them. Shakespeare and eighteenth-century Spenser melt like a trite mirage and we are alone with Keats. It isn't the sudden arrival of the nightingale that presages big things to come, nor even the idea of her blessing the world with song, but the generalised yet potent feel of her "cloister'd" state up there in the trees, foreshadowing the cool filtered light of the *Nightingale Ode's* "beechen green" and the symphonic taste-and-temperature poetry which follows.

It is also possible to pursue the real poet into some of the most glaring absurdities of his Pleasure Thermometer. Of course "men-slugs and human serpentry" is laughable, but not to be derided, quite, because of the feel-situation which has provoked it. True, the mild *frisson* engendered by "wipe away all slime" seems a pretty commonplace effect. But compare it with what occurs fifty lines later in the same book of *Endymion*:

> Bushes and trees do lean all round athwart,
> And meet so nearly, that with wings outraught,
> And spreading tail, a vulture could not glide
> Past them, but he must brush on every side.
> Some moulder'd steps lead into this cool cell . . .[1]

[1] I, 865.

and might occur anywhere in early Keats. In so far as the lines are not absolutely negligible, we must seek the reason in "brush". "Brush", like "wipe", is a small thing but his own. The two verbs mark a stirring of the same feel-dominated fancy. We locate here the impulse which drags that poor vulture in by the scruff of the neck, making him ridiculous in the same way as the men-slugs. He exists simply for the brushing sensation of his wing-tips; when Keats makes a picture of him, that is its principle of composition, and the vulture himself is a very minor flourish of Negative Capability (I can imagine the feel of a bird gliding through a too-narrow gap). There are scores of non-human and human existences like his. Cumulatively, they matter.

Sleep and Poetry and *Endymion* both witness a passing hesitation in which Keats surveys his imagination's competence and wonders if this can be the real thing. The poet answers the doubting man with a firm "Yes" in both works. The programme of *Sleep and Poetry* was to enjoy the tasting-and-touching realm of Flora and Pan for a while, but then to leave it for human pain. However, finding pain resolves itself into seeing "afar" the charioteer, into a business of picture-making; and not merely has the charioteer no bearing on our human condition, he is quite expressly supplanted and dispossessed by "a sense of real things". *Endymion's* Pleasure Thermometer, on the other hand, is intended to be read throughout in the light of the feel-injunction "Fold a rose leaf"; but here the issue is muddied by the vague claim to spiritualise feel, to make a higher thing of it, a religious thing, a "fellowship divine". Cutting across this false story—false for Keats—of the soul's ascent is the true poetic imprint of "essence" and "intensity", a picture of the same again inside nature, only more so: "Life's self is nourish'd by its proper pith."

The reason for his temporary and recurring loss of nerve is broadly this. There ran a vein of sturdy common sense in him, impelling him to view all art, high and low, as indulgence. One writes poetry because one wants to, and to give pleasure to others,[1] but one has to live whether one wants to or not. "Life must be undergone", as he says in one letter, whereas one may, like Keats, consider abandoning poetry for medicine or journalism or the sea. This separation of life and art—a Romantic affair which comes to the surface in Kierkegaard—was aggravated by worldly failure. He would have thought about it less if he could have earned a living at poetry.

[1] "I am sometimes so very sceptical as to think Poetry itself a mere Jack a lanthern to amuse whoever may chance to be struck with its brilliance" (*Letters*, vol. I, p. 242).

On top of this he was troubled by his own imagination's bent. Some poets are, he believed, less indulgent than others, and when he considered the question his instinct led him to the distinction between (in our formulation) open-ended feeling and end-stopped feel. Therefore his bad conscience expressed itself in the urge to tell truths about the world, to deal with it interpretatively. But he has not got it in him to tell truths *about*. The ambition remains purely prescriptive, and the effort self-hortatory. And so we note the hollow magniloquence of *Sleep and Poetry's* address to "the events of this wide world". And the mood in which poetry "is not so fine a thing as philosophy".[1] And the confession "I have been hovering for some time between an exquisite sense of the luxurious and a love of Philosophy".[2] Repeated critical use has been made of such remarks, naturally enough, but I can't think a Keatsian interpretation of "events" has many honest devotees. Or of a god Pan who is

> *Dread opener of the mysterious doors*
> *Leading to universal knowledge.*[3]

The same Pan whose minions labour

> *to surprise*
> *The squatted hare while in half sleeping fit*[4]

is another matter. But that canting "universal knowledge" provides a talking point, whereas the squatted hare is what he is. Many pages have been devoted to the definition of poetry

> *'Tis might half-slumb'ring on its own right arm*[5]

at the expense of the picture which is nevertheless the thing achieved. What to say about such thereness of posture, except that it is Keatsian and fine? And meaningful? That it incarnates what we are all, including him, seeking to define?

We can add that such postures are pleasurable with a pleasure that soaks and soaks through the grieving Saturn "quiet as a stone" as much as it does the strangely contented figure "on a half-reap'd furrow sound asleep" in the middle stanza of the *Autumn Ode*. This saturating pleasure refers us to Keats individually as well as to the universal truth that art gives delight. For pleasure and feel are insistently and aboriginally linked in his work, and it is this bond which gives his bad conscience about his talent the particular stress and direction it has. He sees himself, however dimly, as celebrating the world's feel instead of offering opinions about the world's

---

[1] *Ibid.*, vol. II, p. 81.   [2] *Ibid.*, vol. I, p. 271.
[3] *Endymion*, I, 288.   [4] *Ibid.*, 264.   [5] *Sleep and Poetry*, 237.

meaning—say like Wordsworth. And he recognises that his creative celebration is doubly indulgent; it is satisfied to immerse itself in the stuff which others are busy interpreting, and it immerses itself pleasurably. The object of poetic immersion is pleasure (otherwise why do it?) as surely as the object of interpretation is truth. Here Keats uncovers, anxiously, his impulse to write, and finds it inseparable from his own life's sane appetites, his normal sensuality. He is as much, and as articulately, exercised by the pleasures of feel as are his critics by the tendency they call his escapism, though he has not received much credit for being forthright.

He states the case against his present poetic self very harshly indeed when he sketches his life's programme in *Sleep and Poetry.* His immediate hunger is for air

> *Smooth'd for intoxication by the breath*
> *Of flowering bays,*

and in the country just ahead the fruit and the girls taste nice and the flat line

> *And choose each pleasure that my fancy sees*

appears almost deliberately to withold all possibility of serious merit. He is working, of course, towards his contrast with the "nobler" poetry of suffering. But just as the attempt to oppose visionary interpretation to end-stopped feel collapses, so the subordination of pleasure to pain gets blandly reversed. The charioteer has nothing to tell us about suffering, and it is equally true that he cannot, by any clever stretch, be turned into a Keatsian picture of pain of the sort *Hyperion* will specialise in. If we try to make him actualise "the agonies, the strife" (rather as the "half-slumb'ring" figure incarnates poetry) we are left with a self-portrait of the ardent and happy Keats of 1817, "intent" as everyone who knew him describes him, composing "with hurrying glow".

Thereafter the pleasure-pain reversal becomes explicit. Keats says he will never forget the charioteer, and at once plunges into a passage commending the poetry "of old".

> *Ay, in those days the Muses were nigh cloy'd*
> *With honors; nor had any other care*
> *Then to sing out and sooth their wavy hair.*[1]

---

[1] *Sleep and Poetry,* 178. "Sooth" in the final line looks suspicious, and "smooth" may seem a plausible emendation (no manuscripts survive, so the issue turns on the likelihood of a misprint in the 1817 volume or a dropped "m" in the printer's copy). The missing "e" is then accounted for; the sense is perhaps easier; and the slight embarrassment of "soothe's" repetition 57 lines later (see the passage next quoted) is removed. But see p. 61, below.

Bad times followed, he heavily explains, in which neo-classical standards prevailed and men worshipped "the name of one Boileau". But things are better now, "Now, 'tis a fairer season". Better but not perfect; the Romantic Revolution has happened and brought fresh access of strength—at a price.

> But strength alone though of the Muses born
> Is like a fallen angel: trees uptorn,
> Darkness, and worms, and shrouds, and sepulchres
> Delight it; for it feeds upon the burrs,
> And thorns of life; forgetting the great end
> Of poesy, that it should be a friend
> To sooth the cares, and lift the thoughts of man.[1]

This conclusion he now clinches with an even more emphatic statement of poetry's *sooth*-ing role; making overt, as he does so, the continuity between the feats of the old imagination and the splendid promise of the new:

> All hail delightful hopes!
> As she was wont, th' imagination
> Into most lovely labyrinths will be gone,
> And they shall be accounted poet kings
> Who simply tell the most heart-easing things.
> O may these joys be ripe before I die.[2]

Within a very small space, therefore, *Sleep and Poetry* achieves an astonishing self-contradiction; to save its prose logic by arguing that a man might set out for the land of human pain and "simply tell the most heart-easing things" when he got there, would be a desperate sophistry. Reading the last two-thirds of this poem is like overhearing a dialogue between the creative instinct and the moral will. Instinct asks

> And can I ever bid these joys farewell?

The will replies,

> Yes, I must pass them for a nobler life,

but the severities of this new road are no sooner proposed than the instinct challenges them with "a lovely wreath of girls" and other typical early blisses, finally affirming

> O may these joys be ripe before I die.

[1] *Ibid.*, 241.   [2] *Ibid.*, 264.

The will, forced round in a circle by the literal repetition of "these joys", protests

> *yet there ever rolls*
> *A vast idea before me,*

only to be silenced by instinct's wordless certainty that the idea spends itself in the rolling; as if Keats had been thinking negative-capably about the billiard ball of his boast to Woodhouse. And from now on instinct has the stage to itself, the characterful badness of

> *fingers soft and round*
> *Parting luxuriant curls*

and of nymphs

> *wiping*
> *Cherishingly Diana's timorous limbs*

continuing unchecked, until we come to one of those testing moments which reach—in potentiality—beyond the parting and wiping and the silly sex, and summarise the major talent:

> *as when ocean*
> *Heaves calmly its broad swelling smoothness o'er*
> *Its rocky marge, and balances once more*
> *The patient weeds; that now unshent by foam*
> *Feel all about their undulating home.*[1]

An imagination which perches within the weeds lifted on the tide and made free to feel their whereabouts, does not need to be told its way. What it will one day achieve remains uncertain, however—as we respond to the pompous seaweed's "undulating home", at once endearingly inept (a bit like Hardy) and an authentic isolating stroke. The whole simile is premonitory in its marrying of feel and Negative Capability; and also in its heaving impulse towards some desired consummation—a fruitlike ripening is suggested by the sea's "swelling"; and then, from just a dozen lines earlier,

> *satyrs taking aim*
> *At swelling apples with a frisky leap*
> *And reaching fingers, mid a luscious heap*
> *Of vine leaves.*

Which is enough to impress the desultoriness and "luscious" impossibility of the whole. Yet it also confirms the overthrow of proposed pain by present pleasure, with fingers all the time busy at delicious feel, with that much more interesting seaweed enjoying

---

[1] *Sleep and Poetry*, 376.

its balancing sensation, its clean-washed state ("unshent"), its exploratory groping round its home; and with the "swelling smoothness" of the ocean no less tactile in imagination than that of the apples. Keats's repetition of "swelling" within twenty lines warns us not to hold it against the reading "sooth" (at "sooth their wavy hair") that it reappears so soon at "sooth the cares". He does indeed repeat such words. They evidence the concentration of *Sleep and Poetry*, and the great strain which maintaining his focus imposes on him. The effort forces repetition, and a scraping of the barrel for archaisms like "unshent"; and it provokes freaks like "sooth".[1] Did he spell the verb that way in order to bring it visually—and thus magically-truly—closer to "smooth"? Or perhaps its private rationale is to be found in the private Keatsian adjective "sooth" which exists in his poetry alongside the public "sooth" (meaning of course "true") and appears to conflate "smooth" and "soothing"—at any rate in *St. Agnes Eve's* "jellies soother than the creamy curd". The superlative form "soothest"— again unexampled outside Keats—in the invocation "O soothest Sleep!" of the sonnet to Sleep might well mean no more than "most soothing". But, whatever direction guesses take, his language's importuning of pleasurable feel persists, and his poetry of suffering dwindles further and further into hypothetical remoteness.

Endymion, the next major project after the 1817 volume, phrases his hoped-for "nobler life" differently. Instead of proposing two consecutive stages in the one career, his ambition now is to contain pain within the single sensory dynamic of pleasurable feel—as it were to wall pain up inside the case of the Pleasure Thermometer. The top notch of the thermometer is also the *dénouement* of the absurd story; we leave the shepherd hero secure at last in his enjoyment of life's "chief intensity", love. But in the mean time Endymion was intended to suffer. His career should have been *per ardua ad astra*—against which it needs saying (and this is the overarching reason for judging the Romance a failure) that the aspired-to *astra* are a fraud and the *ardua* he endures, paper-thin. The fraudulent stars of the narrative are simply a long weary elaboration of the pseudo-spirituality of the thermometer itself. The falsity of Endymion's quest for, and union with, his goddess is the falsity of the thermometer's "fellowship divine". The imaginative substance of

---

[1] Keats's autograph fair copy reads "sooth" at "soothe thy lips" in the *Endymion* Pleasure Thermometer (l. 783), and I think he always spelt the word thus. The reason for the manuscript reading "soothe" at *Endymion*, II, 1018 is that the passage is in the hand of John Reynolds who no doubt regularised his friend's eccentricity.

his adventures is exhausted at "I have tasted her sweet soul to the core" in Book Two, and the rest is Arnoldian humbug. Any contrary hope a reader may repose in "soul" is eclipsed by the direct feel-conviction of "slippery blisses", "warm / Between her kissing breasts", and the plain circumstance

> *That the fair visitant at last unwound*
> *Her gentle limbs, and left the youth asleep.*[1]

Keats's attempt to take Endymion beyond life's chief intensity to its chief intensity intensified (since his love is supposed to be divinely required) dies of starvation. A complete spiritual penury leaves Endymion's feel-pleasures bearing the full weight of a four-book narrative.

I stress the flimsiness of the rigours endured by Endymion because the belief (which almost everybody shares) that the poem is too sweet stems as much from the boring insubstantiality of its pains as from the exorbitance of its luxuries. It is as firmly pleasure-based as the thermometer, which remains the true paradigm throughout. The rare moment when pain strikes home as more than a theory is nearly always an assertion of dispersal and autonomy by the single Keatsian organ; thus the tongue of Niobe,

> *Poor, lonely Niobe! when her lovely young*
> *Were dead and gone, and her caressing tongue*
> *Lay a lost thing upon her paly lip.* . . .[2]

Or it is an authorly intervention, a general thought lifted clean out of the poem's action. As when Endymion wakes after his first dream-union and finds the girl has gone. Wandering about disconsolate he comes to a well,

> *when, behold!*
> *A wonder, fair as any I have told—*
> *The same bright face I tasted in my sleep,*
> *Smiling in the clear well. My heart did leap*
> *Through the cool depth.—It moved as if to flee—*
> *I started up, when lo! refreshfully,*
> *There came upon my face, in plenteous showers,*
> *Dew-drops, and dewy buds, and leaves, and flowers,*
> *Wrapping all objects from my smothered sight,*
> *Bathing my spirit in a new delight.*
> *Aye, such a breathless honey-feel of bliss*
> *Alone preserved me from the drear abyss*
> *Of death, for the fair form had gone again.*
> *Pleasure is oft a visitant; but pain*

[1] II, 851.   [2] I, 339.

Clings cruelly to us, like the gnawing sloth
On the deer's tender haunches: late, and loth,
'Tis scar'd away by slow returning pleasure.[1]

Such turns in the story reveal the whole undertaking at its most doomed. The three realities of this passage are the tasting and the adventure of "smothered sight" and the haunch-gnawing, and they all involve Keats in hopeless problems. "I tasted" rings true to the savouring instinct. But what did he taste? In trying to say, he finds himself torn, throughout *Endymion*, between the pale spirituality of soul-words and the euphemism of face-words. Everyone knows that "face" will not do for the essential pithy feel of her. His difficulty is close to that of the decorous pornographer —the same again, but acceptably. His problem is also, as always with intensity, the same again only more so; and in the present passage, piling bliss on bliss, he addresses himself to it by way of his hero's "smothered sight". The sensitive "wrapping" ("shut softly up alive") and introversion of the organ of outward sense faithfully proclaim him; that is why to underscore the resulting "honey-feel" is to do more than establish a point about his vocabulary. But as soon as we wonder what right the little episode has to be here at all, its credit collapses. "When lo! refreshingly", unkindly mimicing "when, behold!", gives the gratuitous, episodic game away. Like many other sudden shifts in *Endymion*, it serves pleasurable feel and feel intensified—the private theme—but has no public narrative status whatever; and our response soon defines itself as incredulous boredom with the story.

Summoning goodwill towards *Endymion* is like trying to get interested in a monstrously overblown and diluted ode. And when the pattern of bliss on bliss is broken at "Pleasure is oft a visitant; but pain . . ." the private logic is being abandoned too; we have lost Endymion's voice and are being addressed from the wings by Keats himself. Unquestionably by Keats, because of haunch and jaw and the "tender" imagination of suffering; unquestionably by early Keats because of the huge unbridged gap between this local touch and the empty vision of cosmic pain.

That reflective "but pain . . ." versifies the memorable passages in his letters where he strives to make sense of the world. It is an extrinsic thought which fails to get inside the Pleasure Thermometer and help *Endymion*. Afterwards, surely, he sensed as much himself, when he sat down in April 1818, at Teignmouth with his dying brother, and wrote a Preface conceding the poem's "mawkishness".

[1] *Ibid.*, 893.

More explicit about the world's pain and his own poetry are some couplets he dashed off to John Reynolds a mere fortnight before the date appended to the Preface, towards the end of the month in which he finished revising *Endymion* for the press, and with the whole poem at the forefront of his mind.

> *Dear Reynolds, I have a mysterious tale*
> *And cannot speak it. The first page I read*
> *Upon a Lampit Rock of green sea weed*
> *Among the breakers—'Twas a quiet Eve;*
> *The rocks were silent—the wide sea did weave*
> *An untumultuous fringe of silver foam*
> *Along the flat brown sand. I was at home,*
> *And should have been most happy—but I saw*
> *Too far into the sea; where every maw*
> *The greater on the less feeds evermore:—*
> *But I saw too distinct into the core*
> *Of an eternal fierce destruction,*
> *And so from Happiness I far was gone.*
> *Still am I sick of it: and though to-day*
> *I've gathered young spring-leaves, and flowers gay*
> *Of Periwinkle and wild strawberry,*
> *Still do I that most fierce destruction see,*
> *The Shark at savage prey—the hawk at pounce,*
> *The gentle Robin, like a pard or ounce,*
> *Ravening a worm—Away ye horrid moods,*
> *Moods of one's mind! You know I hate them well,*
> *You know I'd sooner be a clapping bell*
> *To some Kamschatkan missionary church,*
> *Than with these horrid moods be left in lurch—*
> *Do you get health—and Tom the same—I'll dance,*
> *And from detested moods in new Romance*
> *Take refuge—Of bad lines a Centaine dose*
> *Is sure enough—and so "here follows prose".—*

The story told in these lines is by now familiar: the rooting of present efforts and achievements in pleasurable feel; the aspiration to go on from here 'to philosophize'; the recognition—"I dare not yet" he tells Reynolds—that this desire leaves him gazing into an almost unimaginable future; the philanthropic stress on the power to make sense of pain.

Thus the couplets to John Reynolds form a trinity with *Sleep and Poetry* and *Endymion*. As well as confirming, they extend and clarify the two earlier statements. With the "Periwinkle and wild strawberry" we return to the realm of Flora and Pan—but instead of glancing resolutely ahead to the "nobler life", Keats admits a situation of impasse. His disquiet, and our interest, centre upon the verb to see: "too far into the sea", "too distinct into the core / Of an eternal fierce destruction". They bring to the surface the hard buried truth about vision, about know in relation to feel, in Keats's poetry. Where *Sleep and Poetry* had appealed to the "vision" of the charioteer, had intimated that the way to comprehend pain was to get a clear look at him and his mysterious writings, but had suffered an unexplained, involuntary lapse through the supplanting of vision by "a sense of real things"—where the import of this had before been hidden from Keats, he now interprets it as advisedly (almost) and as lucidly as his reader can claim to do.

Correcting *Sleep and Poetry*, he observes to Reynolds that the trouble with wished-for philosophic vision is not that it refuses to come clear but that it is already "too distinct". The heart of his complaint is that the clear sight of suffering strikes him dumb; he torments himself with something that needs saying, "but cannot speak it"; and for our part we should not ignore the hardening of the pessimism of "not yet" which the continuation "Oh never" brings about. In *Sleep and Poetry*, the spectacle of the world's pain had presented him with a challenge to be met and against which to test his artistic maturity; to press on would call for nerve and dedication, but it could be done. Now, this same spectacle is acknowledged to be merely disabling.

In recognising so much he has faced the worst, and spoken worse than the worst. He proposes:

> *I'll dance,*
> *And from detested moods in new Romance*
> *Take refuge.*

The severest of his moralising critics would be hard put to it to state the escapist case more damagingly, or more unfairly. He ignores, rather movingly I think, the outcome of his own monologue in which the recommendation to avoid seeing has been overtaken by events at "I saw too far". There it is. He cannot unsee. And we, experiencing the impact of this *fait accompli* through the gentle robin and the tortured worm, are bound to interpret his refuge-taking generously.

The couplets to Reynolds are founded on a fruitful self-contradiction, like Coleridge's *Dejection Ode* which is a poem about being unable to write poems. Keats knew in his heart that pleasurable feel was the home field of his poetry, and yet he could not persuade his heart to shut itself to pain. His first reaction to this state of affairs had been to tell himself, in *Sleep and Poetry*, he "must"—and would—get on to pain later. His second had been to try to enclose pain (by narrating the *ardua* of an heroic quest) within the Pleasure Thermometer of *Endymion*. The third is to appear to admit defeat. I say 'appear' because the poet who resolves to bury his head in the pleasures of Romance cannot thus wish away his negative-capable apprehension of the ravened worm. And so while the "Oh never" of the Reynolds couplets seems to stand the "I must" of *Sleep and Poetry* on its head, the final effect is a consolidating one.

His self-tormenting urge to manage pain persists; and persists not merely in the large philanthropic declamation of "high reason" and the rest, but in the detail. For example, in the unobtrusive word "tease". Compare

> *Things cannot to the will*
> *Be settled, but they tease us out of thought*[1]

which he gives Reynolds as his explanation of the sad "Oh never", with the outwardly optimistic programme

> *Then the events of this wide word I'd seize*
> *Like a strong giant, and my spirit teaze*
> *Till at its shoulders it should proudly see*
> *Wings to find out an immortality*

of *Sleep and Poetry*. And one is struck by the way "teaze" fits its context of uncreative fretting in the first case, but is being worked against its natural grain in the second. Then turn to Keats's letters and note the consistent mannerism running through them: "In this world there is no quiet,—nothing but teasing and snubbing and vexation"; "Not that I was so ill, but so much so as only to be capable of an unhealthy teasing letter"; "Do not, my dear Brown,"—so he urges, mortally ill—"tease yourself about me". And then there is the exact repetition of his words to Reynolds in the *Grecian Urn's* "Thou, silent form, dost tease us out of thought"; where one may ask whether he has not unwittingly surrendered the key to the nervous finger-wagging dogmatism—so uncharacteristic—of the ode's ending:

> *that is all*
> *Ye know on earth, and all ye need to know.*

As his own critique of Wordsworth states the matter, "We hate poetry that has a palpable design upon us—and if we do not agree, seems to put its hand in its breeches pocket".[2]

---

[1] L. 76. [2] *Letters*, vol. I, p. 224.

"Teaze" is a truthful enemy within *Sleep and Poetry's* gates, working to discredit its surface optimism; and thus we find Keats's vocabulary mirroring the displacement of the visionary charioteer by "a sense of real things". That poem, and *Endymion*, and the lines to Reynolds, tell the story of a poet whose imagination revolves in tight helpless circles round a "real" world where robins torture worms and "women have cancers".[1] His humanity and his quick practical intelligence, both very evident in his letters, keep his attention turned this way, but they cannot solve his creative problem for him. In a sense they make matters worse by adding a crust of plausibility to the pseudo-vision of the charioteer and the pseudo-spirituality of the Pleasure Thermometer. They are also, of course, both relevant to the creative work; the needed urgency, the wrought-up state of composition, is scarcely conceivable in separation from the painful mystery which can neither be coped with nor forgotten. But we must stand firm upon our old distinction between the poet of feel and the man seeking "universal knowledge". That knowledge, with its heavy philanthropic stress, fails to get into the poetry, it is a voice reaching us from outside—until it learns how to submit itself to the imagination's rule. And when that has happened, when knowledge is at home in the kingdom of feel, one must walk delicately both as regards the man who wants to know and the poet who can't help feeling. When the poet enters negative-capably into the thrush and projects his song:

> I have not read any Books—the Morning said I was right—I had no Idea but the Morning and the Thrush said I was right—seeming to say . . .

> *"O fret not after knowledge—I have none*
> *And yet my song comes native with the warmth*
> *O fret not after knowledge—I have none*
> *And yet the Evening listens—"*[2]

we have to recognise that "fret not after knowledge" is itself a deliberately adopted point of view like the rest; the poet cannot shed other possibilities any more than he can forget the ravened worm by deciding to "take refuge" in a new Romance. Or any more than he can—or really hopes to—sidestep the appalling toil of composition by declaring "That if Poetry comes not as naturally as the leaves to a tree it had better not come at all". On the one hand, man and poet are inseparable. On the other, Keats helps us to a valuable discrimination when, generalising on the basis of his

[1] *Ibid.*, p. 292.   [2] *Ibid.*, p. 232.

own gift, he coins and expounds Negative Capability. The exercise of this power yields him the thrush's song; and the thrush says "fret not after knowledge"; and the poet of Negative Capability is he who can remain "in uncertainties, Mysteries, doubts, without any irritable reaching after fact & reason"; and the thrush's "fret" and the poet's "irritable" both lead back to our touchstone word "tease". Keats knew and dreaded the killing breath of irritability, fret, teasing. But since the poet is also the man who must live in the "real" world of pain, how can he not be teased by it? That question hangs over the 1817 volume, and *Endymion*, and it introduces the later work.

II: THE ABSTRACT IDEA

1 The Choice of a Word

THE "new Romance" which John Reynolds heard about in March of 1818 was *Isabella* or, more probably, the never-finished Hyperion epic. April saw the publication of *Endymion*; and when *Hyperion* finally appeared under the subtitle "A Fragment" two years later, its publishers stated, in a draft Advertisement, "He commenced the Poem just before the publication of his *Endymion*; and he abandoned the intention of proceeding with it, in consequence of the reception that work experienced from some of the reviews".[1]

The first assertion would not be worth much on its own, because of the second's manifest falsity.[2] But all the evidence supports it—provided "commenced" be taken to indicate planning and reflection generally, rather than writing. We have the couplets to Reynolds, and the Preface to *Endymion* which bears the date 10 April and reads: "I hope I have not in too late a day touched the beautiful mythology of Greece, and dulled its brightness: for I wish to try once more, before I bid it farewell." Then there is a letter from the previous September which reports that he is deep in *Endymion*, that the whole thing really needs rewriting—"but I am tired of it and think the time would be better spent in writing a new Romance which I have in my eye for next summer".[3] As he said this he was in the process of falling behind schedule with *Endymion*. The plan, when he began in the spring of 1817, had been to finish before winter came again:

[1] *Poetical Works*, p. 276. This draft was not printed.

[2] Nailing the lie about the blighting effect of the *Endymion* reviews (which lie encouraged the wilting-flower legend) was first undertaken by Keats himself. The Advertisement finally issued ran as follows: "If any apology be thought necessary for the appearance of the unfinished poem of HYPERION, the publishers beg to state that they alone are responsible, as it was printed at their particular request, and contrary to the wish of the author. The poem was intended to have been of equal length with ENDYMION, but the reception given to that work discouraged the author from proceeding."

A copy of the first edition survives in which Keats has fiercely scratched out the whole Advertisement and written above it: "I had no part in this; I was ill at the time." Then he has bracketed off the words about *Endymion* for special denunciation, scribbling underneath, "This is a lie!"

[3] *Letters*, vol. I, p. 168.

O may no winter season, bare and hoary,
See it half finished: but let Autumn bold,
With universal tinge of sober gold,
Be all about me when I make an end.[1]

He would then have had leisure to turn *Hyperion* over in his mind through the winter and spring, and no doubt the next summer would have found him ready to write. In the event he seems not to have put pen to paper until the autumn of 1818, and our first account of him in the throes of composition is in a journal-letter to his brother and sister-in-law newly emigrated to America. On 18 December he writes:

I think you knew before you left England that my next subject would be "the fall of Hyperion". I went on a little with it last night—but it will take some time to get into the vein again.[2]

So he probably discussed his plans with them before they sailed in June. And right back in January he was considering subjects from his poetry for the painter Haydon, telling him "it would be as well to wait for a choice out of *Hyperion*", and adding that he proposes to treat it "in a more naked and grecian manner" than *Endymion*, one great difference being that Endymion is a mortal hero "whereas the Apollo in *Hyperion* being a fore-seeing God will shape his actions like one".[3] All this is pretty circumstantial; it shows that his expression of intention near the close of *Endymion*,

Thy lute-voic'd brother will I sing ere long,[4]

was not lightly made. And when, in October, he warns Richard Woodhouse not to take him very seriously when he threatens to give up being a poet ("Might I not at that very instant have been cogitating on the characters of Saturn and Ops?"),[5] we should think of him as busy composing, almost certainly, and as having been 'cogitating' for many months.

The chronological upshot is, then, an epic plan the beginnings of which were entangled with *Endymion*'s execution, which he worked at seriously during the autumn and on into the winter of 1818-9, which he returned to intermittently and abandoned in the early

---

[1] I, 54.
[2] *Letters*, vol. II, p. 12. The interruption hinted at here was the death of his brother Tom on 1 December.
[3] *Ibid.*, vol. I, p. 207.   [4] IV, 774.
[5] *Letters*, vol. I, p. 387. The word "cogitate" occurs only once in his poetry in all its forms—at the end of Saturn's speech to the defeated Titans (*Hyperion*, II, 169). Among these, of course, is "Ops, uplifting her black folded veil" and revealing her characterful face (113-5).

autumn of 1819. The attempt spans his mature creative life; for the Chapman's Homer sonnet ("Much have I travell'd") is the only very memorable thing to antedate its first stirrings, and the letter which baldly announces "I have given up *Hyperion*"[1] also mentions, immediately before, the Sunday walk outside Winchester which gave rise to the ode *To Autumn*, his last great poem. That Sunday was 19 September, the letter is dated the following Tuesday; and there the story ends, apart from his ill-documented attempt near the end of the year to pick up his narrative again.[2]

Very closely linked to his hopes and disappointments over this long period is the word 'abstract'. It can't be called a general favourite of his, appearing not at all in the poetry and only a handful of times in the letters. It is a *Hyperion* word. I want to give six instances—which is almost the total—in chronological order.

1

. . . for when a Schoolboy the abstract Idea I had of an heroic painting —was what I cannot describe. . . .

2

I wish I could say Tom was any better. His identity presses upon me so all day that I am obliged to go out—and although I intended to have given some time to study alone I am obliged to write, and plunge into abstract images to ease myself of his countenance his voice and feebleness . . . if I think of fame of poetry it seems a crime to me, and yet I must do so or suffer.

3

I never was in love—Yet the voice and the shape of a woman has haunted me these two days—at such a time when the relief, the feverous relief of Poetry seems a much less crime—This morning Poetry has conquered—I have relapsed into those abstractions which are my only life—I feel escaped from a new strange and threatening sorrow.

4

Praise or blame has but a momentary effect on the man whose love of beauty in the abstract makes him a severe critic on his own Works.

---

[1] *Ibid.*, vol. II, p. 167.
[2] Charles Brown, with whom he was living, recounts (*Keats Circle*, vol. II, p. 72) that he spent his mornings writing the silly *Cap and Bells* satire, and in the evenings was "deeply engaged in remodelling" *Hyperion*. Brown's words have led to much argument among specialists. By far the most probable view is that Keats's efforts at this stage can only have amounted to tinkering. Thorough revision does not square with the rest of the evidence.

My own domestic criticism has given me pain without comparison beyond what Blackwood or the Quarterly could possibly inflict—and also when I feel I am right, no external praise can give me such a glow as my own solitary reperception & ratification of what is fine. J.S. is perfectly right in regard to the slipshod *Endymion* . . . I have written independently *without Judgment*—I may write independently & *with judgment* hereafter.

5

The mighty abstract Idea I have of Beauty in all things stifles the more divided and minute domestic happiness. . . . I feel more and more every day, as my imagination strengthens, that I do not live in this world alone but in a thousand worlds. No sooner am I alone than shapes of epic greatness are stationed around me. . . . I am as happy as a man can be—that is in myself I should be happy if Tom was well, and I knew you were passing pleasant days. Then I should be most enviable —with the yearning passion I have for the beautiful, connected and made one with the ambition of my intellect.

6

Forgive me if I wander a little this evening, for I have been all day employ'd in a very abstract Poem and I am in deep love with you— two things which must excuse me.[1]

The four middle passages fall within a space of five weeks in September and October 1818, the time of his first sustained effort at composition; and when the remaining "abstract" cases are joined to them, the unforced consistency of his usage grows even more impressive. Number One is the letter which gives this book its section-headings; it is to Haydon, like the one urging him to wait for the "naked and grecian" *Hyperion* to choose paintable subjects; its date is two days before the Preface to *Endymion* where Keats says he has in mind a fresh attempt at "the beautiful mythology of Greece"; it is tonally close to Number Five where "abstract idea" also appears, and where "shapes of epic greatness" recalls "heroic painting". Number Six belongs to late July of the next year, 1819, when he was making a final assault on *Hyperion* before abandoning it: "I have also been writing parts of my *Hyperion*",[2] as he tells Bailey on 14 August.

Three of the six passages (Two, Three and Six) show him at grips with a poem which he thinks of as somehow, in its nature,

---

[1] *Letters*, vol. I, pp. 265, 368, 370, 373, 403; vol. II, p. 132.
[2] *Ibid.*, vol. 11, p. 139.

essentially abstract. This is *Hyperion*.[1] In the other three he is standing back and brooding, not so much about *Hyperion* as in a Hyperionic climate. "Abstract" forms the thread upon which all six are strung. We ask what the word means, wherein its special relevance to *Hyperion*. And the following pattern emerges. Always the use is determined by some contrast between what exists actually in the world and what exists notionally in Keats's mind. This truth appears at its simplest and quaintest in One; for the answer to the question, what would be a *concrete* idea of an heroic painting? is, I'm certain, Keats's impression of some painting he had seen or perhaps had had described to him, as opposed to one he had imagined—' in his head ' as we say. More subtle is the contrast in Six; but even here we only have to go back to the "Forgive me" at the beginning of the sentence to grasp the central issue. He is apologising for being distracted by the poetry in his head from the actualities of his love-relationship to her. By objecting on our side that all poetry is in one's head, mental, abstract in Keats's sense, we draw attention to the special status of *Hyperion* and so advance the discussion a stage further.

Next consider Two and Three which place *Hyperion* over against Tom and his illness. The dying brother is inescapably actual, so is John's duty to him; whereas the poem indulges the poet's private whim. He need not do it, and in doing it he removes himself from his brother. Hence the pejorative colouring which "abstract" acquires here through the repeated "crime", and, more mildly, through "obliged to write", "I have relapsed". It is a situation which touches his sensitiveness—the bad conscience we have already noted—to the charge of escapism; this is the Keats who asked whether he was lingering with Flora and Pan when he ought to be finding the agonies of human hearts.

[1] In passages Two and Three (and note, also, the contrast between present hopes and *Endymion* running through Four, and the "shapes of epic greatness" in Five) *Hyperion* has no rival worth a moment's thought. It must be said that at the time of his letter to Fanny Brawne (our Six) Keats is also busy with *Otho the Great* and *Lamia*. But *Otho* he always refers to as "a" or "the" or "my" or "our" —his and Charles Brown's—"Tragedy". And in any case a play could not conceivably be called an abstract poem. *Lamia* is one of the "three or four stories" which he mentions to Fanny in a letter immediately before our Six (*Letters*, vol. II, p. 130). These stories may, he says, appear in print "by Christmas". We understand *Isabella, St. Agnes, Lamia*, and perhaps *St. Mark*; he cannot be including a large, and largely unwritten, epic narrative among them, even if we may imagine him calling *Hyperion* a story. Therefore when he goes on to mention to the same correspondent "a very abstract poem", the strong probability is he means *Hyperion*. Strong grows stronger when all the other evidence points this way.

Outside these two passages "abstract" sheds its disesteem, but does not lose its Keatsian and Hyperionic character. Thus in One and Four the contrast of actual and notional is preserved while it is rephrased in terms of performance against unachieved ideal. Four's "love of beauty in the abstract" is the mind's-eye standard, the aspiration, which he brings to bear in the criticism of his own written work; and this introduces the "abstract idea" of One which is the schoolboy's vision of true excellence—obscure no doubt, but again an ideal standard which will enable him, he hopes, justly to appraise whatever pictures Haydon may, in fact, paint. Finally, the same phrase "abstract idea" in Five completely reverses—does more than abandon—the initial disparagement, and even so continues true to our observed type. The contrast, as in Two, Three and Six, is between the poetry running in his head and so-called real life, but instead of thinking it a crime to let poetry prevail, and instead of apologising for the resulting inattention to the demands of real life, he glories in the fact that his abstract idea "stifles" the actualities of "domestic happiness". The whole of Five reads as if *Hyperion* were going well just now ("every day, as my imagination strengthens"); as if the ideal seemed, for the time being, not utterly unattainable. We all know those moments when the gap narrows.

I would stress again there are only a handful of "abstract" occurrences in all Keats, and when they are studied the actual/notional antithesis is seen to undercut everything else. *Hyperion* is not "a very abstract poem" because it got under way while Tom was dying; nor (conversely) because Keats saw in it the promise of an ideal vindicated and fulfilled. The gloomy and the bright shading are both, in Lockeian terminology, secondary qualities. Only the antithesis is primary, and its rationale must be sought, naturally enough, in the poem itself.

2 'Hyperion'

The best introduction to the two versions of *Hyperion* is our clutch of "abstract" letters. These expose both the actual and the notional sides of the matter, in the first place through the recurring ideal standard and the strange phrase "the ambition of my intellect" which plainly relates to that standard. *Hyperion's* abstractness for Keats and its ambitious scope are not finally separable; they share a common root in the fact—obvious but often ignored—that

74

the poem never got written. It seems odd that he should apply "abstract" both to his poem and his ideal standard, until we focus our attention where his is, on what is notionally present but unachieved. Had he finished *Hyperion*, it would have ceased to be abstract; the result would have been an "existence" or a "nothing", depending on whether it satisfied his ambition or not. Here I follow the home-made terminology of one of his Teignmouth letters:

As tradesmen say everything is worth what it will fetch, so probably every mental pursuit takes its reality and worth from the ardour of the pursuer—being in itself a nothing. Ethereal things may at least be thus real, divided under three heads: things real—things semireal—and nothings. Things real—such as existences of Sun Moon & Stars and passages of Shakespeare; things semireal—such as Love, the Clouds &c which require a greeting of the Spirit to make them wholly exist; and Nothings which are made great and dignified by an ardent pursuit.[1]

Thus even the "nothing" of the merest "mental pursuit" borrows a kind of inferior reality from the pursuer's earnestness. But Keats thinks of Shakespeare's verse as real in its own right, so to

---

[1] *Letters*, vol. I, p. 242. As so often, Keats's thinking is going on at the tip of his pen. "Every mental pursuit" seems at first to cover all imaginative work, and that may well have been his own intention initially, especially he has just confided to Bailey: "I am sometimes so very sceptical as to think Poetry itself a mere Jack a lanthern to amuse whoever may chance to be struck with its brilliance." But, if so, he soon realised the need to distinguish; and "at least" marks a check and hesitation. The greatest literature cannot be a "nothing" wholly dependent on finding an ardent pursuer. What he wants to say is that ardent pursuit bestows reality of a sort on the poorest endeavours of mind. And so he offers the real / semireal / nothing trichotomy.

His coupling of love and clouds also invites comment. He is saying that both require a "greeting of the Spirit" wholly to realise their natures. Love has to be acknowledged and requited; clouds have to be characterised. The oddness of the latter notion springs from his very persistent habit of regarding clouds as cloud-shapes after the fashion of Hamlet's conversation with Polonius about camels, weasels and whales. One thinks immediately of the "huge cloudy symbols" in the sonnet "When I have fears". But this happens in an undistinguished way all the time:

> *I watch and dote upon the silver lakes*
> *Pictur'd in western cloudiness, that takes*
> *The semblance of gold rocks and bright gold sands,*
> *Islands, and creeks, and amber-fretted strands*
> *With horses prancing o'er them, palaces*
> *And towers of amethyst. . . . (Endymion, I, 739)*

His cloud-shapes range from "flocks new shorn" ("I stood tiptoe", 8) to "herded elephants" (*Endymion*, II, 289). This is the sense in which a cloud is only semireal until it has received a greeting of the spirit.

speak, like the stars above us. This last coupling demonstrates that the actual/notional antithesis is not Keats's version of the familiar alignment of Nature against Art. Great art like Shakespeare's compels inclusion within the sublime existences of Nature. If he could himself have achieved *Hyperion* he would have given "existence" to something no less real than the sun.

We may further refine the interdependence of abstractness and ambition, observing that *Hyperion* is "very abstract" (as Keats tells Fanny) because it is surpassingly ambitious, and *vice versa*. That "very" bears directly upon the poem's peculiar status, which is expressed by its author once as a desired confluence of "Intellect" and "Passion", and once as a determination to compose "with Judgment". What of poetry coming as naturally as the leaves to a tree? What of the cry from the heart, "O for a Life of Sensations rather than of Thoughts!"? Indeed what of Negative Capability? For the essence of his creative analysis, and self-analysis, was, we recall, a glad acceptance of the condition of having no identity and going out from self to fill other bodies—the consequence of which, for the abstract-ambitious intellect, was to be "capable of being in uncertainties, mysteries, doubts, without any irritable reaching after fact and reason". Even closer to the bone is the neat verbal parallel between the negative-capability letter in which he modestly welcomes it for a healthy sign of his "poetical character" that "the identity of every one in the room begins to press upon me", and the "abstract" letter in which the fact that Tom's "identity presses upon me so all day" is something he fights against and tries to undo.

Moreover his way of resisting Tom's identity is to write, to "plunge into", poetry; and at this point the opposition between the negative-capable and abstract attitudes grows complete. What had been easy and confident and natural (like the leaves to the tree) becomes self-tormented from two directions: the direction of the escapist reproach and that of the abstract-ambitious intellect. Underlying both, of course, is the situation of pain. Keats is prepared to contemplate the abstract idea stifling "domestic happiness", but we may doubt whether *Hyperion's* progress could ever have been sufficiently promising for him to say the same about domestic distress. Pain forces him to ask, in his letter, the heroically simple question, "Why should women have cancers?"; and then he has to choose between condemning his own poetry to the function of Flora-and-Pan escapism and forming the abstract-ambitious resolve to answer that same question satisfactorily.

In *Hyperion* he very deliberately accepts the second alternative, and in doing so imparts to his work an uncharacteristic steeliness, a willed quality, which we find reflected in the "abstract" letters, momentarily belying all I understand by Keatsian end-stopped feel, and all he meant by Sensation and Negative Capability. The issue is well summarised in yet another letter where he re-phrases the question about women.

One saying of yours I shall never forget—you may not recollect it—it being perhaps said when you were looking on the surface and seeming of Humanity alone, without a thought of the past or the future, or the deeps of good and evil. You were at the moment estranged from speculation and I think you have arguments ready for the man who would utter it to you—this is a formidable preface for a simple thing—merely you said; *"Why should Woman suffer?"* Aye. Why should she? "By heavens I'd coin my very soul and drop my blood for drachmas."! These things are, and he who feels how incompetent the most skyey knight errantry is to heal this bruised fairness is like a sensitive leaf on the hot hand of thought.[1]

The question points away from the poetic achievement we admire, the leaf in the hand towards it. But, of course, the leaf is itself a small incarnation of pain. It does not belong to a world of possible answers to Bailey's and Keats's question; there is nothing in it to gratify the abstract-ambitious intellect. But it does re-cast that question by actualising it—like an event in life which cries out for explanation. Unlike life's pains, the leaf evokes an "ah!" of surprised pleasure and recognition, which is our tribute to imagination's little triumph. We know Keats could have made something of that leaf.[2] We know because of the easy effect towards which feel and Negative Capability and the picture-making instinct are beginning to conspire. The incontrovertible thereness of the leaf lying on the hand—an idea so perfectly ordinary and yet so distinguished—belongs to him alone. Whereas any serious-minded young man who had worked and watched in a London hospital early in the nineteenth century would be likely to frame questions about human suffering. Those antipodes, the

---

[1] *Letters*, Vol. I, p. 209. He is writing to his clergyman friend Bailey who will have proposed a Christian answer, of a dull sort, to this question. The second sentence in inverted commas is an adaptation of Brutus's words in *Julius Caesar* (IV, iii), giving Bailey to understand he would go to great lengths to find an answer.

[2] The "sensitive leaf" reappears, now as felt rather than feeler, on his Scottish walking tour with Charles Brown. Brown "kissed a child who was afraid of his Spectacles and finally drank a pint of Milk. They handle his Spectacles as we do a sensitive leaf" (*Letters*, vol. I, p. 347). This incident nicely shows his innerness of apprehension as he watches the object being delicatedly fingered.

question and the leaf, both have a place in the study of *Hyperion*. The epic, as far as Keats got with it, is to do with beauty. We have to lean heavily on the first version in judging overall pattern and tendency, because there he pushed further ahead with his story than when he broke down the second time. However both fragments agree on a war in heaven as the basis of the present narrative. An older race of gods, the Titans, has been overthrown by the younger Olympians. Hyperion, who gives the work its title, is cast in the role of ultimate champion of the Titan cause, for he is the only one of them undefeated when we come in. The main action will apparently be the overcoming or superseding of Hyperion by the Olympian Apollo[1]—but all that is best left on one side since it does not exist on paper.

The fundamental *donnée*, then, of both versions is the war which has just finished. From the outset we stand in the shoes of the defeated Titans, experiencing their bitter sorrow, asking their questions; and the centrality of beauty is asserted precisely here. For the only theoretical response given by either version to the Titan cry, why this pain at the hands of the younger gods? is that beauty should triumph and in the present case has triumphed. The victorious Olympians are more beautiful than the Titans; there is no more to be said,

> *for 'tis the eternal law*
> *That first in beauty should be first in might:*[2]

and this one stroke not only puts beauty at the centre of *Hyperion*, but interlocks it with pain by spelling a metaphysic of suffering out of beauty's triumph. To those who can make no sense of how the world is, Keats says that the less beautiful go to the wall.

And now the "abstract idea" of those letters begins to take shape, and their juxtaposing of "the yearning passion I have for the beautiful" and "the ambition of my intellect" ceases to be just a puzzle. Keatsian beauty had always taken its nature from the pleasures of feel, actual and imaginary, and in *Hyperion* he sees the chance of simultaneously vindicating the beautiful and coping philosophically with pain. This is the force of "connected and made one with". He is involved in a lofty form of the attempt to kill two birds with one stone. The attempt dominates his very ambitious, very abstract poem.

" 'Tis the eternal law", he affirms, hoping to show forth the

---

[1] The letter to Haydon (p. 70, above) in which Apollo is called the poem's divine hero, in contrast with the mortal hero Endymion, shows that a very important part was envisaged for him.

[2] II, 228.

world's pain as the price of beauty's victory. His words have that
ring of steely resolve which we met for the first time in *Sleep and
Poetry*.

> And can I ever bid these joys farewell?
> Yes, I must pass them for a nobler life. . . .

The lines leap off the page in the 1817 volume not, I insist, because
they are good, and not because they are characterfully bad like so
much of the early poetry of feel, but because they are unKeatsian.
Behind the assertiveness, the dogmatism, he has lost touch with his
habitual self-certainty. In the next line,

> Where I may find the agonies, the strife

he fails to achieve even the mildest intimacy with the idea of
"find". And so on our side nothing moves us to wonder what "find"
might mean. It inclines, in brief, towards the abstract idea. At "I
must pass" and "I may find" Keats takes the first step along the
road that ends with the abandonment of *Hyperion*.

Sleep and Poetry divided his future career into two distinct phases,
the first spent with Flora and Pan where the fruit and the girls
taste delicious, and the second among the painful "events of this
wide world". (The same hollow energy belongs to "seize" the
events as to "find" the agonies.) *Endymion*, his next big poem, gave
up the notion of two stages and tried instead to ennoble the
pleasures of feel (to ennoble Keatsian beauty, that is) by trans-
cendentalising them. The tokens of its failure are our disbelief in
the *ardua* of Endymion's spiritual aspiring quest, and our boredom
with the quasi-pornographic repetitiousness of his erotics *en route*.
The climactic revelation in which the pursued goddess Cynthia
turns out to be none other than the human, and humanly desired,
Indian Maid cannot give surprise or interest, because that is the
only sort of conviction she ever carried. Her pursuit and her own
self constitute a damning commentary on Keats's "fellowship
divine", that borrowed plume of the Pleasure Thermometer; and
what he calls the thermometer's "argument" nudges him further
along the abstract path. His Indian Maid, on the other hand,
lives in the land of Flora and Pan, which is just what the abstract-
ambitious intellect is complaining about when it styles *Endymion's*
overall effect sentimental. This severe view is soon elaborated in
the verse-letter to John Reynolds. There, with "take refuge",
Keats consigns his own work to the escapist role, and with the
lines about seeing "too far into the sea" he points, as if across a
guarded frontier, at the whole unmanageable real world of pain.

Hyperion comes over the horizon at this juncture, because of its central concern to show that the things which happen under the sea's pleasant surface are such as art can manage, touch, contain, account for—whatever "find" and "seize" mean in *Sleep and Poetry*. The connection is striking between Keats's despondency in the Reynolds couplets:

> but I saw
> *Too far into the sea; where every maw*
> *The greater on the less feeds evermore:—*
> *But I saw too distinct into the core*
> *Of an eternal fierce destruction,*
> *And so from Happiness I far was gone—*

and his buoyant expository zeal in *Hyperion*.

> *We fall by course of Nature's law, not force*
> *Of thunder or of Jove. . . .*
> *Now comes the pain of truth, to whom 'tis pain;*
> *O folly! for to bear all naked truths,*
> *And to envisage circumstance, all calm,*
> *That is the top of sovereignty. Mark well!*
> *As Heaven and Earth are fairer, fairer far*
> *Than Chaos and blank Darkness, though once chiefs;*
> *And as we show beyond that Heaven and Earth*
> *In form and shape compact and beautiful,*
> *In will, in action free, companionship,*
> *And thousand other signs of purer life;*
> *So on our heels a fresh perfection treads,*
> *A power more strong in beauty, born of us*
> *And fated to excel us, as we pass*
> *In glory that old Darkness: nor are we*
> *Thereby more conquer'd than by us the rule*
> *Of shapeless Chaos. Say, doth the dull soil*
> *Quarrel with the proud forests it hath fed,*
> *And feedeth still, more comely than itself?*
> *Can it deny the chiefdom of green groves?*
> *Or shall the tree be envious of the dove*
> *Because it cooeth, and hath snowy wings*
> *To wander wherewithal and find its joys?*
> *We are such forest-trees, and our fair boughs*
> *Have bred forth, not pale solitary doves,*
> *But eagles golden-feather'd, who do tower*
> *Above us in their beauty, and must reign*
> *In right thereof; for 'tis the eternal law*
> *That first in beauty should be first in might:*
> *Yea, by that law, another race may drive*
> *Our conquerors to mourn as we do now.*[1]

[1] II, 181.

Both passages are committed to "Nature's law", and both interpret that law, in its radicals, alike. The survival of the fittest is the tune to which creation dances; this constitutes the world's outward drama and equally its inner sense. *Hyperion* assents to "the greater on the less feeds evermore" in the couplets to Reynolds, adding that the greater is the more beautiful since Nature's law now has a second clause which reads, "That first in beauty should be first in might".

Hyperion's addition in which the "greater" of the Reynolds couplets acquires the gloss "more strong in beauty" was intended to change the picture decisively. To appreciate Keats's insistence we have to run an eye quickly over the fragment as a whole, beginning at the beginning with Saturn sitting dead still and silent after his defeat. He is joined by the goddess Thea, Hyperion's wife, who rouses him from his stupor in order to stress his total discomfiture and to affirm she has no explanation of these recent events, or consolation, to offer. "I have no comfort for thee, no not one", she pointedly says—and through her Keats's will is beginning to bear down on the reader. In reply, Saturn asks her to

> *tell me if this feeble shape*
> *Is Saturn's; tell me, if thou hear'st the voice*
> *Of Saturn; tell me. . . .*[1]

The hectoring spate of command and question, faintly echoing Lear's "Does any here know me?" speech, reaffirming that Shakespeare is always a bad sign in Keats. Bad here because a mark of knowingness and strain. Here, he wants to settle his poem firmly into its vein of unexplained suffering. Thea only understands that disaster has struck them down. Saturn only understands the pain of defeat. They both want to understand more; and Keats now sends them together (after introducing Hyperion, the one still unconquered) to

> *that sad place*
> *Where Cybele and the bruised Titans mourn'd.*[2]

Some of these are introduced, whereupon Saturn proceeds to address them. His speech burrows deeper still into the sheer puzzle of pain, beginning

> *"Not in my own sad breast,*
> *Which is its own great judge and searcher out,*
> *Can I find reason why ye should be thus:"*[3]

---

[1] I, 98.   [2] II, 3.   [3] II, 129.

"not there", nor anywhere else, he repeats,

> *"Can I find reason why ye should be thus:"*[1]

and he wheels round on one of the listening Titans:

> *"Thou, Oceanus,*
> *Ponderest high and deep; and in thy face*
> *I see, astonied, that severe content*
> *Which comes of thought and musing: give us help!"*[2]

The effect of bathing *Hyperion* in questioning and bafflement is inevitably—and advisedly on Keat's part—to underscore the speech which follows. Oceanus it is who now asks them to see their Titanic woes as part of a process called Beauty's Triumph. How, or even whether, the process justifies the pain, is not easy to determine. Oceanus proclaims his message to be "the pain of truth", but immediately cries "folly" against those who take it for pain. His speech's dominant note is stoic resignation to the truth rather than welcome of it. He concludes:

> *"Receive this truth, and let it be your balm."*[3]

But there is no suggestion of pain's mystic transformation into something other than itself. All he can say is, we suffer, but we suffer in a good cause. So "all calm" is his mandate.

Against the objection that this is only his view, not Keats's necessarily, or the poem's, we remind ourselves once more that the poem never got written, and what we have bends inward upon Oceanus's speech with all possible emphasis. To which I would add that Keats cannot but assent, broadly, to this view; for he is embarked on a narrative in which beauty will indeed and in truth prevail. Oceanus makes his own individual defeat exemplify the general principle he has just laid down.

> *"Have ye beheld the young God of the Seas,*
> *My dispossessor? Have ye seen his face?*
> *Have ye beheld his chariot, foam'd along*
> *By noble winged creatures he hath made?*
> *I saw him on the calmed waters scud,*
> *With such a glow of beauty in his eyes,*
> *That it enforc'd me to bid sad farewell*
> *To all my empire. . . ."*[4]

[1] II, 149.   [2] II, 163.
[3] II, 243.   [4] II, 232.

Following him, the Titaness Clymene reaffirms the earlier per-
vasive bewilderment:

> "*O Father, I am here the simplest voice,*
> *And all my knowledge is that joy is gone,*
> *And this thing woe crept in among our hearts,*"[1]

and then she introduces Apollo:

> "*A voice came sweeter, sweeter than all tune,*
> *And still it cried, 'Apollo! young Apollo!'*
> *I fled, it follow'd me, and cried 'Apollo!'*"[2]

So that our first word of him is his name carried on some unseen
stranger's voice of utmost beauty. And the beauty is, of course, the
point, since the final triumph of beauty will be Apollo's, and therein Oceanus's reading of Nature's law will be vindicated. We
should not be distracted from this firm outline by the next and last
speaker, Enceladus, who now follows Clymene and rejects both
her opinion and Oceanus's:

> *Or shall we listen to the over-wise,*
> *Or to the over-foolish, Giant-Gods?*[3]

For Keats needs to close the debate with a speech that will narrow
attention upon the confronting of mighty opposites, of old and
new, beautiful and more beautiful, shortly to come. A flaunting
militancy is called for.

> *And be ye mindful that Hyperion,*
> *Our brightest brother, still is undisgraced—*
> *Hyperion, lo! his radiance is here!*[4]

Providing it in the person of Enceladus, Keats admits—for the
first time I think—an unqualified and truly abject dependence on
the Great Consult in *Paradise Lost's* second book. Hardly a surprise,
therefore, that devising this speech brings him within two hundred
lines of breakdown.

This sad circumstance gets reported in a letter to John Reynolds:

I have given up *Hyperion*—there were too many Miltonic inversions in
it—Miltonic verse cannot be written but in an artful or rather artist's
humour.[5]

Behind that laconic front, Enceladus (*alias* Moloch) indicates a
Miltonic parasitism of far greater import than *Hyperion's* modest

---

[1] II, 252.   [2] II, 292.   [3] II, 309.   [4] II, 343.
[5] *Letters*, vol. II, p. 167. He is talking about the second, revised version in this
letter, but what he says applies to the whole project.

total of inversions. And behind Milton altogether lies the personal failure. Keats's hyper-Miltonism is a symptom, not the cause, of his loss of heart, though what he says here to Reynolds makes perfectly good shorthand sense.

The profounder observation is the one he helps us to arrive at for ourselves, when he tells Fanny Brawne a fortnight or so before he throws over the epic that it is still "a very abstract poem". The rift between the actual and the notional persists. He knows his way blindfold among the pleasures of feel, but when it comes to

> *the eternal law*
> *That first in beauty should be first in might*

feel's actuality has been abandoned for that concern which his "abstract" letter relegates to "the ambition of my intellect", and which it hopes will sooner or later be "made one with" the Keatsian actual. To its credit, Keats's intellect is a very honest faculty. As soon as it begins asking what is 'real' (a favourite and telltale word) in life, it gladly salutes "Sun Moon & Stars and passages of Shakespeare", but sees too that it must include the fact that "women have cancers". And this is the moment at which creative buoyancy is lost. In terms of *Hyperion*, his sturdy common sense tells him that women do not endure their cancers in the cause of beauty's triumph. So why go on with his taxing epic fiction?

Recognising, with special poignancy, that *Hyperion* was just a story, he decided to give it up. The sharpness of this realisation is attributable to the play of his abstract-ambitious literary hopes against his daily life's humanity, unmetaphysical and very direct; and when we wonder, reasonably, how he can ever have hoped to make something more than a story of *Hyperion*, our only recourse is to point to the obscure resolve in *Sleep and Poetry* to "find" the world's agony and "seize" its events. We stop here, where criticism so often begins, not because the rest is too difficult, but because (like the unwritten triumph of beauty in *Hyperion*) it does not exist.

Or because, like the *Grecian Urn's* coda, it does not exist effectually. Indeed, addressing his urn,

> *a friend to man, to whom thou say'st*
> *Beauty is truth, truth beauty,—that is all*
> *Ye know on earth, and all ye need to know*

he provokes a general showdown. We cannot avoid making up our minds about the mature, the major poet. There, thrust forward, is the opaque and almost featureless assertion about truth and beauty.

Certainly an abstract-ambitious affair, like the first line of Endymion:

A thing of beauty is a joy for ever:

and, like that line, gummed hopefully on to an alien substance. For if *Endymion*, a poem of many blissful feel-unions and desolating separations, has any truth to expound, it is the absolutely Keatsian tautology that a felt thing of beauty is a joy while we feel it. Similarly, the *Urn* destroys its own coda. Out of its beautiful questions, especially the ones surrounding the "little town" of the fourth stanza, emerges the most heart-rending of our satisfactions, which is our assured lack of knowledge. "Beauty is truth, truth beauty" has not had an easy passage. But the head-on assaults and belabourings of it as false or meaningless have been misconceived, I think. They reflect a confused desire to punish Keats for the self-betrayal of "all ye need to know"—the pinched calculation, the nurse-maid's voice—and, what is more serious, the delimitation "on earth".

"On earth" works havoc by insinuating another place or state where the beauty-truth formula might not suffice. This reintroduces Keats's religion: the "fellowship divine" of the Pleasure Thermometer, and the broader spirituality of *Endymion* as a whole. By borrowing two Keats words we are able to say that the *essence* of the matter is *intensity*: the same again only more so. Which recalls the letter conceiving man's afterlife as a repetition of his earthly pleasures, but a repetition "in a finer tone". The importance of taking "finer" for an intensifying and not a spiritualising agent becomes clearer all the time; famous images like

burst Joy's grape against his palate fine

in *Melancholy* shed light on as they draw strength from this distinction, which so far we have been using negatively, to suggest why (in particular) *Endymion's* "clear religion of heaven" should be as bad as it is. And so, when instinct tells us that "on earth" in the *Grecian Urn* is not just otiosely rhetorical but a destroyer let loose within the Keats universe, the reason must be looked for here. We know that the ardent, intensifying Keats was capable of sustaining an unspoken "Beauty is truth, truth beauty" in a poem's heart of hearts; the pictured beauty of the *Autumn Ode* is no other thing than its voiceless truth; the lambs are full grown and/ but (an accepting "and" made one with a regretful "but") the swallows are gathering to go. Nevertheless there can be no saving the stated proposition which has the poet bearing down wilfully upon it with his talk of need, and curtailment to earth. We are left clutching a dictum.

Hyperion presents the same phenomenon writ large, for it seeks to demonstrate, on the scale of myth, that life means what the urn says. At an earlier time, with the failure of *Endymion* still near and sore, Keats had pierced the sea's agreeable surface to the deep truth of "eternal fierce destruction"; and his reaction had been to look away and embrace poetry as something to "take refuge" in. Now he girds himself, in the biggest effort of his young maturity, to look again, to keep looking and to spell out from what he sees, an "eternal law".

His postulated law comes through to us pathetically naked and vulnerable, in just the same way as the beauty-truth formula. We witness the same helpless coming apart of the willed sentiment and the poetic gift. Neither does it avail anything that the sentiment is not to be taken lightly, that it issues, and issues impressively, from a hard struggle to understand; that Keats is almost never superficial—in his letters. Directly relevant to *Hyperion* is the finest thing he wrote outside his poetry, the "Vale of Soul-Making" from a long journal-letter of the Spring of 1819, to his brother and sister-in-law.

The most interesting question that can come before us is, how far by the persevering endeavours of a seldom appearing Socrates mankind may be made happy. I can imagine such happiness carried to an extreme—but what must it end in? Death. And who could in such a case bear with death? The whole troubles of life which are now frittered away in a series of years, would then be accumulated for the last days of a being who, instead of hailing its approach, would leave this world as Eve left Paradise. But in truth I do not at all believe in this sort of perfectibility—the nature of the world will not admit of it—the inhabitants of the world will correspond to itself. Let the fish philosophise the ice away from the rivers in winter time and they shall be at continual play in the tepid delight of summer. Look at the Poles and at the sands of Africa, whirlpools and volcanoes. Let men exterminate them and I will say that they may arrive at earthly happiness. The point at which Man may arrive is as far as the parallel state in inanimate nature and no further. For instance suppose a rose to have sensation, it blooms on a beautiful morning, it enjoys itself—but there comes a cold wind, a hot sun—it cannot escape it, it cannot destroy its annoyances—they are as native to the world as itself: no more can man be happy in spite, the worldly elements will prey upon his nature. The common cognomen of this world among the misguided and superstitious is "a vale of tears" from which we are to be redeemed by a certain arbitrary interposition of God and taken to Heaven. What a little circumscribed straightened notion! Call the world if you please "The Vale of Soul-Making". Then you will find out the use of the world (I am speaking now in the highest terms for human nature, admitting it to be immortal which I will here take for granted for the purpose of showing a thought which has struck me concerning it). I say *"Soul-making"*—Souls as distinct from an Intelligence. There may be intelligences or sparks of the divinity in millions —but they are not Souls till they acquire identities, till each one is personally itself. Intelligences are atoms of perception—they know and they see and they are pure, in short they are God. How then are Souls to be made? How then are these sparks which are God to have identity given them—so as ever to possess a bliss peculiar to each one's individual existence? How, but by the medium of a world like this? This point I sincerely wish to consider because I think it is a grander system of salvation than the Christian religion—or rather it is a system of Spirit-creation. This is effected by three grand materials acting the one upon the other for a series of years. These three materials are the *Intelligence,* the *human heart* (as distinguished from Intelligence or Mind) and the *World* or *Elemental Space* suited for the proper action of *Intelligence* and *Heart* on each other for the purpose of forming the *Soul* or *Intelligence destined to possess the sense of Identity.* I can scarcely express what I but dimly perceive—and yet I think I perceive it. That you may judge the more clearly I will put it in the most homely form possible—I will call the *world* a School instituted for the purpose of teaching little children to read—I will call the *human heart* the *horn book* used in that School— and I will call the *Child able to read, the Soul* made from that *school* and its *hornbook.* Do you not see how necessary a world of pains and troubles is to school an Intelligence and make it a Soul? A place where the heart must feel and suffer in a thousand diverse ways! Not merely is the heart a hornbook, it is the mind's bible, it is the mind's experience, it is the teat from which the mind or Intelligence sucks its identity. As various as the lives of men are, so various become their souls, and thus does God make individual beings, souls, identical souls of the sparks of his own essence. This appears to me a faint sketch of a system of Salvation which does not affront our reason and humanity. . . . Seriously I think it probable that this System of Soul-making may have been the Parent of all the palpable and personal schemes of Redemption, among the Zoroastrians, the Christians and the Hindoos. For as one part of the human species must have their carved Jupiter; so another part must have the palpable and named Mediator and Saviour, their Christ, their Oromanes and their Vishnu.[1]

This stands to *Hyperion* as the letter calling Heaven a finer-tone repetition of earthly pleasures stands to the bulk of his early writing and to *Endymion.* The vale of soul-making marks a shift away from pleasure and towards pain; and one only has to turn back for a second from *Hyperion* and flick through the 1817 volume and its

[1] *Letters*, vol. II, p. 101.

sickly sweets, to acknowledge the broad correspondence of prose development with poetic. No question either that the echoes and resonances of the vale are heard through his greatest verse; they relate to his creative as well as his human history, and we shall be aware of their background murmur always from now on. The vale also contains a present truth about the collapse of *Hyperion*. Vastly though Keats has grown between the "finer tone" letter belonging to the final stages of *Endymion's* composition and the vale of soul-making which comes after his first sustained effort at *Hyperion*, the two letters possess a large common segment.

The earlier one, which provides his tacit and unintended critique of *Endymion*, confines the heavenly quest within his true competence of intensified feel; and one of our reasons for endorsing this restriction has been throughout the toneless, merely received character of his spiritual words, "soul" especially. The later letter frames its master-question at "How then are Souls to be made?" How indeed? The automatic nature of the process is what strikes an observer first. The world is "a place where the mind must feel and suffer in a thousand diverse ways"; and, in the inevitable course of feeling and suffering, it becomes a soul and at the same time furnishes us with a working model of Keats's private (as he supposes) "system of salvation". Provided one stays alive one cannot help growing into a soul, and a saved soul. The scene therefore appears theologically as well as morally empty; for God fails not only to judge his human creation, but to be effectively present for it in any way. Ostensibly the hero of Keats's discourse, he remains absent throughout; and while the words of the letter declare "thus does God make individual beings", what in fact happens in the vale of soul-making is that souls just emerge. God's relation to the world is of the feeblest and coldest Paleyesque outwardness. He even lacks the functional, low-creative *raison d'être* of Paley's divine watch-maker, since Keats does not bother about using him to explain how the vale, which is the world, itself arrived. God's enormously modest part is to support the hypothesis ("which I will here take for granted for the purpose of showing a thought") of personal immortality. And his inert externality stands openly confessed when Keats observes that the "mediators and personages" of religion—including Christ—have been *introduced* in order to make the process of soul-making more easily accessible "for common apprehension".

As he contemplates that august reality, the soul, maturing from out the interplay of worldly actualities, Keats reveals the extent and importance of the agreement between the vale of soul-making and the "finer tone" letter. Both insist on his commitment to the actual, the commitment which has authenticated end-stopped feel from the beginning. In doing so, they both define the area and sense, already touched on, in which his imagination was un-religious. Where the religion of the religious poet works to make poetic sense of life, this particular poet's religion—if the word is to be retained—spends itself making the poetic most of life. It must intensify, I said, or it is a destroyer. And the distinction between making the most and making sense brings us to the non-interpretative heart of the matter, providing a just commentary not merely on Keats's religion but on the entire jungle-growth called, in the books about him, his philosophy. It is no accident that the word "argument", which always sounds right when we hear it (as we often do) on Wordsworth's lips, has a sudden de-naturing effect when Keats uses it (as he never does in his verse) in the letter about the Pleasure Thermometer. The vale of soul-making is, of course, just as much an argument, an interpretation, as anything Wordsworth or anyone else might offer. Which is simply to say Keats's letter is not a Keatsian poem. And, signifi-cantly enough, when the letter-writer is straining forward at his most intent and self-forgetful, we apprehend the poet beginning to take charge.

Not merely is the heart a hornbook, it is the mind's bible, it is the mind's experience, it is the teat from which the mind or Intelligence sucks its identity.

To evoke the actual ("experience"), to say exactly how a mind achieves individual character, is his problem; and at a crisis of this order only the precision of metaphor will serve. The mind *sucks* its identity. The feeding-and-tasting image, most hard-worked among all feel's realisations in his poetry, is the true and—even here, deep in this reasonable letter—the non-interpretative mean-ing. The meaning does not outrun the bitter taste.

Hyperion, though, sets out to interpret the taste of the world's pain, and the venture fails. There are plenty of fine things to admire *en route*: Saturn himself, and even the little nymph who follows immediately and has a line and a half to assert herself in:

> the Naiad 'mid her reeds
> Press'd her cold finger closer to her lips.[1]

She is what Keats *can* do. She reminds us of the letter which poses the question "Why should Women suffer?", which does not

_____
[1] I, 13.

answer that question but gives us the "sensitive leaf on the hot hand". *Hyperion* comes to grief in its answers while gaining many successes in its negative-capable pictures.

The intellectual substance of his answer to the pain of defeat and change, the evolutionary answer that "on our heels a fresh perfection treads", has been overvalued. People suppose, surprisingly often, that Evolution is a Victorian idea, born with Darwin and Lyell's *Geology* and growing up with *In Memoriam* and Herbert Spencer. In consequence Keats gets judged original where he is not, and prescient where he is breathing the historical, metaphysical and even the scientific air of his own generation.[1] This point would not be worth making (since the lack of interesting originality in his "argument" has nothing to do with its failure to engage with the poetry we admire), were it not that such misconceptions make it even harder to accept the unimportance of the high-sounding "eternal law" in relation to the cold pressure of the Naiad's finger against her lip. Pressures like that affirm themselves, in their haunting persuasion, through all his good work. They constitute our present theme because they perplexed as well as inspired him; he felt them personally (so to speak) as well as creatively, and from the beginning—from the 1817 volume and especially *Sleep and Poetry*—we have the spectacle of Keats swinging with the wind and tide of abstract-ambitious intellect, but always moored to feel. The tug of actuality is sharply asserted in the pseudo-spiritual *Endymion,* and even in the couplets to Reynolds where, against the surface wish to "take refuge" in a new Romance he prays for his imagination to be tethered to "something of material sublime", and reminds himself that "in the world we jostle".

The whole affair of Keats and the world comes to a head in *Hyperion.* My conclusion is that he determines somehow to harness his positive affections to the task of explaining why women have cancers—"with the yearning passion I have for the beautiful, connected and made one with the ambition of my intellect", as his letter puts it. His failure is two-sided. The "first in beauty shall be first in might" thesis could never be adequate to human suffering. Second, the poet who resorts to a mythological story to demonstrate this thesis can hardly pretend to be jostling "in the world", he is not setting out the right way to satisfy *Sleep and Poetry's* de-

---

[1] The evolutionary instinct runs deep in his letters. For example, "Here I must think Wordsworth is deeper than Milton—though I think it has depended more upon the general and gregarious advance of intellect, than individual greatness of mind" (*Letters*, vol. I, p. 281).

mand that he shall "find" the world's pain and "seize" its events. Both of failure's faces must be remembered when we appraise the breakdown of *Hyperion.*

3 'The Fall of Hyperion'

The same two faces of failure confront us when we turn to *The Fall of Hyperion*—for convenience *The Fall*—Keats's second, again unsuccessful attempt to get his epic written.[1] Returning to his abandoned first draft, he decided to take a run at the narrative of the defeated Titans by introducing it through an encounter between the poet himself and the prophetess Moneta, whose connection with the main story is that she has been left "sole priestess of his [Saturn's] desolation".[2] The switch to first-person narration puts a master-key in the reader's hand; for Keats's problem, at once primary and ultimate, simple to state and impossible to compass, is to place himself inside his story. If he can build his work out of the authenticities of feel, authentic because his own with a new literalness, it will cease to be abstract, cease to be just a story.

Having put himself inside *The Fall* he sends himself to sleep by drinking—how loyal to instinct!—from

> *a cool vessel of transparent juice,*
> *Sipp'd by the wander'd bee, the which I took,*
> *And, pledging all the Mortals of the world,*
> *And all the dead whose names are in our lips,*
> *Drank. That full draught is parent of my theme.*[3]

The reason for making so large a claim for his delicious drink appears in the next few lines, when he wakes and finds himself in "an old sanctuary with roof august". At its west end he

> *saw far off*
> *An Image, huge of feature as a cloud,*
> *At level of whose feet an altar slept,*
> *To be approach'd on either side by steps,*
> *And marble balustrade, and patient travail*
> *To count with toil the innumerable degrees.*

[1] Now and then doubts are raised as to whether it was *The Fall* that Keats abandoned in the Autumn of 1819. They seem entirely unreasonable, and so I ignore them.
[2] *The Fall*, I, 227.   [3] I, 42.

> *Towards the altar sober-pac'd I went,*
> *Repressing haste, as too unholy there;*
> *And, coming nearer, saw beside the shrine*
> *One minist'ring;*[1]

and the one ministering is the prophetess Moneta, survivor, inter-preter, and even re-enactor of the far-off history of Hyperion's fall.

By thus introducing himself to Moneta, Keats reaches the deci-sive step in his new assault on the poem. Henceforth we need to have those vigorous in-the-world verbs "jostle" and "seize" buzz-ing round the doors of consciousness as perhaps they were buzzing round his. For the prophetess now sets him a strenuous physical task, which he performs.

> *"If thou canst not ascend*
> *These steps, die on that marble where thou art.*
> *Thy flesh, near cousin to the common dust,*
> *Will parch for lack of nutriment—thy bones*
> *Will wither in few years, and vanish so*
> *That not the quickest eye could find a grain*
> *Of what thou now art on that pavement cold.*
> *The sands of thy short life are spent this hour,*
> *And no hand in the universe can turn*
> *Thy hour glass, if these gummed leaves be burnt*
> *Ere thou canst mount up these immortal steps."*
> *I heard, I look'd: two sense both at once*
> *So fine, so subtle, felt the tyranny*
> *Of that fierce threat, and the hard task proposed.*
> *Prodigious seem'd the toil, the leaves were yet*
> *Burning,—when suddenly a palsied chill*
> *Struck from the paved level up my limbs,*
> *And was ascending quick to put cold grasp*
> *Upon those streams that pulse beside the throat:*
> *I shriek'd: and the sharp anguish of my shriek*
> *Stung my own ears—I strove hard to escape*
> *The numbness; strove to gain the lowest step.*
> *Slow, heavy, deadly was my pace: the cold*
> *Grew stifling, suffocating, at the heart;*
> *And when I clasp'd my hands I felt them not.*
> *One minute before death, my iced foot touch'd*
> *The lowest stair; and as it touch'd, life seem'd*
> *To pour in at the toes: I mounted up,*
> *As once fair Angels on a ladder flew*
> *From the green turf to heaven.*[2]

[1] I, 87.　　　　[2] I, 107.

In order that he, and we, shall understand the meaning of this strange exercise, he asks her:

> "Holy Power,"
> Cried I, approaching near the horned shrine,
> "What am I that should so be sav'd from death?
> What am I that another death come not
> To choak my utterance sacrilegious here?"[1]

And the dialogue continues:

> Then said the veiled shadow—"Thou hast felt
> What 'tis to die and live again before
> Thy fated hour. That thou hadst power to do so
> Is thy own safety; thou hast dated on
> 145 Thy doom." "High Prophetess," said I, "purge off
> Benign, if so it please thee, my mind's film—"
> "None can usurp this height," returned that shade,
> "But those to whom the miseries of the world
> Are misery, and will not let them rest.
> 150 All else who find a haven in the world,
> Where they may thoughtless sleep away their days,
> If by a chance into this fane they come,
> Rot on the pavement where thou rotted'st half.—"
> "Are there not thousands in the world," said I,
> 155 Encourag'd by the sooth voice of the shade,
> "Who love their fellows even to the death;
> Who feel the giant agony of the world;
> And more, like slaves to poor humanity,
> Labour for mortal good? I sure should see
> 160 Other men here: but I am here alone."
> "They whom thou spak'st of are no vision'ries,"
> Rejoin'd that voice—"they are no dreamers weak,
> They seek no wonder but the human face;
> No music but a happy-noted voice—
> 165 They come not here, they have no thought to come—
> And thou art here, for thou art less than they—
> What benefit canst thou do, or all thy tribe,
> To the great world? Thou art a dreaming thing;
> A fever to thyself—think of the Earth;
> 170 What bliss even in hope is there for thee?
> What haven? every creature hath its home;
> Every sole man hath days of joy and pain,
> Whether his labours be sublime or low—
> The pain alone; the joy alone; distinct:
> 175 Only the dreamer venoms all his days,
> Bearing more woe than all his sins deserve.

[1] I, 136.

Therefore, that happiness be somewhat shar'd,
Such things as thou art are admitted oft
Into like gardens thou didst pass erewhile,
180 *And suffer'd in these Temples; for that cause*
Thou standest safe beneath this statue's knees."
"That I am favored for unworthiness,
By such propitious parley medicin'd
In sickness not ignoble, I rejoice,
185 *Aye, and could weep for love of such award."*
So answer'd I, continuing, "If it please,
Majestic shadow, tell me: sure not all
Those melodies sung into the world's ear
Are useless: sure a poet is a sage;
190 *A humanist, Physician to all men.*
That I am none I feel, as Vultures feel
They are no birds when Eagles are abroad.
What am I then? Thou spakest of my tribe:
What tribe?"—The tall shade veil'd in drooping white
195 *Then spake, so much more earnest, that the breath*
Mov'd the thin linen folds that drooping hung
About the golden censer from the hand
Pendent.—"Art thou not of the dreamer tribe?
The poet and the dreamer are distinct,
200 *Diverse, sheer opposite, antipodes.*
The one pours out a balm upon the world,
The other vexes it." Then shouted I
Spite of myself, and with a Pythia's spleen,
"Apollo! faded, farflown Apollo!
205 *Where is thy misty pestilence to creep*
Into the dwellings, thro' the door crannies,
Of all mock lyrists, large self-worshippers,
And careless Hecterers in proud bad verse.
Tho' I breathe death with them it will be life
210 *To see them sprawl before me into graves.*
Majestic shadow, tell me where I am,
Whose altar this; for whom this incense curls:
What Image this, whose face I cannot see,
For the broad marble knees; and who thou art,
215 *Of accent feminine, so courteous."*

With that large chunk the overall pattern of *The Fall*, the second Hyperion fragment, has almost declared itself. It remains for Moneta to tell the poet that the image she attends is Saturn's, and this temple the sole relic of his defeat. She then makes her promise of mystic re-enactment, saying that he shall with "dull mortal eyes behold" those distant events which are nevertheless "still swooning vivid through my globed brain", and what is more shall behold them "free from all pain, if wonder pain thee not". Whereupon she parts the veil curtaining her face—a high moment—at the sight of which Keats

> *ached to see what things the hollow brain*
> *Behind enwombed:*[1]

and so he asked her to let him witness them, as she had promised. Which brings us to Saturn and his limp right hand, the dead leaf, the Naiad pressing finger to lip—the pictures, in fact, with which the first version opened, and made largely with the same words.

Keats has prefaced his heroic story with an episode designed to put himself (one wants to say literally) in the picture. Having worked its way into the first *Hyperion*, *The Fall* stops in mid-sentence on the old road, before the Titanic debate has begun. Whether the poet could not face again the "first in beauty shall be first in might" argument, or whether he decided his new introductory section had failed to do its job, we cannot be sure. A bit of both is the likely answer. At any rate he has left evidence that *The Fall's* introduction gave him trouble, certainly made him hesitate over fundamental issues.

To begin with the physical task. Keats rests the main weight of his new hopes upon it because, as Moneta explains, by climbing the altar steps he places himself, if not among, then in a close and richly ambiguous relation to

> *those to whom the miseries of the world*
> *Are misery, and will not let them rest.* (148)

At once we are back inside *Sleep and Poetry*, contemplating the grand endeavour to find our common world's agony and seize, lay hands on—to feel—its painful events. Precisely: to feel. For the poet of *The Fall* rounds on the prophetess with the question "Are there not thousands . . . who feel the giant agony of the world. . .?" So why should he find himself here, at the top of the steps, "alone"? (154-60).

And now the trouble starts. My guess is Keats intended, anyhow at the outset, to lay great stress on "usurp". (147) The idea would then be that those who feel the world's pain are here as of right; or at least they cannot be stopped coming. But in fact they do not come. They are engrossed in the world and its affairs, and have no thought to this altar-step existence beyond. (161-5) They are not "vision'ries" and "dreamers". Keats, on the other hand, is; and Moneta urges him to "think of the Earth". (169)

[1] I, 276.

The force of this injunction, one naturally supposes, is that Keats has hitherto failed to feel the world's pain. But it soon becomes apparent that Moneta is accusing him of something more complicated than a failure to feel. Our first warning is a pair of cancelled lines which Woodhouse records in his transcript of *The Fall*, between 166 and 167 in our text:

> *Mankind thou lovest: many of thine hours*
> *Have been distempered with their miseries.*

Following this pointer we read on from "think of the Earth" and see that the fault of the dreamer lies not in lack of feeling but in failure to keep his "joy and pain" in what he feels "distinct"; with the result that he suffers excessively rather than too little. (170-6) The charge amounts, broadly, to intense confusion of feeling. And Moneta explains that the dreamer Keats is allowed into the temple, and at the top of the altar steps, to give him solace in his muddled pain.

Groping, then, for the principle which distinguishes the dreamer from those who are properly tormented, not allowed to "rest", by the world's sorrows, we begin to suspect that it lies within the words "to whom the miseries of the world / Are misery"—in the distinctly miserable character of their misery, that is, as opposed to the joy-pain medley which the dreamer feels. However the suspicion is dissipated rather than confirmed by what follows, since Keats shows no further interest in this embryonic contrast, but sets off on a new tack with a leading question to the prophetess: Surely true poetry is not "useless"? And (he continues) if I am not a true poet, as indeed I "feel" I am not, what am I? (189-94) From now on the distinction between the wrongly feeling dreamer and the rightly feeling man of the world is abandoned entirely. What had seemed to be central to the dialogue vanishes. In its place emerges the bald opposition of dreamer and poet, the one vexing the world, the other bringing comfort to it. (199-202) We get absolutely no help from Keats over this second contrasted pair. Nothing is elaborated, nothing qualified.

Worse still, in some ways, is the difficulty of establishing his final intention as to the text. In *The Fall* alone among his longer works we have no autograph. Apart from scraps which he copied in a letter to Woodhouse,[1] we are dependent on three transcripts and an early printed text. One of these transcripts appends a note to line 187, "Keats seems to have intended to erase this and the next twenty-one lines". A quick run-through confirms that 211

---

[1] *Letters*, vol. II, p. 171.

might well be the beginning of a second attempt at this passage, following directly after 186 with the intervening lines cancelled. The possibility is strengthened by the fact that the first printed text of *The Fall* appeared in 1856 without 187-210. We know nothing of the manuscript which served as the printer's copy; this may have made Keats's intention plain. The other two transcripts, however, one of them by the scrupulous Woodhouse, give no hint that anything is amiss; so the fair conclusion must be that we read the passage as it stands in Garrod's edition, but read it with mental brackets round the doubtful lines.

The real significance of all this lies in its bearing on Keats's hesitations. They extend beyond the local and transient problems of the twice-abandoned epic, and touch the heart of his abiding self-doubt. Again, though more amply now, we are claiming to know Keats better than he knew himself. And again we are bound —all of us, in different ways—to do just this; because when he tells Fanny Brawne in the early months of 1820, with all his great verse behind him, "Let me have another opportunity of years before me and I will not die without being remember'd",[1] it forms no part of modest caution to wonder if he might be right, and the rest of us wrong. He *has* made himself remembered, we answer, adding a Johnsonian "and there's an end on't".

The two fragments of *Hyperion* and *The Fall* are the main diagnostic tools when one comes to examine his late misjudging mood of failure. He elaborates the mood thus in another letter:

Now I have had opportunities of passing nights anxious and awake I have found other thoughts intrude upon me. "If I should die," said I to myself, "I have left no immortal work behind me—nothing to make my friends proud of my memory—but I have lov'd the principle of beauty in all things, and if I had had time I would have made myself remember'd."[2]

And in trying to assess the delicate and recurring antithesis of failure in great hopes and devotion to the beautiful, one goes first to his epic ruin. *Hyperion* evinces his love of the principle of beauty in all things through its attempt to demonstrate a universal triumph of beauty. But—I mean the "but" in his letter—*Hyperion's* argument never matured into that epic realisation he was hoping for. Instead of the ripe, intense, achieved Keatsian object, we are left with a pale and imageless "universal law".

[1] *Ibid.*, p. 277.
[2] *Ibid.*, p. 263. It was back in October 1818, in the very early days of his Hyperion attempt, that Keats wrote to his brother and sister-in-law, "I think I shall be among the English Poets after my death" (*Letters*, vol. I, p. 394).

That, very roughly, is how he saw it himself when he set about infusing the blood of actuality into *The Fall*. What I have called putting himself into the picture was not to be achieved simply by resorting to first-person narrative. The crux of the matter is feel, dramatised in the physical task of climbing the altar steps and expounded in the ensuing dialogue between Keats and Moneta. That dialogue is meant to reveal the meaning of the task, and no sooner does it begin than all his old abstract-ambitious difficulties return. He is engaged upon a re-phrasing, no less doomed for its being more sophisticated, of the interpretative effort we met first in *Sleep and Poetry*—the effort to write *about* feel. He now proffers two contrasts, the first one feel-focussed but aborted, between the dreamer and the humane dweller in the world; the second completely bare, certainly hesitant, and perhaps abandoned on further reflection, between the dreamer and the true poet. In fact his schematising does not end here, since the opening lines of *The Fall* ("a sort of induction" is his description to Woodhouse[1]) presumably relate to the Keats-Moneta dialogue ahead:

> *Fanatics have their dreams, wherewith they weave*
> *A paradise for a sect; the savage too*
> *From forth the loftiest fashion of his sleep*
> *Guesses at Heaven: pity these have not*
> *Trac'd upon vellum or wild indian leaf*
> *The shadows of melodious utterance.*
> *But bare of laurel they live, dream and die;*
> *But Poesy alone can tell her dreams,*
> *With the fine spell of words alone can save*
> *Imagination from the sable charm*
> *And dumb enchantment. Who alive can say*
> *"Thou art no Poet; mayst not tell thy dreams"?*
> *Since every man whose soul is not a clod*
> *Hath visions, and would speak, if he had lov'd*
> *And been well nurtured in his mother tongue.*
> *Whether the dream now purposed to rehearse*
> *Be Poet's or Fanatic's will be known*
> *When this warm scribe my hand is in the grave.*

But how related to that dialogue, impossible to say. Instead of the poet-dreamer contrast we are presented with three kinds of dreaming man: the fanatic, the savage, the poet. The savage (true to Romantic type) has poetic dreams but fails to write them down. The fanatic's dreams are certainly—but very obscurely—a different matter; because, despite his weaving "a paradise for a sect"

---

[1] *Letters*, vol. II, p. 172.

with them, the passage comes to a double-paragraph close at the uncompromising opposition of "Poet's or Fanatic's", before launching into the first person with "Methought I stood" in the poem's nineteenth line. There is something unpoetic about this sort of dreaming. But the fanatic is never heard of again. Conceivably he is the dreamer of the dialogue's poet-dreamer contrast. And yet even if he is, he does not help us to understand that exchange.

Fanatic, savage, humanist, poet, dreamer: the final chapter in the story of Keats's interpretative effort is a spawning of empty distinctions. The passage has one merit, which is his address to his own hand. This phenomenon of life within the mindless bodily part I called Keatsian dispersal, and I admired the self-sufficiency he bestows on eye, ear, forehead, fingertip, or Porphyro's "warm, unnerved arm". It saves many a passage from total undistinction, as when Endymion's friends

> *feelingly could scan*
> *A lurking trouble in his nether lip,*
> *And see that oftentimes the reins would slip*
> *Through his forgotten hands. . . .*[1]

Forgotten but how insistently present. How present in being forgotten. An ounce of such hands is worth a ton of large distinguishing. *The Fall's* contraries, unresonant in themselves, spread a logic-chopping aura over the poet in his climbing of the altar steps—a feat which saves his life, we are told—and reduce the episode to farce. They drive us to view the circumstance of life pouring in "at the toes" in the light of intellect, of a promised analysis, of thoughtful philanthropic missions ahead. And the light is a killing light which renders the whole climbing exploit absurdly physical. Absurdly here means 'merely'. It becomes merely physical because of the interpretative expect ions which are bent upon it; just as Keats's true gift becomes 'merely' sensual when placed over against the intellectual and spiritual anti-self concocted by Matthew Arnold. At such moments Keats plays, and compels his reader to play, Arnold's game. We cannot help apprehending some intended symbolism whereby the poet who performs the painful set task proves his capacity to feel, as well as to observe, the defeat of the Titans which he is about to relate. The plot to put himself inside his story, experiencing what he sees, cannot escape us entirely. But the facts of the task and its symbolism fall apart; and both then fail. Neither the feeling toes nor the paper-thin

[1] I, 178.

argument (just consider "Therefore, that happiness be somewhat shar'd . . .") are able to carry *The Fall*. Their very apartness frustrates them. It is as if the *Nightingale Ode's* "drowsy numbness" had got separated from the assertion "Beauty cannot keep her lustrous eyes", and the reader were trying to use the sentiment to validate the sensation.

The "therefore" of "Therefore, that happiness be somewhat shar'd" will always ring like a bad penny; it is the sign of a futile interpretative zeal, claiming house-room within a Keatsian poem. The stifling cold, on the other hand, and the toe-sensation attending the set task, have no "therefore" to shed. They belong inside a Keatsian poem already—though not in the reduced circumstances of *The Fall* where their meaning is supposed to lie somewhere beyond themselves, and where the disappointed searcher after their meaning turns against their own poetic natures, resentful of their naïve clarity. Expecting a revelation, he finds something not far removed from the girl "who cannot feel for cold her tender feet" in the most juvenile Keats.[1] The thing he is waiting for turns out to be perfectly simple after all.

And yet the whole force and virtue of this endured cold is its pain; and pain is the theme both of *Hyperion* and *The Fall*, and especially of the poet's task; and who can deny that Keats's imaginative projections of pain—"drowsy numbness" and so forth —are indeed simple? But this task has to support an elaborate superstructure of temple, altar, divine image, prophetess with her inspired admonition and pseudo-theology of "sins" and what those sins "deserve"—an apparatus designed, in short, to put the poet in the picture.

Nothing could be more earnest than his desire to put himself there; nor harder to satisfy. Nor, on our side, does it lend itself to neat assessment. Its basis is as broad as the justly famous letter in which he tells John Reynolds he has been thinking about Wordsworth and "how he differs from Milton":

And here I have nothing but surmises, from an uncertainty whether Milton's apparently less anxiety for Humanity proceeds from his seeing further or no than Wordsworth: and whether Wordsworth has in truth epic passion, and martyrs himself to the human heart, the main region of his song. In regard to his genius alone—we find what he says true as far as we have experienced and we can judge no further but by larger experience—for axioms in philosophy are not axioms until they are proved upon our pulses. We read fine things but never feel them to the full until we have gone the same steps as the author. I know this is not

[1] *Specimen of an Induction to a Poem.*

plain; you will know exactly my meaning when I say that now I shall relish *Hamlet* more than I ever have done. Or, better, you are sensible no man can set down Venery as a bestial or joyless thing until he is sick of it, and therefore all philosophizing on it would be mere wording.[1]

Out of this tangle of art and life I should like to extricate the phrase "proved upon our pulses". It relates to all men in their daily living—in their venery, for example, and their philosophising thereon—but also in their appreciation of great imaginative writings, since we cannot "feel them to the full until we have gone the same steps as the author". It relates, finally, to the poet himself, in this case Wordsworth, who, in so far as he "has in truth epic passion", appears to Keats in the likeness of one who "martyrs himself to the human heart". At each stage of proving on the pulses, pain dominates. So he continues: "Until we are sick, we understand not; in fine, as Byron says, 'Knowledge is Sorrow'; and I go on to say that 'Sorrow is Wisdom' "—until his mood eases into his own sort of buoyant scepticism, and thence into jokes.

The poet's mode of proving on the pulses is what chiefly concerns us. Keats's associating of true epic passion with self-martyrdom, while it refers to Wordsworth sheds light on himself. The phrase "or, if I can bear" in *Sleep and Poetry* marks the decisive shift from feel to vision. But what about the apparently gratuitous masochism with which the power to experience "visions of all places" and seize "the events of this wide world" is made dependent on the undergoing of an ordeal? We had nothing to say earlier because there was then no clue to his hitching of vision to ordeal. But now there is, since the task imposed by Moneta on the poet is an elaborate dramatisation, and her subsequent talk with him is a rationalising, of this vision-ordeal association. *The Fall* gives us "or, if I can bear" much magnified.

Also we now have two of the finest things in his letters, the vale of soul-making and the proving on the pulses, to help us construct the human background to the poetic ordeal. He welcomes the vale we all know—"a world of pains and troubles"—because "a place where the heart must feel and suffer in a thousand diverse ways" is necessary for the heart's possessor to grow into a soul. He accepts the painful experience of proving on the pulses as the price we must pay if we are ever to form judgments about the world that shall weigh heavier than words, and if we are to have the direct Keatsian feel of our art, both as makers and audience. The two letters are his life's running commentary on his art. And the two

[1] *Letters*, vol. I, p. 278.

Hyperion fragments commemorate the long struggle to establish his art on a footing grand enough to satisfy that commentary.

The first *Hyperion* fell victim, I said, to Keats's worldly good sense as much as to his philanthropic idealism. It was no use pretending that human beings suffer so that beauty may prevail. *The Fall's* abandonment, too, is caused by a failure of the facts of life, as he must see them, to fit the bent of his art, as he must pursue it. No amount of care lavished on *Sleep and Poetry's* "or, if I can bear" will make the poet's undergoing of a feel-ordeal qualify him for the proposed heroic task which is nothing less than to "feel the giant agony of the world". He cannot convince himself that getting to the top of the steps amounts to a real proving on the pulses. It will never lift *The Fall* from the realm of very abstract, very ambitious projects to that of existences like the sun and moon and Shakespeare's plays.

Thus when I maintain that *The Fall* fails to place the poet in the picture, my first thought is to the separation of his task's actual circumstances from its symbolic rationale. The idea of the task is irrelevantly abstract, and the sensation of life pouring in at the toes is ludicrously concrete; and Keats's big achievements know no such separation.

Secondly, I am saying that lines which are often and admiringly quoted as an index of *The Fall's* imaginative heart, lines like

> *"None can usurp this height," returned that shade,*
> *"But those to whom the miseries of the world*
> *Are misery, and will not let them rest",*

do not engage with its inner creative economy at all. Such lines give us pause, of course; but that is because they versify the very impressive humanity of his letters. They illustrate our point, which is just this: that the man who wrote about proving on the pulses and the poet of feel are not co-extensive.

The Fall leaves us with an impression of the letter-writer looking over the poet's shoulder and half-consciously exploiting him. "Feel is your thing," he seems to say; "so get on with it." The poet then comes up with talk about people who "feel" the world's agony, clinging to his own word, but his own word drained of its virtue, become ordinarily general. Or he resorts, more exactly, to his proved home territory of stationed posture, of smelling, tasting, shuddering and aching sensation, and the palate:

> *Blazing Hyperion on his orbed fire*
> *Still sits, still snuffs the incense teeming up*
> *From man to the sun's God: yet unsecure,*

> *For as upon the Earth dire prodigies*
> *Fright and perplex, so also shudders he:*
> *Not at dog's howl, or gloom-bird's Even screech,*
> *Or the familiar visitings of one*
> *Upon the first toll of his passing bell:*
> *But horrors, portion'd to a giant nerve,*
> *Made great Hyperion ache. His palace bright,*
> *Bastion'd with pyramids of glowing gold,*
> *And touch'd with shade of bronzed obelisks,*
> *Glares a blood red through all the thousand Courts,*
> *Arches, and domes, and fiery galeries;*
> *And all its curtains of Aurorian clouds*
> *Flush angerly: when he would taste the wreaths*
> *Of incense breath'd aloft from sacred hills,*
> *Instead of sweets, his ample palate takes*
> *Savour of poisonous brass and metals sick.*[1]

But leaves his reader uncomfortably aware of a self-manipulating process, in which the letter-writer is trying to convert the poet into a classic model in order to get *The Fall* written on the lines he has laid down for it. Hence the rather weary decorum of much of the verse, and the separation (once again) of the cosmic theme and its articulation: for this interested coaxing of his own gift cannot save the feel of the world's pain from bloodless abstraction, or the taste of poisonous brass from Arnoldian mereness.

Keats grows into a silver-age exponent of his own manner, complaining to Reynolds of the "artful or rather artist's humour" which this demanded of him, while we are left watching an academic film form over the truths we have been telling about his genius. The dispersal, for example, which projects Hyperion's sorrow through his palate remains Keatsian, but one cannot get excited about it any longer. "This warm scribe my hand" certainly possesses a life which the rest of *The Fall's* Induction is without. But Endymion's "forgotten hands" have more life, and the emprisoned "soft hands" of *Melancholy* more still.

At the end of his dialogue with Moneta, the poet says:

> *I had no words to answer; for my tongue,*
> *Useless, could find about its roofed home*
> *No syllable of a fit majesty*
> *To make rejoinder to Moneta's mourn.*[2]

Dispersal again. The snail-like containment of the organ—compare "soft-conched ear"—is entirely authentic. Yet its impact is dulled by just a hint of calculation, as if Keats had himself lighted

---

[1] II, 15. [2] I, 228.

on our distinction between meaning and picture-making, and so lost his creative innocence. "I had no words to answer" betrays a crafty purpose; the interpretative effort is being shuffled out of sight, and the microcosmic groping of the tongue round the dark cave it lives in appears instead. So on to the altar-flames "fainting for sweet food", and Moneta's "globed brain" and the events which it "behind enwombed"; and the poet's "heart too small to hold its blood". On, finally, to our last impressions of the old defeated king, fixed in the beauty of his pain:

> *only his lips*
> *Trembled amid the white curls of his beard.*
> *They told the truth. . . .*[1]

They did indeed. But alas that Keats should have been driven to say so.

[1] I, 450.

III: SNAILHORN PERCEPTION

1 To See as a God Sees

THE self-consciousness which the two Hyperion fragments
display is a complicated business and needs delicate handling. The initial focus here is the artful humour in which—
on occasion—Keats manipulates his talent; but that is only one
part of the story, and not the most important. This problem's knot
tightens as we go. For the longer we admire the fine things in
Hyperion and *The Fall*, the harder it becomes to call either version a
failure; while the impossibility of claiming success for either of
them is at every step confirmed. The exploiting touch is deathly,
and yet it is his own true gift which he exploits.

At the heart of these difficulties, deeper than the question of an
overdriven talent, lies the poet's subtle but passive understanding
of what he is trying to be and do. This gets expressed through the
Olympian Apollo in *Hyperion*, and then through Keats himself in
The Fall.

Apollo, as the letter to Haydon explains, was to be the hero of
the finished epic. In the event his contribution amounted to the
merest coda tacked on to a narrative of the older gods, their sorrows and their long debating: the first two books, culminating in
the entry of Hyperion the only undefeated Titan, are devoted to
them. Book Three is Apollo's, but it had run to less than half the
length of the other two when Keats gave up.

The time is early morning, and Apollo enters listening to the
first thrush and the sound of the sea.

> *He listen'd, and he wept, and his bright tears*
> *Went trickling down the golden bow he held.*[1]

He arrives (as Endymion so often did before him) with state of
mind and physical fact hilariously juxtaposed. All Keats's imagining has gone into Apollo's tears, into their ordinary palpable
lapsing wetness; and there is none left for his sorrow. We disbelieve
the mysterious cosmic allegation but hold to the trickling. And,
naturally, when the interpreter of his distress appears, as she
immediately does—

> *With solemn step an awful Goddess came—*[2]

every stride proclaims the false profound.

[1] III, 42.   [2] III, 46.

She herself, Mnemosyne, Goddess of Memory, mother of the Muses and foster-mother of Apollo the God of Verse, cuts no ice at all. Her face is a different matter. The last ninety lines of *Hyperion* constitute Apollo's attempt to "read" that face. In the story, as Keats tells it, he succeeds painfully. The truth of his reader's reaction however (and the silent witness of the abandoned epic poem) is more confused: painful again, but doubling back on itself with a thwarted energy which is the mark of both these fragments. In a hidden but easily recoverable sense, moreover, Keats is compelled to accept the reader's standpoint for his own, since he can only make Apollo succeed by killing his poem. The pattern of those final ninety lines of *Hyperion* is declared as soon as the "awful Goddess" and Apollo meet, the next line continuing

> *And there was purport in her looks for him,*
> *Which he with eager guess began to read*
> *Perplex'd. . . .*

There is something familiar about her. Puzzled by a vague consciousness of *déjà vu*, he exclaims:

> *"Goddess! I have beheld those eyes before,*
> *And their eternal calm, and all that face,*
> *Or I have dream'd."*[1]

She answers "Yes"—

> *"Thou hast dream'd of me; and awaking up*
> *Didst find a lyre all golden by thy side,*
> *Whose strings touch'd by thy fingers, all the vast*
> *Unwearied ear of the whole universe*
> *Listen'd in pain and pleasure at the birth*
> *Of such new tuneful wonder. Is't not strange*
> *That thou shouldst weep, so gifted? Tell me, youth,*
> *What sorrow thou canst feel. . . ."*[2]

But instead of telling, Apollo looks at her face again "with sudden scrutiny"[3] and resorts to the old trick of demanding why he should explain to her things she knows already:

> *"Why should I tell thee what thou so well seest?*
> *Why should I strive to show what from thy lips*
> *Would come no mystery?"*[4]

leading to further questions, large resounding ones like "Where is power?",[5] the purpose of which is not to be answered or even

---

[1] III, 59.   [2] III, 61.   [3] III, 80.
[4] III, 84.   [5] III, 103.

answerable—whatever Keats may have thought—but to keep her quiet while Apollo and the poem concentrate on her face:

> *"Mute thou remainest—Mute! yet I can read*
> *A wondrous lesson in thy silent face:*
> *Knowledge enormous makes a God of me.*[1]

Then on immediately to the guillotined climax of *Hyperion*, with Apollo just looking and looking, and Mnemosyne silent:

> *Thus the God,*
> *While his enkindled eyes, with level glance*
> *Beneath his white soft temples, stedfast kept*
> *Trembling with light upon Mnemosyne.*
> *Soon wild commotions shook him, and made flush*
> *All the immortal fairness of his limbs;*
> *Most like the struggle at the gate of death;*
> *Or liker still to one who should take leave*
> *Of pale immortal death, and with a pang*
> *As hot as death's is chill, with fierce convulse*
> *Die into life: so young Apollo anguish'd:*
> *His very hair, his golden tresses famed*
> *Kept undulation round his eager neck.*
> *During the pain Mnemosyne upheld*
> *Her arms as one who prophesied.—At length*
> *Apollo shriek'd;—and lo! from all his limbs*
> *Celestial*

where Keats's autograph breaks off. While stopping in mid sentence and mid line it records the cancelled variant "Apollo shreikd and lo he was the God!"; and a transcript by some unknown person connected with Woodhouse, perhaps his clerk, has the words "Glory dawn'd: he was a god!" pencilled in after "Celestial". Thus it cannot fairly be doubted that Apollo's strange convulsion is a proving and an acting out of the assertion "Knowledge enormous makes a God of me". And we know that the book which yields him this deifying knowledge is Mnemosyne's face.

In his second attempt, *The Fall*, it is Keats who undergoes a momentous looking into a face. This simple act is the outcome of his determination to put himself in the picture. First he switched from third- to first-person narrative. Then he got Mnemosyne (who is also, and more often, called Moneta in *The Fall*) to impose on him a task of painful feel which he performs. And now he stands

[1] III, 111.

beside the altar watching the "lang'rous flame" of a sacrificial
fire:

> till sad Moneta cried,
> *"The sacrifice is done, but not the less,*
> *Will I be kind to thee for thy goodwill.*
> *My power, which to me is still a curse,*
> *Shall be to thee a wonder; for the scenes*
> *Still swooning vivid through my globed brain*
> *With an electral changing misery*
> *Thou shalt with those dull mortal eyes behold,*
> *Free from all pain, if wonder pain thee not."*
> *As near as an immortal's sphered words*
> *Could to a mother's soften, were these last:*
> *But yet I had a terror of her robes,*
> *And chiefly of the veils, that from her brow*
> *Hung pale, and curtain'd her in mysteries*
> *That made my heart too small to hold its blood.*
> *This saw that Goddess, and with sacred hand*
> *Parted the veils. Then saw I a wan face,*
> *Not pin'd by mortal sorrows, but bright blanch'd*
> *By an immortal sickness which kills not. . . .*
> *I ached to see what things the hollow brain*
> *Behind enwombed: what high tragedy*
> *In the dark secret Chambers of her skull*
> *Was acting, that could give so dread a stress*
> *To her cold lips, and fill with such a light*
> *Her planetary eyes; and touch her voice*
> *With such a sorrow—.*[1]

His wish is no sooner expressed—

> *"Let me behold, according as thou said'st,*
> *What in thy brain so ferments to and fro"—*[2]

than he finds himself "Deep in the shady sadness of a vale" with
Saturn, the dead leaf, the Naiad: experiencing the opening lines of
Hyperion, and describing this highly singular experience at the
moment he plunges into it:

> *Whereon there grew*
> *A power within me of enormous ken,*
> *To see as a God sees, and take the depth*
> *Of things as nimbly as the outward eye*
> *Can size and shape pervade.*[3]

I kept *Hyperion* and *The Fall* apart before in order to make their
common segment stand out as clearly as possible now. They share

[1] *The Fall,* I, 240.   [2] I, 289.   [3] I, 302.

a thematically central element of deep gazing into faces; and the moment of deep gazing is the moment when Keats's self-knowledge, the distinguishing mark of both fragments, shows itself. It was also important, in "The Abstract Idea", to use all due severity against the bloodlessness of *Hyperion's* "first in beauty should be first in might" proposal; and against the inadequacy of the set task in *The Fall*: meaning by inadequacy the failure of the "palsied chill" of the steps to measure up to a proving of the world's "giant agony" upon the pulses of the feeling poet. Because, in contrast with those crude devices, the two faces of the two versions evoke respect for a fine initial conception.

In fact the two faces are one face. Keats intends the face of life's tragic beauty, exposed totally, at a stroke, in a sudden maplike revelation. Ultimately this is why *Hyperion* and *The Fall* constitute attempts to write the same poem. In *Hyperion*, Apollo "reads" this face; he spells out a "wondrous lesson" there; it discloses "knowledge enormous". And we should not doubt that a certain deep apprehension of surfaces—a painted urn, an autumn landscape— is Keat's true way. But, for the very reason that his feel is end-stopped, the fruit of such apprehension belongs within the feeling act—as in *Melancholy's* "feed deep, deep upon her peerless eyes". Moneta's face, the one Apollo is feeding on, provokes an uncomfortable half-assent because, while its features submit to his initial gazing urge, they resist the poet's attempt to deploy them interpretatively. They will not co-operate in a lofty prostitution of feel to know. And so the 'lesson' which is supposed to be learnable in them carries no conviction. Calling his own bluff as to what Moneta's face *means*, Keats gives up and starts again.

The Fall shows understanding of the nature of *Hyperion's* failure. Keats now lays a probing and to some extent a healing touch on the weakest point of his first version, which was its affirmations about the face's discoverable meaning. This time, with the poet replacing Apollo as the gazer into Moneta's (Mnemosyne's) features, he does not pretend to find any lesson there. The exercise in face-reading is changed to one in sympathetic feel.

Moneta gives advance warning of this when she mentions the scenes "swooning vivid" through her brain, the scenes which in due course, she tells Keats, he will "behold" for himself. At

> *but not the less,*
> *Will I be kind to thee for thy goodwill*

there is the familiar contrast between a pantomime morality (compare "Therefore, that happiness be somewhat shar'd") and the serious "electral" business of feel. "Behold" was Moneta's word, and it is his too in his appeal to her "let me behold", but this is no ordinary seeing, as the swooning and electral talk indicates. Moreover when he comes to watch Saturn and the others, he experiences their "shapes" as "ponderous upon my senses"; his brain is left "burning" and he himself "gasping".[1] It seems hard to reconcile such sensations with Moneta's promise that he will witness these things "free from all pain, if wonder pain thee not". The truth is that all remoter considerations are overborne by his main and central anxiety to place himself inside that little theatre of feel, Moneta's "globed brain". Thus, he hopes, the rather ludicrous duality of *Hyperion* in which the prophetess has to ask Apollo

> *Tell me, youth,*
> *What sorrows thou canst feel*[2]

will be overpassed in the single feel-situation shared by Moneta and Keats and the events they are contemplating.

The reader of the epic, too, is given a tacit promise of access to this inward drama; to

> *what things the hollow brain*
> *Behind enwombed: what high tragedy*
> *In the dark secret Chambers of her skull*
> *Was acting. . . .*

As he pauses on the threshold, he finds he has two distinct achievements to salute. The meaning of Moneta's face has been thrown overboard, so that the reward of looking into it is now not a lesson but a story. Second, the task of climbing the altar steps has been recast into a more sophisticated shape. We still have a feel-ordeal (as the burning and gasping indicate), but one which ministers to an ideal of sympathetic involvement in fact and event, and so escapes the arbitrariness—pantomimic again—of the prescribed task.

The poet's appeal to Moneta, "Let me behold", marks the final stage of his attempt to put himself in the picture. The whole enterprise is anchored in a persistent debate, or running fight, between Keats's philosophic and his sensual natures. Early on this became polarised, in his own mind, into a state "ambitious of doing the

---

[1] I, 391-8.

[2] *Hyperion*, III, 68. The convenience of a single theatre of feel for the two principals is obvious. Whereas Keats in *The Fall* is admitted inside Moneta's head, Mnemosyne in *Hyperion* remains outside Apollo's and has to be told about the things which "pour into the wide hollows of my brain" (III, 117).

world some good"[1] and a counter-determination to indulge his gift
the only way he could, which was through immersion in feel. His
maturer thought is that feel may, with luck and careful art, be
turned philosophical. And here the concept of reality emerges,
bewilderingly, to be invoked on both sides of the debate at once.
The problems which philosophy poses are 'real', but so is the poet's
feel. The humanitarian question "Why should woman suffer?"
and the Pleasure Thermometer mandate "Fold a rose leaf round
thy finger's taperness" confront each other unyieldingly. Here the
speculative emphasis is philanthropic, and this happens again and
again—most neatly perhaps in the charming portmanteau expression "human friend Philosopher".[2] Keats's ambition, as he wonders about bringing feel to bear upon philosophy, is that the human
friend philosopher shall prove himself a human friend poet too. He
would then earn the title "miserable and mighty poet of the human
heart",[3] and the passage about proving on the pulses suggests how
this might happen. The briefest summarising statement appears in
yet another letter: "Nothing ever becomes real till it is experienced."[4] Easier said than done. The dread word "real" infests the
whole scene, and both versions of the Hyperion myth break their
backs trying to placate it.

Complete success would have meant investing his narrative with
the credentials of history. As it stands, the undertaking is befogged
in a very private, near-religious atmosphere, as if Keats had
thought up the doctrine of the Incarnation all on his own, and
then, to provide a home for his idea, had decided to invent the
New Testament. He wants the creature of his fancy to be manifestly as real as real. "Let me behold" expresses his yearning for
eye-witness authority, but eye-witness in a quite personal fashion
since the longer we consider his "behold" the more exactly does
it conform to the familiar innerness of Keatsian vision. He tells us
that a "power" grew within him "to see as a God sees". And we
are able to add that such seeing is performed upon the palate or
finger-tip or eye-lid of the "burning brain". To see as a God sees
becomes, very naturally when verse is to be written, to see as
Keats sees; and to see as Keats sees is to feel. Finally, in the philosophic hopes attending the two Hyperion fragments, to feel is to
authenticate. It is to realise.

Keats is telling us what we have been busy finding out for ourselves: that the gift of end-stopped feel and the picture-making
talent are inseparable; that this poet has to spatialise event, indeed

---

[1] *Letters*, vol. I, p. 387. [2] *Ibid.*, vol. II, p. 139.
[3] *Ibid.*, p. 115. [4] *Ibid.*, p. 81.

the whole temporal order, in order to prove it on the pulses, which is to make it 'real'. And so *The Fall* places *Hyperion's* narrative from beginning to end inside Moneta's head where Keats can hope to get at it on his own terms, where it becomes an extended, simultaneous, swooning merry-go-round of feel.

In *The Fall*, therefore, Keats completes a voyage of self-discovery. He returns armed with the truth—but with the unavailing truth since its nature is critical and not creative. The converting of *Hyperion* into a revolving internal drama, or dramatic tapestry, is an elaborate way of trying to guarantee for *The Fall* an effect which his best poetry produces anyhow. That is why the transcendental machinery of this second version puzzles the judgment; it is at once subtle and futile, relevant and inert. What it intends has either been achieved already or it cannot be gained by this means at all. To go through the internalising, feel-promoting rigmarole is not to paint the Keatsian picture but merely to sign it. Nothing is added to his art thereby. The story is successfully set within inverted commas; a one-man epic convention is established. But such aids are unnecessary since no one bothers to look for a signature when he finds himself in front of the recumbent Saturn.

He recognises Keats's work at a glance because of his instinctive response to that power which *The Fall* cumbrously defines as seeing the way a god sees. He knows (without necessarily knowing he knows) that seeing is feeling, and that in exercising his gift the poet gratifies a double urge: to articulate his material spatially, without which there would be no pictures, and to characterise negative-capably the object thus rendered, without which his pictures would lack their vital differentiation. Saturn and Hyperion, for example, are both suffering portraits. The one is gripped in "icy trance", the other has the taste of "poisonous brass" haunting his palate. Their pains are distinct but grounded equally in end-stopped feel. And both are credible portraits. Again and again, caught at a loss for words, we stand and admire the sheer achieved presence of these pictured figures in Keats: this is our tribute to his spatialising energy, and it easily gets forgotten that unfelt space is no space. Ruth, in the *Nightingale Ode*, is what she is both for the deprived feel of her heart and for the bare unqualified extension of her standing in the corn. The naiad of *Hyperion* and *The Fall* is an even simpler case. Ruth's "alien corn" has become just "her reeds", but the spatial conviction of "'mid" and "amid" is imaginatively no less than verbally the same with both of them.

Then it isn't surprising that the Pre-Raphaelites wanted to lure

Keats's secret out onto their canvasses.[1] Or that Keats the painter-poet has become a commonplace of criticism. Or even that one hears talk of his visual imagination.

The last is a disaster, because altogether misconceived. If someone wants to paint the naiad it is because her insistent thereness commands him. Yet he must know his power before he tries, since the maid's authority was won for her, in the poetic act, by the joint and inseparable working of the spatial imagination and the cold pressure of finger against lip; and that pressure is something no mere illustrator could manage.

2 Sensation, Imagination, Intellect, Beauty, Truth, Pleasure

I argued just now that we have to beware "let me behold" and the whole business of seeing the way a god sees in *The Fall* because of the singular, Pickwickian application of these words. What in fact goes on inside Moneta's head is a revolving, yet timeless, dramatic tapestry of "scenes" which the poet wants to guarantee by proving them on his pulses, and so make them 'real'. By feeling them is the short way of stating it.

To feel Keats-fashion is to apprehend inwardly, immediately, blindly, certainly. The poet himself suggests the image of the snail's horn. First, in November 1817, he writes to John Reynolds with a quotation from *Venus and Adonis*:

> As the snail, whose tender horns being hit,
> Shrinks back into his shelly cave with pain,
> And there all smothered up in shade doth sit,
> Long after fearing to put forth again:
> So at his bloody view her eyes are fled,
> Into the deep dark Cabins of her head.[2]

He does not say what he likes about the stanza beyond remarking that the simile brought it to mind as an example of Shakespeare's "fine things said unintentionally—in the intensity of working out conceits". But during the next April "intensity" reappears in the "havens of intenseness" of our focal letter to Haydon, and so does

---

[1] As others did too. There used to be a rendering of Ruth amid her corn in the dining-room of the Grand Hotel in Plymouth, by a forgotten Victorian RA.

[2] *Letters*, vol. I, p. 189. Keats's "put forth", misquoting Shakespeare's "creep forth", may result from his attention being primarily on the horns, the indrawn organs.

the snailhorn. He speaks of "the innumerable compositions and decompositions which take place between the intellect and its thousand materials before it arrives at that trembling delicate and snail-horn perception of Beauty".

"Snail-horn perception" is quite simply right. It awakens memories of Keats's eyes, ears, fingers, foreheads, tongues, palates, and all the familiar landmarks. We may apply it up and down the whole length of his work. It underlines feel itself, that large initial truth, and sets in train a host of cross-references between situations otherwise remote: for example, between two microcosmic and inward theatres of feel, Moneta's "globed brain" and the "shelly cave" where the snail withdraws its "tender horns" and sits "smothered up".[1]

The snailhorn, like the rest of this letter, has nevertheless not had its due. This may be partly because of the unpromising company it keeps; for "intellect", "beauty", "perception" itself, make up a smooth-worn generalised currency which encourages little hope of close contact. No surface oddity catches the eye as it did with Keats's "abstract".

"Perception" reintroduces Arnold's—and the common reader's —sensual poet. There is no knowing how much Keats understood about the physiology of the snailhorn, but one can be sure he is using the organ to exemplify a tactile sort of vision or a visionary sort of touch—no matter which, since both possibilities point with equal directness to the genius of feel. Not that "feel" enjoys a snail-horn monopoly; we have already found Keats using "sensation" and "sense" in contexts of the purest end-stopping.

"Sensation" denotes the fact of feel, and "perception" the act of feel. "Sensation" occurs over thirty times in his correspondence, and ranges no less widely than feel itself; starting out from the "quart of cold water" in the Teignmouth letter, it branches further and further into his moral and poetic concerns. He explains his anxiety to reach a clearcut financial arrangement with his publisher by saying that he has to be on his guard against "a too lax sensation of life".[2] Having described the pipe-smoking old Irishwoman in her sedan, he exclaims: "What a thing would be a history of her life and sensations."[3] Writing to Jane Reynolds, again in a negative-capable mood, he tells her "I now hear the voice [of the sea] most audibly while pleasing myself in the Idea of

---

[1] "Smother" is very much a Keats word, ranging from the "pleasant smotherings" of the 1817 volume to "smother" (together with stifling, choking, and allied sensations) as an agent of painful feel in both Hyperion fragments.
[2] *Letters*, vol. II, p. 143.   [3] Page 22, above.

your Sensations".[1] When he tells John Reynolds he has thrown over the Hyperion venture, his words are "I wish to give myself up to other sensations".[2] Breaking the same news to his brother and sister-in-law, he employs virtually the same phrase: "I wish to devote myself to another sensation."[3] He asks George and Georgiana Keats, "With what sensation do you read Fielding?"[4] Later he tells them that his own *Lamia* has a "sort of fire in it which must take hold of people in some way—give them either pleasant or unpleasant sensation";[5] and that his *Eve of St. Mark* "will give you the sensation of walking about an old county town in a coolish evening".[6] A famous generalisation runs: "The Genius of Poetry must work out its own salvation in a man: it cannot be matured by law and precept, but by sensation and watchfulness in itself."[7] More personally but still in a generalising vein, he writes to Benjamin Bailey, his parson friend, about "the great Consolations of Religion and undepraved Sensations—of the Beautiful—the poetical in all things".[8]

That last example completes the circle; for the snailhorn perception of beauty is, in its trembling delicacy, neither more nor less than the undepraved sensation of the beautiful, the poetical. I want first to note an omission: "imagination" is not among the words Keats uses although he is repeatedly touching on the poetic process. The reason is interesting; it is that imagination's place has been usurped by perception and sensation.

To run an eye over our small (but representative) stock of "sensation" occurrences is to observe more than a surprisingly wide reference. While Keats is put on his guard by his own casualness in practical affairs, we are made alert by the word he prefers. Something like a lax "attitude to life" might have been expected. In fact he chooses "sensation of life", and the impression he leaves is not one of shallow affectation. So far so good, or rather so merely puzzling. The force of his unspectacular yet piquant usage grows clearer in the remaining cases, all of which have a bearing on the literary art—potential with the old Irishwoman and John Reynold's sister, and actual with the other seven. Take *Hyperion*. We are not so much concerned with the singularity of his expression (though this is indeed an odd way of saying goodbye to his epic poem and welcoming the "northern" temper of our "purest English") as the threat which his "sensation" offers to the concept of imagination. Moreover the threat is, as our examples together

[1] *Letters*, vol. I, p. 158.
[2] *Ibid.*, vol. II, p. 167.
[3] *Ibid.*, p. 212.
[4] *Ibid.*, p. 18.
[5] *Ibid.*, p. 189.
[6] *Ibid.*, p. 201.
[7] *Ibid.*, vol. I, p. 374.
[8] *Ibid.*, p. 179.

show, persistent and cumulative. How can the maturing of poetry's genius by sensation not be an encroachment on imagination? Where does the line come between sensational and imaginative reactions to Fielding, to *Lamia* and to *St. Mark*? And as to *Hyperion*: if Keats really thinks he is registering the biggest creative crisis of his life, then where will the word "imagination" be needed?

Of course he does use the word. One can't conceive of a second-generation Romantic not doing so; it was everywhere. But the question is, how does he use it?

O I wish I was as certain of the end of all your troubles as that of your momentary start about the authenticity of the Imagination. I am certain of nothing but the holiness of the Heart's affections and the truth of Imagination. What the Imagination seizes as Beauty must be truth—whether it existed before or not—for I have the same idea of all our passions as of love: they are all, in their sublime, creative of essential Beauty. . . . The Imagination may be compared to Adam's dream—he awoke and found it truth.[1]

Not, in the first place, creatively, but apprehendingly, touchingly, like the ubiquitous finger-tips of his own poetry. "Seizes" is his word in a sentence which often gets quoted with the clause "whether it existed before or not" chopped off. That phrase matters, however. It confirms "seizes", it anticipates the sleep-and-wake doubleness of the Adam's dream conclusion, and it shows that imagination has, for Keats, been drawn into the orbit of sensation and perception.

His mind, as he writes this letter, is running round the imagination's touching and grasping function, and around the "what" which is touched and grasped; and at once—and characteristically —the commonsense difficulty occurs to him that sometimes there is no "what", anyhow no immediately obvious "what". Imagination may work fantastically, fictively, spinning from its own entrails—in a word, and in a rather special Keatsian sense, creatively. When Fanny Brawne gives rise to—inspires as they say—a poem, there is no problem about the "what" which imagination seizes as beauty. But suppose the nameless mistress of the *Ode on Melancholy*, or Lamia, had no original, no amalgam of originals, no apparent ground in actuality: what of the "what" and its "truth" then? Keats dashes off "whether it existed before or not" to indicate that this truth still stands.

His dilemma arises straight out of the utter conviction of his snailhorn. Having made imagination subservient to an ideal of sensitive feel, he cannot help considering imagination's object,

[1] *Letters*, vol. I, p. 184.

the thing felt. But rather than say, initially, that imagination creates its object, he leaves Bailey to make what he can of the unstressed but potent paradox of the touched and grasped thing which may not have existed before imagination did the touching and grasping. The passage does then go on to talk of creation— by "all our passions" though, not by imagination specifically; which ought not to surprise us since we have already seen him elaborate just this thought in another letter to Bailey: the one about "things semi-real which require a greeting of the spirit to make them wholly exist—and Nothings which are made great and dignified by an ardent pursuit".[1]

Keats's aesthetic, which he never develops systematically, which scarcely exists at the theoretical level, begins and ends in a combination of ardent pursuit and snailhorn feel. Pursuit is creative, feel visionary (both in a very idiosyncratic sense); and the imagination tends either to be squeezed out altogether or to be admitted as famished and pursuing feel's humble pensioner.

The largest single source of misunderstanding, in commentary, is the assumption that some version of creative imagination must have held the centre of his thoughts. Next to that, and not much less grievous, has been the Platonising of his beauty. The means of studying this second error lies at hand, for there in the letter to Haydon we find Keats's snailhorn flanked on one side by "intellect" and on the other by a capital-letter "Beauty". Writers have sought to justify an Arnoldian critical posture by appealing to this intellect-beauty collocation and to the word "truth" (or "reality") which haunts all such talk of Keats's. Playing with the counters of intellect, beauty, and truth, commentary accommodates its subject to its own educated expectations; the sovereign fact of the snailhorn is laid on one side, and the rest is shuffled together into a Platonic-Keatsian Idea of Beauty: beauty apprehended by intellect and lying beyond the stars, the one and the true beauty which knows no chance or change.

There can be no denying, any more than there was with imagination, that these words are freely used by Keats. And again the relevant question is, how? My conclusion over imagination was that the usual coarse generalising about Romanticism obscures the particular truth. With the other words, we have to beware of presuppositions vaguer even than Romantic. 'Intellect' first. Prepared for a narrow use suggesting developed, specialised mentality and the life of cerebration, we are surprised to find that intellect's dominant meaning in Keats is simply mind. A Negative Capability

[1] Page 75, above.

letter will serve for illustration, where he says that his friend Dilke "cannot feel he has a personal identity unless he has made up his mind about everything. The only way of strengthening one's intellect is to make up one's mind about nothing—to let the mind be a thoroughfare for all thoughts".[1] So, too, intellect means mind in the striking phrase which suggests that the points wherein Wordsworth is a more profound poet than Milton depend rather "upon the general and gregarious advance of intellect, than individual greatness of mind".[2] In fact it may be because "mind" appears in both passages (three times in the first) that the letter-writer casts around for a synonym. But the same thing happens when "mind" is absent. The sentiment that "America will be the country to take up the human intellect where England leaves off"[3] covers the whole mental history of the West, as well as showing yet once more his ingrained Evolutionism. Then he praises the scenery he is meeting on his walking tour by speaking of "the tone, the coloring"; and elaborates: "or, if I may so say, the intellect, the countenance of such places".[4] Here nature's face is the index of her mind, and it was open to Keats to write "the mentality" or "the mental colouring" of such places. But he preferred "intellect" (as again at "this countenance or intellectual tone" in the next sentence), and his choice is significant.

I mean we should not hesitate to interpret the "intellect" of his letter to Haydon in a residual and colourless sense. Keats is not speaking—not even untechnically—of the faculty of intellectual intuition which, in the Platonic tradition, directly grasps reality. Nor is he setting out to promote the analytic function of mind and thus turn upside down such affirmations as Wordsworth's "we murder to dissect". He is exclaiming to his fellow artist about the large and mysterious space (so that a heavy stress falls on "labyrinthian path" and "innumerable compositions and decompositions") dividing everyday mentality from the life of poetry and painting. His reference is to uncategorised mind.

This liking of his for "intellect" is not a mere verbalism. It belongs effectually within the snailhorn complex, and shows the same subordination to feel's master-image as his "imagination" does. Indeed sensation's encroachment on the province of imagination is only one aspect, though perhaps the most important, of its general tendency in Keats's letters to bend all mind and spirit to its rule. To take an example from the vale of soul-making:

---

[1] Page 17, above.
[2] Page 90, above.
[3] *Letters*, vol. I, p. 397.
[4] *Ibid.*, p. 301.

The point at which Man may arrive is as far as the parallel state in inanimate nature and no further. For instance suppose a rose to have sensation, it blooms on a beautiful morning, it enjoys itself—but there comes a cold wind, a hot sun—it cannot escape it, it cannot destroy its annoyances—they are as native to the world as itself: no more can man be happy in spite, the worldly elements will prey upon his nature.

He does not say "suppose a rose to have consciousness", and we can see why. His attention is upon the feel of heat and cold and of delicious cool summer mornings. But—a very large but—what are we to make of "it enjoys itself"? Certainly not that he is anxious about the line which divides mind and sense.[1] Rather the opposite —that sensation naturally and easily assumes a dominance over mind throughout the notorious no-man's-land (or both-men's-land) of pleasure and pain. And further, that the command which sensation shows in appropriating enjoyment and its opposite is not peculiar to the rose, the mindless rose. His assertion of a "parallel state" in man has the entire poetry of feel sustaining it. The apples and strawberries and girls of *Sleep and Poetry* taste nice, and the poisonous brass on Hyperion's palate tastes nasty.[2] Early and late, in his good verse and in his bad, sensation means the rose's postulated sensation in the vale of soul-making, with the same quasi-mental amplitude.

The rose enjoying the cool morning has sensation. The rose which said to itself "I am enjoying the morning" would have intellect. This gives Keats's characteristic usage. In essence it is a defensive gesture, since mind lies in the shadow of feel, and yet mind's sensationless, concept-kneading power must somehow be conceded. The result is the residual flavour of his "intellect". It is the flavour which the word "neutral" suggests in another Negative Capability letter: "Men of Genius are great as certain etherial Chemicals operating on the Mass of neutral intellect".[3] The result is also a kind of inert centrality; for its concept-forming does not incline intellect towards rare cerebrations; it keeps it busily employed in mundane, unintellectual, yet still of course concept-forming activities like "I am enjoying the morning".

So it appears that Keats's much-quoted cry "O for a Life of Sensations rather than of Thoughts!"[4] was framed and uttered in the privacy of his own passions. The sensuality of those sensations

---

[1] Though eighteenth-century epistemology was obsessed with this question; and so was Keats's philosophical mentor, Hazlitt.

[2] On Keats's also: "The last two years taste like brass upon my palate" (*Letters*, vol. II, p. 312).

[3] Page 17, above.   [4] *Letters*, vol. I, p. 185.

is not quite what generalising commentary would have it to be; nor the intellection of those thoughts. He wants—just now at least—to be a rose enjoying the morning and not a man telling himself about it. He is in the mood of the unrhymed sonnet which he wrote for a thrush, making the bird say "O fret not after knowledge".[1] When we apply the Haydon letter to the situation of the rose, or the thrush, it is plain that "it blooms on a beautiful morning, it enjoys itself" instances the snailhorn perception of beauty; but the letter's "intellect" has dropped out; the rose is not a man; one need acknowledge no composing and decomposing process with residual, sensationless mind at the other end of it.

Beauty, on the other hand, is present and named both for the rose and for the human being. By recognising Keats means the summer morning to be not just "beautiful" when he calls it that, but beautiful *for the rose*, we set our faces against the Platonising tradition. And as soon as we allow his universe—men and roses —to test, authenticate, the beautiful by its pleasure to sensation, we are treading the opposite and right path. Matthew Arnold took one step along it, thought he saw a "merely sensual" conclusion, and turned back. He wanted, with an earnestness which may seem strange at first (for Arnold was not against joy), to disembarrass himself of "enjoys", of that omnipresent Keatsian pleasure, especially as it appears in the love letters. He will have begun to read:

My sweet Girl,
Your letter gave me more delight than any thing in the world but yourself could do; indeed I am almost astonished that any absent one should have that luxurious power over my senses which I feel. Even when I am not thinking of you I receive your influence and a tenderer nature stealing upon me. All my thoughts, my unhappiest days and nights have I find not at all cured me of my love of Beauty, but made it so intense that I am miserable that you are not with me: or rather breathe in that dull sort of patience that cannot be called Life. I never knew before, what such a love as you have made me feel, was; I did not believe in it; my fancy was afraid of it, lest it should burn me up. But if you will fully love me, though there may be some fire, 'twill not be more than we can bear when moistened and bedewed with Pleasures.[2]

And his eye will have lingered regretfully over "my love of Beauty". If only this promising phrase could be extricated from its "luxurious" prologue and from that decorum-threatening continuation which envisages the moistening agency of pleasure amid fierce erotic flames. Here and throughout the love letters, no rescue operation is worth even contemplating; but elsewhere one can,

[1] Page 67, above.　　　　[2] *Letters*, vol. II, p. 126.

some do, draw a notional ring round phrases like "the yearning passion I have for the beautiful", and hope to fabricate a spiritual and intellectual poet out of them.

The force of Keats's "yearning passion" here derives from its being placed over against "the ambition of my intellect". Ignore the specific context, abstract, ambitious, Hyperionic, and trouble follows. What is local to the epic venture, what proves self-refuting, is asked to express the norm. And we ourselves are then tempted to avert our gaze from the desired and dreaded fire and the moistening pleasures of that love letter. But if we do, many other things, small things often like

> *at thy supreme desire,*
> *Touch the very pulse of fire*
> *With my bare unlidded eyes*

will probably be neglected too, things which are, each in its degree, the real achievement.

The dictum that great poets are not merely sensual has a corollary, which is that great poetry is not merely indulgent. That is the motive for playing down Keatsian Pleasure. His own sensitiveness to this consideration has already emerged; philanthropy—disinterestedness, doing the world some good—gets ranged against the poetry of pleasurable feel, from the beginning in the 1817 volume where human agony and strife bears down accusingly on the delights of Flora and Pan, to the end in *Hyperion* where Keats struggles to maintain that Beauty is Might is Right, and in *The Fall* where he pours his strength into the sands of an inchoate dialectic involving, as chief participants, the world's beauty-seeking poets (who may mature into something higher?) and its humanitarian sufferers on behalf of all of us in all our pain.

But the love letter, the letters as a whole, confirm what the poetry demonstrates—that humanitarian "philosophy" is helpless to uncouple beauty from pleasure. The painful touch of fire against bare eyes is another story, one which lies ahead, but otherwise beauty retaliates against the uncoupling effort by remaining "in the abstract". A state of impasse is reached, with the philosophic mood anxious, in Keats and his critics, to disown a poetry of appetite and a poet who apparently just goes after what he wants. The licence of it is disconcerting; so the Arnoldian game of drawing protective rings round acceptable phrases and sentences goes on.

To do this one must forget the poetry and then proceed against the deep self-consistent strain of the letters. The last is something their writer hardly ever does, outside his philosophic mood. Whether talking about beauty's creation by our passions, or affirming that the object seized as beautiful must be true *even if it had no prior existence*, beneath the perplexing, choppy surface he is paying homage to the snailhorn; he is asking us to picture what he called "the mere yearning and fondness I have for the Beautiful"[1] as a venturing forth in search of pleasurable feel. Why pleasurable? invites the commonsensical Keatsian answer that if it were not so, in hope at least, the creature would stay inside his shelly cave. Here we touch the heart of his bad conscience about his poetic impulse; and I appeal to the "ardent pursuit" letter by way of commentary on this "yearning and fondness" which is his own sort of venturing forth. The letters offer no coherent doctrine, but they do strike, in the mass, an attitude recognisable as his; which is the best reason for saying they belong with the poems.

3 The 1817 Poems

Keats achieved—had to achieve—a lot in a short time, because he died young and also because he was less precocious than people like to think. He was born in 1795 but wrote nothing of importance until 1816. He seems to have written no verse at all before he was eighteen.[2] And he died in February 1821, not quite four months beyond his twenty-fifth birthday. In fact the span is even shorter than a bare recital of dates would suggest; for the lung haemorrhage which struck him down in February of 1820, and the subsequent decline into consumption, left him without strength or inclination to attempt anything new in the last year of his life: he just tinkered with old work. In so far, finally, as the winter months before that first haemorrhage were productive of any extended writing, they produced the worthless *Cap and Bells* and so were largely wasted.

The snailhorn trinity, sensation, pleasure, ardent pursuit, belongs equally to his slow start and his rapid development. "Belongs" is the word he chose himself for the opening line of the earliest of his verse epistles,[3]

Sweet are the pleasures that to verse belong,

[1] *Letters*, vol. I, p. 388.
[2] Charles Brown says so in his *Life* (1937, p. 41) and only Charles Cowden Clarke among Keats's contemporaries has suggested anything else.
[3] *To George Felton Mathew.*

and it advises where first to look when we marvel how the 1817 volume contrives to foreshadow his familiar and great things while it is being quite extraordinarily tiresome. For the pleasures of verse extend beyond the reading, and even the writing (as writing is usually understood) of poetry, beyond the conceiving to the formless desire to conceive, to the nameless need, the blank unhoused restlessness, the premonitory aura. These pleasures "belong" particularly and personally to Keats's creativeness; they are its secret premiss, proveable in retrospect like footprints in the snow. Their progress involves him in tacit, unintended self-definition, as at the "death of luxury" climax in *Sleep and Poetry*:

> *or, if I can bear*
> *The o'erwhelming sweets....*

And the same thing happens at the only other point in the book where his philanthropic ("philosophical") voice breaks in:

> *Could I, at once, my mad ambition smother,*
> *For tasting joys like these, sure I should be*
> *Happier, and dearer to society.*[1]

The belonging pleasures, like the poetry-philosophy antithesis, are entirely his own—his own first and foremost through his manner of appropriating them. There is a smothering sensation implicit in *Sleep and Poetry's* "o'erwhelming" which comes out into the open in the other passage, and likewise with the buried taste of "sweets". The association of smothering and tasting with pleasure, arbitrary enough outside the little world of his first book, becomes inescapable within it. To smother ambition may seem a morally severe proposal, a disagreeable "smother", but one's response to it here is complacent and touched with delicious irresponsible fantasy; our own feel teaches us to exploit the gap dividing Keats's overall sentiment from the pleasures he has narrowly but truly imagined.

> *The soul is lost in pleasant smotherings*[2]

is the fact of the matter, prompting us to forget "ambition", to take a hint from "tasting joys"—the idea next door—and indulge "smother" for ourselves.

Richness, softness, palate-metaphors of feeding, drinking, sipping, tasting, are the common stuff of his earliest verse and the odes and other mature work of 1819. The list may be extended to cover those centralities "tender" and "smooth", and the whole area of

---

[1] *To My Brother George*, 110.　　　[2] "I stood tip-toe", 132.

temperature—"warm", "cool", "chill", merging into sensational halfway houses of the "fresh", "clear", "airy", "balmy" sort. All this is shared material; and to say so is to begin exploring the strange relationship, at once intimate and remote, between what goes on in 1817 and two years later. Attentiveness is not always easy to command. Familiarity and the anthologising habit domesticate long-acknowledged masterpieces, teaching them to lie down by the fire as good classics should. It is a process of inverted patronage in which short, completely famous poems like the odes of 1819 are bound to suffer most. So we receive the *clamminess* of the honeycomb cells in *Autumn* as just what to expect and nice to live with. While *Melancholy's* "strenuous tongue" fails to make its effect; ceases even to catch the eye.

But the moment always returns when the tenderness of the *Nightingale's* night, palpable, the snailhorn's joy, cannot be taken for anything other than Keats's very own, and hard won, and a fragment of his poem's greatness. We ask why "tender" in the ode amounts to more than the "tenders" of the 1817 poems: a question with a serious core to it in so far as phrases like "the tender greening / Of April meadows"[1] show him beginning as he means to continue, coaxing his reader towards a mind's-fingertip solicitation of that young responsive surface to the year's Spring. Obviously, the answer turns upon context and the larger whole.[2] And the damaging, diminishing thing about context, everywhere in the 1817 volume except the Chapman's Homer sonnet, is the crude tyranny of the pleasure principle: not the fact but the fashion of pleasure's rule.

The bad and the characterful elements of the book are held together by Keats's radical assumption about poetry and pleasure. "For what has made the sage or poet write," he asks—what but "the fair paradise" of natural joys?[3] His question sustains both the venturing snailhorn and the insufferable monotony. Always with this poet, and especially in his first book, monotony means a very obvious failure of thematic momentum. It is as if he had appreci-

---

[1] *Sleep and Poetry*, 170.
[2] A quick way of noting the book's immaturity lies through the oscillation of "tender" between prosaic primary uses like "tender feet" (*Calidore*, 185; *Specimen of an Induction to a Poem*, 14) and ineffective extensions like "tender pondering" ("I stood tip-toe", 122). The same is true of "tender's" first cousin "soft"; it yaws violently between "soft dimpled hands" ("Light feet", 2) and "soft humanity" (*To George Felton Mathew*, 55). Later, in the "tender-taken breath" of the "Bright star!" sonnet and the "soft-dying day" of *Autumn*, we find these words reposing securely within an intermediate position of Keats's own making.
[3] "I stood tip-toe", 125.

ated that the breeze of pleasurable feel blowing insistently in his
face was the force filling the sails of invention and driving him
forward, but had supposed that the best way to make progress was
to steer straight ahead. So he stands motionless in the eye of the
wind, held in irons as the sailors' metaphor has it.

How to use the wind is the lesson he eventually learns. In the
meantime, not surprisingly, doubts assail him about the thing itself, the wind in his face; and in *Sleep and Poetry*, the last poem of
1817—last in the book and last written—he begins to fly his kite of
laborious painful knowledge. We have already studied that recurring move—the interpretative effort, the various forms which
know-against-feel takes—and it only remains to acknowledge the
size of his difficulty. He was not one of nature's self-doubters. We
have to put ourselves in his shoes as he stood in the flat sweet middle of his book and pondered its involvement with sensation,
pleasure and ardent pursuit, like a man contemplating his fate. He
was preoccupied, initially, with "the pleasures that to verse
belong"; and following pleasure through the 1817 volume we find
that his rather elaborate coupling of it with the creative impulse
in the "o'erwhelming sweets" section of *Sleep and Poetry* has several
primitive and unworked forerunners like

> *No sooner had I stepp'd into these pleasures*
> *Than I began to think of rhymes and measures:*[1]

while that section itself gets further developed in Keats's distinction
between "strength alone" and true poetry whose office is strongly
"to sooth"—without an "e" and deliciously assimilated to
"smooth".[2] Moreover, the scheme of generalised pleasure runs
true to the book's individual sweets. Just as key words like "soft"
and "tender" swing helplessly between a trite concreteness and the
vaguest abstraction, so the pleasure principle has one foot in a
"world of blisses"[3] and "pleasures of the bard",[4] and another in
specific indulgencies like "I pillow my head on the sweets of the
rose";[5] and neither will do for a proper home.

These facts inform the little nautical trope of Keats lying head
to pleasure's wind: the essence of his 1817 situation is it unpro-
gressiveness. The figure can claim the further merit that it is not

---

[1] *To Charles Cowden Clarke*, 97.
[2] Lines 230-47. This logic-chopping in *Sleep and Poetry* is comparable with the
argument about poets, dreamers and humanitarians in *The Fall*, and should be
taken for an equally sinister sign.
[3] "I stood tiptoe", 54.   [4] *To My Brother George*, 67.
[5] *On Receiving a Curious Shell*, 38.

just a roundabout way of observing he has not enough to say. That observation is true of course, but inadequate, and misleading too in that it tempts one to repeat his own know-against-feel mistake, or something like it. Diagnosing his trouble as a poverty of external impetus, rather than innate impulse, is our job; learning to use the wind, with no thought of disavowing it, is his. For there are things in the pleasure-drenched 1817 volume which anticipate (without embodying) truths of the first importance about the poet we all admire. The fish in "I stood tiptoe" which "nestle / Their silver bellies on the pebbly sand" show the same dedication to sensory environment as Madeline lying between her cold, lavendered sheets; and when Keats makes them stick their heads out of the cool water "to taste the luxury of sunny beams"[1] he is playing contrastingly with temperature as he does throughout *St. Agnes*. It follows, when we wonder why *St. Agnes Eve* is a masterpiece and "I stood tiptoe" extremely poor, that we should not be afraid to welcome their very formidable common element: formidable because vitalising rather than because large. A certain steadfastness is needed, within the confines of 1817, to say again and again that an effect is ultimately Keats's and ultimately futile. Those fish out of water have everything and nothing to do with the real feats of Negative Capability.

I would further refine this point by quoting six horrible lines from a sonnet with a serious claim to be judged the worst in the book:

> *Yet these I leave as thoughtless as a lark;*
> *These lures I straight forget,—e'en ere I dine,*
> *Or thrice my palate moisten: but when I mark*
> *Such charms with mild intelligences shine,*
> *My ear is open like a greedy shark,*
> *To catch the tunings of a voice divine.*[2]

The palate, were it an isolated palate, would be nothing, despite its suspicious gratuitousness. But, incarnate in metaphors of taste, the palate is everywhere in 1817; and here the organ is joined to, or meets half way, the "greedy" ear; and this infolding of sensation's externalities is the sure sign of the pleasure-seeking snailhorn at work. Then in for a penny in for a pound as regards the worst of 1817.

> *The inward ear will hear her and be blest*
> *And tingle with a joy too light for rest*[3]

[1] Lines 72-7.
[2] "Light feet, dark violet eyes". The "lures" and "charms" referred to are the poem's light feet and violet eyes and other pleasures.
[3] Two cancelled lines after "I stood tiptoe", 64.

shows the threadbare image of the inward ear serving as it were a literal purpose. The innerness is a real shelly-cave affair, a snail-horn-tingling, and does not follow poetic convention. Just now Keats was invoking the moon.[1] Why "closer of lovely eyes"? Because the eye is not for seeing with. Or rather, it is there for snailhorn-seeing, which Keats called "perception". You can snail-horn-hear with your "greedy" and tingling ears too. And you can snailhorn-touch with your lips. In "lips have trembled with a maiden's eyes"[2] an eloquent reciprocity of sensation, which will be the special province of the odes, begins to stir. Also something of the odes' murky, pungent syntax. I take that "with" joining lips and eyes to mean "at the inward feel of". Not that it matters much now; and not that such prepositions need glossing later on, when they do not matter.

4 'Endymion'

This lip-and-eye exchange in the 1817 volume summarises Endymion's tender plight; and the continuation "Ah! I will taste that dew", tells us what the shepherd prince decides to do about it. He wants the moon (which is another way of saying he isn't sure what he wants; but he *does* want, and wants absolutely); and he goes out to get her.

The four-book Romance describes his quest. The thing is in effect one unbroken ardent pursuit in which "I will taste" emblazons the hero's motto, uniting the snailhorn trio but giving precedence to pursuit over the other two. While, certainly, the cardinal palate metaphor pays court to sensation and pleasure, all eyes are on the future tense and the snailhorn's venturing forth. At least that is the intention, for the story proves a very boring one.

Keats was a severe judge of what he called "my first-blights", and in trying to make his narrative lean forward expectantly he is addressing himself to the failure of momentum in the 1817 poems, now finished and published. He must get his muse moving. Hence the uncharacteristic resoluteness of his approach, and the harping on "invention", a word which emerges with *Endymion* and disappears with it again. This poem alone is "a test, a trial" and "a task"—a test "chiefly of my invention which is a rare thing indeed

[1] Immediately before the "pleasant smotherings" of "I stood tip-toe".
[2] "Had I a man's fair form".

—by which I must make four thousand lines of one bare circumstance and fill them with Poetry. . .".[1] He wants to get the job finished by the next winter, and through one period sets himself a composing stint of fifty lines a day.

All this is very unlike the poet who wanted his poetry to come as naturally as leaves to a tree. *Otho the Great,* his five-act Tragedy, affords a parallel in that it too was written with an eye on the clock. But it is a parallel which stresses the other work's oddity. For *Otho* was aimed directly at Drury Lane and the star actor Kean, who might (and in the event did) go away at short notice and spoil the plan; it was devised and executed in close collaboration with his worldly friend, Charles Brown, appearing usually as "our Tragedy" in his letters; and immediate financial gain was the leading motive throughout.[2] Whereas Endymion's forward urging was coupled with the loftiest, most detached ambition. Keats wrote it, as he says in his Preface, with "a great object" before him. Both works suffer dreadfully from being composed on the will. That brings them together in the end. But it is also true, and important, that they constitute two very different tests, trials, tasks.

Endymion's solemn despatch isolates it therefore. The Romance brings a remedy called Invention to the ills of 1817—"the Polar Star of Poetry", Keats calls it, still talking about *Endymion:* "This same invention seems indeed of late years to have been forgotten as a poetical excellence."[3] What he means by Invention is never very clear; without exactly denying its long and respectable neoclassic past he overlays it with the opaque semi-privacy—compare "abstract"—of the word which is becoming, for a season, a Keats word. He leaves us to refer it both to his "great object" in writing *Endymion* and to the trivial ingenuity (as it must appear) of spinning out "one bare circumstance" for four thousand lines.

Invention he also calls the Pole Star, the star to steer by; which image confirms the forward-thrusting, forward-thinking drift of everything else we hear, and at the same time recalls our own figure of his 1817 muse lying head to pleasure's wind. Invention sums up his response to this state of affairs. As I say, it is the remedy he proposes.

To consider how efficacious a remedy is to go on talking about pleasure. *Endymion* is a rambling storehouse of pleasures, but of

[1] *Letters,* vol. I, p. 169.
[2] He had three good reasons for trying to make money quickly. He was in debt. He wanted to get married. He needed a capital sum to lend his brother George in America.
[3] *Letters,* vol. I, p. 170.

pleasures which claim a new gravity by doting on their own fair features and murmuring from time to time, "Beauty!" This narcissistic exercise does more than anything else to make the poem the airless, eventless, self-caressing thing it so disagreeably is. Nevertheless there is occasion here for respectful thought as well as condemnation, because the voice murmuring "Beauty!" in *Endymion* acquires, on and off, the tone we are waiting for, showing there is such a thing as snailhorn-speech too.

In the 1817 poems, the relation between sensation, pleasure and ardent pursuit is nearly everywhere stable and predictable: that guarantees the book's monotony. When, however, in the Spring of 1818 Keats presented Haydon with the phrase "snailhorn perception of beauty", he had just finished revising *Endymion,* and a certain rigid primitive lucidity is now lost for ever. Taking first things first, I brusquely assimilated beauty to pleasure, stating that the snailhorn goes after its desire. Attempting next things next—*Endymion* that is—we have to add a rider that the assimilation may work the other way round. Of course the creature still chases its desire, whether in search of beautiful pleasures or pleasurable beauties, but precisely this openness of possibility can be made significant.

We only have to begin reading, with the 1817 volume fresh in mind, to become aware of an obstinate and spreading patch of indeterminacy within the desire of the snailhorn.

> *A thing of beauty is a joy for ever:*
> *Its loveliness increases; it will never*
> *Pass into nothingness . . . .*

Exploiting this openness of possibility—exploiting emphasis—is one of the ways in which he learns to use the motive wind of pleasure; it is one of those trials of Invention he talks about, though he might be surprised to hear me say so. I should like to ply him with a little Socratic coaxing. "This Invention of yours. You aren't, are you, really talking about multiplying incident. You are fumbling after, dimly preconceiving, the stone-dropped-in-water effect of the odes. Your instinct here is not for making matters longer, not linear and temporal; indeed your own statement in the 'Invention' letter about readers of poetry liking 'a little region to wander in' suggests the spatial and time-mocking truth. And what about your 'one bare circumstance'? This isn't an event, surely, or a fact in the ordinary run of facts, but a proposition. Bare and single as you say, but a proposition. It is your poem's first line."

F   129

Joining us now and resting his eye on

A thing of beauty is a joy for ever

Keats might agree that the "great object" he was striving after when in the throes of *Endymion* was this line's decisive vindication; and, taxed gently with his own certainty of having failed, he might begin to wonder why his verdict upon a long, patently uneven work had been so cut and dried. Think of him rounding off the dialogue: "Your prompting, Socrates, and my hindsight urge this conclusion. The nine words of Line One were a bare circumstance which grew heroic—became a great object—while I struggled to make them good within my poem. Fulfilling their secret potentiality of growth, ripening, dilation on the page, was the task given to Invention, that neglected poetic faculty. The task was not fulfilled. Therein my certainty of failure."

He and we part company just here, because for us *Endymion* does not stand or fall by any single, absolute test. Nevertheless he happens to be broadly right; we only want to make minor qualifications; and in any case, an agreed initial focus on "beauty" and "joy" and on the "for ever" claim still unites us in our differences. That first line compels every student of Keats to make up his mind about an unmistakable widening of pretensions which has taken place since the 1817 volume. *Sleep and Poetry* (which Keats finished while the book was in the press) has grand resolves of the "I must pass" and "I may find" sort; but there is all the difference, in this connection, between a proposal and a proposition. Not any old proposition. One which reveals its pretensions in its careful rhetorical abandon, mounting an imaginative assault on time, attempting a two-way assimilation of beauty and pleasure—both placed within a situational openness mentioned before and needing closer study now.

Two candidates have appeared for the doubtful honour of acceptance as *Endymion's* motto. *Per ardua ad astra* was the badge tied to the Pleasure Thermometer long ago, and just now I borrowed "I will taste" from the 1817 volume to express the shepherd prince's quest. Both may be justified because both are there, persistently there, in the poem. In fact there is room for both within the thermometer itself, as we saw when we poured scorn on its "fellowship divine" but were prepared to take seriously its invitation "Fold a rose leaf". The first shares the general discredit of *Endymion's* spiritual stars; the second lives by the tasting truth of the snailhorn.

We might have brought the two mottoes even closer together by observing that Keats's autograph fair copy has no sign of any "fellowship divine" but offers instead a "blending pleasurable". The change must have occurred at the last minute. Here and throughout, reaching for the stars and pursuing the snailhorn's pleasure are most closely confused. They wind in and out in dismal fugue through four interminable books, and are already at it the opening lines. The *ardua* of Endymion's journey are foreshadowed in

> *the unhealthy and o'er-darkened ways*
> *Made for our searching:*

the "thing of beauty" and "shape of beauty" postulate his goal, and it is very soon apparent that he will have to wade through many lines of diluted Wordsworth ("A flowery band to bind us to the earth"—or simply homage to Leigh Hunt?) before he gets there, and pick his way through flocks of "simple sheep" that have strayed in from olden pastoral. But twenty lines have not elapsed when the other theme, the counter-process, begins to assert itself. The opposition of "health" and "unhealthy" is a queer thing but Keats's own—and more of that later—while the classic temperature contrast at "cooling coverts" and "hot season" prepares the ground for a kind of homecoming at

> *Rich with the sprinkling of fair musk-rose blooms:*

a celebration and gathering of the clans. This little indulgence greets the

> *clear air,*
> *Smoothed for intoxication by the breath*
> *Of flowering bays!*[1]

from the first book he published, *Endymion* being the second, and ushers in the later roses of *Hyperion* and *The Fall*: the cry

> *Let the rose glow intense and warm the air*[2]

and the poet's waking dream, "Methought I stood . . .

> *In neighbourhood of fountains, by the noise*
> *Soft-showering in mine ears; and, by the touch*
> *Of scent, not far from roses.*"[3]

That is snailhorn perception. Sense-transference does not go to the root of the matter; for while it is true, and worth remarking, that "musk" pulls the touch-effect of "sprinkling" towards smell,

---

[1] *Sleep and Poetry*, 56.   [2] *Hyperion*, III, 15.
[3] *The Fall*, I, 19.

that "smoothed" pulls the smell-effect of the bay's "breath" towards touch, that the whole visuality of the rose's colour is brought against our receiving mind in the fancy of a glowing source of warmth, that "soft-showering" strokes the ear and "touch of scent" is a straight sensory cross—none the less, the fact to prefer with all possible stress is the snailhorn's desire which it embalms in the master-image of taste. Taste is the active principle within *Isabella's* triple sensory cross:

> *O turn thee to the very tale,*
> *And taste the music of that vision pale.*[1]

The description "Groanings swell'd / Poisonous about my ears"[2] discreetly recalls that the Keatsian ear is for tasting with. These and all such sense-transferences are moves made to appease the snailhorn's hunger; they are the surface show of the determination "I will taste". Beneath them, imaginatively prior to them, an unmoved mover watches and waits, urges and sustains: a sensory solar plexus, a hidden confluence of all sensation's externalities. Sense-transference turns inward upon this centre, in the interest of snailhorn perception, and the snailhorn is the organ of end-stopped feel.

Inevitably the snailhorn's hunger drives it to draw to itself and appropriate, to savour what it sees.

> *Sideway his face repos'd*
> *On one white arm, and tenderly unclos'd,*
> *By tenderest pressure, a faint damask mouth*
> *To slumbery pout; just as the morning south*
> *Disparts a dew-lipp'd rose.*[3]

What begins visually turns towards feel at "pressure" (compare the naiad and her cold finger) and the boldly repeated tenderness, at last provoking the extraordinary *fait accompli* of the verb "disparts". Here comes confirmation of the infelt, negative-capable pressure, but confirmation salted with aggressive sensuality: the old familiar, the erotic Keats. As so often, we must both admit—indeed let rip with—the grossest fantasy over this labial disparting and yet refuse to isolate sex; for he has swamped sex within his larger reverie. We are after all (to state the bigger thing very simply) talking about roses. And have been talking about *Endymion's* roses since

> *Rich with the sprinkling of fair musk-rose blooms.*

[1] Stanza XLIX.   [2] *Endymion*, III, 490.
[3] *Ibid.*, II, 403.

To try and separate the erotic strand in "disparts a dew-lipp'd rose" would be as destructive as it would be futile. One might as well pull his chosen epithet "rich "apart in order to get at the sex in it.

The last point is well taken, I venture to say. When Keats comes to write the poetry of 1819 "rich" will acquire strategic importance: at moments like

> *Now more than ever seems it rich to die*

in the *Nightingale Ode*, and

> *Or if thy mistress some rich anger shows*

in *Melancholy*. Its earlier history, like that of those other 1819 words "soft" and "tender", records his progressive mastery of a vocabulary which had been his own from the start. "Rich" already went with roses in 1817; with roses and with sex:

> *Yet must I dote upon thee,—call thee sweet,*
> *Sweeter by far than Hybla's honied roses*
> *When steep'd in dew rich to intoxication.*

With roses, sex, with the scent and cool touch of dew, and with tasting: "Ah! I will taste that dew" he continues here, and his future tense picks up and maintains the expectancy, the stretching towards consummated pleasure which already informs "rich to intoxication".

Precisely this thrusting forward of the snailhorn gives "I will taste" to Endymion as his true motto, just as the hollow spirituality of the Pleasure Thermometer proves *per ardua ad astra* to be his false one. But it does not follow that Keats would have succeeded with his four-book Romance if he had stuck to the true motto. Let "rich" be our touchstone still, for the 1819 phrases "rich anger" and "rich to die" neatly pose the problem of *Endymion* by allowing us to look back on it from the vantage point of success. In 1817 "rich" went primarily with roses. In 1819 it goes with anger and death. *Endymion*, published in 1818, is in this as in other respects transitional. Its first line intends, and merely intends, what the "rich" happenings of 1819 will realise. That is why

> *A thing of beauty is a joy for ever*

might be tacked on to the singing of the nightingale or the scene pictured on the grecian urn as an author's comment on his own work, but seems not to belong to *Endymion* at all. An 1819 phrase like "rich to die" sets us playing at cats' cradles with Keatsian beauty and Keatsian pleasure; this is the situational openness I spoke of, the two-way assimilation. Whereas the interpenetration of beauty and pleasure announced by *Endymion's* first line remains a pious hope and rhetorically pathetic, because of what ought to follow but never does.

When we echo Keats's verdict on his poem, we conceive two reasons for its failure. The journey *per ardua* was doomed from the start; and "I will taste", while true to the snailhorn's nature and especially its habit of ardent pursuit, nevertheless lacks a *rich* continuation. The potential wealth of "I will taste" becomes a casualty—the main casualty—in the struggle between the two rival mottoes. I trace the outcome in the fact that beauty provides a theme and province for the spiritual quest, while the snailhorn is left to make what it can of sheer, bare pleasure. The poet is thus forced back, as regards pleasure, into his 1817 posture. In a way he is worse off than he was then because of the tight restriction which his epic story imposes on him. In 1817, his freedom to "choose every pleasure that my fancy sees"[1] was made catholic use of. But now he has to follow the fortunes of a particular hero as he goes after the girl in the moon and, after various half- and dream- and trance-consummations, finally wins her. Her beauty, her goddess quality, has been hived off into a world of supernaturalistic mumbo-jumbo, leaving the snailhorn genius completely but narrowly occupied with the pleasure to be had out of her. With her sex, that is. And so this long poem turns out to be erotic Keats *par excellence*, providing the main documentation for Matthew Arnold's merely sensual criticisms, and also the main ground for his deeper fear and distaste.

Keats not only has to cope with a bulky narrative lying head to pleasure's wind (if we may ignore the asserted *ardua* for a moment) but with pleasure which is far more closely tethered to sex than it had been in 1817. We encounter now the shifts and shuffling embarrassments that unite him, momentarily, with the very humblest erotic writers. From *Endymion* may be borrowed

> *the fair visitant at last unwound*
> *Her gentle limbs, and left the youth asleep*

in order to point the tonal clash between the visitant and the unwinding. If we turn to the earlier draft preserved in Woodhouse's transcript, we find evidence that Keats himself came to notice the frankness of his verb. The transcript reads "Her prison'd limbs".

---

[1] *Sleep and Poetry*, 104.

"Prison'd" confirms and draws attention to "unwound". Therefore (I guess) he altered "prison'd" to "gentle"; and so the outspokenness gets muffled.

Amusement can be drived from breasts in *Endymion*:

> *To linger on her lily shoulders, warm*
> *Between her—breasts*. . . .[1]

Keats first tried "budding"; then he hesitated, and without crossing out "budding" wrote "pouting" above it. Then he scrapped both and settled for "kissing"—which is our text. All these possibilities are, nevertheless, tinged with distinction as well as mirthful. "Budding" has noble associations with the ripening process throughout his work: metaphorical at the "budding morrow in midnight" of the fine and underrated sonnet to Homer;[2] quasi-literal, as here, in "my fair love's ripening breast" from "Bright star!"; and literal with all trace of "quasi" removed in *Autumn*:

> *to set budding more,*
> *And still more, later flowers for the bees*. . . .

"Pouting", while it does not abandon Keatsian ripeness, inclines the issue towards sex. It silently assimilates what the trite lyric voice comes out with:

> *You say you love—but then your lips*
> *Coral tinted teach no blisses,*
> *More than coral in the sea—*
> *They never pout for kisses—*

contrast the dreamy, invested sex of "slumbery pout" which preceded the disparting of the dew-lipped rose and was itself heralded by "tenderly unclos'd, / By tenderest pressure". That "pout" managed to keep its kissing to itself.

But it is also true that the movement from "budding" *via* "pouting" to "kissing" presents a just three-word paradigm of *Endymion's* erotic constriction, an ungenerous and therefore untypical state, an Arnoldian "mere" state with the marvellous potentiality of ripening all forsaken. By this token *Endymion* becomes odd man out, while the 1817 volume joins hands—in its idiocies even—with the work of 1819.

---

[1] II. 946.

[2] "Standing aloof in giant ignorance". Matthew Arnold, Robert Bridges and H. W. Garrod all compiled lists of Keats's "best sonnets", but none of them included this.

Yet this is vain—O Mathew lend thy aid
To find a place where I may greet the maid—
Where we may soft humanity put on,
And sit, and rhyme and think on Chatterton ;[1]

where "soft humanity" is both indefensible and acquainted with the fearless dilating ardour of the best Keats. *Endymion's* soft themes on the other hand, hem us round with their tight circle of "soft ravishment", "soft caressing sobs", "soft embrace", "soft kiss", "soft arms".[2] Even such ordinary (for Keats) and central usages as "soft slumber" and "soft ear"[3] reach us as grateful exceptions to the local rule; while once, with the hero's "soft poppy dream",[4] a *St. Agnes* vista opens suddenly.

Her dawning love-look rapt Endymion blesses
With 'haviour soft.[5]

This one, like the others, reveals a predicament which inevitably grows most acute as the erotic writer confronts the act of sex. When Keats cannot leave matters at "'haviour soft" we observe him running for the cover of double negatives and other shielding devices:

And then she hover'd over me, and stole
So near, that if no nearer it had been
This furrow'd visage thou hadst never seen.[6]

That, of course, is Endymionese for "she seduced me".[7] As soon as the narrator has laid his smokescreen and negotiated the awkward step behind it, he feels free to exclaim

"Who could resist? Who in this universe?"—

while the announcement

"thus particular
Am I, that thou may'st plainly see how far
This fierce temptation went"

leaves us smiling at the impudence of "plainly". Another recourse is to proceed like this:

So fond, so beauteous was his bed-fellow,
He could not help but kiss her :[8]

[1] *To George Felton Mathew*, 53. [2] II, 715, 736, 756, 806; III, 270.
[3] II, 329; III, 974. [4] IV, 786.
[5] IV, 463. [6] III, 446.
[7] Conversely, "to doff / Thy shepherd vest, and woo thee mid fresh leaves" (II, 699) is Endymionese for "to undress you and. . .".
[8] IV, 448.

where, in the same year that Thomas Bowdler produced his ex-
purgated Shakespeare, *Endymion* offers one thing and its reader
substitutes another.

This might all be called good sadistic fun at the expense of poor
Keats, sex-committed throughout four thousand lines and under
the surveillance of a correct publisher.[1] Superficially, the literary
roasting he endures is that of the pornographic writer who has one
thing to say and has to go on saying it, but printably. The scene
under the surface, however, the personal issue, is the one we are
exploring through the rivalry of *Endymion's* two mottoes. What
suggests a pornographic analogy is the deprivation which "I will
taste" suffers; worse than merely sensual, the threat to our
Arnoldian composure is merely sexual. Now mere sex is a mere
abstraction in any persisting human contact, and here we have the
strong if unobvious link between Keats's two epic narratives. The
"abstract idea" of his Hyperion project is most lucidly expounded
in the falling apart of the enjoined feel-exercise of climbing the
altar steps and the rationale of that task. *Endymion's* abstraction
betrays itself in a very similar and equally disabling separation, of
the erotic adventure from the value attributable to it. That is why
I find the first line so revealing. The "beauty" of its pleasure, and
the substance of its "for ever" claim, must live within the adventure
to come, or they are nowhere. They prove to be nowhere; they
drag out their non-existence, that is, in bodiless transcendental
commentary; and the first line has to be rephrased "A feel-
pleasure is a pleasure while we feel it". True in that form, and the
stuff of Keats's poetry; but raw, unworked, potential only. And
fraught with peril for the poet determined to hitch pleasure to sex
through thick and thin.

Older and perhaps wiser, he will give up *Hyperion* and *The Fall*
—both versions. Now he presses on with *Endymion*, fifty lines a day
and so forth, changing his scene from under the earth to under the
sea to up in the air, calling in aid subsidiary feel-pleasures with
flagrant disregard of relevance ("I started up, when lo! refresh-
fully, / There came upon my face, in plenteous showers, / Dew-
drops")[2]; but committed utterly to sex. Sex has to go it almost
alone. The three inset stories extend the poem while emphasising
its narrow focus; Venus and Adonis, Arethusa and Alpheus, Circe
and Glaucus—all these intermezzo relationships say it again.[3] At
the same time Keats must appear to have other means of holding

---

[1] But a very generous friend. Mr. Edmund Blunden's book about John Taylor
is called *Keats's Publisher*.

[2] I, 898.   [3] II, 454-533, 936-1017; III, 397-806.

his narrative together. This demand comes from his own good sense as much as from his public or publisher, and he is often mechanical in fulfilling it, resorting to threadbare linking devices of the "when lo!" sort we have just witnessed. Often too he allows his rumbling carriage to stop dead, axle-deep:

I left poor Scylla in a niche and fled.[1]

After which he has the weary job of cranking it into motion again. Or he may prefer a novelistic transition, however clumsy and glaringly unpoetic:

> *At length, to break the pause,*
> *She said. . . .*[2]

So we conclude that Endymion's sexuality is carried through with stifling insistence; and also (which is no contradiction) that the whole is cobbled more or less anyhow, in sagging openstitch.

We are meant to get interested in a mortal shepherd prince who loves a goddess and is finally, and eternally, united to her. In other words, Keats asks us to take seriously the "beauty" and "for ever" of Line One. We cannot do so because the hero's quest lacks imaginative substance, and I tried to prepare the ground for this conclusion by making the "fellowship divine" of the Pleasure Thermometer my point of entry into the poem. Our concern then was with characterlessness and sheer vacuity; with the fact that *Endymion's* spiritual pretention is a great yawning hole.

But Keats converts the hole into a positive mischief by using Endymion's quest to further and cement and—much most ruinous —to sanctify the action. Disaster strikes in the first book when the hero, now "ripe for high contemplating", settles down with a priest and some wise old shepherds to philosophise

> *upon the fragile bar*
> *That keeps us from our homes etherial;*
> *And what our duties there. . . .*[3]

Everything wrong with *per ardua* may be spelt out of that little nut-shell of verse: the two-tier universe which division by the "bar" entails; the conceiving of eternal "homes" on the other side of the divide; the strenuous programme implicit in our being kept from these homes where we want to be; and a scheme of "duties" to be performed when we get there. Wrong, as always, because un-Keatsian. There is nothing here to awaken his gift, the thing is posited merely.

---

[1] III, 635.　　　[2] I, 720.　　　[3] I, 360.

Talk of "duties" begins to attract attention to itself when it persists in dangling a parcel in front of us with the poem's true merit supposedly wrapped up inside it. Endymion meets a naiad who tells him,

> *"thou must wander far*
> *In other regions, past the scanty bar*
> *To mortal steps, before thou cans't be ta'en*
> *From every wasting sigh, from every pain,*
> *Into the gentle bosom of thy love.*
> *Why it is thus, one knows in heaven above:*
> *But, a poor Naiad, I guess not. Farewel!*
> *I have a ditty for my hollow cell."*[1]

Her job is to give utterance to the *per ardua* motto. For our part we do not believe in the reappearing "bar"; nor do we believe that "one knows", in heaven or anywhere else. That does not mean, though, that we find it easy to shake off the tissue of proffered meanings in which the guileless erotic tale becomes enmeshed.

One result is that *Endymion's* worst vulgarities adhere to its upper sphere rather than its lower, to the supernatural apparatus rather than the candid sex. As the poem proceeds, its habit of gesturing towards withheld divine significances becomes increasingly tied up with human (so to speak) coyness and retreat and blushes and snooping and arch comment. Thus the goddess herself to Endymion:

> *I love thee, youth, more than I can conceive;*
> *And so long absence from thee doth bereave*
> *My soul of any rest: yet must I hence:*
> *Yet, can I not to starry eminence*
> *Uplift thee; nor for very shame can own*
> *Myself to thee. Ah, dearest, do not groan*
> *Or thou wilt force me from this secrecy,*
> *And I must blush in heaven. . . .*
> *And wherefore so ashamed? 'Tis but to atone*
> *For endless pleasure, by some coward blushes:*
> *Yet must I be a coward!*[2]

Once admitted, this imbecile morality is never got rid of. Anybody in doubt where exactly to locate the suburban Keats he reads about in hostile commentary, will be hard put to improve on the provocation of

> *Ah, have I really got*
> *Such power to madden thee?*[3]

[1] II, 123.   [2] II, 774.   [3] II, 955.

or the reasoning process which binds

> *would thou hadst a pain*
> *Like this of mine, then would I fearless turn*
> *And be a criminal.*[1]

As I say, this vulgar extreme is met with in *Endymion's* heaven. On earth the goddess's "secrecy" and "coward blushes" have no place; her "wicked me!" sentiment disappears, she holds her shepherd to her and relishes the last drop:

> *and will press at least*
> *My lips to thine, that they may richly feast*
> *Until we taste the life of love again.*[2]

Scarcely good writing, and certainly not decorous, but it belongs. It might be worked up, might be made good. It belongs as softness and pressure and tasting always belong, and as the fear lest "I must blush in heaven" which the same speaker utters ten lines later cannot belong.

The goddess's fear forms part of the divine superstructure, which itself follows a perfectly familiar neo-Spenserian pattern, worn into rags by the tradition, often lightheartedly assumed by individuals. Assuredly, and however hard this individual may have tried, Keats's heaven is a poor thing. But I still do not think we are being oversolemn about it here and now; for the rivalry between his broadly Spenserian *per ardua ad astra* and his personal "I will taste" extends beyond *Endymion* and has a close bearing on the work of the next two years, no matter how unseriously we take the allegory itself. Our concern, ultimately, is not whether its meaning adds up to this or that, but why the poet should be going through the motions of delivering a meaning in the first place. We care because of the quite specifically Keatsian problems that arise whenever meaning threatens to outrun feel. For example, one way of considering the failure of the Hyperion venture—I think the most fruitful way—is to stand the feel-ordeal

> *(the cold*
> *Grew stifling, suffocating, at the heart)*

directly against the priestess's exposition

> *(Therefore, that happiness be somewhat shar'd*
> *Such things as thou art are admitted oft)*

in order to establish the cardinal truth that each of these is forcing the other to appear ridiculous. And turning back then to *Endymion*

---

[1] II, 961.   [2] II, 770.

we observe the same phenomenon writ large across four thousand lines, but here channeled into sex.

> *O state perplexing! On the pinion bed,*
> *Too well awake, he feels the panting side*
> *Of his delicious lady.*[1]

A bad mistake to have the perplexity and the lady in bed together. When he comes to write the *Ode to Psyche* in the Spring of 1819 he has learnt his lesson; now the poet keeps his puzzlement (which is the poem's mentality) to himself as he gazes through the picture-frame of the ode, while inside the frame Cupid and the questionable Psyche lie in one another's arms, a study of dozing intensity, of blind trusting absorption, of saturation in feel:

> *They lay calm-breathing on the bedded grass;*
> *Their arms embraced, and their pinions too;*
> *Their lips touch'd not, but had not bid adieu,*
> *As if disjoined by soft-handed slumber,*
> *And ready still past kisses to outnumber*
> *At tender eye-dawn of aurorean love:*

the snailhorn's feast. Whereas in *Endymion*, mind (which was always a fraud) and body (which has become "mere" in Arnold's sense) are both inside the frame destroying each other. How desolate the "feels" I quoted there! How characteristic of *Endymion* as a whole this oscillation between the real but reduced physicality of "panting side" and the pert cosmetic "delicious lady". And so the observation that "delicious" fits the classic taste-and-smell pattern becomes, in its truth, entirely impotent. We witness a thoroughgoing cheapening of the sensual gift; in which process colourless interjections like "O state perplexing!" play a bigger part than at first appears. They are not disposed of by remarking the vacuity of the "decrees of fate" to which Keats finally refers them. I say again that the spiritual pretension of *Endymion* is not a lacuna, not just a hole.

To ponder, in fact, *Endymion's* two mottoes is to ask how mind, and thus how men, can be a manageable subject for this poet. Apprehensions like "panting side" catch the eye for no other quality than their animal truth. And a longer example:

> *far upward could be seen*
> *Blue heaven, and a silver car, air-borne,*
> *Whose silent wheels, fresh wet from clouds of morn,*
> *Spun off a drizzling dew,—which falling chill*
> *On soft Adonis' shoulders, made him still*
> *Nestle and turn uneasily about.*[2]

[1] IV, 439.   II, 517.

141

It comes to life most weirdly. And the "it" round which our awareness of a poet at work begins to settle is the bare animal existence. Adonis lies stretched before the mind's eye like a sleeping dog in the grip of violent dreams. The welter of commonplace disperses and Keats remains: the chill drizzling touch of dew, the nestling and uneasy stirring.

Doglike Adonis brings a return towards familiar ground. Isabella sweeping her hair aside as she dug was like a horse troubled with summer flies; Madeline was like a bird settling into its nest. I sketched an answer to the question about mind and humanity in Keats when I remarked that his people are imagined at moments of deep instinctive solidarity with the world's wider life. Now this is equally true of those for whom no specific animal likeness suggests itself: the figure "sound asleep" in the middle, in the utter wellbeing, of the *Autumn Ode*; even the idea of Lorenzo embalmed in "warm Indian clove". These carry the same conviction as the others, and so do many more whose self-enfolded presence is flowerlike—more vegetable than animal. It makes sense, but dangerous sense, to say that they all buy their way into this larger brotherhood at the price of their mentality. If they are mindless, then so is Keats's rose which he supposes to "have sensation" and feel the morning air and *enjoy* itself.

Endymion, unluckily, must live up to a mental mission which has nothing to do with the wider life we respond to in Keats's poetry. When that life is encountered here, it seems for once a stranger and even an enemy. Adonis, and others like him, have wandered in from some unwritten Keats poem which is their real home. To find Adonis at that imaginable point where men and dreaming dogs meet is to acknowledge one typical creative stroke, but it is also to denounce *Endymion* for the absurd rigmarole it is. There is no place for this real life in that factitious scheme—and so much the worse for the scheme. In fact there is no place for any sustained Keatsian reality outside the shorn and "mere" lovemaking. So no wonder an air of near-delinquent loafing hangs over the piece:

Some idly trailed their sheep-hooks on the ground . . . .[1]

Its narrative futility is stressed rather than mitigated by its vital starts, and at once all its professions collapse. Here again, the loosewoven Romance permits a leisurely view of something which reappears in more compressed form in the two Hyperion fragments:

[1] I, 145.

Blazing Hyperion on his orbed fire
Still sat, still snuff'd the incense....[1]

It is not our irreverence which ousts the Miltonic hero and replaces him with a bearlike creature sitting back and indulging an urge to use his nose. It is imagination, however damaging to Keat's epic solemnities.

In its stripped and vulnerable state *Endymion* provides a very handy text, shaping alien bodies like Adonis in the simplest isolation. Just because he is an intruder, Adonis is an adequate illustration, which the people who belong where we find them can never be. If we take Isabella with her eyes buried in her pillow, or Madeline laying a hand on "her warmed jewels" (warmed by her own body), they will help us discuss Keatsian feel, and the feel of other existences which he called Negative Capability. But this must always be a cruel sort of surgery performed on his poem's spatial tissue. *Endymion* does not need the knife, Adonis comes away of his own accord; so when we call the cold drizzle on his bare shoulders an example of end-stopping, and the total impression of restless repose an exercise in Negative Capability, that really will do.

Endymion is also, and for the same reasons, a valuable catalogue of snailhorn perceptions which have become neat, tractable, unspreading, almost verbal. A phrase like "so cool a purple"[2] gives a text for a two-minute sermon on sense-transference in Keats, leading to the thought which matters and which we want to send our congregation away with: sense-transference serves taste and the snailhorn. A sermon based on the "purple-stained mouth" of the *Nightingale Ode's* second stanza would take longer and be more intricate. Something like this. "Purple-stained mouth", visual and observed on the surface, is a mouth nevertheless, and Keats fosters our dormant awareness of what mouths are for, especially wine-stained mouths, by placing the "brim" of his beaker immediately on one side of it and "that I might drink" on the other; and back we go through the footloose enveloping syntax (both beakers and drinkers have mouths) to the wine itself, an affair "of the warm South" but also "cool'd a long age", until we finally stand with the wishing poet ("O for a draught") outside the stanza's picture-frame and contemplate the Saturnalia of feel going on inside—very much as the wondering poet of the *Ode to Psyche* looks through his frame at the mythical lovers on the grass. The same truth holds good here, but contained—as I hope the last sentence

---

[1] *Hyperion*, I, 166.   [2] II, 444.

hints—within a complex which resists, while never contradicting, talk of an inward and unitary focus of sensation, turning that talk to dust and theory.

"So cool a purple", on the other hand, does have a theoretical taint, and no great harm results from reducing it to the level of Sitwellian sensory tinkering. For the snailhorn is at a loose end in *Endymion* with nothing to savour except love and language. It must always, of course, simply because it is Keats's, vindicate itself up to a point. Thus my scorn for the goddess's notion of atoning for her sexual pleasure "by some coward blushes" was at bottom directed against its mental emptiness; the cheapness of her shame, certainly there and offensive, is undercut by its incredibility. This sort of blushing Keats can never substantiate. But there is another sort, the sort of

> *that cheek so fair and smooth;*
> *O let it blush so ever! let it soothe*
> *My madness! let it mantle rosy-warm*
> *With the tinge of love,*[1]

which proves the object ripe for tasting. This blushing unmental proof, while it reaches forward to possess, has a way of respecting the object's freedom. In urging "let it mantle rosy-warm" Keats apprehends something alive on its own, self-charged, a separate and secret centre. He is appealing to the same imagined hidden source as when he asks the rose to "glow intense and warm the air". This life-fostering fancy of his spills over into the many attempts to guess admiringly not just at phases of other lives but at their latent principles; and then to transpose his conclusions into language which the snailhorn understands. Blushing joins with glowing and flushing, with smothering and stifling and obscure inner pressures, with floating and heaviness and aching and languor—a central knot of conditions which hover on the verge of namelessness, all hard worked by him and all striving to mature an account of how one feels into a revelation of what one is.

> *As with us mortal men, the laden heart*
> *Is persecuted more, and fever'd more,*
> *When it is nighing to the mournful house*
> *Where other hearts are sick of the same bruise;*
> *So Saturn, as he walk'd into the midst,*
> *Felt faint. . . .*[2]

[1] IV, 311.   [2] *Hyperion*, II, 101.

The point to hang on to is that "felt faint" is trying to mean more than "felt faint"; its struggle with a crushing semantic load is obvious enough, though one may spend a long time groping for the explanation. The sequence of feel-conditions, presented by *Hyperion* with its usual compression, will be seen to embrace "laden" and "fever'd" and "faint" itself; but "bruise" is the word I want to pause at. Bruises, like blushes, are felt from the inside. When the shadow of a mildly disconcerting literalness crosses our sensibilities as we read—and after all "bruise" is at one level the most ordinary Shakespeare-plus-Milton pastiche—we should look to that innerness of apprehension which Keats himself hailed gratefully when he quoted the *Venus and Adonis* snail shrinking painfully back into his shell and sitting there in the dark, "all smothered up". That is how his own people are.

The struggle to get a bare "felt faint" to do its special Keatsian work is distressing to watch in the two Hyperion fragments. *Endymion*, desultory and very inferior, lets us proceed through similar country with a light heart. In intention, that poem's "ears / Whose tips are glowing hot"[1] are just as serious as *Hyperion's* "felt faint". They are meant to mean more than they would mean if we met them elsewhere; Keats wants them to be adequate to the condition of their owner.

This is an epic of implausible encounters, of

> *scaring out*
> *The thorny sharks from hiding-holes,*[2]

so that while we are going through the motions of observing the fierce visible creatures, our imaginations are busy with their skins. Journeys up in the air and under water bring with them their special feels:

> *To interknit*
> *One's senses with so dense a breathing stuff*
> *Might seem a work of pain; so not enough*
> *Can I admire how crystal-smooth it felt,*
> *And buoyant round my limbs.*[3]

But they leave behind in the reader a weary oppression at the inconsequence of it all. The deeper fault with that "crystal-smooth" sentence is not its slackness and garrulity, but its unattachment; it advances no theme; the snailhorn has to feed on itself. "Thorny sharks", by contrast, is as taut as one could wish. It is pure snailhorn as to the thorniness, and pure licence and verbalism as to the

---

[1] II, 840.   [2] III, 88.   III, 380.

sharks; and behind the phrase can be heard the narrator's voice reporting that

> shapes unseen
> Would let me feel their scales. . . .[1]

Keats's draft proves that he was sometimes capable of discipline. His first thoughts for a tender encounter between Endymion and his sister Peona ran like this:

> She tied a little bucket to a Crook,
> Ran some swift paces to a dark wells side,
> And in a sighing-time return'd, supplied
> With spar cold water; in which she did squeeze
> A snowy napkin, and upon her knees
> Began to cherish her poor Brother's face;
> Damping refreshfully his forehead's space,
> His eyes, his Lips: then in a cupped shell
> She brought him ruby wine; then let him smell,
> Time after time, a precious amulet,
> Which seldom took she from its cabinet.[2]

A neater example of the snailhorn's single inward focus (a conspiracy of touch, taste, smell, with eyes in the same feel-employment as lips and forehead) would be hard to find; but it probably struck him—even him—as too flagrantly excursive. For his printed text contents itself with the two sensitive apexes of lips and finger-tips.

> Soon was he quieted to slumbrous rest:
> But, ere it crept upon him, he had prest
> Peona's busy hand against his lips,
> And still, a sleeping, held her finger-tips
> In tender pressure.[3]

With what gain, however? Too well we know those tender pressures. They keep *Endymion* on the path of feel, the straitness and narrowness of which is a reminder that it leads nowhere.

As well as pruning and trimming and denying the snailhorn some of its pleasures, Keats braced himself for a tremendous keying-up of the rhetoric of taste and touch. He had exclaimed, lazily, in the 1817 volume:

> O for three words of honey, that I might
> Tell but one wonder of thy bridal night![4]

---

[1] III, 343.   [2] *Poetical Works*, p. 77.   [3] I, 442.
[4] "I stood tiptoe", 209.

Endymion witnesses a getting down to business; the words of honey are now forthcoming: "a breathless honey-feel of bliss"; "honey-whispers"; and the memory that

> *One kiss brings honey-dew from buried days.*[1]

All within a hundred lines. "Honey-dew" (two years after Coleridge gave the world his honey-dew in *Kubla Khan*) reinforces "a drop of manna-dew"[2] and is buttressed round with "sigh-warm kisses"[3] and a vast armoury of taste metaphors. Indeed the scope of taste in *Endymion* is our surest and simplest index to the snailhorn's ceaseless, furious stylistic doodling. I am thinking not so much of the range of objects tasted—"the gentle moon", "a long love dream", "the same bright face"[4] and so on—as of the grotesqueries and obscurities which Keats's straining of this small linguistic area leads him into. What on earth does

> *to count, and count*
> *The moments by some greedy help that seem'd*
> *A second self,*[5]

mean; or rather, what does "greedy" mean, since this is the pitch-dark centre of a murky few lines? And touch:

> *To linger on her lily shoulders, warm*
> *Between her kissing breasts, and every charm*
> *Touch raptur'd!*[6]

Is "touch raptur'd" a compound adjective? And if so, if we supply the hyphen, what then? Keats is still being drawn on and on, tempted to ask too much of his feel-language: *überfragen*, if there is such a word. His reader tends not to bother because *Endymion* has made him sleepy—quite a different thing from the power of great art to dictate its own terms.

But what about "as mere as marble"?[7] Surely, "as pure, sheer, perfect, as marble". And this is a perfection in the eye of the beholder. When the snailhorn approaches marble, it finds that its work of internalising the visible surface has already been done for it. The "liny marble" of *Sleep and Poetry* has already been elaborated in a very early sonnet:

> *Through the dark robe oft amber rays prevail,*
> *And like fair veins in sable marble flow;*[8]

---

[1] I, 903, 955; II, 7.   [2] I, 766.   [3] I, 967.
[4] III, 110, 440; I, 895.   [5] I, 657.   [6] II, 946.
[7] III, 845.
[8] *To Lord Byron*, dated December 1814 in Woodhouse's transcript.

so that here the snailhorn's way of apprehension in depth is the only way; marble makes snailhorn-seers of us all.
Much later, in *Lamia*,

> *so new,*
> *And so unsullied was the marble hue,*
> *So through the crystal polish, liquid fine,*
> *Ran the dark veins, that none but feet divine*
> *Could e'er have touch'd there.*[1]

The warmth implicit in "dark veins" is countered by marble's coldness to the touch; this temperature contrast is a property of the substance itself, and demonstrates again its fitness for the snailhorn's immediate loving attention. When Endymion

> *lowly bow'd his face*
> *Desponding, o'er the marble floor's cold thrill,*[2]

his indulgence tells the truth about "as mere as marble".
Tracing such cloudy assiduities as

> *their gaze*
> *Ripe from hue-golden swoons took all the blaze*[3]

through *Endymion* is like studying rejected drafts of Keats's best work. They ring prematurely true. He has not finished wrestling with the angel of his daydreams. And even when—especially when —his meaning is clear, the poem's verbalism has him in its toils. He knew "the moist languor of thy breathing face"[4] would not do; then tried "the most soft completion of thy face"[5] and let that stand. But the second with its dash of Herrick is as doodling as the first. We carry on, therefore, rather heartlessly using *Endymion*, declaring: if you want a demonstration of that wrapping up of sense which is the essence of snailhorn perception, consider

> *her lips and eyes,*
> *Were clos'd in sullen moisture,*[6]

and where eyes are not mentioned, note how the two small words "pressed lashes"[7] whisper their origin. *Endymion*, of course, is the home of "eyes shut softly up alive". But the same hushed palpability attends many phrases where sensation enjoys no obvious privileges, but which call with the insistence of a familiar deep pain: "warm with dew at ooze from living blood".[8]

[1] I, 382. [2] II, 337. [3] III, 860.
[4] *Poetical Works*, p. 119. [5] II, 757. [6] II, 468.
[7] *Poetical Works*, p. 79. [8] IV, 667.

This poem marks a turn towards a new kind of sensual abstractness. Assuredly

> *Muffling to death the pathos with his wings*[1]

is a strange line, as Keatsian as

> *Fondles the flower amid the sobbing rain—*[2]

but more subtly so. You find nothing like that muffling-pathos collocation anywhere in the diction of 1817, though there are plenty of smothering and stifling words, and much abstraction. This is the potentiality which he will realise at moments like "glut thy sorrow" in the *Ode on Melancholy*. And when *Endymion* gives us, as if from nowhere,

> *Obstinate silence came heavily again,*
> *Feeling about for its old couch of space*[3]

all talk of the poem's verbalism begins to crumble and fall apart, making it time to stop. This solitary confinement of the snailhorn cannot be pursued any longer without damage to the larger whole.

[1] II, 421.   [2] I, 331.   [3] II, 335.

IV: HAVENS OF INTENSENESS

1 Natural Sculpture

APOLLO in *Endymion*, nestling and stirring "uneasily" at the drizzle of dew on his shoulders, might be called a picture. Picture conjures up individuals: Isabella, Madeline, Saturn, involving many words; Ruth, the little Naiad, Apollo himself, involving very few. Picture conjures up *tableaux vivants* like Cupid and Psyche lying in the grass, and the figures grouped round the Grecian urn. Picture conjures up the landscape of the *Autumn Ode*. Beyond and including all that, picture touches something vital to our whole way of receiving Keats's poetry.

Well, he is a painter-poet in the Spenserian tradition. But that does not mean he is a visual poet[1]. Our primary urge is to enter and occupy his pictures, not to see them. Their compelling presence is a kind of in-feeling; we envisage only because we have in-felt.

The Germans have a word for in-feeling: *Einfühlung*. Early in the twentieth century, one Tichener who must have known a little Greek coined "empathy" to stand as English equivalent to *Einfühlung*; and since then empathy has proved a useful term. Nevertheless we usually understand by it not in-feeling in any confined and controlled sense, but the unqualified ability to imagine oneself in somebody else's shoes. And so empathy has its dangers for the student of Keats[2]—and for Keats himself.

His home-made phrase Negative Capability is my in-feeling, and it extends across the entire spectrum of his creative instinct, from knowing (and wanting to say) what it feels like to be a billiard ball, to his total apprehension of Madeline in *St. Agnes Eve*. He was a man of very impressive self-knowledge who nevertheless made, it seems to me and almost everybody, one huge blunder. He thought he was destined to write plays. And the stubborn centre of this conviction will be found in the letter—the only one—in which Negative Capability is expressly mentioned. That, he says, is the thing "which Shakespeare possessed so enormously"; and the

---

[1] Keats is painterly, not pictorial. It is the Pre-Raphaelites with their vision cut in lengths—Inchbold, Yardtimid—their shallow understanding of what it means to paint what you see, who have betrayed the bond between Keats's snailhorn and the master-painter's groping eye.

[2] An example is Professor Walter C. Bate whose admirable biography employs the word half a dozen times without qualification.

other letters bearing on this theme make the connection between drama and the negative-capable gift abundantly clear, as it appeared to Keats. Shakespeare's genius was supremely negative-capable and supremely dramatic. Keats was himself, he knew, a negative-capable poet ("that sort of which, if I am anything, I am a member"), and would develop, he supposed, into a dramatist, the sort of writer who "has as much delight in conceiving an Iago as an Imogen". We, with the advantage of hindsight, can detect a *non sequitur* in this transition from Negative Capability to the drama: the first is Keatsian and works through space and feel; the second is generic and involves a diversity of temporal and mental circumstances. Keats confused the two, or believed the one would lead to the other. He thought of *St. Agnes Eve*, the most negative-capable poem he ever wrote, as a practice run before settling down to his plays.

The little dramatic skill I may as yet have, however badly it might show in a Drama, would I think be sufficient for a Poem—I wish to diffuse the colouring of *St. Agnes Eve* throughout a Poem in which Character and Sentiment would be the figures to such drapery—Two or three such Poems, if God should spare me, written in the course of the next six years would be a famous gradus ad Parnassum altissimum—I mean they would nerve me up to the writing of a few fine Plays—my greatest ambition—when I do feel ambitious.[1]

His view of such an obviously undramatic poem as *St. Agnes* is bound to remain mysterious until we make his assumption our own for a moment and see his triumphant conceiving of a Madeline as a step along the road to conceiving an Imogen. The suspension of disbelief called for here is acrobatic.[2] What God did, in the event, spare him to accomplish demonstrates a lyric gift plainly and several-sidedly, and also a narrative gift which we need to delimit with care. For the rest, his tally is one dramatic failure (*Otho*) and one fragment (*King Stephen*), one epic failure (*Endymion*) and two fragments (*Hyperion* and *The Fall*), and one unfinished satire (*Cap and Bells*) which reads doomed.

[1] *Letters*, vol. II, p. 234. Compare his statement that the Pleasure Thermometer in *Endymion* "is my first step towards the chief attempt in the Drama" (*Ibid.*, vol. I, p. 218). And again: "One of my ambitions is to make as great a revolution in modern dramatic writing as Kean has done in acting" (*Ibid.*, vol. II, p. 139).

[2] Though a Keatsian strain is very evident in Shakespeare's two narrative poems, and in some of the sonnets, and in the dramatic verse up to the time (roughly) of *Romeo and Juliet*.

Space and feel is his thing then, Negative Capability, the picture. The authentic Keatsian picture, whether of individuals or *tableaux* or natural scenes, belongs almost entirely to his later writing. Apollo in *Endymion* is exceptional; but in *Isabella*, which follows immediately, picture-making goes on all the time; and *Isabella* is the earliest of the big poems of the 1820 volume, the third and last book he published. The reason why we find so few pictures in early Keats was uncovered when we were talking about feel in the 1817 poems. There a certain helplessness prevails, with the writer or some implausible *alter ego* tasting and fondling, sipping and smelling, motionless in the eye of pleasure's wind. The boredom of this, our severe conclusion as to its self-indulgent repetitiousness, can be most simply accounted for by the inevitable coupling of poet to feel. Certainly there is good rough justice in this complaint, enough to show why we make such a fuss when we suddenly come upon the seaweed in *Sleep and Poetry*, feeling the bumpy rock under and around it as it sinks with the retreating wave. We are hailing one of those very rare moments in 1817 when feel has become un-tethered from the poet, a free moment of in-feeling, of achieved out-thereness: a picture. We are also asserting a clear but fathom-less continuity with Madeline "trembling in her soft and chilly nest" and Porphyro when his "warm, unnerved arm / Sank in her pillow". This is the Keatsian sublime.

Whereas the general rule in 1817, and *Endymion*, is that the "pictures" are not in-felt, and so are not true pictures at all. The corollary of a poet-fettered tasting and touching is a starving of the spatial imagination. One damaging account of 1817—the one already given—deals with its feckless riot of feel. The other, start-ing now, runs through its gallery of vacant pictures.

Vacant but sometimes, I would claim, arresting. The problem of characterful bad Keats returns once again, now in the form of 1817's eye-catching and held, and yet empty, attitudes. Our re-cognition of attitude, arrest, stasis, may amount to no more than a passing twinge at something familiar about the set of a figure in a sonnet's opening line:

> *Nymph of the downward smile, and sidelong glance,*

after which, the usual rubbish:

> *In what diviner moments of the day*
> *Art thou most lovely? When gone far astray*
> *Into the labyrinths of sweet utterance?*
> *Or when serenely wand'ring in a trance*

> *Of sober thought? or when starting away,*
> *With careless robe, to meet the morning ray,*
> *Thou spar'st the flowers in thy mazy dance?*
> *Haply 'tis when thy ruby lips part sweetly,*
> *And so remain, because thou listenest.* . . .

But even so he continues to peck feebly at his human object, trying to catch and sustain it out there through intentness, abstraction, and a sort of abrupt surprise: in "far astray", "in a trance", "starting away"—until at

> *thy ruby lips part sweetly,*
> *And so remain, because thou listenest*

we react with that involuntary "Ah" which signifies "not good, but unmistakably Keats".

The Victorian illustrator who painted Ruth standing in the corn should have contented himself with the nymph smiling downward and glancing sidelong. He could have managed her nicely; the poet has already posed the painter's model for him, as he does twice more in "I stood tiptoe":

> *O let me lead her gently o'er the brook,*
> *Watch her half-smiling lips and downward look.* . . .

> *And lovely women were as fair and warm,*
> *As Venus looking sideways in alarm.*[1]

And again in *Sleep and Poetry*:

> *Sappho's meek head was there half smiling down*
> *At nothing.* . . .[2]

Having collected these four, we take the whole 1817 volume—a slim book—at a run, and find a struggle to realise angle and tilt everywhere apparent. Keats's persistence in this effort creates the family likeness which marshals an otherwise ragbag assemblage.

> *the sweet buds which with modest pride*
> *Pull droopingly, in slanting curve aside,*
> *Their scantly leaved, and finely tapering stems.* . . .[3]

> *Just as two noble steeds, and palfreys twain,*
> *Were slanting out their necks with loosened rein.* . . .[4]

> *with an incline so sweet*
> *From their low palfreys o'er his neck they bent.* . . .[5]

[1] Lines 101, 219. [2] Line 381. [3] "I stood tiptoe", 3.
[4] *Calidore*, 77. [5] *Ibid.*, 86.

He slants his neck beneath the waters bright
So silently. . . .[1]

Archimago leaning o'er his book. . . .[2]

Another, bending o'er her nimble tread. . . .[3]

Some with upholden hand and mouth severe. . . .[4]

One, loveliest, holding her white hand toward
The dazzling sun-rise: two sisters sweet
Bending their graceful figures. . . .[5]

Without much searching the list could be doubled and trebled. It could be extended into Keats's juvenile stanzaic compliments:

> *'Tis morn, and the flowers with dew are yet drooping,*
> *I see you are treading the verge of the sea:*
> *And now! ah, I see it—you just now are stooping*
> *To pick up the keep-sake intended for me.*[6]

And one might claim membership for some of his smallest and feeblest tropes:

> *Let there nothing be*
> *More boisterous than a lover's bended knee;*
> *Nought more ungentle than the placid look*
> *Of one who leans upon a closed book. . . .*[7]

All 1817's bending, leaning, slanting, stooping, tells the same story. The spatial imagination is busy staking its claim. It does so, in the first place, by asserting that space has in fact been occupied, is being used. Its root proposition is

> *And now! ah, I see it—you just now are stooping.*

This kind of thing amounts to no more than crying "Snap!" But, as with the endless tasting in 1817, so with the stooping: we need to sweep our attention's foreground as clear as possible of the greatness of Keats in order to begin with the Keatsness of Keats. The right way round is to get to know the bond uniting the bending and leaning figures of 1817 with the statuesque Titans, with Cupid and Psyche, with "thou dost keep / Steady thy laden head across a brook" in *Autumn*, with the *Grecian Urn's* lowing heifer, before contemplating the distance between them. The heifer "lowing at the skies" serves the spatial imagination of 1817, but tactfully. We all

---

[1] *To Charles Cowden Clarke*, 3.   [2] *Ibid.*, 37.
[3] *Sleep and Poetry*, 113.   [4] *Ibid.*, 143.   [5] *Ibid.*, 366.
[6] *To Some Ladies.*   [7] *Sleep and Poetry*, 259.

know that upturned tilt and stretch, and we respond to it—as we respond with our mind's fingertip to the invitation implicit in the "silken flanks" of the next line. The naturalness of our response acclaims the discretion of his art.

All Keats does in these 1817 examples is to declare a pose. That, indeed, makes them interesting, since the unvindicated words of attitude give us access to the crucial distinction between visual and spatial imagining. No pandering to vision will help him fill his attitude-words, because he is not that kind of poet. He must move in the direction of the lowing heifer. And so he does, intermittently. One could present, in one's fancy, the *downward* smile and *sidelong* glance of the sonnet we began with to some poor hack painter and tell him to get on with it. These are empty attitudes awaiting their conventional visual filling, and he can supply it. But the phrase which gave us momentary pause,

> *thy ruby lips part sweetly,*
> *And so remain, because thou listenest:*

is on a different plane. An illustrator would be at a loss here because the attitude has already been filled, and the filling is not visual except in one of its effects.

A stasis, spatial and time-defying, is the feat of imagination we are saying yes to. While we struggle to admire stasis justly, the need to relegate vision to a secondary, consequential status grows clearer. Our sympathetic joy in Keats's picture-making takes the form of a sudden grasp which, while not excluding sight, is never vision-dominated. To insist on this is not just to continue our running fight against the queen of the senses, on behalf of inwardness and snailhorn perception. Nor is it just to draw attention away from the pictorial "sources" of his poetry. It is also to recognise that in-feeling, Negative Capability, has two sides. Keats's "feel I have" of other existences is partly the ventriloquism with which he feels through them—the seaweed and its undulating home for example. That side we have been discussing all along. The other (to stay inside the 1817 volume) is modestly exemplified by the girl listening with her mouth open. His feel of her is of the caught and held object, all alive, coming through in one piece, nothing left behind, nothing added.

In finest Keats the two sides work together, and the distinction between them is formal and analytic, our concern not his. Retrospectively, we conclude that the in-feeling of *St. Agnes Eve* is partly a matter of sensual ventriloquism (Madeline's wintry bedroom, her warmed jewels, her lavendered sheets and so on) and partly the stasis in which we have and hold her all there and all engaged, completely present for us in her filled attitude—

> *and suddenly*
> *Her blue affrayed eyes wide open shone:*

and in which the dynamic arrest is powerful enough to absorb any amount of narrated movement; so that

> *She danc'd along with vague, regardless eyes*

is no less "held" than the other. During the reading, though, we are conscious of no such separation into snailhorn and stasis, only of Madeline.

In the rest of Keats this distinction exists on the page, being a fact of his immaturity. The 1817 volume especially falls apart into a language of taste-and-touch and a language of attitude; and this remains true when the tasting is the snailhorn's and the attitude has been filled. We become aware, in consequence, of two sorts of picture-making, the seaweed sort and the open-mouthed girl sort, both radically Keatsian and neither able to live with his finest things. Once in 1817 we have the strange experience of observing the two kinds assert themselves side by side within the narrow bounds of a sonnet, that *On First Looking Into Chapman's Homer.*

> *Much have I travell'd in the realms of gold,*
> *And many goodly states and kingdoms seen;*
> *Round many western islands have I been*
> *Which bards in fealty to Apollo hold.*
> *Oft of one wide expanse had I been told*
> *That deep-brow'd Homer ruled as his demesne;*
> *Yet did I never breathe its pure serene*
> *Till I heard Chapman speak out loud and bold:*
> *Then felt I like some watcher of the skies*
> *When a new planet swims into his ken;*
> *Or like stout Cortez when with eagle eyes*
> *He star'd at the Pacific—and all his men*
> *Look'd at each other with a wild surmise—*
> *Silent, upon a peak in Darien.*

Those who judge, rightly, that this is by far the most successful entity in the book, ought also to concede the feebleness of the octave. Ignore the sestet, and there remains no honest way of extricating the first eight lines, their watery classicism and their puce album-verse diction, from the bulk of 1817. Particularly striking is the failure of the five times repeated "I", beginning with the club bore's "Much have I travell'd", to attract attention to itself.

The astronomer changes all that—on the face of it a remarkable achievement, since the "I" is after all the experiencing poet while the astronomer is just a figure made for a simile. In poetic fact the "I" drops out now, and so does the "like", and the sonnet has arrived. It begins to set, to be fixed; a process of still and silent intensification, like frost. In the emancipation from time which picture-making brings, the more specific intentness of Cortez's staring and his men's wild looking at each other spreads backwards like a stain over the sky-watcher, calm now and ennobled, but still "held". The *feeling* sky-watcher, we must add. For while the "I" and the "like" fall away from "then felt I like" and disappear, the "felt" dilates into a vast ocean of sensation through which the swimming planet is received; this image translates "felt" into no less a thing than the touch of the snailhorn, endlessly curious and discovering, at the opposite pole to the abstract idea. Everything the creature knows, his horn has first received, has had swim into its ken.

Then the astronomer is a token of mature Keats because of the intertwining and joint working of snailhorn and stasis in him. Cortez and his party not so. They are filled attitude, mere stasis. Indeed it is astonishing how the painterly analogue quails into obvious impossibility with the astronomer, whereas the leader and his men on their mountain top really do accost the fancy like an heroic canvas, the sort of subject Haydon was always pondering.

One could not have a clearer case of prose logic (an astronomer's business is to see and interpret) turned on its head by Keats's poetry (an astronomer feels a swimming approach). The controverting of "see" bears upon everything I have said about vision and externality in general. The disappearance of a separable "interpret" provokes the subtle theme of mind. The whole situation, the comparing of poet and astronomer, glosses my cardinal distinction between open-ended feeling and end-stopped feel. Another Romantic poet would have used the simile to float an insight, some vista of other worlds and other modes of being; to gesture on and away. Keats compels us from poet to astronomer and round to our own delighted sensibilities again. The closed circuit yields its own kind of illumination, as we shut our eyes and savour "swims into his ken"; but it is different: luminous like all aesthetic pleasure, but itself. No doubt, driving "sensation" so hard in his letters, he was himself a bit in awe of the spongelike sopping up of mental categories which end-stopped feel effects. One impact of this process on his language is the enchantment undergone by words of intellection and understanding, like "ken" here; a spell which grows, at the top of his bent, into a complete metamorphosis of the abstract. That, we may suspect, is why I found

> *Obstinate silence came heavily again,*
> *Feeling about for its old couch of space*

so very fine; instinct with 1820, and so unexpected in *Endymion*. We learn from it something about the impersonal resources of Keats's sensuality, especially in the odes, those lyric and (as is loosely said) very personal poems. This, of course, is the lesson which the disappearing "I" has been teaching in the Chapman's Homer sonnet.

First there are the empty attitudes scattered everywhere across the surface of 1817. The more absurd the better for our present purpose:

> *let there nothing be*
> *More boisterous than a lover's bended knee;*
> *Nought more ungentle than the placid look*
> *Of one who leans upon a closed book. . . .*

Bend and lean, bend and lean. Then the filled or vindicated attitudes, like that of the girl (but what poor writing!) absorbed by what she is listening to, and (much better) of the explorers in the grip of their "wild surmise". And finally there is the easy interpenetration of snailhorn and stasis in the "watcher of the skies", the stamp of great Keats.

But even 1817 attitudes as empty as Venus's "looking sideways in alarm" are trying to become filled, are seeking virtue; "in alarm" beats a primitive verbal gong for the summoning of the human object which will continue, better but the same, to the end. That is how Keats is. And the summoned, rallied self runs foul of our preconceptions about stereotyping and bad art. His people are so formidably sheer.

Here emerges a cheap-seeming paradox, which is that their sheer quality affords the handhold we are looking for. When we say sheer, we mean that these filled attitudes in Keats marry the catching-and-holding of the human object to its human credit, so that the arrest and the truth to nature become one. Our humblest and simplest example, the open-mouthed girl, demonstrates this well enough. She also shows that the only terms on which such a marriage can take place are those of all or nothing; the projection of the self within the attitude must be entire, unqualified, unfaceted even, if it is to happen at all. And when it does, the result is imponderably simple, like an animal's presence. The lowing heifer, in fact; and hence our constantly reviving sense, as we read Keats, that his human creation stands on common ground with those withdrawn, vivid lives which our imaginations are accustomed to placing firmly, if affectionately, in the hedgerow. His letter-writing, naturally enough, sometimes catches him at a point between our habit and his own verse.

I go among the fields and catch a glimpse of a stoat or a fieldmouse peeping out of the withered grass—the creature hath a purpose and its eyes are bright with it. I go among the buildings of a city and I see a man hurrying along—to what? The creature has a purpose and his eyes are bright with it. But then as Wordsworth says, "we have all one human heart".[1]

And thus he starts to do our job for us. And even summarises the rest; for his sudden turn at "But then" is enormously revealing. The Keatsian "one human heart"—forget Wordsworth—emerges at precisely this moment of catholic existence, of disposition shared with stoat and mouse; and he articulates the heart whole in the purposeful bright eye: compare the familiar marvel of the ship in the bottle. No wonder we have to tread warily with consciousness, with the status of thought in his poetry. "Purpose" in the letter is a mental word, just as the "surmise" of the Spanish explorers is mental, and a context of intentness—the staring eye—sustains both. It seems a narrow context, but proves wide enough; genius has what it can use.

Staring eyes, parted lips, "upholden hand and mouth severe" situations, are already familiar because they recall the pheno- menon of dispersal in which Keats's human theme of the moment— fear, anger, love—gets carried into the body's separate parts. There is a special reason for holding on to the notion of dispersal late in his career, in the two Hyperion fragments. The delibera- tion of his practice matches that of our invented term:

> One hand she press'd upon that aching spot
> Where beats the human heart; as if just there
> Though an immortal, she felt cruel pain;
> Thr other upon Saturn's bended neck
> She laid, and to the level of his hollow ear
> Leaning, with parted lips, some words she spoke. . . .[2]

Bend and lean still. But nowhere else in Keats is the attitude and its emotional filling carried from hand to heart to neck to ear to lips so cleanly, so advisedly, as in these late pieces. He betrays what

[1] *Letters*, vol. II, p. 80.
[2] *The Fall*, I, 344. Compare *Hyperion*, I, 42.

he is up to when he stations Saturn "an awful presence" before us, while at the same time

> *his lips*
> *Trembled amid the white curls of his beard.*
> *They told the truth—*

which is what they are there for. And the effect of Keats's saying so is baneful. Conceive of Madeline:

> *she panted quick—and suddenly*
> *Her blue affrayed eyes wide open shone:*
> *They told the truth. . . .*

The knowingness directing, and diminishing, these Hyperionic dispersals is only one aspect of the impotent clarity with which the poet addresses his task. Certainly he could not have too much of the right kind of knowledge, and certainly there are kinds of knowledge possessed by poets about poetry (including their own) which can be fruitfully exploited, like T. S. Eliot's, in literary criticism and other work. But there is also such a thing—and Eliot's verse plays may be a case in point—as incapacitating penetration by an artist of his problems. With Keats, the main grounds for suspecting he was coming to know more than was creatively good for him have been declared already. In *Hyperion* his intelligent if partial appraisal of his poetry's basis in the end-stopping habit leads him to buttress feel with know: "for 'tis the eternal law / That first in beauty should be first in might." Then in *The Fall*— cutting closer to the bone—he aims for the area he knows he can command by polarising his action round the feel-ordeal of climbing the altar steps and the feel-reward of mystically grasping the scenes (a sophisticated feel this) "swooning vivid" through Moneta's brain. It is also true, of course, that he was tinkering with the epic far too long and interruptedly, that parts of it read overstudious, that his self-accusation of Miltonic artfulness has substance; but the other thing needs saying first.

When we respect this priority we discover a Philoctetes in our late epic Keats. He is armed with the bow of knowledge and crippled with the festering heel of self-consciousness. The self-consciousness is Hamletish. The name of the snake which bit him, and is still very much alive and biting, is Romanticism.

His sickness displays common *Zeitgeist* characteristics and is poignantly his own; the feel which places him at the centre of the Romantic Movement, also isolates him; and so it is with the in-feeling of his pictures. In mature Keats, stasis and snailhorn interfuse. In immature Keats they do not, which is why the Chapman's Homer sonnet leaps off the page in the 1817 volume. The two versions of *Hyperion* are anything but immature; they groan under treasures of snailhorn perception and hoarded nobilities of attitude. But it is only in tiny thrown-off *aperçus* like the line-and-a-half Naiad that the two act together instinctively. And when this happens, it would be pedantic to insist on the dispersal of cold finger and pressed lip.

How unlike the general progress of the fragments, where we can use our term of art profitably, and where the separate manipulating of a poetry of taste and a poetry of attitude comes near to being their principle of composition. The tasting suffers more than the attitudinising, as always in Keats; its fortunes are more immediately and pathetically dependent on his; it cannot look to the tradition for inert confirming solace and expectations roughly squared with: so the snuffing of incense and savouring of brass are blatantly indecorous, if touching, in their candour; while the broad Spenserian-Miltonic tide carries the pictures along, even the feeblest, towards an unearned fitness for epic society. Against this background the more direct influence of Cary's *Dante* gets analysed by Keats specialists, half-approvingly.

And some of the pictures are very memorable. We think of Saturn sitting there so cold and still, a beautiful little picture-poem on his own. Then the goddess Thea joins him and the two form a tableau:

> *And still these two were postured motionless,*
> *Like natural sculpture in cathedral cavern;*
> *The frozen God still couchant on the earth,*
> *and the sad Goddess weeping at his feet:*[1]

in which "natural sculpture" recalls Saturn by himself "quiet as a stone" at *Hyperion*'s opening. "Stone" was right, and "sculpture" is right now; Keats's spatial imagining has become more emphatic about the third dimension, and more resourceful.

The sculptural analogy needs to be just as narrowly contained as the painterly, since in neither case is the realisation—what I called the filling—of these objects primarily visual. The roots of the whole process run down to the arrested bendings and leanings and sideways posings of the 1817 volume. Keats's impulse, endlessly thwarted in his bad early verse, is to occupy space effectively, and the vastly greater success of the Hyperion fragments is due in part to the way they explore depth. The kingdom of space's third

---

[1] *Hyperion*, I, 85. Compare *The Fall*, I, 382.

dimension is their special charge. Things are groined, scooped out, followed lovingly

> *Even to the hollows of time-eaten oaks,*
> *And to the winding in the foxes' holes. . . .*[1]

"Deep" is *Hyperion's* first word, "Deep in the shady sadness of a vale" its first imagined tunnelling. Those unpromising grots and bowers and scoured shell-shapes of *Endymion* may have been tending this way after all. Anyhow, when Haydon took his friend to see the Elgin Marbles newly arrived from Greece, the enthusiastic but dismally thin pair of sonnets[2] with which Keats responded ought not to be taken for the experience's true fruit; but rather, a handful of isolated observations such as

> *These raven horses, though they foster'd be*
> *Of earth's splenetic fire, dully drop*
> *Their full-vein'd ears, nostrils blood wide,—*[3]

and then *Hyperion* and *The Fall*. Those ears and nostrils were not taken from nature; they were studied in Pheidias's reliefs from the Parthenon metopes on show at the British Institute, where Keats repaired "again and again", Severn tells us, after his first visit with Haydon.

The Hyperionic sculpture, like everything in this epic attempt, is tinged or obscurely tinged with Milton. In one of his notes on *Paradise Lost* Keats singles out an effect of "stationing or statuary"; speaks of Milton fostering this particular felicity and "gorging it to the producing his essential verse".[4] Our interest in this thought recalls our interest in Shakespeare and Negative Capability, and in Wordsworth and the "one human heart": the light falls on Keats. We can see what he means, more or less, for the connection between Milton's "stationing or statuary" and Milton's poetry at large is easy to assert and accept:

> *Forthwith upright he rears from off the pool*
> *His mighty stature;*

and so on. But "essential verse" is not so simple. There are all sorts of things one might want to say about the essence of Milton. Not, however, about Keats in his two Hyperion versions. First Saturn, then Saturn and Thea, then Hyperion, and then the de-

---

[1] *The Fall*, I, 408.
[2] *On Seeing the Elgin Marbles* and *To B. R. Haydon, With the Foregoing Sonnet on the Elgin Marbles*.
[3] *Endymion*, IV, 398.   [4] The Hampstead Keats, vol. V, p. 303.

feated Titans one by one: they are all caught and held. They share, and share *essentially*, the dynamic arrest of Keats's stasis. This force unites Saturn in his "icy trance", Thea caught-and-held very differently "to the level of his ear / Leaning with parted lips", Hyperion fettered tight by pain:

> *At this, through all his bulk an agony*
> *Crept gradual, from the feet unto the crown,*
> *Like a lithe serpent vast and muscular*
> *Making slow way, with head and neck convuls'd*
> *From over-strained might. Releas'd, he fled. . . .*[1]

The group of Titans,

> *Dungeon'd in opaque element, to keep*
> *Their clenched teeth still clench'd, and all their limbs*
> *Lock'd up like veins of metal, crampt and screw'd;*[2]

and Iäpetus individually, with the stasis extending to the throttled snake in his hand:

> *Iäpetus another; in his grasp,*
> *A serpent's plashy neck; its barbed tongue*
> *Squeez'd from the gorge. . . .*[3]

And his neighbour:

> *Next Cottus: prone he lay, chin uppermost,*
> *As though in pain; for still upon the flint*
> *He ground severe his skull, with open mouth*
> *And eyes at horrid working.*[4]

Here where by the criterion of common sense Keats stands closest to Milton, the result is not insufferably Miltonic. That happens later, when the debating starts. And yet the speeches are only plotted on the model of the "great consult", direction and tone of argument leaving Keats his own master, whereas the situation of the ruined Titans so closely follows that of the rebel angels lying "abject and lost" on the burning flood, he would seem to have very little room to manoeuvre.

I think the explanation lies in the imaginative effort underpinning "convuls'd", "clench'd", "lock'd", "crampt and screw'd". The agonised stasis, the arousing of direct sympathetic feel, is his own, unlike the arguing. These variations upon the Laocoön theme assert themselves with a contained violence which "its

---

[1] *Hyperion*, I, 259.   II, 23.   [3] II, 44.   [4] II, 49.

barbed tongue / Squeez'd from the gorge" epitomises; until the Miltonism of the whole, while remaining apparent, ceases to be servile.

In short, the Titans are intensely sculptural: not only the completest illustrations, outside the *Grecian Urn*, of stasis and the filled attitude, but sincere gropers after depth; so much so that we forsook the painting analogy and applied his remark about Milton's "stationing and statuary" to himself. The Titan goddess Thea, whom we met earlier bending and leaning "with parted lips", also knows about the Hyperion world of excavated tree trunks and winding foxes' holes:

> *Thoea arose,*
> *And stretch'd her white arm through the hollow dark,*
> *Pointing some whither :*[1]

not pointing anywhere in earnest, but celebrating the third dimension with her own sort of aesthetic disinterestedness, like Saturn and the reaching trees around him:

> *Still fix'd he sat beneath the sable trees,*
> *Whose arms spread straggling in wild serpent forms,*
> *With leaves all hush'd. . . .*[2]

Through the disjunction of snailhorn and stasis, this verse progresses towards a blighted moonscape of the spatial imagination's own making. Trying to speak with the voice of his "essential" poetry, we designate this a country without feel. But an unforgettable country—as we remind ourselves whenever the failure of the Hyperion fragments is being debated.

2 Imagination Again

It does not follow that everthing Keats says and implies about imagination hangs together, for the snailhorn-poet has the counter-thrust of the instinctive picture-maker to reckon with. There is one Keats who conceives Imagination through the blandishments of pleasurable feel ("Sensations—of the Beautiful—the poetical in all things") and ardent pursuit ("I will taste"); then another Keats who talks about making and feigning.

No prose reconciliation can be found, nor should it be hoped for. In his snailhorn mood, as we saw, creative imagination cannot make much headway against the master-term sensation and the

---

[1] *The Fall*, I, 454. "Thoea" is "Thea".　　　[2] I, 466.

dependence on actuality which sensation brings with it. The poet's sensation cannot be of a nothing. Or can it? At the thought of art, even great art, dancing to the tune of what he called "present palpable reality",[1] a rebellious spirit, a dormant autonomy, begins to stir, and the words "whether it existed before or not" get added. Now this is a flagrant case of trying to have one's cake and eat it. The link between art and the actual which Keats wants to deny, or vaguely to mitigate, in defence of imagination's freedom he also wants to assert for the sake of imagination's truth. Behind his "what the Imagination seizes as Beauty must be Truth" lies the invincible sustaining fact of his "sensations—of the Beautiful—the poetical in all things". He has felt what he has felt. His clinging to the word sensation is the form taken by his individual appeal from art to life.

For the snailhorn, then, imagination is dominantly unfeigning and true with its own truth to touch; and, in consequence, sensational rather than creative. The picture-maker naturally enough (since we have reason to be in earnest about the spatial imagination) opposes the snailhorn-poet on both issues. Making and feigning are tidily coupled in the *Ode to Psyche*:

> *Yes, I will be thy priest, and build a fane*
> *In some untrodden region of my mind . . .*
> *A rosy sanctuary will I dress*
> *With the wreath'd trellis of a working brain,*
> *With buds, and bells, and stars without a name,*
> *With all the gardener Fancy e'er could feign. . . .*

The stanza has its blemishes, particularly in the Wendy House of the "rosy sanctuary", but they do not affect the sharpness of the contrast between this poetry of building and make-believe and the whole way of the snailhorn.

Probably Keats's "Fancy" has caused a general dulling of interest, or allaying of anxiety. People tend to read Coleridge's distinction between Imagination and Fancy into the usage of contemporaries, and to assume a light-toned, playful sense for Fancy whenever they meet the word. They have no warrant for doing so here. Coleridge's view had just been given sketchy publicity in the *Biographia Literaria* of 1817; but whether Keats knew and was deliberately ignoring it, cannot be an important question; for if he had not read Coleridge he was Hazlitt's friend and must have been aware of the widespread fashion for playing the higher organic-creative powers of genius against the lower whimsical-mechanical ones of cleverness and talent: thus the spirit of the age.

---

[1] *Letters*, vol. I, p. 325.

Whatever he had or had not heard and read, Keats knew his own mind and refused to take part in the nineteenth-century downgrading of Fancy.[1] Once—only once—he distinguishes Fancy and Imagination himself, in the letter about *Endymion* and the importance of Invention: ". . . Invention which I take to be the Polar Star of Poetry, as Fancy is the Sails, and Imagination the Rudder". The interpretation of his shipboard images may not be obvious, but nobody will deny that sails are as necessary and dignified as rudders. Elsewhere in the letters a lofty use of Fancy persists. When he tells his publisher of his "determination not to publish anything I have now ready written, but for all that to publish a Poem before long and that I hope to make a fine one", adding "I have been endeavouring to persuade myself to untether Fancy and let her manage for herself",[2] he is pointing in the direction of Invention and "the marvellous"—of making and feigning—but he does not mean Taylor to take anything but the highest view of the enterprise. Fancy and a very noble making come together again in a beautiful letter written from his sick-bed, after the lung haemorrhage:

Like poor Falstaff, though I do not babble, I think of green fields. I muse with the greatest affection on every flower I have known from my infancy—their shapes and colours are as new to me as if I had just created them with a superhuman fancy. . . . The simple flowers of our spring are what I want to see again.[3]

Nor will Fanny Brawne have understood the "Fancy" of his love-letter to be commonly fanciful:

I never knew before, what such a love as you have made me feel, was; my Fancy was afraid of it, lest it should burn me up.[4]

All these occurences are in deadly earnest, and there is nothing untypical about them. They comment on "the gardener Fancy" of the *Ode to Psyche*; they should preface our thinking. And then the gardener may himself be compared with "the fancy" of the *Nightingale Ode*. The *Nightingale* was written within a month, perhaps a few days, of *Psyche*. "With all the gardener Fancy e'er could feign" says *Psyche*, unquestionably. "Adieu! the fancy cannot cheat

---

[1] Of course he was not alone in this. Leigh Hunt and John Reynolds both affected a high employment of Fancy, and so did some of the Sensibility specialists, including Mary Tighe whom Keats admired and later grew out of. ("Mrs Tighe and Beattie once delighted me—now I see through them and can find nothing in them—or weakness": *Letters*, vol. II, p. 18.)

[2] *Letters*, vol. II, p. 234.   [3] *Ibid.*, p. 260.   [4] *Ibid.*, p. 126.

so well / As she is fam'd to do" is our received text of the *Nightin-gale*. I have my doubts about it. Study of Keats's one surviving autograph in the Fitzwilliam Museum at Cambridge leads me to think that he wrote, there at least, "fain'd" (feign'd).[1] He was a notoriously eccentric and inconsistent speller. I have not found an exact parallel to "fain'd", but I can produce an exact converse, which is almost as good: "feign" for "fain". "I would feign, as my sails are set", he tells Fanny Brawne, "sail on without an inter-ruption for a brace of months longer."[2] In any case "fain" for "feign" is commonly met with in the older writers. And, further-more, the scrupulous Woodhouse borrowed another manuscript, now lost, which belonged to John Reynolds; and above "fam'd", in his own transcription of the ode, Woodhouse records: "*feigned* J.H.R.*" A plausible reconstruction is that Keats's spelling of the word was orthodox in Reynolds's manuscript (as it was in his letter to his brother and sister-in-law in which he copied the *Ode to Psyche*); and that Woodhouse, who certainly had access to the Cambridge manuscript as well as to Reynolds's,[3] was deceived by the former's bizarre spelling and by the fact that the dot of the "i" is missing or has been lost in the tail of the "y" of "fancy" in the line above.[4] It never occurred to him he was looking at the same word differently spelt.

Right or wrong, however, "fain'd" or "fam'd", the *Nightingale* with its "cheat" and its continuation "deceiving elf" gives us a Fancy no less feigning than *Psyche's*. Keats's combining of artistic seriousness with making-and-feigning is the crux; one which needs stressing because it affronts expectations. The work of the gardener and the flight to join the nightingale ought, in Romantic parlance, to be imaginative. His word is Fancy. But we gain no comfort by saying that he used Fancy and Imagination interchangeably in a relaxed pre-Coleridgean fashion, as he surely did;[5] we still have to explain his linking of a serious deep-toned Fancy with the sort of untruthful making, the pleasing invention, which might have been

---

[1] If the reader finds himself in Cambridge, let him compare the "ain" of the word I take to be "fain'd" with the "ain" of "plaintive", and then contrast it with the much tighter and differently formed "am" of "dream" in the same stanza.

[2] *Letters*, vol. II, p. 141.

[3] Because his transcript records eleven variants taken from it.

[4] Keats quite often forgot to dot his i's. In the case of "plaintive" the dot is just visible at the tip of the comma after "do" in the line above.

[5] Thus at *Endymion*, IV, 750, the printed text read "my own fancies" against the draft "my own imaginations". I have no doubt that the change was promp-ted entirely by metrical considerations.

dredged up from any repository of eighteenth-century common-places. And here the old-fashioned look is the clue to follow, for the picture-maker does owe a central eighteenth-century allegiance. It is no accident that the gardener Fancy leaves behind him an aftermath of tired conceit. The serious makebelieve of Keats's Fancy is based on the *ut pictura ita poesis* premise of neo-classical mimetic aesthetics.

It would be foolish, though, to regard the picture-making Keats as a pre-Romantic figure standing over against the Romantic poet. English Romanticism being the complex thing it is, we can recognise old and new features on both sides of the fence. Secondly, and personally, the whole debate takes place under a single bright star: under the interpenetration of snailhorn and stasis which is the mark of his best work. Within the realm of Imagination and Fancy, what comes through to us is not so much an awareness of speaking with two voices as a sensitive, largely unselfconscious hovering, neither stressful nor complacent. The tacking of "whether it existed before or not" on to "what the Imagination seizes as Beauty must be Truth" hits this poise off exactly.

So does a consistent slight oddness in his use of the word "imaginary". "Imaginary" only comes once in his poetry, when Endymion is telling his sister how he sailed through the air in a dream:

> *So kept me steadfast in that airy trance,*
> *Spreading imaginary pinions wide.*[1]

His chosen word brushes against the meaning "non-existent because an illusion" and also against "real with the reality of imagination"; but settles on neither. It hovers.

I very much doubt if Keats is consciously equivocating. He is behaving with the self-preserving instinctiveness of his own stoat and fieldmouse, and "imaginary" is becoming, by a process of linguistic osmosis, a Keats word. If we feel impatient with the hovering attitude and want a scapegoat; or if the world of his creative scepticisms (the gardening employment of *Psyche's* Fancy, its cheating in the *Nightingale*, the implications of the *Grecian Urn's* "cold pastoral", the unforced "as if" status of "until they think warm days will never cease" in *Autumn*) begins to unfold before our quickening critical sense: then it is time we examined his "imaginary" in the light of his "real".

Imaginary grievances have always been more my torment than real ones. You know this well. Real ones will never have any other effect

---

[1] I, 585.

upon me than to stimulate me to get out of or avoid them. This is easily accounted for. Our imaginary woes are conjured up by our passions, and are fostered by passionate feeling; our real ones come of themselves, and are opposed by an abstract exertion of mind. Real grievances are displacers of passion. The imaginary nail a man down for a sufferer, as on a cross; the real spur him up into an agent.[1]

Once again, "imaginary" is neither non-existent nor is it the Romantic reality of Imagination, challenging the actual. We cannot compel it either way. This is always true in his letters. And the sensitive point for our probing, as we prepare to leave "imaginary" for larger issues, is the status of Imagination. Again the modesty of Keats's claim troubles our Romantic preconceptions:

My dear Reynolds—I cannot write about scenery and visitings—Fancy is indeed less than a present palpable reality, but it is greater than remembrance—you would lift your eyes from Homer only to see close before you the real Isle of Tenedos. You would rather read Homer afterwards than remember yourself.[2]

Another deep-toned Fancy, this one, but a feigner just the same when it comes to "the real Isle of Tenedos". To lift one's eyes from Homer's immortal fiction and salute the actual as somehow more real might seem a denial of the dictum "What the Imagination seizes as Beauty must be Truth". Yet who would call Homer unreal, especially when he found himself preferring the poetry to his own memories? The question is, what is more real than what? "One kiss brings honey-dew from buried days" interjects the poet in *Endymion*, a story in which remembered feel, imagined feel and actual feel hustle one another perpetually. He loves naming the things he considers as real as real can be: "Sun, Moon and Stars"[3] (and of course "the real Isle of Tenedos"); his brother's "happy marriage" and "the pleasure of loving a sister-in-law" ("things like these, and they are real");[4] an unspecified present to Hazlitt ("After all there is certainly something real in the world—Moore's present to Hazlitt is real");[5] Bailey's unselfishness in tearing up and rewriting a gloomy letter ("It was to me a real thing").[6] These most assured realities possess either a simple physical warrant or the heart-certainty of human kindness. Already in the 1817 volume Keats's "real" ambitions for his poetry can be seen gravitating

---

[1] *Letters*, vol. II, p. 181.   [2] *Ibid.*, vol. I, p. 325.
[3] Page 75, above. And recall that he included "passages of Shakespeare" among these physical natures in a sudden idolatrous impulse. Shakespeare was a great god too.
[4] *Letters*, vol. I, p. 325.   [5] *Ibid.*, p. 282.   [6] *Ibid.*, p. 209.

towards the touchable, tastable one ("O for three words of honey")
or the philanthropic other ("a nobler life"). The nearer it
approaches to either, the more reality-stuff a poem will contain;
and the question, what is more real than what? will go on obtruding
itself. A bottomless relativism, perfectly secular and unmetaphysical, promotes and sustains the hovering attitude.

Coleridge, who was an absolutist and a religious man and a
metaphysician, once jotted down the following thought:

> If a man could pass through Paradise in a dream, and have a flower
> presented to him as a pledge that his soul had really been there, and if
> he found that flower in his hand when he awoke—Aye! and what then?[1]

He asks the question which never enters Keats's universe, and
which would destroy it if it did. Keats's version of Coleridge's
dream runs like this:

> I am certain of nothing but the holiness of the Heart's affections and
> the truth of Imagination. . . . The Imagination may be compared to
> Adam's dream—he awoke and found it truth.[2]

Adam dreamt of a beautiful creature "man-like but different
sex", and awoke to "behold her not far off".[3] To which the
Coleridgean response is "So what?" Or as Wittgenstein will sum
up the issue: "The meaning of the world must lie outside the
world.".[4]

But Keats's reaction is Adam's: "My dream come true!"—and
all humanity knows how they feel. Whereas if Adam had awoken
and found no Eve, he and Keats would have said, "It was just a
dream". And we know that feeling too.

"Dream come true", then, or "just a dream". This alternative
is the subject of Keats's poetry. I say so with great emphasis
because I have been dealing severely with meanings throughout;
narrowly circumscribing the humanity and mental life of his work,
cavalierly dismissing the surface narratives of *Endymion* and the
two *Hyperions*, championing feel against know; and I am anxious
not to be misunderstood. To maintain that his poetry moves on a
"dream come true" / "just a dream" axis, is not to discredit the
various tissues of argumentation spelt out of Keats by other poeple
in order to substitute my own. For nothing worth calling argumentation comes of this true/false alternative. You dream of a
beautiful girl, or you don't; you wake up and there she is, or she
isn't. The alternative provides Keats with a viable dialect (as

---

[1] *Anima Poetae*, p. 282.   [2] *Letters*, vol. I, p. 184.
[3] *Paradise Lost*, VIII, 452-89.   [4] *Tractatus Logico-Philosophicus*, 6.41.

opposed to the dialectic of know against feel which he conceives but cannot use) only in the sense that feel acquires thereby two counter-masks of sleep and wake. In his dream, and again on waking, he can taste the girl and make infelt pictures of her, thus paying her the tribute of snailhorn and stasis. But no dreaming means no poems. While a dreamed-of girl who vanishes on waking means a memory of that "face I tasted in my sleep" and of the dream-tributes it called forth. Keats can, of course, without progressing into argumentation, without forcing open feel's closed circuit, be unsure whether he is awake or asleep: as in

> *Surely I dreamt to-day, or did I see*
> *The winged Psyche with awaken'd eyes?*

at the beginning of the *Ode to Psyche*; and in

> *Was it a vision, or a waking dream?*
> *Fled is that music:—Do I wake or sleep?*

at the end of the *Nightingale*, with its unsatisfactory but suggestive semi-privacy in the distinction between visions and waking dreams. He can also claim "Real are the dreams of Gods",[1] thereby affirming a power, beyond the command of a human Adam, to actualise the dream. A divine Adam would only have to dream of Eve to produce the girl. And, in *Lamia*, such "real" dreaming goes on within the same limits as that other "real" taste-and-touch which follows soon afterwards:

> *Let the mad poets say whate'er they please*
> *Of the sweets of Fairies, Peris, Goddesses,*
> *There is not such a treat among them all,*
> *Haunters of cavern, lake, and waterfall,*
> *As a real woman. . . .*[2]

But the "real" implicit in Coleridge's "Aye, what then?" as he looks at the flower in his hand rises free of the phenomenon and of history. Had that Coleridgean "real" ever come home to Keats, all creative urgency would have been drained from his "dream come true" / "just a dream" alternative. It would cease to matter much whether Eve was there when Adam woke up, or not.

One does not have to labour the fact that Keats thought of Imagination as a kind of dreaming, because of what is generally accepted about Romanticism and Dream, and because of his own clear preoccupations from *Sleep and Poetry* onwards. The range of his dreaming is wider than the word, however, and embraces

---

[1] *Lamia*, I, 127.   [2] Line 328.

things as apparently unlike as the love which the *Grecian Urn* depicts and the persuasion of *Autumn's* bees that the sun will shine for ever. But it is the coupling of dream with waking and finding it truth that most easily gets missed or understressed or falsely rendered. The point of the prayer in his verse letter to John Reynolds, that "our dreamings all of sleep or wake" should take their colours "from something of material sublime", is the Adam's dream point. His mind is on dreaming and waking simultaneously: the quality of the dream and the situation—the "truth"—on waking.

This interplay of imagination and the actual, which we encountered first in the two voices of feigning fancy and the snailhorn's touch, runs through everything he writes. He is a dreaming man and a realist. The two come together in his firm habit of proving his dreams upon his pulses; for to prove, inside Keats's poetry, is to celebrate the feel; the proving is no less imaginative than the dream. Outside his poetry (an outside which includes his ambitious poetic failures) the proving on the pulses by the philanthropic and speculative Keats is not imaginative. But the naïve clinging to how things are and happen persists. Moore gave Hazlitt that present; and "after all there is certainly something real in the world". What about the real things that might be and happen outside the world? His "finer tone" letter conceives our earthly joys coming to us again in Heaven intensified, the very same only more so; it will be (he continues) like hearing again "an old melody" and seeing again "the singer's face", only "more beautiful that it was possible" on earth. A Heaven where we hear new melodies, where Moore and Hazlitt experience for the first time joys of giving and receiving which were denied them in their lives, is not Keats's.

The "vale of soul-making" letter in which he returns to this subject is far more mature than the "finer tone" one, but equally committed to how things are. There he describes a heavenly community of souls; and souls are human beings who have been sufficiently pressed upon by the facts of life. Our immortal part is that which carries the marks of having felt enough. It is hard, as I said, to find room or a role for God here. And by entitling his second and final attempt at the philosophical epic *The Fall of Hyperion—a Dream* he recalls *Lamia's* dictum "Real are the dreams of Gods". For once again, though much more earnestly, the reality of supernatural dreaming must be understood as an actualising power. The poet in *The Fall* is privileged to experience the inside of Moneta's head, which is the history of the Titans' defeat, the events themselves.

In all sorts of connections we have to keep Keats's poetry separate from the rest of his life. But in the authority of the actual we identify a factor common to, and crucial to, his creative work and what we are obliged to call his philosophy and religion. This accounts for the most lovable thing about him, his trustful scepticism. This or that or the other may be hailed, ardently grasped as "real", but the silent question, what is more real than what? persists, and likewise the *Nightingale's* uncertainty, "Do I wake or sleep?" Amid the horrors of the voyage to Italy and far advanced consumption, he asks "Shall I awake and find all this a dream?"[1]

Imagination has thus a modest front discoverable both in its fanciful-feigning and its snailhorn-touch. And in both these it flaunts an amazingly impudent pretension; for it claims to produce Eve as well as dream about her. Keats is the hero of English Aestheticism less profoundly for the reasons that are always given—reasons connected with beauty—than in his rapt meditation on the possibility of art spinning reality from its own entrails. "Real are the dreams of Gods" might mean "real are the dreams of poets", just as "to see as a god sees" could only mean "to see as Keats sees". Altogether like Moneta bringing to pass the story in her head. He is the first English poet to be hit, and hit hard, by Jowett's thrust in Max Beerbohm's cartoon: "And what were they going to do with the Grail when they found it, Mr. Rossetti?" This joke echoes through the nineteenth century, beyond English Aestheticism and beyond England. It only vulgarises Coleridge's "Aye, what then?" as he contemplated the flower he had dreamed of, lying in his grasp.

3 To Ripen or to Wither?

Keats would not be the great writer he is were his wild theme of art—'real are the dreams of poets'—not intimate with his fear of waking and finding no Eve. She (*alias* Endymion's moon-goddess Cynthia, his Indian Maid, Lamia, la Belle Dame, with a male counterpart of the very first importance in Madeline's Porphyro) carries the main burden of his hovering attitude, his judgment's suspension between "just a dream" and "my dream come true".

In *Endymion*, the hide-and-seek by which this alternative is

---

[1] *Letters*, vol. II, p. 346.

borne aloft becomes comical. Pursuing "my thrice-seen love",[1] tasting her, losing her, believing, doubting, tasting again and losing again, Endymion sets the narrative adither between the showing forth of Adam's dream and the enactment of a counter-proposition, The Lady Vanishes.

Both Cynthia and the Indian Maid disappear, the latter abruptly. Endymion and she are together under a fine rising moon,

> While to his lady meek the Carian [Endymion] turn'd,
> To mark if her dark eyes had yet discern'd
> This beauty in its birth—Despair! despair!
> He saw her body fading gaunt and spare
> In the cold moonshine. Straight he seiz'd her wrist;
> It melted from his grasp: her hand he kiss'd,
> And, horror! kiss'd his own—he was alone.[2]

And that was that. In Cynthia's case, The Lady Vanishes is played out in extended contradiction of Adam's Dream. Again and again she melts, leaving Endymion to awake, a counter-Adam, and find it falsehood.

When he finds her gone, the imaginative effort sustaining Keats's "just a dream" conclusion shows itself first at the level of vocabulary. The paradisal setting of this vanished love becomes "full of pestilent light", its water tastes "sooty" and is "o'erspread with upturn'd gills / Of dying fish", the scene is "sullen", "leaden", "faded". The poppies hang their heads and a curious dead stillness hangs over everything.[3] Now appears the unhealthy side of the "health" / "unhealthy" antithesis enunciated in the first ten lines of Endymion.

These negative outcomes are as true to Keats as the positive, which means that the sooty taste of tainted water is the kind of thing he can do. And the larger question of context—where can this ability be profitably used, deployed, enlarged?—is neatly indicated by those poor poisoned fish. We are back with Hyperion and the "savour of poisonous brass" on his palate. That, I said, is a grotesque effect, coming across naked and touchingly absurd, because Keats has harnessed it to the huge philanthropic and intellectual pretensions of his epic. Likewise with many appealing strokes of the "sooty" sort in Endymion; they are true but impossible. The per ardua ad astra Romance makes them appear ridiculous without enhancing its own spiritual height in the least. Yes but not here, is the judgment on them.

Then what is the right place for the "sooty" imagination? I

----

[1] II, 168.   [2] IV, 504.   [3] I, 681-98.

point to *La Belle Dame sans Merci* where Keats turns his preoccupation with The Lady Vanishes into a lyric triumph. *La Belle Dame* opens

> *O what can ail thee, knight-at-arms,*
> *Alone and palely loitering?*
> *The sedge has wither'd from the lake,*
> *And no birds sing.*

It closes,

> *And this is why I sojourn here,*
> *Alone and palely loitering,*
> *Though the sedge has wither'd from the lake,*
> *And no birds sing.*

In the body of the poem the questioner of the knight-at-arms observes

> *on thy cheek a fading rose*
> *Fast withereth too.*

The knight tells of his meeting "a lady in the meads", and how she took him "to her elfin grot",

> *And there she lulled me asleep,*
> *And there I dream'd—*

the converse of Adam's dream;

> *And I awoke and found me here,*
> *On the cold hill's side.*

Like Cynthia, she had gone. And like the entire "just a dream" aspect of *Endymion*, *La Belle Dame sans Merci* reveals an eerie dead-white motif running through Keats's head. But the lyric concentrates, gives a rondeau form, to what was fatally dissipated and thwarted in the self-refuting Romance. Thus Circe, the "vulture-witch" of one of *Endymion's* inset stories, is and is not like la Belle Dame, and the effect she produces ("A clammy dew is beading on my brow")[1] invites and repels comparison with the lyric. Those vanishings in *Endymion* aspire rather pathetically towards

> *The sedge has wither'd from the lake,*
> *And no birds sing.*

That, in the long run, is what the "sooty" side of *Endymion* will be capable of.

Together with the bitter smell (which is the snailhorn-taste) of

---

[1] III, 568.

soot, an entirely new verbal cluster appears in *Endymion*. "Wither" comes to mind first because we have just noted three "withers" in the tiny compass of *La Belle Dame*. There are no "withers" in the 1817 volume; they arrive in strength in *Endymion,* as with the

> undescribed sounds
> *That come a swooning over hollow grounds,*
> *And wither drearily on barren moors.*[1]

Sounds simply do not wither drearily in the 1817 poems. Behind that fact looms the problem of pleasure as I discussed it in relation to early Keats. He must get his muse moving. The ambitious opposing of pleasure by "the giant agony of the world" begins in *Sleep and Poetry* at the end of the 1817 book, and proves calamitous. Then, with a thought to *Endymion* and the 1820 poems and the collapse of the Hyperion venture, I made three sweeping assertions: that the "just a dream" / "dream come true" alternative is what his poetry is most really about, that this presents him with a viable dialectic (and us with an effect of debate, progression, theme) where the various forms of know-against-feel must and do fail; that the Eve Adam dreamed of and who was there when he woke up (but who equally might have disappeared) is the plainest and most insisted-on expression of the Keatsian alternative.

Eve in her numerous guises is that alternative incarnate. As disappeared and absent heroine she enjoys her great moment, certainly her purest triumph, in *La Belle Dame sans Merci*, but that lyric is not the only reason for denying that the negative outcome is a mere prelude to the positive. Eve as Lamia—"with a frightful scream she vanished"—lies ahead. And the fuss I made earlier about the "Drear-nighted December" piece may be justified by the mushrooming out of Keats's struggle to articulate the feel of not to feel into the literature of The Lady Vanishes. Not to feel, in "Drear-nighted December" with its repeated "ne'er remember", means no longer to feel; it does not here or anywhere else, and could not, mean never to have felt. Whence arises the phenomenon of "wither drearily" ("*drear*-nighted" was a broad hint); of ashes in the mouth, "a parching tongue" with the *Grecian Urn,* the country where "no birds sing". Indeed this is the "forlorn" situation of the *Nightingale Ode*. It falls within a valid Keatsian discourse, it works, precisely because the experience we all share of awakening out of some idealising or hopeful vision—imaginative, intellectual, self-aggrandising, sensual, pious, no

---

[1] I, 285.

matter what—and finding the world not so, is itself realised in terms of end-stopped feel.

> *There, when new wonders ceas'd to float before,*
> *And thoughts of self came on, how crude and sore*
> *The journey homeward to habitual self!*[1]

No cruder than *Endymion's* attempt to render it. But this same "crude and sore", the backward waking to a state of lost feel, "alone" like the knight-at-arms—this is what art will educate into

> *Forlorn! the very word is like a bell*
> *To toll me back from thee to my sole self!*

where the waking moment, the fading feel, is boldly entrusted to the sound-and-sense of "forlorn", spelt "folorn" both times in the *Nightingale* and nearly everywhere else. No doubt Keats spelt it as he pronounced it, and pronounced it as his imagination savoured it. He had, he told Bailey,[2] a private musical system of complementary and contrasting vowels. Accepting "forlorn" does not, though, entail understanding the system, or much believing in it even.

Later again, a raw, primitive non-feel returns in a poem to Fanny Brawne belonging to his desperation in love and, one guesses, to advancing illness.

> *Where shall I learn to get my peace again?*
> *To banish thoughts of that most hateful land,*
> *Dungeoner of my friends, that wicked strand*
> *Where they were wreck'd and live a wrecked life;*
> *That monstrous region, whose dull rivers pour,*
> *Ever from their sordid urns into the shore,*
> *Unown'd of any weedy-haired gods;*
> *Whose winds, all zephyrless, hold scourging rods,*
> *Iced in the great lakes, to afflict mankind;*
> *Whose rank-grown forests, frosted, black, and blind,*
> *Would fright a Dryad; whose harsh herbag'd meads*
> *Make lean and lank the starv'd ox while he feeds;*
> *There bad flowers have no scent, birds no sweet song,*
> *And great unerring Nature once seems wrong.*[3]

The haste of this is obvious. He probably meant "wretched" for the second "wrecked", as H. B. Forman suggests. "Bad flowers" is also suspicious. Perhaps he wrote "bud", changed his mind to "flowers", but, pressing on in full career, forgot to delete the first.

[1] II, 274.   [2] *Keats Circle*, vol. II, p. 277.
[3] "What can I do . . . ?"

He certainly forgot to close his enormous sentence with a question mark. And what is "that most hateful land"? With frosts and famine and scentless flowers and silent birds to come, we think of the knight-at-arms on his cold hillside. Yet "my friends" and their "wrecked (?wretched) life" seem circumstantial; and as a matter of history his newly-emigrated brother and sister-in-law were having a tough time in America, land of "great lakes" and "forests", just now. No manuscripts survive. If Milnes, who printed the poem in 1848, was right in dating it October 1819, it must be among the last poems Keats wrote. Anyhow, roughly finished as it is, we find more here than a reversion to the "unhealthy" side of *Endymion*: partly because of the mature *Belle Dame* associations, and partly in the hint of a lurid horror, unlike the wan distemper of *La Belle Dame*, lurking within the "wrong" courses of Nature it describes. "Monstrous" is its key word. A sudden thought brings back *Endymion's* Lady Vanishes passages, not in their withering but in their appalling quality:

> *Straight he seiz'd her wrist;*
> *It melted from his grasp: her hand he kiss'd,*
> *And, horror! kiss'd his own . . .*

not the fact that she vanishes, but how she vanishes on this particular occasion. (Contrast the dull, almost complacent unalarm of such disappearances as

> *half awake*
> *I sought for her smooth arms and lips, to slake*
> *My greedy thirst with nectarous camel-draughts;*
> *But she was gone.*)[1]

She vanishes like Lamia when she melted with a scream at the end of her poem,

> *And Lycius' arms were empty of delight. . . .*[2]

This is the nightmare strain in Keats, the "monstrous" strain, rare but recognisable.

Very occasionally *Endymion* treats health and unhealth with a certain antithetical sharpness, and this tends to be in lyric asides or intermezzi as we might expect. The action of Book One is held up by a choral hymn to the god Pan.[3] Here we recognise the dreary, dank, desolate, overgrown, hemlocky complex at once. This is the *timbre* and taste of "wither drearily", where the lady vanishes (as

---

[1] III, 477. "Nectarous camel-draughts" deserves a place in any museum of snailhorn curiosities.

[2] II, 307.   [3] I, 232–306.

Pan's "fair Syrinx" herself vanished, the song tells us) and we are left struggling to express the feel of not to feel. But the other and healthy side is new. It may fairly be called *Endymion's* message and final conviction, since the hero's aspirations all mature. He wakes and finds it truth. His girl is there, as Adam's was, and the fear that it will turn out just a dream is put to flight. Thus the positive alternative prevails; and Stanza Two of the hymn summarises an entire phase of Keats's imagination by enunciating the ripeness metaphor. The opposite to "wither drearily" is a powerful forward thrust (thus "foredoom") towards "ripen'd fruitage" and replete honeycombs and the birth of the linnet's young and—haunting abstraction—all the year's manifold "completions".

The victory of health and the positive outcome, stated like this, sounds more like the final Chorus of the *Oresteia* than *Endymion*, whose *dénouement* is utterly confused. Book Four, the last, introduces a fresh and notorious complication in the unfathomable person—or is it the straightforward seductive shape?—of the Indian Maid. Suddenly Keats confronts the reader with a second woman in *Endymion's* young life. In herself, and in her relations with the first (Cynthia the moon-goddess, sometimes called Phoebe), the Indian is meant to test and define the hero's affirmations, and then, with doubts set at rest and all knots untied, to find her place in the last triumphant stage. Undercutting her creator's cheerful intention, however, her effective role is that of destroyer. Again, never trust the artist—trust the tale. And so much Keats may have come to suspect for himself. Some sense of having dragged a Trojan Horse into *Endymion* may have helped him to his retrospective certainty of failure; for the Indian is the chief means whereby Book Four exposes the sandy foundations of which his Preface speaks.

An overall pattern emerges in which the new girl is cast, for the time being, opposite Cynthia (*alias* Phoebe) as body to soul, sense to spirit, earth to heaven, sex to love. Keats throws the weight of his scolding on Cynthia's side in a funny mixture of highmindedness and of jogging Endymion's memory through such appeals as "Is Phoebe passionless?" to help him recall that love—hers anyway—includes sex.

Endymion is in turmoil. Keats again wags his finger at his hero:

> *He surely cannot now*
> *Thirst for another love: O impious*
> *That he can even dream upon it thus!*[1]

[1] IV, 86.

But being, unlike Keats, inside the story, he has the full force of the Indian's sensuality to contend with.

So Book Four is fast moving towards a sexual climax. And Keats, in the same boat with every erotic writer in the world, must handle the resulting constriction as best he can. This dedication to sex—this aesthetic counterpart to Ivan Ilyich's sensation of death as a being thrust into the belly of a sack—is eased in Keats's later poetry by food and music. Both appear in *St. Agnes*, where the need to gain time and light and air and a broader sensual basis for his language overrides the probabilities of Madeline's bedroom; and again in *Lamia*. Here in *Endymion* the burden falls entirely on music. The hero's response to the Indian girl's suggestion that they spend the night together is, very implausibly,

> *I love thee! and my days can never last.*
> *That I may pass in patience still speak:*
> *Let me have music dying, and I seek*
> *No more delight—*

whereupon she sings a song, a "roundelay" to Sorrow.[1]

The chief sign that *Endymion* has shut the door of the 1817 volume behind itself is this dialectical adventure of health and un-health which I have been examining. The master-metaphors of ripeness and withering now, and increasingly, make their presences felt. Where the hymn to Pan opposes the two in successive stanzas, the song to Sorrow further concentrates this same antithesis and renders it down into oxymoron. Sorrow's borrowing "the natural hue of health" in the opening stanza ends with the Indian girl telling Sorrow "I love thee best" towards the close of her song. An uneasy state of affairs, since one does not borrow what one has already—and so in what sense "sweetest Sorrow"? What is this bitter sweetness and loving enmity? The Indian does not sing any old song here, on the verge of sexual consummation, but one that projects the unhealthy health, the withering ripeness, of a girl—herself—born to fulfil a sensual destiny ("how I could love!") but left mateless in her "maiden prime". Like Endymion, we are supposed to think. He is ripe and mateless too. Their encounter is being brought to the boil. And her vague grumble about being "cheated by shadowy wooer from the clouds" furthers the same purpose, laying her course and his side by side. For Endymion also has been cheated up to now, or half-cheated, by a celestial wooer. Keats's intention, clearer in his summary of the story to his little

[1] IV, 146.

sister than in his execution, was that the initiative should be Cynthia's from the start.[1]

The song ends; the oxymoron persists in

> the wind that now did stir
> About the crisped oaks full drearily,
> Yet with as sweet a softness as might be
> Remember'd from its velvet summer song.

And next, by way of the *bienséance* of Endymion's

> I've no choice;
> I must be thy sad servant evermore

the two move swiftly towards physical union, but are caught on the brink (his "I am so near" shows how near) by a voice calling out of nowhere, "Woe to that Endymion! Where is he?" It strikes the approved moral note, and yet "went echoing dismally" as Keats reports, thus sustaining contradiction at all levels before he prods his narrative forward on its final stage.

The essentials, with a mass of supernatural nonsense cut away, are our two conclusions of Adam's dream, healthy and unhealthy, opposed face to face in antithesis or locked within oxymoron. First Endymion falls asleep, with the Indian still beside him, and in his sleep "the mournful wanderer dreams" of a face which at first he does not recognise:

> He looks, 'tis she,
> His very goddess: good-bye earth, and sea,
> And air, and pains, and care, and suffering;
> Good-bye to all but love! Then doth he spring
> Towards her, and awakes—and, strange, o'erhead,
> Of those same fragrant exhalations bred,
> Beheld awake his very dream:[2]

his dream come true. But, "O state perplexing!"—perplexing and embarrassing, since the Indian girl is in bed with him. And she is

---

[1] "Many years ago there was a young handsome shepherd who fed his flocks on a mountain's side called Latmus. He was a very contemplative sort of person and lived solitary among the trees and plains little thinking that such a beautiful creature as the Moon was growing mad in love with him. However so it was; and when he was asleep on the grass, she used to come down from heaven and admire him excessively for a long time; and at last could not refrain from carrying him away in her arms to the top of that high mountain Latmus while he was dreaming" (*Letters*, vol. I, p. 154).

[2] IV, 430.

"so fond, so beauteous" that he cannot help being fond too; which evidently distresses Cynthia, because

At this the shadow wept, melting away.

Then just a dream? We must wait. Endymion's vain urging of Cynthia to stay rouses "the stranger of dark tresses" and he and she proceed to make love, though Endymion is naturally bothered by what has just happened. More so when, at moonrise, he turns to the Indian and

Despair! despair!
He saw her body fading gaunt and spare
In the cold moonshine.

Then doubly just a dream? We must go on waiting. While the issue hangs in doubt Keats surprises his reader with the news that Endymion experiences a sort of negative happiness at this of all moments, with both his loves vanished and no reason to suppose either will come back. He is in a state of mind designated "this Cave of Quietude":[1]

There anguish does not sting; nor pleasure pall:

but whereas a numbness which keeps pain at bay is easy to under-stand and accept, what sort of "pleasure" are we to imagine for Endymion here? The question is no sooner asked than those 1817 pleasures undergo metamorphosis before our eyes. The Keatsian word is itself becoming enveloped in the oxymoronic mist of the song to Sorrow; for the cave of quietude proves to be a place of ripe peace and consummation where rest may be had "calm and well";

Yet all is still within and desolate.
Beset with painful gusts, within ye hear
No sound so loud as when on curtain'd bier
The death-watch tick is stifled.

Yet also, therefore, a "desolate" deathly void. Certainly a place where no birds sing. A place where the negative outcome of Adam's dream achieves a sort of positive intensity, though an intensity distinguishable from the wanhope of *La Belle Dame* on the one hand and from the rare, "monstrous" nightmare of "frightful scarlet" on the other. And I believe the much-canvassed meaning of the cave of quietude, as Keats halts his action in order to plant

[1] IV, 512-551.

this passage in our lap, ought never to have been allowed to out-run its office of sustaining the oxymoron:

> *Happy gloom!*
> *Dark Paradise! where pale becomes the bloom*
> *Of health by due; where silence dreariest*
> *Is most articulate; where hopes infest;*
> *Where those eyes are the brightest far that keep*
> *Their lids shut longest in a dreamless sleep.*

The tight centre of the knot is again that highly idiosyncratic "health". Its meaning is a fraud except at the level of Adam's dream. Endymion's two women have been—and gone; and there is no other sort of wisdom to be extricated from the cave. Indeed one of the many things wrong with Book Four is its recourse to statements like "pale becomes the bloom / Of health by due", which cannot stand up to the inspection they solicit. Why "by due"? We are left irritably thinking how easy it is to write in riddles. No light falls on Endymion's bereft condition from this drawing tight and infolding of the health-unhealth complex. The cave of quietude is a device enabling Keats to float the two opposite conclusions of Adam's dream simultaneously; and the poised, doubting consciousness which it illuminates—after a fashion—is his own. Of course if the whole story were not so silly the comings and goings of Endymion's women might dramatise his personal history for us, instead of prefiguring in a thin schematic way what Keats's best poetry will be about. But then if *Endymion* were a deeply imagined poem, long like *St. Agnes* or short like *La Belle Dame*, its versions of Adam's dream would have been negative-capably housed and directed throughout. The moral pretentious-ness of "by due" would never have struck root.

Instead, and demonstrating the truth of his own "we hate poetry that has a palpable design upon us", Keats puts his thumb squarely in the healthy, positive, ripe balance, and compels his poem to end happily. Endymion, in his mental cave, is reached by the sound of yet another song,[1] sung by

> *voices sweet*
> *Warbling the while as if to lull and greet*
> *The wanderer in his path.*

What kind of song, the singers reveal by enquiring, artlessly,

> *Who, who away would be*
> *From Cynthia's wedding and festivity?*

[1] *Ibid.*, 563-611.

This is where all that blushing in heaven was leading us. And the function of the wedding hymn is firmly to announce that the oxymoronic tension of the Cave of Quietude is being favourably resolved.

> *Ah, Zephyrus! art here, and Flora too!*
> *Ye tender bibbers of the rain and dew,*
> *Young playmates of the rose and daffodil,*
> *Be careful, ere ye enter in, to fill*
>   *Your baskets high*
> *With fennel green, and balm, and golden pines,*
> *Savory, latter-mint, and columbines,*
> *Cool parsley, basil sweet, and sunny thyme;*
> *Yea, every flower and leaf of every clime,*
> *All gather'd in the dewy morning. . . .*

Harvest and plenitude mark the beginning of the end for the unsuspecting happy bridegroom. He is brought down to earth, literally, in the middle of the prothalamion, and there he finds the Indian maid waiting for him:

>   *now I see*
> *The grass; I feel the solid ground—Ah, me!*
> *It is thy voice—divinest! Where?—who? who*
> *Left thee so quiet on this bed of dew?*[1]

His dream finally come true; there will be no more vanishings. He does not recognise this fact at once, though, since his dreaming has been of Cynthia, and it seems he must lose Cynthia in order to win the Indian. So he accepts a qualified victory and settles down in a businesslike way to life with the dark sexual girl:

>   *Now,*
> *Where shall our dwelling be?*[2]

saying goodbye, as he thinks, to all his hopes of heaven. But there is a surprise in store, heralded mysteriously by the Indian who declares "I may not be thy love: I am forbidden", without saying why. Then Endymion's sister, Peona, arrives to sound the note of Cynthia and health once more:

>   *on this very night will be*
> *A hymning up to Cynthia, queen of light;*
> *For the soothsayers old saw yesternight*
> *Good visions in the air,—whence will befal,*
> *As say these sages, health perpetual*
> *To shepherds and their flocks;*[3]

[1] L. 621.   [2] L. 669.   [3] L. 827.

and to prepare us for the last and decisive twist which is the magical transformation of the Indian into Cynthia, giving Endymion a mystic two-in-one. "Sister", he addresses Peona,

> *"I would have command,*
> *If it were heaven's will, on our sad fate."*
> *At which the dark-eyed stranger stood elate*
> *And said, in a new voice, but sweet as love,*
> *To Endymion's amaze: "By Cupid's dove,*
> *And so thou shalt! and by the lily truth*
> *Of my own breast thou shalt, beloved youth!"*
> *And as she spoke, into her face there came*
> *Light, as reflected from a silver flame:*
> *Her long black hair swell'd ampler, in display*
> *Full golden; in her eyes a brighter day*
> *Dawn'd blue and full of love. Aye, he beheld*
> *Phoebe, his passion! joyous she upheld*
> *Her lucid bow, continuing thus; "Drear, drear*
> *Has our delaying been. . . ."*[1]

That last has its truth for all of us, and inspires the briskness of the present survey. "Drear" also exemplifies Keats's uncanny self-consistency in diction; the ripening fact of "swell'd ampler" and the sterile threat that has been lurking throughout in "wither drearily" continue their intertwined career to the last minute. It all looks like bare bones, put in this way, but *Endymion's* meagreness invites summary treatment. In fact the thousand sprawling lines of Book Four give us all the conciseness we could possibly ask for when it comes to testing large conclusions, to arguing the case of John Keats.

Book Four offers Adam's dream, and offers it unnaturally clearly. This lucidity, while useful, reveals the miserable unhoused state of both the "dream come true" and "just a dream" alternatives in the poem. Then why are they so poor and thin, so unlike Adam's dream in the best Keats? Because of the enforced separation of the object of Endymion's dreaming (the spiritual Cynthia) from his living feel (the earthly Indian). Once again, the poet is doing Matthew Arnold's work for him, postulating a high spiritual and intellectual theme and a merely sensual one.

Both are ghosts, but the second is the shadow of a poetic substance. The first is nothing at all and provides the main reason why the writing is so very very bad. So verbose and so penurious. "Pseudo-spirituality" is meant to stigmatise the infantile supernatural machinery, and the failure to get any moral dignity into

---

[1] L. 975.

Endymion's heaven (producing a state of affairs where "foolish fear /
Witheld me first; and then decrees of fate"—and so forth), and the
emptiness of the whole Cynthia conception.

Pseudo-spirituality also proposes to explain the muddle Keats
finds himself in over the status of dream in *Endymion*, and especially
in this last book. By making two different girls out of the one we
dream about idealisingly and the one to whom we say "Now,
where shall be our home?" he disarms his imagination. The creative interdependence of the dreaming man and the realist is viola-
ted. For in memorable Keats, witness *St. Agnes*, the girl who "rose
like a mission'd spirit" is capable of walking downstairs in the same
stanza "to a safe level matting".[1] Whereas in *Endymion*, because
dream is shackled to Cynthia and Cynthia is *ex officio* unactual, all
manner of doubts arise regarding the credentials of the hero's
dreaming. True, Keats turns the Indian maid into Cynthia at the
close—but what a merciless self-criticism! The poem is now over,
the damage done, this final external manipulation quite futile
except by way of verse postscript to the confession of failure made
already in the prose Preface.

And so dream in *Endymion* keeps groping behind itself for firm
ground to stand on.

> *"Endymion, how strange!*
> *Dream within Dream!"*[2]

interjects Peona early on. But if we take the Romance seriously
and possess the mental stamina to sort the layers out, "dream
within dream" proves only a beginning. We have to undertake the
peeling of Peer Gynt's onion, counting visions within faints or
trances within dreams within apparently dreamless sleep within
the story.[3] A strenuous burrowing dispossesses the straight cross-
rhythm of "just a dream" / "dream come true", and it is a sad
symptom.

The purpose of the pseudo-spiritual label is, finally, to entrust
to the Indian girl the promise of growth and better verse to come
which we deny Cynthia. To some extent Keats is our ally in this.

---

[1] XXII.   [2] I, 632.

[3] At the close we have to make what we can of Keats's assertion that "all
were dreamers" (IV, 900). Presumably he wants to contrast the world of their
present consciousness with the imminent "real" event of the Indian's metamorphosis. And there is the further difficulty that *Endymion's* happy outcome
has already been anticipated in a dream dreamt by Sleep personified (IV,
367-380). The longer I spend with dream, trance and allied states in *Endymion*,
the surer I become that it is a waste of time trying to be nice about them.

Through the Indian he voices his disquiet about Endymion's dreaming. He makes his hero say, at the new sheer feel of her,

> I have clung
> To nothing, lov'd a nothing, nothing seen
> Or felt but a great dream. . . .
> There never liv'd a mortal man, who bent
> His appetite beyond his natural sphere,
> But starv'd and died. My sweetest Indian, here,
> Here will I kneel, for thou redeemed hast
> My life from too thin breathing: gone and past
> Are cloudy phantasms.[1]

Now "too thin breathing" is the plain Keatsian truth; his Cynthia never had the scantiest sustenance. Therefore when the poet steps in forcibly to correct this natural bias against Cynthia, and has Endymion decide "a hermit young, I'll live in mossy cave", alone, and the Indian dedicate herself to "white Chastity" so that the "higher" pleasures of the spirit may not be obscured by lower ones,[2] we do not believe a word of it. This is the ground for saying Cynthia is just a ghost whereas the Indian is the shadow of a palpable poetic substance. A shadow, though, and not the real thing, because her attenuated role in Book Four is merely to oppose the transcendental dream by sex and her actual touch. That refutes the dream decisively enough; but it is a mean little victory over an opponent of straw, unglorious compared with the intensifying continuity and confirmation that should be hers. She punctures the pro-Cynthian invocation at the opening of Book Four:

> Great Muse, thou know'st what prison
> Of flesh and bone curbs, and confines, and frets
> Our spirit's wings:[3]

but replaces it with her own crude power to make Endymion feel "this is this world".[4] Keats can make noble poetry out of Adam dreaming of Eve and then finding her gone—the lady vanishes—and also waking and finding her there. Or out of Eve finding Adam:

> Her eyes were open, but she still beheld,
> Now wide awake, the vision of her sleep:[5]

but not out of Adam dreaming about a neo-Platonic allegorical abstraction and waking to find

---

[1] IV, 636.   [2] Ll. 849-883.   [3] L. 20.
[4] L. 320.   [5] St. Agnes, XXXIV.

> *My Indian bliss!*
> *My river-lily bud! one human kiss!*
> *One sigh of real breath—one gentle squeeze,*
> *Warm as a dove's nest among summer trees,*
> *And warm with dew at ooze from living blood!*[1]

The Indian is not the real thing. She is the actual and distinguishable thing. She is relevant to the real thing, and hence Keats's "human" and his unavailing "real", and his routine immature gesture of the secret warm dove's nest, and even his extraordinary idea of the oozing blood-dew. That last is a "sensation" within the meaning of the letter which says *Lamia* has "that sort of fire in it which must take hold of people in some way—give them either pleasant or unpleasant sensation". Cynthia fails to convey any sensation, pleasant or unpleasant, while the Indian makes us "feel the solid ground" of Keats's fantasy. We salute the pure end-stopping of Endymion's appeal to her,

> *Do gently murder half my soul, and I*
> *Shall feel the other half so utterly!*[2]

Kicking its heels idly, that authentic "feel" mischievously incites the Indian to grow too big for the sexual role into which Keats has crammed her. She keeps protesting that

> *When yet a child, I heard that kisses drew*
> *Favour from thee, and so I kisses gave*
> *To the void air, bidding them find out love:*[3]

but we know she could be imaginatively richer than that, having seen her step, fleetingly, into the *Nightingale Ode*,

> *with dew-sweet eglantine,*
> *And honeysuckles full of clear bee-wine.*[4]

She eats and sleeps sex, of course, in so far as she is there for us at all; but the ripe ideal she serves forces the issue on and outward, while an almost inarticulate domestic tenderness surrounds her—everything Endymion left unsaid when he talked to her about "our quiet home". The rest has to be guessed from such simple contacts as

> *so these both*
> *Leant to each other trembling,*[5]

in their gothic fear, after the bodiless voice has burst upon them with "Woe to that Endymion!" on behalf of Cynthia. They seek

[1] IV, 663. [2] L. 309. [3] L. 738.
[4] L. 697. [5] L. 328.

the animal nearness that will inform and strangely elevate the love of Isabella and Lorenzo, and then of Madeline and Porphyro. For all these reasons the Indian is a destroyer let loose inside *Endymion*, but a destroyer of lies and not to be regretted.

4 *The Chief Intensity*

When Adam woke out of his dream "and found it truth" he had two Eves to compare and reconcile. The second manifestation must have more to it than the same again since it brings with it the truth which the first is waiting for. The same again, I said, only more so. What is this more? While Keats invokes Adam's experience in *Paradise Lost*, Coleridge the natural metaphysician places a bomb under this form of the dream-imagination analogy by asking "Aye, what then?" of the flower in the waking poet's hand. The direct surface clash of "just a dream" and "dream come true" is thus dismissed and replaced by a different set of considerations. These are not potentially less poetic, of course, but they happen to be unKeatsian. We only have to look at the sterile "dream within dream" gropings in *Endymion* to assure ourselves he can make nothing of them, and never will.

The ardent, affirmative Keats is the poet whose dreams come true. This truth, the something more of Eve's second manifestation, he calls intensity, and its vehicle is the master-metaphor of ripeness. "The excellence of every art," he tells his brothers George and Tom, "is its intensity."[1] That must sound a jaded observation unless we recall that in 1817 intensity was not the smooth-worn critical and social coin it will become by the middle of Victoria's reign. On the contrary, it was an *avant-garde* word, favoured by Shelley and Hazlitt as well as Keats (compare Hazlitt's "gusto"); helped forward by the vogue of Byron; usurping, isolating, emphasising the enthusiastic and powerful connotations of the declining eighteenth-century "sublime"; partner to those other emergent criteria "sincerity" and "originality", and contained, like them, within the overall shift from objective-mimetic theories (art imitates nature) to subjective-expressive ones (art declares emotions).

Keats's shared Romantic intensity, like his Romantic feel, is also entirely his own. The letter to his brothers attributes intensity not to the artist but to the work of art. This is quite untypical. The

[1] *Letters*, vol. I, p. 192.

early nineteenth-century norm, illustrated by Shelley's image of the composing sensibility as a white-hot but fading coal, is insistently subjective. And the same is nearly always true of the older Romantics who, as we should expect, use and imply intensity less than their juniors: for example Coleridge, when he observes that Wordsworth sometimes displays "an intensity of feeling" disproportionate to the "value of the objects described".[1] But Keats speaks with two equally firm voices, objective and subjective, even in the same letter and in successive sentences:

I spent Friday evening with Wells and went the next morning to see *Death on the Pale Horse*. It is a wonderful picture, when West's age is considered; but there is nothing to be intense upon; no women one feels mad to kiss; no face swelling into reality. The excellence of every art is its intensity, capable of making all disagreeables evaporate, from their being in close relationship with Beauty and Truth. Examine *King Lear* and you will find this exemplified throughout; but in this picture we have unpleasantness without any momentous depth of speculation excited, in which to bury its repulsiveness.

Being "intense upon" the work of art is of course Coleridge's "intensity of feeling". But in Keats the Romantic commonplace has to come to terms with the intensity that is inherent in the artifact, just as—precisely because—the poet of feel must reach a *modus vivendi* with the picture-maker. The old-fashioned objective strain is reappearing in a different guise; and we shall see that the achieved, held-for-ever picture can advance as good a claim to the adjective "intense" as the hungry snailhorn eye.

The two intensities become the same intensity, as surely as the two Keatses are finally one; and the ground of their identity is the ripeness metaphor. Keep patience a moment while the words "no face swelling into reality" have time to simmer. And throw into the pot with them another letter about another picture—one of Haydon's:

I shall expect to see your Picture plumped out like a ripe Peach—you would not be very willing to give me a slice of it.[2]

Then refer both letters to the metamorphosis of the Indian maid at the close of *Endymion*, when, as we have just seen, "her long black hair swell'd ampler". A transformation into the goddess Cynthia is supposed to be going on. The poem's dualistic form dictates this process. It is the poorest of pretences. The true impulse,

[1] *Biographia Literaria*, Chapter XXII.
[2] *Letters*, vol. II, p. 221.

thwarted and desperately corrupted in *Endymion*, was to have had
the Indian "swelling into reality". This should have been the poem's
supreme instance of the same again only more so, of taking the
"merely" out of the merely sensual Keats, of proving Cynthia a
hollow ghost but the Indian, *au contraire*, reality's dark alluring
shadow; and it should have let us see, at the same time and by the
same token, why picture-making is the right name for an activity
which is not dominantly visual. For if in those final lines the Indian
had swelled into reality, had become the matured peach of the
letter to Haydon, ourselves and our admired object would have
been caught and held together within the ripeness metaphor:
ourselves gratified, intense on our desire, and the Indian brought
to her nature's acme and so at last perfectly herself in the intensity
of art.

Intensity's importance rests, throughout Keats's writing life,
on his childlike juxtaposing of the actual and the real. The same
again only more so is a language spoken by simple souls; "I want
a brighter word than bright, a fairer word and fair" is the cry to
Fanny Brawne:[1] this very simplicity articulate, the same again
only more so in the mouth of the intensifier himself, the linguistic
artist. One can scarcely be too emphatic about the unreflective
innocence of such pronouncements in Keats, or too quick to admit
the crudity which his appeal to aesthetic criteria like "no women
one feels mad to kiss" thrusts under our noses. Everybody is
simple and crude sometimes, and understands, beneath his sophistication, what Keats means. In this sense the ripeness metaphor is
the commonest of common property. General de Gaulle declared
at a French Cabinet meeting, with reference to Britain's entry into
the European Common Market: "La problème semble mûrir
lentement dans un sens positif." The positive ripening which
repels intelligent scrutiny also demonstrates the touch of the successful man of affairs. His words impress their unspecific optimism
not on thin air but on our one human, teleological heart. Wise
purposeful nature feels a real thing, as Keats would say.

His own version of positive ripening is, most insistently, these
swellings into reality which his letters and the Indian maid have
just introduced us to. *Endymion's* pseudo-spirituality continues to
the bitter end doing its best to confuse the issue. Cynthia tells the
hero finally,

> 'twas fit that from this mortal state
> Thou shouldst, my love, by some unlook'd for change
> Be spiritualiz'd.[2]

[1] *Ibid.*, p. 123.   [2] IV, 991.

Writing of that quality destroys its own pretensions effectively enough. Asking where things have gone wrong we concentrate, as always, on the spiritual word, and find it vainly attempting to shore up the dualism of "some unlook'd for change" (what a give-away!) against Keats's natural intensifying rhythm of the same again only more so. *Endymion's* pleasure thermometer has already told this story in a nutshell; the rest is confirmation and elaboration. Our grounds for attacking the thermometer's "fellowship divine" become clearer with every step the poem takes, and likewise our reason for defending the imaginative truth (but not the execution) of the thermometer's unbroken ripening progress

> *leading, by degrees,*
> To the chief intensity:

and furthermore it becomes possible to resolve the hesitation with which we greeted phrases like "fellowship with essence". The fact is, Keats finds himself short of intensity-words. I take my cue from the undereducated strain in the 1817 volume:

> *And gave the steel a shining quite transcendent.*

Endymion, readier, verbally more adroit, brings up reinforcements in the shape of "etherial", "Aeolian", "aerial", "empyrean" and "empyreal", "Elysium" and "Elysian" ("It feels Elysian"), the dread vulgarised "divine", "essence" of course, and even "spiritual" itself. There are employments like

> *every sense*
> *Filling with spiritual sweets to plenitude,*
> *As bees gorge full their cells*[1]

which show that even "spiritual" can be drawn by poetry unambiguously into the right service. We stand here at the opposite pole to Cynthia's wilful, lying "spiritualiz'd". The ground between is strewn with oddities like "fellowship with essence", which hint the truth—since essence suggests selfhood intensified rather than subjected to "unlook'd for change"—but which also invite misunderstanding. Any number of metaphysical Keatses can be built with those bricks. Thus while essence is an honest intensifier it also helps, by appearing in the singular case, to foster the impression of a transcendentalist (Shelley, say) with his mind's eye fixed on some philosophic or religious One beyond the stars. In this respect Endymion's talk of exploring

[1] III, 38. Woodhouse records "spiritual honey" from Keats's draft.

all forms and substances
Straight homeward to their symbol-essences[1]

deals more justly than "fellowship with essence" does with Keats's aesthetic nominalism: I mean with his universe of distinct intensifiable singulars. Which is why it is so important to appreciate the force of the last three words in both those letters, frequently quoted and wrongly Platonised, about his pursuit of "the poetical—the beautiful—in all things" and about having "loved the principle of beauty in all things".

But we have to add at once that such borrowed plumes as "form", "substance" and "symbol" are grotesquely unbecoming. Endymion's "essences once spiritual" in

> *Now I have tasted her sweet soul to the core*
> *All other depths are shallow: essences*
> *Once spiritual, are like muddy lees,*[2]

are the best words he can find to talk about experiences which had seemed to him very, very intense. Keats will improve on them in due course.

Again in the letters, exactly the same pattern of vocabulary emerges. The spiritual words either repudiate the creative gift or they are assimilated privately and more or less misleadingly to that gift. When he writes to his sister-in-law about his "unearthly, spiritual and etherial" attitude of mind towards "John Howard, Bishop Hooker rocking his child's cradle and you my dear sister", the three epithets mean what they appear to mean; we only have to recall that Howard was a philanthropist, Hooker (never a bishop in fact) the author of *The Laws of Ecclesiastical Politie*, and George Keats's wife a person for whom John Keats's love has, John is plainly indicating, no trace of sensuality in it; and at once the total separation of this unearthly, spiritual and etherial state from the world of his verse becomes apparent.[3] On the other

---

[1] III, 699.   [2] II, 904.

[3] *Letters*, vol. I, p. 395. Keats's "spiritual" train of thought has been touched off here by his meeting a girl called Jane Cox. The month before he tells John Reynolds, "the voice and shape of a woman has haunted me these two days" (*Ibid.*, p. 370); and in the present letter he expatiates: "She is not a Cleopatra; but she is at least a Charmian. She has a rich eastern look; she has fine eyes and fine manners. When she comes into a room she makes an impression the same as the beauty of a leopardess. . . . I am at such times too much occupied in admiring to be awkward or on a tremble. I forget myself entirely because I live in her. You will by this time think I am in love with her; so before I go any further I will tell you I am not—she kept me awake one night as a tune of Mozart's might do—I speak of the thing as a pastime and an amusement than

hand, when elsewhere his Adam's Dream letter suggests "a conviction that Imagination and its empyreal reflection is the same as human life and its spiritual repetition", the two spiritual words need to be kept firmly in check and glossed on the authority of our hard-earned deeper understanding. If we did not know about those faces which art's imaginative intensity makes one "mad to kiss", and about a heaven where earthly pleasures will come again intensified ("repetition" is the truth), we should be floundering.

What—to follow de Gaulle's lead—is a negative ripening? It is waking up alone on the cold ground, like *La Belle Dame's* knight-at-arms. But Adam, and Keats sometimes, witness a positive ripening; they discover a face swelling into reality, a secular epiphany. And just as Keatsian sex occupies its very important place within—but within—Keatsian feel, so the ripeness metaphor comprehends all love's longed-for possibilities within an impulse as spacious as great heedful Nature herself: a coaxing and fostering impulse to nurse forward, to bring on as we say, the absent and merely potential phases of things; to consummate the actual.

In his earliest work one gets a "sidelong view of swelling leafiness", bees "buzz round two swelling peaches", apples are naturally "swelling" on the branch[1]—naturally because of the open or thinly veiled invitation to taste which the poetry of snailhorn perception everywhere conveys. And naturally also, as we now see with the unbroken history of his ripeness metaphor opening before us, because of the latent dynamism of these 1817 swellings. They are swellings *towards*, as well as static indulgencies of touch and taste. However only the advantage of hindsight renders this silent forward pressure observable with any confidence; were it possible to find and feel it inside the 1817 volume, that book's lack of momentum would have been at least partially cured. What emerges from an enclosed reading of 1817 is, yet again but in a

which I can feel none deeper than a conversation with an imperial woman the very 'yes' and 'no' of whose lips is to me a banquet."

Now it is against this very affirmative reaction to Miss Cox that his spiritual feelings about Georgiana Keats and the others get introduced; he sees them himself in polar opposition. Thus the letter is doubly interesting. After his neat demarcation of an area closed to his creative powers (though not of course to his humanity and intelligence), we turn back to Jane Cox and meet the authentic words ("rich . . . fine . . . fine"), the authentic image (" the beauty of a leopardess"—compare Lamia especially and the common ground of human and animal throughout Keats), Negative Capability itself ("I forget myself entirely because I live in her"), and the internalising of sight and sound—of seen lips and heard voice—in that final snailhorn "banquet".

[1] *Calidore*, 34, 66; *Sleep and Poetry*, 361.

new analytic context, the falling apart of his self-dictated personal programme and his poetry's discernible strength, direction, character. These swellings towards ripeness remain genuine only so long as they are tethered to apples and peaches, the realm of Flora and Pan. They have no means of acquiring humanity. In the poet's prayer

> *O may these joys be ripe before I die*

his master-metaphor stands rebuked, a gatecrasher from a different party.

The metaphor cannot help its primary attachment to Flora's realm, since Keats is Keats and

> *The flower must drink the nature of the soil*
> *Before it can put forth its blossoming.*[1]

All hope of something better to come rests, as it always did, on the unawakened resources of his sensuality. Intensity, ripeness, cannot disown these naïve "imaginary" fruits, but it must somehow humanise its attachment to them. And already in 1817 two things are beginning to happen. The swelling process is being extended through territories of sound and sight ("the sonnet swelling loudly" for example, and "as when ocean / Heaves calmly its broad swelling smoothness")[2], and it is being deployed magically in simultaneous, all-of-a-piece ripenings which pander to Keats's time-banishing, picture-making urge:

> *What next? A tuft of evening primroses,*
> *O'er which the mind may hover till it dozes;*
> *O'er which it well might take a pleasant sleep,*
> *But that 'tis ever startled by the leap*
> *Of buds into ripe flowers. . . .*[3]

The heard sonnet and seen ocean are not so much fruitlike as destined to meet Keats's apples and peaches on common ground; his power to bend sound and sight inward upon the one sensory solar plexus is beginning to stir. And stir in two complementary directions. For his ripening—like his blushing and bruising—is felt from within as well as appreciated from without. It teaches the grammar of negative capability. Likewise it defines the wishful dream wherein buds "leap" miraculously towards and into their mature fate. Keats is determined, like the photographer with his

---

[1] "Spenser! a jealous honourer of thine"—one of his most uneven sonnets.
[2] *To Charles Cowden Clarke*, 60; *Sleep and Poetry*, 376.
[3] "I stood tiptoe", 107.

"Hold it!", to compel the facts into a picture, and potentially an infelt picture, and a picture endowed with the very special momentum of the ripeness metaphor, the swelling into reality which his letter about Benjamin West's painting introduced us to.

Endymion proliferates extended swellings of the sonnet and sea sort, and also magical ripenings. To put the word ripe in the middle of the map is to get entangled in a maze of conceit, sometimes literary:

> *Her soft arms were entwining me, and on*
> *Her voice I hung like fruit among green leaves:*
> *Her lips were all my own, and—ah, ripe sheaves*
> *Of happiness! ye on the stubble droop,*[1]

and almost inert; sometimes more obscure, personal, and interesting—the situation of "for earth too ripe" or "ripe from hue-golden swoons".[2] We also commit ourselves to follow the word into weird blendings of epic-conventional and the private fancy:

> *and, full oft,*
> *When a dread waterspout had rear'd aloft*
> *Its hungry hugeness, seeming ready ripe*
> *To burst. . . .*[3]

where the insensitive pounding verse may borrow a second's life from the picture of the vegetable sea,

> *while ocean's tide*
> *Hung swollen at their backs,*[4]

and, once at least, miraculous ripening and the budlike bursting of foam-bubbles reinforce each other fantastically yet cogently:

> *sweeter than the rill*
> *To its cold channel, or a swollen tide*
> *To margin sallows, were the leaves he spied,*
> *And flowers, and wreaths, and myrtle crowns*
> *Up heaping through the slab: refreshment drowns*
> *Itself, and strives its own delights to hide—*
> *Not in one spot alone; the floral pride*
> *In a long whispering birth enchanted grew*
> *Before his footsteps; as when heav'd anew*
> *Old ocean rolls a lengthened wave to the shore,*
> *Down whose green back the short-liv'd foam, all hoar,*
> *Bursts gradual, with a wayward indolence.*[5]

[1] III, 270.   [2] I, 142; III, 861.   [3] III, 345.
[4] III, 312.   [5] II, 339.

Thus his ripeness brings our thoughts about intensity to a head, so to say literally. In a letter, one—he—can talk easily about "reality" which is the end of all swelling towards and into. The poet has to work to make reality good.

In the heart of a poem's crystal alone can the Spring come true.[1]

While the letter-writer ties reality, with a tacit "you know what I mean", to the tail of passion intensified and the sort of face one feels mad to kiss, the poet has to do the thing. The girl in the poem is the stranger who overwhelmed one at the bus stop or wherever it was, only more so. She is the girl Keats "saw for some few moments at Vauxhall"[2] and addressed a sonnet to five years later:

> *Time's sea hath been five years at its slow ebb;*
> *Long hours have to and fro let creep the sand;*
> *Since I was tangled in thy beauty's web,*
> *And snared by the ungloving of thine hand.*
> *And yet I never look on midnight sky,*
> *But I behold thine eyes' well memoried light;*
> *I cannot look upon the rose's dye,*
> *But to thy cheek my soul doth take its flight;*
> *I cannot look on any budding flower,*
> *But my fond ear, in fancy at thy lips,*
> *And harkening for a love-sound, doth devour*
> *Its sweets in the wrong sense:—Thou dost eclipse*
> *Every delight with sweet remembering,*
> *And grief unto my darling joys dost bring.*

Robert Bridges, preposterously judging that the sonnet "might have been written by Shakespeare",[3] does scratch the exposed tip of the pastiche question, provoking thought on its layers and limits, its spots of abjectness and its latent creative force. The story begins with *King Lear*. In the first of the references to *Lear* scattered through his letters, Keats tells John Reynolds: "From want of regular rest, I have been rather *narvus*—and the passage in *Lear*— "Do you not hear the sea?"—has haunted me intensely."[4] He then copies out for Reynolds a sonnet ("It keeps eternal whisperings")

---

[1] "Shepherd's Bush Eclogue", by John Heath-Stubbs.

[2] Note to a transcript of the poem made by the person whom Garrod tentatively designates Woodhouse's clerk. Woodhouse himself records in a second transcript: "Keats mentioned the circumstances of obtaining a casual sight of her at Vauxhall, in answer to my enquiry."

[3] *Critical Essay* written for the Muses Library Keats.

[4] *Letters*, vol. I, p. 132.

prompted by his present state of mind, not obviously about *Lear* itself, but "On the Sea". Shakespeare is a buried influence, local and trivial first of all, in the line "Oh ye! who have your eye-balls vexed and tired"; for while that appeal to the organ of sight's feel comes straight from Keats, it is also true that the passage haunting him "intensely" concerns the newly-blinded Gloucester; so those intrusive eye-balls of the sonnet are, bizarrely ("Out vile jelly!"), Shakespearian too. The sea begins to dominate the scene in the sonnet-length speech delivered by Edgar, as if looking over the English Channel from the brink of a high cliff. Keats draws attention to these lines in the very next reference to *Lear* in his letters, by quoting "I am 'one that gathers Samphire dreadful trade' the cliff of Poesy towers above me".[1] After the samphire, in Shakespeare, comes

> *The murmuring surge*
> *That on th' unnumb'red idle pebble chafes*
> *Cannot be heard so high.*

And after Keats's early references to *Lear* (in April and May of 1817) no more is heard about his actually reading the play until 23 January of the following year, when he tells parson Bailey "I have sent my first book [of *Endymion*] to the Press—and this afternoon shall begin preparing the second"; and in the next paragraph: "I sat down to read *King Lear* yesterday."[2] At the beginning of *Endymion's* second book we find

> *Wide sea, that one continuous murmur breeds*
> *Along the pebbled shore of memory!*[3]

This is Edgar's sea, tinged strongly with the sixtieth sonnet:

> *Like as the waves make towards the pebbled shore. . . .*

It is Edgar's sea explicitly in its pebbles and its murmuring, implicitly in its width to the mind's high-stationed eye and in being an ocean of memory and feigning fancy. Twelve days later, on 4 February, Keats composes the "Time's sea" sonnet, supremely a sea of memory, with the girl he had once glimpsed at Vauxhall for his theme. *Endymion's* word "memory" has gone, together with the murmur and the pebbles. The sea's touch remains, the rubbing and fretting and insistent physical pressure that link Edgar's "chafes" and Keats's "to and fro let creep". This is now not so much Edgar's sea as a sea big enough for both Shakespeare and Keats to imagine in.

[1] *Ibid.*, p. 141.   [2] *ibid.*, p. 212.   [3] II, 16.

"Let creep" leads to "tangled" and thence to "snared" in the high and held moment of the octave:

And snared by the ungloving of thine hand.

There is the infelt picture. Visual on top, underneath how remote from all seeing except the snailhorn's. He did indeed see the girl; but the truthful origin of what we are reading comes through, while strongly, very strangely. It feels like an old tale.

Now as to the snailhorn, Keats should not have let matters stand at "in the wrong sense" in his twelfth line. The phrase suggests where to begin in demonstrating, against Bridges, that Shakespeare could not conceivably have written the sonnet. At the same time, not surprisingly, the phrase indicates who did write it. "In the wrong sense" carries the familiar prose honesty of Keats's attempts to observe his own poetry from within—which means, feel being what it is, from without; its plight is that of all such versified commentary on poetic fact. The words point to the sense-transference between sight and sound. This is what may be said to happen, but not what gets achieved. For our glad reception of "devour" elevates the "wrong sense" of honest commentary into the right sense of poetic intensification. The whole comes to rest within that consummation of both "look" and "harkening", that ripening of the unobtrusive and apparently conventional "budding flower" where the whole process began. Run straight through the sonnet, and surely the shock of change does not pass unnoticed from

I cannot look upon the rose's dye,
But to thy cheek my soul doth takes its flight

which is nothing (or if you like sub-Shakespearian, together with "grief unto my darling joys" and so on), to the next four lines where something is beginning to move. Like so much of what he wrote in 1818, the sonnet is suspended between vigorous crudities of the

My ear is open like a greeedy shark

sort belonging to the year before or earlier, where the "wrong sense" comment would do quite well, and the poetry of the year following.

"Time's sea" takes the Vauxhall girl, the actual one, and does two things with her: pictures her intensely and savours her intensely. In so far as the sonnet succeeds, the girl swells into reality. Keats treats her—her dispersed gloveless hand and her taste—as he would like to treat the Indian Maid. But *Endymion* has four thousand lines against fourteen and is committed to a neo-Platonic scheme in which the reality she swells into has to be Cynthia.

Against this betrayal of true intensity, the "swell'd ampler" of the Indian's metamorphosis can achieve little or nothing; and no wonder, since the ripening instinct has been set to transcend the very actuality it longs to perfect. Therefore that instinct rebels in small, almost wordless gestures of natural consummation. Accompanying her metamorphosis is heard

> *The vesper hymn, far swollen, soft and full—*[1]

the real and fruitlike thing, the achieved object of Endymion's and Adam's dreaming, what the poem intends when it makes statements like "every sense had grown / Ethereal for pleasure".[2] Again, immediately before her metamorphosis, the hero returns to the forests of Latmos he grew up in, and

> *the very stream*
> *By which he took his first soft poppy dream;*
> *And on the very bark 'gainst which he leant*
> *A crescent he had carv'd, and round it spent*
> *His skill in little stars. The teeming tree*
> *Had swollen and green'd the pious charactery,*
> *But not ta'en out.*[3]

That tree has been growing during the poem, behind the many words, as if *Endymion* had possessed from the start and through its worst follies a secret life hidden with the god of all fulfilments. One recalls

> *the birth, life, death*
> *Of unseen flowers in heavy peacefulness;*[4]

also running back to the beginning of the poem, and also prefiguring the 1819 Keats of finished purposes, whose poems are arrivals rather than voyagings, havens of intenseness within the memory, the personal past, of every reader.

But we remember too the perfunctory magical ripenings of *Endymion*. The rather fine "floral pride" which

> *In a long whispering birth enchanted grew*
> *Before his footsteps,*

was not a fair example. More typical is

> *Delicious symphonies, like airy flowers,*
> *Budded and swell'd, and, full-blown, shed full showers*
> *Of light, soft, unseen leaves of sounds divine.*
> *The two deliverers tasted a pure wine*
> *Of happiness, from fairy-press ooz'd out.*[5]

[1] IV, 967.   [2] II, 671.   [3] IV, 785.
[4] I, 234.   [5] III, 798.

And sure enough, all this sense-transference comes to rest in "tasted", and taste itself gets concentrated, becomes an intensity, an Endymionic essence, in the squeezed oozings from the press. We have here one of those situations of simultaneous nearness and remoteness between the Romance and the 1820 volume: nearness to the words "last oozings" in the *Autumn Ode* and the idea of the press; remoteness from the occasion of the oozings and the employment of the press. *Endymion* lacks the imaginative juxtaposing of actual and real which breeds intensity in all the great odes. Its "fairy-press" (against *Autumn's* "cyder-press") reaffirms the sad central fact of four thousand lines squandered on an inane subject. All the oozy concentrations in the world, the essential "dew of her rich speech", the "distilling odorous dew", the ringing of "rich" changes and "honey" compounds, cannot help the girl in the moon to satisfy the criterion which Keats applied to Benjamin West's painting.

> *Whence that completed form of all completeness?*
> *Whence came that high perfection of all sweetness?*[1]

Endymion asks. The first is a picture-making question, the second a savouring one. They are both intense devices aiming to thrust the issue, via "completeness" and "perfection", towards a consummation of the actual; and they will both fail until the answer to "whence?" can truthfully be given as Vauxhall or somewhere near and comparable in imagination.

One final magic ripening:

> *Now he is sitting by a shady spring,*
> *And elbow-deep with feverous fingering*
> *Stems the upbursting cold: a wild rose tree*
> *Pavilions him in bloom, and he doth see*
> *A bud which snares his fancy: lo! but now*
> *He plucks it, dips its stalk in the water: how!*
> *It swells, it buds, it flowers beneath his sight;*
> *And, in the middle, there is softly pight*
> *A golden butterfly. . . .*[2]

The butterfly lacks the obvious connection with ripeness and intensity which the bud possesses here, or even the "upbursting" spring-water. Its climactic significance falls within its nature as a butterfly, and Keats makes this clear to Fanny Brawne in the first letter he wrote her.

---

[1] I, 606.   [2] II, 53.

I almost wish we were butterflies and liv'd but three summer days—three such days with you I could fill with more delight than fifty common years could ever contain.[1]

The butterfly is his dream of ripeness incarnate. The creature celebrates its earliest appearance in his poetry by compressing the three crammed days of the letter into a single ecstatic spasm:

> *A butterfly, with golden wings broad parted,*
> *Nestling a rose, convuls'd as though it smarted*
> *With over pleasure—*[2]

intensity intensified. "Convuls'd" simultaneously evokes the held state of Keats's picture and his butterfly's apogee of feel. Stasis and snailhorn. We both contemplate the natural sculpture and endure the quasi-orgasm.

The butterfly's natural ripeness, the intensity it cannot help, precedes Keats's interest in the Greek Psyche which was their butterfly-emblem of the human soul. Academic discussion, which has been plentiful, of Psyche in his poetry ought to be judged in the light of that negative-capable "convuls'd" which forbids us either to make capital out of the traditional separateness of soul and body—the separateness at the root of his and his critics' troubles with *Endymion*—or to be persuaded by the Greek habit of depicting the butterfly-soul on gravestones into promoting death above life. Neither is primary; the fullest feel of life and immediate neighbourhood to death meet in the ripe fact. The

> *June that breathes out life for butterflies*[3]

in another early poem also harvests that life. Indeed "convuls'd" articulates the ripe fact single-handed, for it is a kind of little death and a tremor of sheer life too. Doing justice to both is always Keats's business, specially in his later work:

> *Why did I laugh? I know this Being's lease,*
> *My fancy to its utmost blisses spreads;*
> *Yet would I on this very midnight cease,*
> *And the world's gaudy ensigns see in shreds;*
> *Verse, Fame, and Beauty are intense indeed,*
> *But Death intenser—Death is Life's high meed.*[4]

The final couplet rings hard, sententious, uncomfortable, because it is not quite true. He has been worrying at the intense

---

[1] *Letters*, vol. II, p. 123.   [2] *Sleep and Poetry*, 343.
[3] "What is there . . .?"
[4] "Why did I laugh to-night?", dating from the Spring of 1819.

idea; will not let the word go, nor the climactic role of death. Intensity and life and death jostle one another in a butterfly-triad. Then the fundamental honesty of this attitude gets betrayed in the attempt at a clinching close. To clinch the sonnet is to caricature the ripe fact. We cannot stand by unprotesting, but neither is it easy to be sure what is wrong since our dissatisfaction amounts to more than an unwillingness to hear death called pre-eminently intense. The last line of "Bright star!"

And so live ever—or else swoon to death

will not do either, and there life and death weigh equal; two comparably intense alternatives are being asserted. ("Swoon", committed to neither, partaking of both, is the line's frail truth-bearer: compare "ripe from hue-golden swoons" in *Endymion*.) In our bones we demand neither priorities nor alternatives but the flowering of the poet's singular vision; intensity itself; ripeness palpable, as it were growing up out of the wish. "Death is Life's high meed" sounds false because it is remote from the haven of intenseness Keats knows how to make us seek and find. The gap between falsehood and truth here is that between "Death intenser" and "or else" on the one hand, and the butterfly's "convuls'd" and the poet's "swoon" on the other. We find the second, the existential thing, stated thus to Fanny:

I have two luxuries to brood over in my walks, your loveliness and the hour of my death. O that I could have possession of them both in the same minute.[1]

Two luxuries but one possession. He lays bare in this love-letter a fact—perhaps an odd fact—of his own psychology, and also what I have distinguished as the affirmative impulse in his verse: positive ripening over against withering drearily. His "O that" cry to Fanny issues from a heart in which commonplace sensual longing and the ambition of genius are hopelessly entangled. Hence the delicacy of the escapist question, and of all judgment upon the wish-fulfilling characteristics of his poetry. The Indian Maid suggests to Endymion

We might embrace and die: voluptuous thought![2]

Not false, her indulgent proposal, but horribly unworked. A cruder rendering of the single possession of two luxuries contemplated

---

[1] *Letters*, vol. II, p. 133.   [2] IV, 759.

in the love-letter would be hard to find. Indeed it is just such lapses that expose the desperate human poverty of *Endymion*, and the doubtful status of this and every other "thought" in it. Thus our enquiry gets driven back again and again upon the same ground—but not in a purely destructive spirit since the mental and human failure continues to illuminate the non-human success. Round the central disaster of the Romance, round the willed climax in which the Indian has to become Cynthia, are clustered many small triumphs like the "short-liv'd foam" (even shorter lived than the butterfly) which "bursts gradual", and those "apples, wan with sweetness"[1] in which a man may read the *Autumn Ode* writ small. We simply have to follow instinct when it tells us "wan with sweetness" is Keatsian and fine, whereas "Death is Life's high meed", though it has been admired, is pretentious rubbish. What seems important, about great issues, is flatulent, a vain lending of *rotunditas* to the canny Scotch sentimentality of J. M. Barrie's "Death must be an awfully big adventure". What seems trivial, about apples, and is about apples, will dilate into *Autumn* and the *wan* "rich to die" sensuality of the *Nightingale*, where single possession of two luxuries comes true in the heart of the poem's crystal, and where the distinction between human and non-human ceases to mean anything worthwhile. For it does not help, I think, to talk about a humanising development from the foam-bubbles of *Endymion* to the grape of the *Ode on Melancholy* which a "strenuous tongue" might burst. Humanity enters the five odes on equal terms with "beaded bubbles" and "globed peonies" and plumped "hazel shells", and grapes for that matter, rather as morality has to take its chance, and of course does take it, in *Antony and Cleopatra*.

As always in great Keats, humanity stands on common ground with a wider life, and to apprehend his ripe forms is to learn something of this truth. A kind of depersonalisation presages the authentic and shared human theme. He has to forget the people, but not the passion, of "We might embrace and die: voluptuous thought!" for the end of the *Ode to Psyche* to become imaginable:

> *Yes, I will be thy priest, and build a fane*
> *In some untrodden region of my mind . . .*
> *And there shall be for thee all soft delight*
> *That shadowy thought can win,*
> *A bright torch, and a casement ope at night,*
> *To let the warm Love in!*

[1] IV, 683.

This is the butterfly's, and the kindred moth's, moment of moments. The Greek word Psyche means both "soul" and "moth" or "butterfly". Noting this fact, H. W. Garrod remarked in 1926:

Keats will be the priest of Psyche, priest and choir and shrine and grove; she shall have a fane "in some untrodden region of the mind", and shall enjoy

> all soft delight
> That shadowy thought can win.

There shall be a "bright torch" burning for her, and the casement shall be open to let her in at night. I do not find that any commentator has seized the significance of this symbolism. The open window and the lighted torch—they are to admit and attract the timorous *moth-goddess*, who symbolizes melancholic love.

For this is the deity which these inspired eyes have created. It is only when we come to the last lines with their

> bright torch, and a casement ope at night
> To let the warm love in

that we realize Keats has in fact identified the Psyche who is the soul (love's soul) with the Psyche which means *moth*.[1]

Which was a suggestive thought, but plainly vulnerable. The objections were neatly stated by Professor N. S. Bushnell three years later:

There are a number of reasons for rejecting this interpretation of the close of the *Ode to Psyche*. From the time of *The Golden Ass* to Mrs Henry Tighe the Psyche story has always, as far as I know, dealt with a maiden Psyche who slept in a palace, to whom the god Cupid came, silently and by night, first to fall himself a victim to her charms, and later as a lover and husband. The opened window and the flaming torch have served since time immemorial as a lure and a signal for the lover that walketh in darkness. Moreover Keats is promising specifically to build for Psyche a fane, a rosy sanctuary. . . . Can there be any doubt that "the warm Love" is Cupid himself? Even Professor Garrod's startling identification of the soul with love's soul can hardly render plausible his suggestion that Keats is promising to Psyche an open window and a lighted candle—traditionally fatal to moths!—by which she may attract herself in the guise of a moth to her own sanctuary.[2]

Nevertheless the rebuttal is less complete than may appear. Both Cupid and Psyche have wings—are pictured as the same species of winged creature—in the poem:

> Their arms embraced, and their pinions too;
> Their lips touched not,

[1] *Keats*, p. 95.   [2] *Modern Language Notes*, 1929.

so that when the impression of a butterfly-Psyche is strengthened in the third stanza

> (*thy lucent fans*
> *Fluttering among the faint Olympians,*
> *I see*)

she carries Cupid with her, to the satisfaction of Keats's unstraining, receptive reader. Moreover she carries him, the "winged boy" of that first embrace, from the daylight ("I see") to the night and flaming torch of the next, which is the final stanza. This new darkness changes butterfly into moth, and advances the whole towards consummation; maturing love explicitly but whispering death in our ear as it does so: earnest to prove the oxymoron which has been drifting unsupported in this stanza, the

> *branched thoughts, new grown with pleasant pain,*

and to bring the poem alongside its near neighbour among the odes of April and May, *Melancholy*, where the poet urges

> *Make not your rosary of yew-berries,*
> *Nor let the beetle, nor the death-moth be*
> *Your mournful Psyche. . . .*

Psyche's "pleasant pain" ushers in a *Liebestod* where the burning torch comes through to us, as no doubt it did to Garrod, in the shape of an inspiration not easy to pin down; and where Bushnell's parenthesis "traditionally fatal to moths!", aimed at the other scholar, inadvertently hits the ode's most imaginative effect of all. Garrod was wrong to confine "the warm Love" to Psyche, and Bushnell likewise to Cupid. It takes two to make Love, and there is no cause to think of either winged creature as particularly inside, or outside, the "fane" which Keats says he will build "in some untrodden region of my mind". Love itself, the poetic butterfly-moth idea, is drawn towards the torch.[1] Thus the entry of "mind" and "thought"—the harvest of "a working brain"—into Keats's universe becomes not merely undestroying but beautiful and true. Thus he finds his single possession of two luxuries. The ode articulates "this wide quietness" of his erotic daydreaming, and then ripens it; brings on the night of love and death; so that when the conclusion crowds inward upon the "sanctuary" which lies, he says, "in the midst" of his feigned mindscape, we find that the

---

[1] Compare the odd phrase "at the kiss / Of Psyche given by Love" by *Otho the Great* (V, v). The focal kiss holds the kissing pair together.

"Yes, I will be thy priest, and build a fane" promised at the opening of the final stanza has been performed.

The bowers, grots, dells, nests of his early work are the unintense forerunners of *Psyche's* sanctuary, all meaning well but wanting art. He dreams them without building them. *Endymion* most obviously provides no "fane", no common consummative ground for butterfly and human theme to meet on. There, every reader admires the creature—as he admires the "wan" ripe apple—and scorns the story, in his heart. Each aspect of *Endymion's* failure is touched by this thought, but since the present contrast is with the *Ode to Psyche*, it falls to the butterfly to add a certain sharpness and even a comic twist to our reaction: the "pent up" crocuslike butterfly of "the fresh budding year"[1] that takes no part in anything the poem intends, indeed whose irrelevancy is a precondition of its merit. And likewise the infelt picture:

> his eyelids
> *Widened a little, as when Zephyr bids*
> *A little breeze to creep between the fans*
> *Of careless butterflies:*[2]

where the creeping feel between the wings insists on being itself alone. In fact there are signs that Keats attempted to mend the breach between the objects his imagination gave him and the tale he had set himself to tell; for at the end of the Romance his hero brings about a shotgun wedding of creature and theme by declaring "I have been a butterfly"[3] and foreseeing his own death with the going down of today's sun. Talking thus he anticipates the "pleasant pain" oxymoron of *Psyche*,

> *in sort of deathful glee*
> *Laughing at the clear stream and setting sun,*[4]

only to be driven into the false haven of the Indian's metamorphosis: *Endymion* has a mere fifty lines to go.

The idea of a butterfly-hero living and dying intensely with the summer day is given no chance. How could it, *Endymion* being what it must be? And so "king of the butterflies"[5] joins the crowd of rootless fancies that get uttered.

Keats's desire to humanise his vision of intensity has repercussions up and down his work, not always easy to recognise for what they are. The scribbled verse-letter to John Reynolds contrasts

[1] I, 258.   [2] I, 762.   [3] IV, 937.
[4] IV, 945.   [5] IV, 952.

"things all disjointed" with things effectively imagined; then pokes its thumb towards the meaning of effective:

> *But flowers bursting out with lusty pride;*
> *And Young Aeolian harps personified,*
> *Some, Titian colours touch'd into real life.*

Very odd those three lines must appear to anyone unfamiliar with magic ripening in Keats, and with his talk of pictured objects swelling into reality. This is shorthand verging on hieroglyph, and needs interpreting. "Personified" is a singularly opaque attempt at the usual more-real-than-reality effect. But the picture of the sacrifice which follows immediately and anticipates the *Grecian Urn* requires no gloss, for here Keats is practising what he has just so obscurely preached; and the key to his practice, the agent of surprise accessible to his reader, is the power to drown visuality in stasis:

> *The sacrifice goes on; the pontiff knife*
> *Gleams in the sun, the milk-white heifer lows,*
> *The pipes go shrilly, the libation flows:*
> *A white sail shews above the green-head cliff*
> *Moves round the point, and throws her anchor stiff.*

About "stiff" it might be said, cynically, that he is writing at speed—which is obvious—and has grabbed any old rhyme for "cliff"; or a grammarian might suggest that the epithet has been transferred to anchor from anchor-chain. Both points are worth considering. Keats's hard-driven rhymes have a way of blurting important truths, as we know already, and the results of the epithet's transference are far-reaching. The effect of "throws her anchor stiff" is to destroy succession in time; we instantaneously, and no matter if unconsciously, assimilate the process of casting anchor to the distant sight, in itself very "like a picture", of the ship riding at anchor with the chain standing away taut, "stiff", from her stem. The small stroke by which Keats attributes the throwing to the ship herself helps to secure this running together of the final held picture and the preliminary strenuous activity. He thus heaps up sheer gratulation upon his next line:

> *The Mariners join hymn with those on land.*

They, we, the picture are home. The true haven indeed.

And like *Psyche's* haven with its torch that draws the moth to love and death, the one projected in the Reynolds couplets has an inexplicit drama at its heart. The satisfaction of arrival is only formally separable from the tension of "throws her anchor stiff". That is why the comfort of the whole stands in the grip of an entirely Keatsian stress, like the butterfly

> *convuls'd as though it smarted*
> *With over pleasure*

whose sensational poise at the height of, and between, pleasure and pain is particularly nice.

Or the painful end of the seesaw may descend sharply, leaving us with the dragon's tail in the stanza of the *Ode on Melancholy* which he wisely suppressed.

> *Though you should build a bark of dead men's bones,*
> *And rear a phantom gibbet for a mast,*
> *Stitch creeds together for a sail, with groans*
> *To fill it out, blood-stained and aghast;*
> *Although your rudder be a dragon's tail*
> *Long sever'd yet still hard with agony,*
> *Your cordage large uprootings from the skull*
> *Of bald Medusa, certes you would fail*
> *To find the Melancholy—whether she*
> *Dreameth in any isle of Lethe dull.*[1]

That severed tail starts up, then attracts the "large uprootings" painfully to itself, because it is not like the stuff round it; and when one asks why not, one must look to Keats's true imagining of all such "convulse" situations for the answer. The butterfly will do. Or the "natural sculpture" of *Hyperion* and *The Fall*, wherever its wrung and wrought and tortured attitudes bear the mark of *Melancholy's* banished dragon-tail.

The stasis of picture-making, I said, is a bit like the photographer's "Hold it!" Or Van Gogh's practice of spilling a glass of milk over a drawing to "fix" it into "a peculiar saturated black".[2] Visual analogies break down, though, as soon as the business of holding and fixing is gone into. We have had this happen repeatedly. The longer we live with a picture like

> *the Naiad 'mid her reeds*
> *Press'd her cold finger closer to her lips*

the less visual it becomes, and the more importunate the combination of pressure and temperature within it: the tiny stressful drama and the feel. Because they do combine, the concepts of snailhorn and stasis make no final sense wielded separately; and out of their

---

[1] *Poetical Works*, p. 503.   [2] *Complete Letters* (1958), vol. I, p. 337.

combination comes intensity: long, languid, drowsy—or agonised. Keats coupled the fixing of his pictures with their infeeling by means of Negative Capability, his home-made and ultimate criterion. It gets put to the test at every turn, most decisively in his struggle to be intense—"the excellence of every art is its intensity", he says, carrying conviction for his own art at least. And when he compresses his dream of intensity into three lines for John Reynolds, into bursting flowers, personified harps, Titian colours touched into reality, I remark that the gap between these gestures and the achieved poetry of intensity is precisely that between telling a dream and inhabiting it negative-capably. Of course he can oblige Reynolds without getting inside his intense proposals, but it is also true that the couplets cannot help trying; the ship throwing her "anchor stiff" does not just point towards the spatial imagination's world of infelt stress and climax; it begins very tentatively to body forth what the letter-writer is idly propounding. The poet never enjoys a complete holiday.

Negative capability becomes our own criterion too whenever, reading Keats, we conclude that to dream intensely is not enough; that the dream must house the dreamer. Such clearcut terms match the second Hyperion fragment, *The Fall*, which brings an uncreative sophistication to bear on the problem by placing its narrative inside the head of the prophetess. Thus it seeks to prearrange intensity, and is partially rebuffed. At the other extreme lies the callow verse of 1817, busy loading its dreamed-up objects with soft, tender *richesse*, and its dreaming subjects with "pleasant smotherings" of every sensual joy. Poles apart from the Hyperions in accomplishment, the juvenile book is already fully committed to intensity, and its policy is one of saturation. The simple-minded hope is to bribe or pre-empt, rather than foreordain, the intense outcome; but 1817's actual legacy—our hazy recollection—adds up to little more than a world of melting fruits confronting a second world of greedy devourers. Now in great Keats fruit and feeder meet in the ample haven which his ripeness metaphor affords: in the "gathering" consummation of *Autumn*, the strenuous tongue and burst grape of *Melancholy*, the perfecting torch blazing within the built fane of *Psyche*, the *Nightingale's* "embalmed darkness". But in 1817, a straitened version of his master-metaphor matches the linguistic and thematic narrowness. Every time the poet tells us how ripe his fruit is grown, he prevents himself from meaning more than that. And each description of full-stretch tiptoe sensation in the feeder endorses Arnold's merely sensual judgment. His purpose in reaching out towards sex, drink, trance, swoon, dream itself, is to shepherd the dreaming subject into a held climax of feel—like the "hung swollen" of the high tide. That accounts for the ghostly metasexual orgasm hovering over so much early Keats. The "bursts gradual" of the bubbles becomes the "convulse" of the dreaming man, and the human poverties of such intensities is then seen to underlie our greater satisfaction with his butterflies than his people.

Endymion grows artful, far beyond 1817, in its lavishing of intense devices. Nevertheless the Romance remains stuck at the stage of trickery and poeticising *Wortkünstelei*; it discovers many ingenious ways of depicting people "ripe to taste" this or that—

> *O he had swoon'd*
> *Drunken from Pleasure's nipple—*[1]

but none of maturing the allegory they are all involved in.

Hyperion pursues a different course, equally resolute upon intensity and ripeness, also defeated by its own kind of baneful sophistication. At the moment when Keats breaks off in mid-sentence Apollo is being transformed into a god before our eyes. This becomes quite explicitly a ripe manoeuvre in the light of *Hyperion's* entanglement, as to its first promptings, with the actual writing of *Endymion*. In the earlier poem, Apollo suddenly emerges from a mob of Endymionic shepherds:

> *next, well trimm'd,*
> *A crowd of shepherds with as sunburnt looks*
> *As may be read of in Arcadian books;*
> *Such as sat listening round Apollo's pipe,*
> *When the great deity, for earth too ripe,*
> *Let his divinity o'er-flowing die*
> *In music. . . .*[2]

He is the Apollo of *Hyperion*, reminding us again that Keats had his second Epic in mind long before he put pen to paper. At least he had already conceived a figure too ripe for earth, and so ripe for heaven, so to be deified.[3] *Endymion* has scarcely begun, and a two-and-a-half year fascination with heroic ripeness stretches ahead. The "too ripe for earth" idea is the buried *raison d'être* of all those magical and extended ripenings we have noted and quoted, to smile at or admire. It slowly comes to the surface towards

---

[1] II, 868.   [2] I, 138.

[3] A strange deification (as several people have observed) since Apollo is some kind of god already. All the more reason not to bother about religion as such.

Endymion's close. And with it, the very tone of *Hyperion* grows audible:

> He did not stir
> His eyes from the dead leaves, or one small pulse
> Of joy he might have felt.[1]

That heaviness and sad finished feel. Endymion swears

> By old Saturnus' forelock, by his head
> Shook with eternal palsy,[2]

and the name sounds almost due, as does the advance notice of Saturn's "palsied" state in *Hyperion*.[3] Indeed the poet affronts our sensibilities by warning Endymion,

> Thy lute-voic'd brother will I sing ere long,[4]

because we possess other more imaginative means of observing Apollo and his world draw near.

Hyperion begins to dominate *Endymion* when all side-issues have fallen away and left the "too ripe" preoccupation naked. In the earlier epic confusion reigns, as we saw; the transforming of the Indian into Cynthia is forced against the natural Keatsian grain of swelling into reality. Here *Hyperion* shows itself clear-sighted. The dualistic pretence is abandoned, and the climax of *Endymion* is done again with Apollo remaining Apollo—only more so, more intense, a god and perfectly real. He consummates the actual in his own person.

So *Hyperion* provides the classic illustration of the ripe ideal. And by breaking down in the throes of Apollo's "fierce convulse" it shows Keats asking intensity to bear a burden which was never suited to that pair of shoulders. Instead of a haven to repose in, the ripeness metaphor tenders a significance to be scrutinised, which is intolerable. The way *Hyperion* has been disposed, we are bound to ask what the deification of Apollo portends; and in asking this we awaken the old anxieties about meaning in Keats in their acutest form. The whole poem looks to Apollo's swelling into reality as to its own truth, with the familiar result that the theme of dying "into life" remains bodiless while the described process compels a mere and therefore a ludicrous physical solicitude:

> so young Apollo anguish'd:
> His very hair, his golden tresses famed
> Kept undulation round his eager neck.

---

[1] IV, 780. [2] IV, 956.
[3] The dispersed "palsied tongue" at *Hyperion*, I, 93. [4] IV, 774.

Our imagination opens up a gap between these goings on and the treasured, unspeakable dream of truth; and all is lost. Most particularly, we ask the deathly question, what happens on the other side of ripeness? The genius of end-stopped feel knows no such curiosity. The intense haven, the spatial fancy's capacious solipsism, enfolds no such abstract moment. Keats had nothing to say about the other side of ripeness, and no stomach to continue his poem once he had entertained a thought of it. So he looked back when he had written

> *Apollo shreikd and lo he was the God!*
> *And godlike*

and drew his pen through the last six words. Then tried again with

> *and lo! from all his limbs*
> *Celestial*

and stopped once more, this time for good.

V: THE LABYRINTHIAN PATH

1 Space, Time and the Odes

THERE is a gloomy and unvital sense in which both the
Hyperion Fragments may be called completed poems.
Hyperion makes Adam's dream come true by deifying Apollo;
The Fall houses the dreamer by thrusting him inside that miniature
theatre of feel, Moneta's "globed brain". The price of these
stratagems is an art which does not come as naturally as the leaves
to a tree.

The astronomer back in 1817, from the Chapman's Homer
sonnet—

> *Then felt I like some watcher of the skies*
> *When a new planet swims into his ken—*

already shows how realising the dream and housing the dreamer
can appear with the certainty of green leaves in Keats's poetry.
This points his mature way, as we acknowledged when the talka-
tive "I" surprised us by dropping out and we knew we had
arrived. The end of such pure stasis as the watcher, and such pure
snailhorn as the swimming, is one of those "many havens of
intenseness" he mentioned to Haydon.

Haven is his word, and the last word. We never escape from
spatial imagining. Nor do we want to (since here is his strength
and our delight) until the struggle to be honest about the mentality
of his writing begins. And then each idea in turn falls, as soon as
we wield it, under the suspicion of serving not the poetry but our
wish to be articulate.

We pick our way between the sensualities of the peach-sucking,
which are banal, and the talk about death being life's high meed,
which is bogus. Always the goal is his mastery of infelt space, whatever the ostensible theme. Death is one example, for to have no
use for the "high meed" talk must be held consistent with believing
that an aside like

> *Though young Lorenzo in warm Indian clove*
> *Was not embalm'd*

brings its own oblique comprehension and reveals a poet at work.
The direct feel of death has a tucked-away back door through
which his own kind of mentality enters.

The path which mind follows in Keats is always labyrinthian, as the *Nightingale Ode* shows when death reappears grandly there. What holds us in the declaration

> *I have been half in love with easeful Death*

has in poetic fact been emerging and defining itself, swelling into reality, in the dark foetal safety and warmth and utter enclosure of the stanzas before and their "winding mossy ways".

> *The murmurous haunt of flies on summer eves*

is the lesson Tennyson could learn. And perhaps it needs saying that some favourite turns of the poem like

> *haply the Queen-Moon is on her throne,*
> *Cluster'd around by all her starry Fays*

are very inferior, at least when they are expected to fend for themselves. The consistency, simple yet unteachable, that issues out into the ode's flowers "cover'd up in leaves" characterises the masterpiece. About this hushed and done with and yet unborn feel of death, this end of all end-stopping, we are making an aesthetic as well as a Freudian observation; for

> *I cannot see what flowers are at my feet*

initiates a surprise which we may have ceased to be aware of in the domesticated classic, but respond to all the same. This privation of sight seems to anticipate complaint and constriction; instead, it blossoms into the keenest sensual joy:

> *But, in the embalmed darkness, guess each sweet*

and leaves us securely possessed of the poet's "I have been half in love with easeful Death". Assenting, we each appropriate the ripeness metaphor (and will go on, alas, to taste "forlorn"). There is more to admire here than in the little aside about Lorenzo, but how much more is there to say? The mental burden of Keats's "half in love" condition, its human interest, still falls from the ode like an uncovenanted mercy. Again too, as with the astronomer, the "I" drops out in an access of impersonal, revelatory passion, and the intense haven of art lies open.

All this needs and uses space. Without objects in space, no embalming. Space's exploitation reveals the same fierce creative hunger here as when

> *Thoea arose,*
> *And stretch'd her white arm through the hollow dark*

in *The Fall*, though the end of Keats's winding and twisting and burrowing and covering up in *The Nightingale* is entirely different. But then space differs in its sameness through all the odes; the principle of organisation persists, the deployment is as various as the poems. So we stand stock still as we travel from *The Nightingale's* forest of darkness to the scene pictured on *The Grecian Urn* to the stubble-fields of *Autumn*: from dream to art to recalled actuality. And the close neighbourhood in separation between *Psyche* and *Melancholy* which we noted before with the death-moth, we encounter again in terms of the root fact that these are the two odes of consciousness, one treating "the warm Love" and the other "the melancholy fit"; and in both of them consciousness is spatialised into a landscape of the head. It is rendered into mental stuff—what Keats calls "branched thoughts" that "shall murmur in the wind"—in a way which we distinguish instantly from the dream-space, art-space and actual space of the other odes. *Psyche* speaks straightforwardly of its mind-space, while *Melancholy* presents without comment a cloud and some spring flowers and a green hill which are no less recognisably the creatures "of a working brain". As in *Psyche*, we are witnessing a spatial drama of consciousness. And just as *Psyche* moves inward upon the mindscape's central "sanctuary", so this ode discovers the melancholy truth it is seeking in the "temple" of the last stanza with a "sovran shrine" inside. This correspondence cannot be undercut, since space forms the imaginative substance of both odes; and neither can the separation of the mind-space of these two from the mutually independent spatial selves of the other three.

The spatial imagination was dormant, or feebly stirring, as far back as *Sleep and Poetry* when he spoke of his immediate task as an exploration of Flora and Pan's "realm". This realm, the "little space"[1] of poetry, marks the beginning of a development which

---

[1] "I stood tiptoe" answers its couplet

> What first inspired a bard of old to sing
> Narcissus pining o'er the untainted spring? (163)

with

> In some delicious ramble, he had found
> A little space, with boughs all woven round. . . .

And from the start he likes spatialising the passage of time in such images as "The gradual sand that through an hour-glass runs" ("After dark vapours . . . "). In the early *To Some Ladies*, the line "To possess but a sand in the hour of leisure" looks wrong. The autograph has, among other signs of haste, no "d" to its "sand". I propose: "To possess but a sand in the hourglass of leisure".

was crammed into four of five years. It is of course the story of the pictures occupying Keatsian space, in their infeeling, their stasis, their aspiration towards ripeness and an explicit maplike status. Ripeness is a kind of simultaneity; and magic ripening, that rather pathetic device, has its counterpart in the "all together" idea of the lyric "Ever let the Fancy roam":

> *Fancy, high-commission'd:—send her!*
> *She has vassals to attend her:*
> *She will bring, in spite of frost,*
> *Beauties that the earth hath lost;*
> *She will bring thee, all together,*
> *All delights of summer weather;*
> *All the buds and bells of May,*
> *From dewy sward or thorny spray*
> *All the heaped Autumn's wealth,*
> *With a still, mysterious stealth:*
> *She will mix these pleasures up*
> *Like three fit wines in a cup,*
> *And thou shalt quaff it:—thou shalt hear*
> *Distant harvest-carols clear;*
> *Rustle of the reaped corn;*
> *Sweet birds antheming the morn:*
> *And, in the same moment—hark!*
> *'Tis the early April lark,*
> *Or the rooks with busy caw,*
> *Foraging for sticks and straw.*
> *Thou shalt, at one glance, behold*
> *The daisy and the marigold. . . .*

Thus his deep-toned "Fancy" crops up again, and the trotting verse must not obscure the seriousness of magic simultaneity; he is handling an earnest preoccupation lightly. Its occurrence in Cynthia's wedding-hymn near the end of *Endymion* is lyrical once more, but solemn; and the call for "every flower and leaf of every clime"[1] is buttressed, obscurely it must be admitted, by the medley of stellar constellations which follows immediately. These are clustered untidily round Autumn and Spring[2]—corresponding to the opposed seasons which are brought together in "Ever let the Fancy roam".

[1] IV, 579-610.
[2] The constellations are: Aquarius, Andromeda, Perseus, the Twins, the Lion (why does Keats say "the planet Lion"?), the Bear, the Centaur. The Centaur is a southern hemisphere constellation but a few of its northernmost stars may be visible due south in April. The Bear, while always visible, appears due south in March. So these belong with the Twins and the Lion in the Spring group, whereas the others could all be called Autumn stars.

Endymion's "every flower and leaf of every clime" is a reworking of

> *every leaf and every flower*
> *Pearled with the self-same shower*

which the feigning Fancy treats. That lyric appears in a journal letter at the very beginning of 1819.[1] How much of *The Fall* was then on paper, how much in Keats's head, how much dreamed of, we can't know. Unquestionably the first lines of the narrative pick up the thread of magic simultaneity once again:

> *Methought I stood where trees of every clime,*
> *Palm, myrtle, oak, and sycamore, and beech,*
> *With Plantane, and spice blossoms, made a screen. . . .*

They repeat *Endymion's* "every clime" and turn again to Fancy's wishful dream of "all together". It becomes obvious in the large heroic context of *The Fall* that Keats's ripe and his simultaneous ambitions are ultimately one, both ambitions meeting in his perfecting instinct. The odes confirm this truth, and sharpen it to a fine point.

So far all our talk has been of space, while the odes themselves are emphatically to do with time. But how is the distinction of these poems related to their treatment of time? People worry away at the nightingale which was "not born for death" as if the relationship were, however hard to understand, direct; as if Keats were saying something immediately temporal about time.

Well, what about the *passing* night and the *mortal* poet and the *undying* bird? On one side of them is the womblike, tomblike enclosure of "embalmed darkness" where to "guess" blind is to perfect the life of sensation, a ripe darkness, a truth which "death is life's high meed" may have intended but which the "violets cover'd up in leaves" enact and the "musk-rose, full of dewy wine" indulges; and on the other, the stasis of Ruth held for ever standing in the corn. But also, on the one side, the musk-rose is unripe ("coming") and the violets are over ("fading"); while on the other Ruth's corn begets, quasi-magically, the rhyme "forlorn", which then produces its own echo for the last stanza. These opposed presences, the ripe and the withering, make up the poetic substance of man and bird and passing night.

The poet wants to join the nightingale, this is his wishful dream. He reaches out in desire ("And with thee fade"), then in assertion ("for I will fly to thee"), and finally in achievement ("Already with thee!"). Nevertheless their union is haunted by the transience

---

[1] *Letters*, vol. II, p. 21.

of "this passing night", and by soft yet climactic death in whose arms it is *perhaps* safe (hence "half in love"); but it cannot be sustained otherwise, as the repeated "forlorn" is about to show. "Forlorn" turns the song "plaintive" for the listening man, it does not touch the bird. The bird is "immortal".

For the nightingale enjoys an estrangement from death which the poem denies to human beings. What Keats has to say about such immortality and such transience is his own, and belongs to the poem's greatness, because time has been subsumed under space's rule, or (preferring geometry to logic), it has been projected upon the plane of infelt space.

The darkness of the poem's dream-space, of the forest where the snailhorn guesses each sweet, is the house built for the mortal poet. The nightingale survives the ruin of the house because she lives in the forest anyhow, naturally, timelessly, Her immortality is her perfect yet living containment within the mid-May of the ode, which is why "the voice I hear" and "this passing night" are centrally juxtaposed. Her song of summer expresses her embalmed and (in the special Keatsian sense) mindless feel. She is like the trees of the "drear-nighted December" lyric which, unlike the men of the same poem, do not have their good times spoilt by anticipation of bad, nor in bad times do they torment themselves with memories of "their green felicity". The idiosyncratic "too" of "too happy, happy tree" reappears with the poet who finds himself, momentarily, "too happy" in the bird's happiness; and beneath the word lies the truly imagined theme of sensation and poisoning mind. Unlike the poet, the nightingale is invulnerably wrapped within the summer night which brought them together. She was "not born for death" but he was. He needs his house to dream in, and his house is at once the work of true imagination and feigning fancy.

Keats shows his hand more openly in *The Grecian Urn* where the wishful "for ever" dream is crucified upon the spatial fact: on the unliving and inexorable dispositions, that is, of the urn's surface. This is the poem of art-space, and its subject is poetry and life. It tells the story of ripeness and simultaneity—the intense outcome—being paid for by the "cold" feel of the "pastoral". Its address to the urn, the object,

> *Sylvan historian, who canst thus express*
> *A flowery tale more sweetly than our rhyme*

is one of Keats's iceberg statements; the visible tip airs the vague and questionable commonplace that painting is, or can be, more eloquent than poetry; the rest, the hidden seven-eighths, is immersed in his struggle with his chosen medium. Language is a discursive symbolism and takes time. Painting is not and does not. The crux of "canst thus express" is to be solved by space: by Keats's ambition of simultaneity and therefore of ripeness. He wants to *write* a Grecian Urn.

This he sets about doing at once, the poem's first four words, "Thou still unravish'd bride", tugging sharply at the temporal continuum along which they are strung. Obviously—I dare say obviously—he is not thinking about the interval between a marriage's celebration and its consummation; his words are after the ripe and spatial solution—there she was—of Adam's dream; they are intended to say what the urn is; and we, reading, are meant to rub our eyes and find "it truth". Hereafter every linguistic deed ventured by the ode eggs us on to wonder if Adam's "it" is sayable. The little space-drama of "still unravish'd bride" is only a beginning. Starting from this, we come to accept that the time-words which litter the *Grecian Urn* only take on life and sense through a process of derivation from space. "Sylvan historian", for example, is a courtesy title. History is one thing after another, the urn declares things all together in a picture. But the poet's hopes rest on our final glad adopting of the courtesy; for to echo "historian" with all our heart would demonstrate the unqualified triumph of his poem. He is trying, as I say, to write the urn, he is the linguistic picture-maker showing forth his subject.

And so,

> *For ever warm and still to be enjoy'd*

verbalises the urn's painted surface in the spirit of that "still unravish'd bride" which was his first essay at the thing itself. This consonance reminds us that nowhere, except in the dream-consummation of *St. Agnes*, does Keats's mature verse place so heavy a burden on sex.[1] Sex sustains the private metaphysic of intenseness in both poems. *St. Agnes* inclines towards the perfection that lies within the haven of all ripe savouring

> *(like a throbbing star*
> *Seen mid the sapphire heaven's deep repose*
> *Into her dream he melted, as the rose*
> *Blendeth its odour with the violet)*

---

[1] The consonance also provides one ground for rejecting "still [i.e. unmoving], unravish'd" which is the unsupported reading of the journal *Annals of the Fine Arts* where the poem first saw the light of print, in January 1820. The 1820 volume has "still unravish'd". So have all four transcripts. No autograph survives.

whereas the *Urn*, striving to realise the distended bubble, the full-blown flower, in evident space, is supremely a poem of stasis and "natural sculpture".[1] Both these emphases are Keatsian, and both poems run into trouble on account of sex. Their sex drains conviction from other imaginings in them—a much less serious matter in *St. Agnes* which is erotic through and through, and in which many other sensualities like food and chill solitary sleep are sex-tinctured. But the *Urn* claims to tell a much larger truth about life "on earth" and the things we "need to know" there.

That boast, as we turn the completed urn-poem round in our hands, makes it the most ambitious and the least successful of the five major odes. It deserves its place with the others because it expresses the ripeness / withering polarity with a brilliant pathos which is its own and which places it next to the *Nightingale* in the series. "Historian" is a reminder that the feigning Fancy which comes out into the open in *Psyche*, and perhaps in the *Nightingale*, is at work within all the odes, producing the shrine and other mind-scape features of *Melancholy*, and the unactual figure in *Autumn's* middle stanza. The need to challenge a low fictive estimate of feigning is plain in all these, and again in the *Urn* where what is most vigorously imagined is the central pretence of spatialised history—and thus of immortality. The poet questions the historian,

> *What men or gods are these? What maidens loth?*
> *What mad pursuit? What struggle to escape?*
> *What pipes and timbrels? What wild ecstasy?*

and finds his answer:

> *Bold Lover, never, never canst thou kiss,*
> *Though winning near the goal—yet, do not grieve;*
> *She cannot fade, though thou hast not thy bliss,*
> *For ever wilt thou love, and she be fair!*

The large confidence of his temporal "never" and "ever" arises, it might be thought oddly, from their utter dependence on the picture. If we think of them as free, like the student who pores over these lines in the hope of extracting some immediate temporal significance which he can make available to common sense, or to science, or philosophy, we shall be faced with the self-imposed task of evading nonsensical conclusions. But if we make no attempt to resist their bondage, then we allow Keats to endow them with the very special certitude of his *Urn's* art-space—just as the bird's

---

[1] Of course both poems contain a muted statement of the opposite stress; *St. Agnes* has an underthought to "deep repose" and the *Grecian Urn* to the feel caught in stasis and waiting "to be enjoyed".

immortality grew out of the "embalmed darkness" of the *Nightingale's* dream-space. The difference between any old whimsical hyperbole and what we have here resides in the picture-making and the feel: in Keats's genius, naturally. The *Grecian Urn* is his purest exercise in the held animation of stasis, the *Nightingale* his most eventful snailhorn exploration. In both odes the language of time is as true as the imagination's grasp of ripe fulfilment and of the feel of not to feel.

That is very true. But the stubborn relativism of the "what is more true than what?" question remains. Both odes confront ripeness with the thing I have called withering; the *Nightingale's* "forlorn" becomes the "desolate" attaching to the little town in the *Urn's* fourth stanza. A hand, a sudden shadow over the heart in the bereft personal feel ("my sole self") and then in the sadness, so hauntingly objective, of the infelt picture of silent streets.

Here the two poems part company. The *Nightingale* closes on the hostility of Keatsian opposites. "What the Imagination seizes as beauty must be truth—whether it existed before or not." But also, "The fancy cannot cheat so well / As she is fam'd [? feign'd] to do". The *Grecian Urn* attempts to decide. Therein its singular ambition. Singularly huge both in its confirming of "What the Imagination seizes . . ." by the dogmatic "Beauty is truth, truth beauty" of the final stanza, and in the superficially modest "on earth" demarcation that goes with it.

"On earth" reaches back to the music of the second stanza, and particularly to the distinction drawn there between "the sensual ear" and "the spirit":

> *Heard melodies are sweet, but those unheard*
> *Are sweeter; therefore, ye soft pipes, play on;*
> *Not to the sensual ear, but, more endear'd,*
> *Pipe to the spirit ditties of no tone:*

where the "unheard" music addressed to the spirit is an abstraction, like Endymion's transcendental quest and the two Hyperion attempts which Keats repeatedly calls abstract in his letters. Love addressed to the spirit would be abstract too, of course, and some equivalent to "unheard" would have to be found for it; but the higher love of the *Urn*, although "all breathing human passion far above", is nevertheless "warm", "panting" and "young". Or rather, it becomes these things. The wishful dream is progressive. Just as Keats works his way into the "embalmed darkness" of the *Nightingale's* dream-forest, so his convinced passion mounts from the *Urn's* judicious second stanza ("never canst thou kiss, /

Though winning near the goal") to the intensifications of the third. In being thus perfected his love remains the thing we know, the same only more so, only held "for ever" within the *Urn's* art-space, a ripeness which has no other side to it, no beyond and therefore no experience of "a burning forehead, and a parching tongue". The warmth and the panting of the *Urn's* surface-love cannot be received as light, still less polite, fictions, but they have only dauntless ardour of imagination to sustain them, and when the break comes at "desolate" and "Cold Pastoral!" it hurts in the way Caliban was hurt, and we cry to dream again.

The supervening coldness answers and opposes, it does not refute, the warmth, in a pattern of hostile antiphon which puts the *Grecian Urn* alongside the *Nightingale*. On the other hand the coldness does not engage with "the spirit" at all; the superiority of "unheard" music remains something asserted and putative, involuntarily defining the area of pretentious failure in the finished poem. By separating the music from his snailhorn-listening to it (in starkest possible contrast to his hearing of the nightingale) Keats grinds his beautiful urn-poem between an upper spiritual millstone and a lower sensual one. During this ordeal suffered by the genius of feel, his talk about time and immortality becomes tainted with stupid bombast, and the sexual imagery begins to read intolerably raw. In retrospect "unravish'd" will not do,[1] but this is a retrospect created by his evoking of meanings which are not his to manage. Likewise the "for ever" reiterations grow uncomfortable because of their helpless freedom; they have been unhooked by "the spirit" from the art-space which determines the poem's tight logic, its beauty and truth. The *Urn* is the aesthetic ode of the series, the one about art. Its form is antiphonal, like the *Nightingale's*, but instead of opposing ripe immortal song by forlorn mortal selfhood it counters warm immortal love with the desolation of aesthetic experience. At the words

> *Who are these coming to the sacrifice?*

the poet is still scrutinising the urn. In the next line,

> *To what green altar, O mysterious priest,*
> *Lead'st thou that heifer. . . ?*

[1] The "bride" now enters the world of the plaintiff in a libel action (*Youssoupoff v. MGM*, 1934) who was awarded a hundred thousand pounds damages on account of a film which suggested that she had been raped by Rasputin. Had the court thought in terms of a human being suffering an outrage, rather than of damaged goods, it probably would not have persuaded itself that a libel had been committed, and in that case the plaintiff would have lost her action altogether.

his attention is shifting and expanding to embrace the scene beyond. This great moment belongs utterly to the spatial imagination. It signals the poeticising of art-space, the transition from urn to urn-poem; for the "green altar" and what follows are not on the urn, they are only in the words. They must survive the envisageable end of this and all urns,[1] and entering the fancy of our race they are "for evermore"—but within the frame "thy streets for evermore / Will silent be". When Keats exclaims "Pastoral!" he re-affirms in sober triumph the claim made by "historian" in stanza One. He has written a Grecian Urn. "Cold Pastoral!", however, completes the picture, invading Adam's dream of love with a serene unhumanity which is art's silent presence with us and its eternal cold. The aestheticism of this ode is very keenly personal. We are led to understand—what is true for all—that the deepest and most powerful art cannot make the world young again and warm, but only known. And then we see what is a special truth for Keats: that the motive of a great creative gift may be rarely, perhaps uniquely sensual, and experienced from within as sensual, and yet the poem is no place to embrace in, no better a place than Marvell's grave. To house the dream must involve shrouding the corpse of the dreaming poet's feel; and so questions like "What wild ecstasy?", exhortations like "yet, do not grieve", invest the whole with a tragic playfulness. The *Grecian Urn* shows us art disporting with itself, and with the man its maker. Keats knew well that the first function of ancient urns was to preserve the ashes of the dead.[2]

The spatial "for ever" of the *Autumn Ode* is a great deal less vaunting and formidable, to the immediate perception, than the *Grecian Urn's*. Now the wishful dream rests with the busy trusting bees who work on persuaded "warm days will never cease". The reader knows the bees are wrong, so does not worry or, perhaps, sufficiently admire their Vergilian perseverence, and the poetic reason in their hearts. The bees live within the scene Keats saw-and-imagined when he left his lodgings in Winchester one fine Sunday and walked in the fields outside the suburbless city. This was 19 September, 1819. Two days later he wrote to John Reynolds.

How beautiful the season is now—How fine the air. A temperate sharpness about it. Really, without joking, chaste weather—Dian skies—I

---

[1] Hence, amid the general shipwreck of the ode's conclusion, the impertinent and slightly grovelling taste left by "Thou shalt remain . . . a friend to man". The sad and fine fourth stanza is partly undone.

[2] This particular urn falls, in time, between *Endymion's* "urn of tears" (III, 432) and the "dusty urns" of *Lamia* (II, 94).

never lik'd stubble fields so much as now—Aye better than the chilly green of the spring. Somehow a stubble plain looks warm—in the same way that some pictures look warm—this struck me so much in my Sunday's walk that I composed upon it.[1]

Without those stubble-fields there would have been no ode *To Autumn*. His pleasure in them is as simple and direct, and appealing, as anything in the 1817 volume. They stretch. How like the real thing, we say, turning to the poem and experiencing their un-alloyed extension:

> *While barred clouds bloom the soft-dying day,*
> *And touch the stubble-plains. . . .*

This is the actual space which constitutes the *Autumn Ode's* special province. It is the September scene, the Hampshire scene. It documents the Sunday walk. And then we read the ode again and savour the "touch" and "bloom" and so on, and the thought comes quietly to the mind's gateway: and yet how like a picture! For sure. But this time Keats has said it first.

I want to magnify hugely his words about the stubble-fields, and especially his assurance that their warm look "in the same way that some pictures look warm" was the thing—this and no other—that he "composed upon". The letter tells the truth about the poem, and a cardinal truth about all his poetry. As the *Nightingale* is supremely the snailhorn adventure among the odes, so the *Grecian Urn* is the infelt *picture* and *To Autumn* the *infelt* picture. The sovereign principle of infeeling is temperature, and this last and greatest of the odes was fostered by an autumnal warmth which now affects us as a thing simultaneously observed and feigned. The fields looked warm, Keats says, the way some pictures look warm; whereupon his reader adds that the poem looks warm too. It holds its heat like sun-soaked stone. We know that hanging autumn warmth and saturation; we meet the familiar and shared pleasure, we meet nature, inside the made poem with a greeting so intimate that the Keatsian tension between the actual and the real almost disappears. Thus while the ode looks like a picture, its space is not the art-space of the *Grecian Urn*. The stress on infelt *picture* in the *Urn* lies at the root of that poem's aestheti-cism and its juxtaposing of warm love and cold pastoral. Whereas *Autumn's* stress upon *infelt* picture gravely awakens joy in the natural prodigy of autumn. Its structure is not antiphonal but climactic, its living form is the season's. The ripeness metaphor

---

[1] *Letters*, vol. II, p. 167.

becomes as accessible as those fields outside Winchester in which Adam can do his dreaming wide awake. This means, within the poem, a certain modest sensitiveness to fact—to the day's death and the "last oozings" from the cyder-press. It is also a matter of fact that the warm scene is held for ever in the poem; the cunningly phrased "hours by hours" of the oozings is not a time that clocks and calendars tell, and the poem's bees are not failing to be realists when they conceive their way into the lap of invulnerable warm plenty. Like the "many havens of intenseness" of Keats's original letter to Haydon, their comfort refuses to be contained by art; it invades life. The sense in which the ode will never cease to feel *autumnally* warm is the one in which the bees are not deluded.

The time which the odes are all about is their time, not a detachable subject but time living and prospering under the aegis of space. I remarked the helpless freedom of "the spirit" in the *Grecian Urn*, and might have added that this sudden deadness of *timbre* epitomises the nullity of Endymion's long quest and the troubles (to do with the further, "abstract" side of ripeness) which Apollo's proposed deification brings. These failures, all superficially different, all reflect the thing which happens so neatly in the *Urn*: the granting of an unusable freedom, the cutting of the kite-string.

The mental vacuity of bad, verbal Keats is always essentially temporal. Language takes time, as I said. Mind takes time, human beings take time. Language and mind and men are what he makes of them because time projects itself on the plane of infelt space. No Christian reader of *Endymion* can take exception to the poem's "clear religion of heaven", for it is just words. But the time-mocking picture in which Sleep holds Madeline's soul "clasp'd like a missal"[1] threatens disquiet, may excite resistance. This is poetry. Keats's religious reader knows a rival show is being mounted.

By now we scarcely need the clasped missal to be assured that "the same way that some pictures" of his letter about *Autumn* is a creative and therefore solitary way. His private struggle to appropriate time is unremitting, and appears most plainly in his attitude to narrative and dialogue. Ordinary consecutiveness is not for him, and so, as he grows and learns, the desultory, dribbling "and next" character of *Endymion* becomes the leap from tableau to tableau in *Hyperion's* natural sculpture, and the infelt magic-lantern show of the 1820 stories, especially *St. Agnes*. The ode stanzas, with

[1] *St. Agnes*, XXVII.

their involute syntax and carefully pondered rhyme-schemes, build the labyrinthian path before our eyes; paramountly, theirs is the language of space; and about them, as about all serious art, questions of form and technique ought never to be raised in isolation.

Ordinary talk is not for him either. Failures in dialogue reflect the one comprehensive inability to render the changing (as distinct from the changed or the persisting) mind in any form:

> aye, all so huge and strange,
> The solitary felt a hurried change
> Working within him into something dreary,—
> Vex'd like a morning eagle, lost, and weary,
> And purblind amid foggy, midnight wolds.
> But he revives at once. . . .[1]

Time's trajectory is not there for the reader to follow and believe in. No imaginative trust can be fostered in such changes and revivals; the Keatsian "felt" and the *Endymion* word "dreary" remain impotent. And while here and there *Endymion* can escape from these mental motions, *Otho*, the five-act Tragedy, is utterly discredited by the fact that its author has condemned himself to a private hell of space-free dialogue-writing.

ERMINIA. I see you are thunderstruck. Haste, haste away!
ALBERT. O I am tortured by this villainy.
ERMINIA. You needs must be.[2]

Psychological information gets ladled out like this through the whole play.[3] The factitious talk proceeds from empty minds, and the minds inhabit a play where all temporal values are null. Against the many incidental havens of intenseness in *Endymion*, *Otho* can boast only one:

> Certes, a father's smile should, like sun light,
> Slant on my sheafed harvest of ripe bliss.
> Besides, I thirst to pledge my lovely bride
> In a deep goblet: let me see—what wine?
> The strong Iberian juice, or mellow Greek?

---

[1] *Endymion*, II, 632.   [2] II, ii, 71.
[3] The unintended humour of *Otho's* dialogue stretches from the bartender's "Coming, sir!" to Queen Victoria after dinner: "Is this clear-headed Albert?" and "No more wine; methinks you've had enough." There are also many simplicities to set beside "Dear Endy: weep not so" in *Endymion's* draft: "Did you ever?" "You may be made a duke"; "Well, I give up"; "We must obey the prince from A to Z"; "An uproar, Duke, you would not hear the end of".

227

Or pale Calabrian? Or the Tuscan grape?
Or of old Aetna's pulpy wine-presses,
Black stain'd with the fat vintage, as it were
The purple slaughter-house, where Bacchus' self
Prick'd his own swollen veins!—

a violent premonition of the *Autumn Ode*.[1] That purple slaughter-house offers momentary *lebensraum* to the spatial imagination, like those other constructions made with the hands of feigning fancy, the sanctuaries of *Psyche* and *Melancholy* and the "husky barn" (changed to "granary floor") of *Autumn*. The slaughter-house has no dramatic business in *Otho*; its job is to contain the fierce and climactic sensuality of the wine god's vein-pricking. Yet in deserting the play it restores the poet to himself. *Otho's* abundant, sometimes agreeable Shakespeare pastiche cannot live with it. Fresh from the odes, we know why; its fleeting strength is the light by which we read the total urgent *faiblesse* of Keats's dramatic venture. His attempt to render the play's mentality through its sensation appears at once inevitable and doomed: "It does make me freeze. . . . You make me tremble. . . . You suffocate me!"— all within fifteen lines.[2] Likewise his recourse to one of the oldest of his allies, the dispersed and feeling organ: finger, lip, palate, eye. Or tongue:

the sharpen'd axe
Will make thy bold tongue quiver to the roots[3]

recalls the dragon's tail "hard with agony" in *Melancholy's* discarded first stanza, but nothing that *Otho* is meant to be about.

In the longer poems published in 1820 he can and largely does avoid the trap which *Otho* forces him into; dialogue, and talk generally, get compelled his way, not he theirs. *Lamia* shows a certain ruthless efficiency in its stripping words of their mental status and turning them into objects of snailhorn perception. There can be no doubt, when

the words she spake
Came, as through bubbling honey, for Love's sake,[4]

what is to be done with them . Or how an oath such as this is to be understood:

through the serpent's ears it ran
Warm, tremulous, devout, psalterian.[5]

---

[1] V, v, 116. On 23 August 1819, about four weeks before he wrote *To Autumn*, Keats told his publisher he had "just finished" *Otho* (*Letters*, vol. II, p. 143). This passage comes in the final scene.
[2] IV, i, 118. [3] III, ii, 86. [4] I, 64. [5] I, 113.

The serpent understood perfectly, she tasted the words, she pressed them deep in upon her sensory solar plexus, and she "blush'd a live damask". Thus *Lamia* reveals in its own sharp fashion that speech like "her new voice luting soft, / Cried 'Lycius! gentle Lycius!'"[1] carries the feel-import of "she breath'd upon his eyes".[2] *Isabella* and *St. Agnes*, the earlier poems, are more tender and instinctive and hazy-edged. Nevertheless their workmanship tells a similar tale. At full pelt—my "full" of speed becoming his "full" of shape—Keats wrote "Her anxious lips mouth full pulp'd with rosy thoughts";[3] then struck the lot through but went on nursing the idea for a few stanzas, to emerge with

> *Sudden a thought came like a full-blown rose,*
> *Flushing his brow, and in his pained heart*
> *Made purple riot:*[4]

which saves the fulness he wants, the ripe completion, while disposing of the impossible pulped mouth. The cancelled draft remains instructive in its neat pointing of the truth that the talk problem is one aspect of the mind problem. Keats is trying to thrust the blown rose of consciousness forward into the seat of utterance, thus asking his ripeness metaphor to embrace a perfection of non-temporal, non-discursive expressiveness. Hence the honest but intolerable "mouth full pulp'd with rosy thoughts". And of course "lips" is no better. The thing has to be driven inward upon the heart's riot of wordless volubility: in fact

> *No uttered syllable, or, woe betide!*
> *But to her heart, her heart was voluble,*
> *Paining with eloquence her balmy side. . . .*[5]

And such is the highest and amplest eloquence of his people. Because it is also silence, this voice of his spatial imagining, a dumb counter-thrust follows at once and he concludes his stanza

> *As though a tongueless nightingale should swell*
> *Her throat in vain, and die, heart-stifled, in her dell.*

But in noting the silence we take "swell" to ourselves, with the straining intensity and the climactic "die", as a power of held expressiveness peculiar to the picture: just as Lorenzo's heart both

---

[1] I, 167. [2] I, 124. [3] *Poetical Works*, p. 239.
[4] *St. Agnes*, XVI. [5] *Ibid.*, XXIII.

"stifled his voice" and speaks its scarlet passion to posterity, an unfading articulate flower:

> and all day
> His heart beat awfully against his side;
> And to his heart he inwardly did pray
> For power to speak; but still the ruddy tide
> Stifled his voice. . . .[1]

The transmuting of ordinary narrative and ordinary talk belongs for obvious reasons to those longer stories in verse which he published in 1820. Not to the odes whose form he devised to suit himself. Nor to the smaller pieces flanking odes and verse-tales; for here, having picked his "little space", he can—so to say—indulge his fancies singly. *La Belle Dame sans Merci* is a song sung by the spirit of withering, fading, in the tones of no longer to feel. Its one moonlight-pale strand is beautifully simple to follow. Like the more memorable sonnets, it states a particular, though primary, form which Keats's world assumes: like the Chapman's Homer sonnet whose groping astronomer and staring human tableau are the manifestations for which snailhorn and stasis can never be more than thought-up names, however apt, no matter how earnestly we breed them out of admiration. Or "Time's sea" whose unity and unShakespearean identity are that of the inner sensory focus devouring "its sweets in the wrong sense". Or the fine sonnet which is effectively "To Sleep" in so far as it gives its subject, the "soft embalmer", Keatsian fingers to press its Keatsian eyes with. Or "Bright star!", the last (it seems) of the important sonnets, and certainly harbouring the sad and craftsman knowledge of his last writing year. There the separation of the star in the octave

> hung aloft the night
> And watching, with eternal lids apart,

from the man in the sestet

> Pillow'd upon my fair love's ripening breast,
> To feel for ever its soft fall and swell,
> Awake for ever in a sweet unrest,
> Still, still to hear her tender-taken breath
> And so live ever—or else swoon to death

touches all five of the odes. Its initial gesture, its dramatic proposition, is antiphonal like the *Nightingale* and the *Urn*. Its closing affirmation is climactic: a natural consummation like *Autumn's*, but also a *Liebestod* like the blazing summoning torch in *Psyche*,

[1] *Isabella*, VI.

and a metasexual orgasm like the burst grape of *Melancholy*. This accounts for the sonnet's haunting potential grandeur. While the *Urn* fulfils itself by infelt *picturemaking* and *Autumn* turns to *infelt* picturemaking, "Bright star!" aspires simultaneously to the tragic artifice of the first and the sublimely grateful naturalism of the second. "Watching", of the star, and "to feel", of the man, are the poem's fixed and clear points; to these polar truths everything else rallies, summoning the whole sonnet beyond the relative stresses of the odes to a sheer and ultimate division of picture and feel.

But in vain, if the great achievement is to be measured against the almost unimaginable hope. Only within the frame of the infelt picture (no matter which way the stress goes) can Adam's dream (no matter its outcome) be housed. Remove that frame, and Keats is undone by a sort of admirable good sense. Putting it another way, actuality takes over the poem, it does not permeate the poem as in *Autumn* or work within the larger pattern of the antiphon as in the *Urn* and the *Nightingale*. Actuality reduces the dream to the first line's "would I were", to mere wish, and the dreamer to the human lover. And actuality whispers in the lover's ear "Watch steadfastly or feel transiently—but not 'feel for ever'". And the lover whispers back "Yet o how I wish". This is sincere and beautiful, but it is not Keats at his amplest; and the reader of the poem shifts joltingly between its modest sane estimations and its vast postures. The steadfastness of the star shares the immense "for ever" of the *Urn's* pictured lovers, but not their "for ever warm". The "soft fall and swell" experienced by head on breast belongs with the firm living pulse ("borne aloft / Or sinking") of *Autumn*, but not with the "never cease" persuasion of its bees. The sonnet's two "steadfasts" and three "evers" are and also are not the things we have just encountered in the odes; the watch / feel antiphon is and is not theirs; that "ripening" strikes very familiar yet so alas does the telltale sexual narrowness of its appearance here; the "swoon to death" conclusion brings the Keatsian climax, but unperfectingly, snatched rather than achieved, which is why it tastes a bit cheap.

"Bright star!", like the odes, may be said to be all about time. Its time either resolves itself into the thin wish "and so live ever" (which is anybody's time) or it begins to be Keats's time; it would, if it could, enter and shelter within the pulse of "fall and swell", giving us an *Autumn Ode* eroticised and grown impossibly, individually human. Keats's eternity of feel, his wish, is left groping for its poetic voice, for its space, its picture; it stands on the threshold of creative dream. And the picture, the bright watching star, is secretly famished for the life of feel. Its "steadfast" and "eternal" also begin to be Keats's own, seeking to avoid their fate of cold separation in gazing on sea and snow. They do not want their fixity to be mere, as we recognise when we find the idea of a star watching up there unremarkable but the expression "with eternal lids apart" a consolation which, in its lurking effort and stress (the eyelids are *held* apart), breathes a faint breath of infeeling into the picture. The star is one of the intent gazers thronging his verse, close in negative capability to the angels of *St. Agnes*,

> *The carved angels, ever eager-eyed,*[1]

who "star'd" with "wings put cross-wise on their breasts". But because of the wall between watch and feel which the lover builds and torments the dreamer with, the effect of "lids apart" in the sonnet is ghostly. Once again, the star is and yet is not like *St. Agnes's* angels; still less can we make secure comparison—but whence the urge to do so?—with the fondle-and-squeeze presences in earlier Keats, the sturdy blatancies, the weight of face against arm which

> *tenderly unclos'd,*
> *By tenderest pressure, a faint damask mouth*
> *To slumbery pout. . . .*[2]

2 'The Eve of St. Agnes' *and* 'Lamia'

So tightly self-consistent is the writing in *St. Agnes* that the effect of any deviation, when it occurs, which is seldom, gets enormously exaggerated. Coming upon the bloodhound who

> *shook his hide,*
> *But his sagacious eye an inmate owns*[3]

is like falling through a gothic trap-door, backwards in time, into a world of *Night Thoughts*. Whereas

> *The music, yearning like a God in pain,*[4]

pitches one forward into *Salome*.

These rare shocks are the measure of our overall assurance. The style's conviction expresses the poem's, and the poem stands firm on the truth of Adam's dream: Madeline went to bed, obeyed the rules of the St. Agnes legend, dreamed of a lover, and awoke to

[1] IV.   [2] *Endymion*, II, 404.   [3] XLI.   [4] VII.

find him kneeling there beside her. Such forthrightness might be envied by any purveyor of escapist fantasy. But then it is a Romantic rather than a specifically Keatsian trait to be able to exist on easy terms with pulp literature; *Wuthering Heights* is one of the earliest tales of love and lust on the Yorkshire moors, Jane Eyre and Mr Rochester live again in every timid hospital nurse and brusque surgeon of the women's magazines.

The work of art is distinguished by the thing we like sometimes to call its reality, and sometimes its imagination. In *St. Agnes* the two become very quickly, and actively, entangled with each other. This happens during, indeed this provides a method for studying, the process of composition. The autograph draft helps to initiate Madeline's escape with Porphyro from the hostile castle, after their union, with his words to her: "Put on warm clothing sweet." They are replaced in the 1820 text by "Awake! arise! my love".[1] What about reality? And what about imagination? The discarded words possess an unheroic actuality, the ones we are left with are brassy, mannered, operatic. Keats seems to have abandoned what was low but (in a much-used sense) real for something neither real nor imaginative.

The admonition about sensible warm clothes was not sacrificed because it was unlofty. Such touches of bourgeois realism as German critics, following Nietzsche, used to find and castigate in Euripides are scattered throughout *St. Agnes*: the cobwebs of the thirteenth stanza, for example, and the old woman's spectacles in the fifteenth, and the safe level matting in the twenty-second. They anchor the wishful dream in domestic detail, and Keats is unbothered about them. Nor is there anything alien or irrelevant in the thought of the cold outside and the need to pile clothes on: on the contrary, from the "bitter chill" of the first line his poem lives by temperature and especially by temperature contrasts:

> *Full on this casement shone the wintry moon,*
> *And threw warm gules on Madeline's fair breast. . . .*[2]

Porphyro's address to Madeline has to be changed for no other reason than that it is an address *to*. It is replaced by words which are addressed *at*—operatic words. Thus we return to Keats's dialogue, which means back to his time and his human beings. His subduing of time concerns his people as much as it does his picture-making; it includes mental time. We cannot admire the picture in

> *She danc'd along with vague, regardless eyes*[3]

[1] XXXIX.   [2] XXV.   [3] VIII.

I*   233

without taking pleasure in the rapt introversion of the girl. Her oblivious active life is her stillness for the reader. She goes about her business in the same state of impenetrable, pictured otherness as the animals of the first stanza:

The hare limp'd trembling through the frozen grass—

which is why, discussing Negative Capability, I spoke of the ground which Keats's human creation shares with a wider life, and of that creation's pure objective status.

Madeline is desired and admired, but never known. Her story fulfils at delicious length the impulse of the ode *On Melancholy*, to emprison the hand and feed upon the eyes. There can be no entering into personal relations with the human object; there can, that is, be speaking at ("Ah, silver shrine")[1] but not to. Every catching of the object's eye is a threat to Keats's power of illusion. When we try to lay hands on that power, we should think of the deep feeling in *Melancholy*, and then of Porphyro as he "gazed upon her empty dress"[2] after Madeline had gone to bed. We may think we too can command the human object like that in its warm, ponderable, breathing separation. In fact we lack the nerve, the concentrated simplicity, which makes the impression so strong and so amazingly youthful and unreflective. The dream of love in *St. Agnes* compounds awe and veneration and hunger. That gazing on the dress awakens sex, but sex enclosed by the perfecting dream; it is a high desire too. Of course Porphyro wants to possess his object; he also wants to worship it, and he wants the sun to shine on it always. The undressed body can shift towards "ring-dove fray'd"[3] and become the fragile unfleshy bird "trembling in her soft and chilly nest";[4] the girl who followed the St. Agnes rules and lay on her back expectantly ("with upward eyes for all that they desire"[5]) is the same one whose "blue affrayed eyes wide open shone"[6] on the brink of the fact. The life of the pure object is not unsubtle for the reader, nor easy for herself as she dreads what she wants, nor easy for Porphyro whose passion, schooled by her fear, now forces him into a half-suppliant, adoring posture "upon his knees". His sensibility—compare "still un-ravish'd bride" in the *Urn*—is tinged, very faintly, with that of Goya's caption to his etching of a soldier setting about one woman while a second prepares to knife him in the back: "They don't like it!"

[1] XXXVIII.   [2] XXVIII.   [3] XXII.
[4] XXVII.   [5] VI.   [6] XXXIII.

This is the reality of *St. Agnes*, and equally its imaginative force. Porphyro's "Put on warm clothing" was true to the poem in temperature and domesticity. Those truths are safe because diffused through the whole, and the actual words have to go because in them Porphyro catches Madeline's eye; Keats is reacting to the threat of personal relations.

The comparison with *Isabella* becomes instructive at this juncture, both for the words which go and for the ones which replace them. In its early stanzas *Isabella* maintains the instinctive silent rapport of the lovers by the tact of its talk. The poem's creative premise, enunciated at once, is that

> *They could not sit at meals but feel how well*
> *It soothed each to be the other by;*

and while both of them proceed to speak "to their pillows".[1] and he "to his heart";[2] and while she responds "to every symbol on his forehead high";[3] and while his diction anticipates Porphyro's "Awake! arise!"—

> *Love! thou art leading me from wintry cold,*
> *Lady! thou leadest me to summer clime—*[4]

they nevertheless avoid talking *to* each other until forced into a situation which that operatic "Love!" and "Lady!" try to retrieve. So far, as Keats's autograph draft and fair copy show, and as the reading ear confirms, the poem has been moving very easily, seeming to sing itself; but now, between stanzas seven and eight, it runs into trouble. Isabella's "quick eye"—the authentic animal quickness—rests on his forehead:

> *She saw it waxing very pale and dead,*
> *And straight all flush'd; so, lisped tenderly,*
> *'Lorenzo!'—here she ceas'd her timid quest,*
> *But in her tone and look he read the rest.*

The same quickness directs "he read the rest". They are recognisably the pair who were eating silently together in the first stanza. Moreover the girl's sensual lisping of "Lorenzo!" appears fine in its naturalness here, whereas in *Lamia* this kind of thing becomes tricksy. And I would say the courtly-conventional "Love!" and "Lady!" are right too because upheld by the serenading style of these stanzas. It is as if Keats had found a rich piece of empty ground lying between Leigh Hunt and William Morris, in order

---

[1] IV.   [2] VI.   [3] VII.   [4] IX.

to assert his own superiority. The grateful light which shines on the lovers when they come

> *close, and share*
> *The inward fragrance of each other's heart*[1]

also reveals Keats's convinced and convincing apprehension of the two loving presences—imagination and reality again—and brings the human stuff of the poem and its sweet singing style into sumptuous accord.

But the felt closeness of Isabella and Lorenzo, cunningly sustained by such touches as

> *his erstwhile timid lips grew bold,*
> *And poesied with hers in dewy rhyme:*[2]

cannot stave off personal relations altogether. The trouble at the end of Stanza Seven centres on Lorenzo reading "the rest" instinctively. Keats reaches this just conclusion after five or six attempts to find something for Isabella to say in addition to her "Lorenzo!", and after writing and then cancelling an entire stanza in which Lorenzo replies to that something. While "he read the rest" is simply right for Lorenzo, Keats has Boccaccio's tale to tell and cannot leave it at that. So the poem ceases to sing itself, and the reader's complacency turns into yes-and-no; there are some fine things, and many occasions where a radical strength—*the* radical strength—obtrudes: that was the point of using *Isabella* so freely in the exposition of end-stopped feel. But there are also many small disasters like "Good bye! I'll soon be back"[3]—Lorenzo's farewell before he rides off, unsuspecting, with his murderers. This is not bad because it is low, but because it catches her eye; the parallel with Porphyro's "Put on warm clothing" is exact. Keats's final choice for the beginning of Stanza Eight ("O Isabella, I can half perceive / That I may speak my grief into thine ear") is anything but low, and yet the firm light pulse of *Isabella* turns thready the moment it is uttered. When we recover that fragrant rhythm, and observe the girl waiting and longing for her lover,

> *Spreading her perfect arms upon the air,*
> *And on her couch low murmuring 'Where? O where?'*[4]

we recognise at once the exploring spatial gesture (compare *The Fall's* "stretch'd her white arm through the hollow dark"), and likewise the supporting role of the spoken words: that question,

[1] X.   [2] IX.   [3] XXVI.   [4] XXX.

poised between sigh and caress, helps to hold the picture of her spreading arms.

Above all, we recognise the human object; and so the nature of Isabella's similarity to Madeline becomes clear: to Madeline carrying her taper upstairs, saying her prayers, undressing, lying awake in bed, asleep—

> *And still she slept an azure-lidded sleep,*
> *In blanched linen, smooth and lavender'd.* . . .[1]

And sleeps like that still, the precious human object caught and hushed in the arms of the soft embalmer, haunting us now as she haunted Porphyro and Keats.

Do not resist this conclusion on the ground that a literature of human objects must be less ample than one of personal relations. For of course it must; Keats's defining narrowness has occupied us from the start. The argument is that his limitation becomes Madeline's poetic character, with the mistress of the ode *On Melancholy* once again abridging the process and providing Madeline's epitome. The mistress's peerlessness of eye recalls Isabella's "perfect arms", and both of these pinpoint the driving thrust to consummate the actual which makes his grasp of Madeline so majestic, dilating his own sensual constriction into her human sublimity. "Peerless", *Melancholy's* perfecting word, withdraws the object, adds an admiring dimension to the desiring one, and in doing so casts a glance of rancourless scepticism upon the proposals "emprison" and "feed deep". What could possession of the peerless object mean? To taste, certainly—but to taste the admired perfection? It is the pathos of such love as Keats has heart-knowledge of—and he makes us reflect upon all male loving, upon love itself—that desire and admiration are found together always and never entirely at peace.

Poetry, the *Grecian Urn* invites us to whisper to ourselves, gives a man the moon he asks for—on poetry's terms; he cannot keep his unfading love and forego his cold pastoral. Poetry frames the wishful dream in various ways; we have studied *Sleep and Poetry* and *Endymion*, the two Hyperions, and then the antiphonal and the climactic odes. Poetry expresses the dream in a single way endlessly modified, the ripeness metaphor. *St. Agnes* frames the dream in narrative, outward and human narrative, which raises its own very acute problem as to the metaphorical nature of Keats's ripeness. The *Nightingale* (for example) articulates ripeness through embalmed forest darkness and a bird's voice; *Psyche*, through a

---

[1] *St. Agnes*, XXX.

contrived mindscape, a torch, a shrine. *St. Agnes* has only its story to rest its metaphor on. We are inside a convention where the story shall be read as if true, as if its reference were actual. Plausibility is neither here nor there. We have no other way. And thus the perennial tension between the actual and the real in Keats's work is given a new sharp emphasis. If we stand back from the poem for a moment and ask what happens, the answer is, Adam's dream. The truth of the dream is the climax of the story, and the expression of both is ripeness. Truth, climax, ripeness, belong to the stanzas after Porphyro has found his way to Madeline's bedroom; they quite simply are the coming together of the lovers. We now approach closer and study the narrative. How does ripeness, the expressive form, emerge? Porphyro drew near, he gazed at her dress and listened to her breathing, he prepared a feast for her, he "took her hollow lute" and sang her a song. These are all modes of standing over against Madeline; they instil life into our dry phrase "human object".The music and the food (which remains uneaten) are addressed neatly and forcefully *at*. We may regard them as extensions of Porphyro's first operatic words:

> '*And now, my love, my seraph fair, awake!*
> '*Thou art my heaven, and I thine eremite:*
> '*Open thine eyes, for meek St. Agnes' sake,*
> '*Or I shall drowse beside thee, so my soul doth ache.*'[1]

Here he lays bare his love. He could scarcely have voiced the desire-and-admire complex more economically. Until, at last,

> *Beyond a mortal man impassion'd far*
> *At these voluptuous accents, he arose,*
> *Ethereal, flush'd, and like a throbbing star*
> *Seen mid the sapphire heaven's deep repose*
> *Into her dream he melted, as the rose*
> *Blendeth its odour with the violet,—*
> *Solution sweet: meantime the frost-wind blows*
> *Like Love's alarum pattering the sharp sleet*
> *Against the window-panes; St. Agnes' moon has set.*[2]

The peculiar challenge of this poem presents itself in Keats's entrusting his real dream of ripeness to his actual tale of love. The castle, Madeline's bedroom, the objects and events there, must be taken for what the story declares them to be—unlike the *Nightingale's* forest, *Psyche's* shrine, *Melancholy's* burst grape, which float free of literal determination and make it easy for us to dream with

[1] XXXI.   [2] XXXVI.

Keats. In *St. Agnes* the poet dares a situation where his master metaphor is given a series of pseudo-historic contexts to fight for its life in. The hazards become evident as ripeness emerges. An advance through music and food threatens to be too oblique (what are these doing in the bedroom? and beware the killing critical afterthought that they stand for something else); and an advance through speech too explicit: the almost open declaration, I want to worship you and I want to sleep with you—"Thou art my heaven . . . I shall drowse beside thee"—risks mirth and an alien hard clarity. Finally, development through sex is likely to prove at once too direct and too narrow. We cannot stand by while the gap between the actual and the real is forcibly bridged by sex, for we know that sex does not fulfil the desire-and-admire impulse. We know too that an experience of sex which did fulfil that impulse would quench the dream of love.

It remains, crucially, to ask in what sense the sex of *St. Agnes* is an experience. As "solution sweet" sex gets called on to embody and vindicate the dream. *St. Agnes's* moon sets on this climax. Wondering, as we must, what sort of triumphant proving is intended here, and what is achieved, we return to the start of the sequence with Madeline "blissfully haven'd", secure, sealed tight in sleep, withdrawn,

> As though a rose should shut, and be a bud again.[1]

And with Porphyro staring at her clothes and inferring the body. The point throughout is desire-and-admire on his side, and innerness of absent perfection on hers:

> Shaded was her dream
> By the dusk curtain:—'twas a midnight charm
> Impossible to melt as iced stream. . . .[2]

She sleeps through his preparation of the food, and through his talk. Then he plays his music "close to her ear" and wakes her. Or does he?

> Her eyes were open, but she still beheld,
> Now wide awake, the vision of her sleep:
> There was a painful change, that nigh expell'd
> The blisses of her dream. . . .[3]

She is awake but still possessed of her dream—just. She suffers a flicker of cross-reference between this world and that. It is a very familiar anguish, an instant of the purest naturalism which Keats

[1] XXVII.   [2] XXXII.   [3] XXXIV.

has observed, and which he now exploits in imagination. Madeline's distress causes her to ask Porphyro to help her find her way back, somehow, within total dream:

> *Give me that voice again, my Porphyro,*
> *Those looks immortal. . . .*[1]

He responds:

> *Into her dream he melted,*

and now we see how it is that the sex of *St. Agnes* does not become overburdened.

At least we see this in analytic retrospect. While we read we experience the actuality of the "solution sweet" being set atremble by the narrative course of things, and likewise the metaphorical status of ripeness. Not that the delicate relation between dream and tale now looks like a solved problem. It appears a fact of life, no more but no less, and its firm fair basis—its beauty and truth—is Madeline's oscillation between sleep and wake. The burden of ripeness has not been eased from sex's shoulders. But rather, Keats has anticipated the final stanza of *Psyche*; for there the winged Cupid and the Psyche-moth coalesce in "the warm Love"; and when I said, not facetiously, that it takes two to make love, I had the deployment of this fact in *St. Agnes* on my mind's horizon. The ripe burden can be sustained by sex because Porphyro and Madeline share its weight. His entry into her dream is not a movement away from literal sex (from the real thing, as a man might crudely assume) into fantasy. For women's sexuality, not just their sexual imagination, is worldliness wrapped in dream, to our male understanding. It was then a supreme insight that restrained Keats from trying to fill the dream she dreams in his story. The hope before she goes to bed, is that

> *Young virgins might have visions of delight,*
> *And soft adorings from their loves receive*
> *Upon the honey'd middle of the night. . . .*[2]

We don't know what *happens* in that hidden sleep of hers. The record after she is awake (but still clinging to "the blisses of her dream") is simply that she recognises and accepts Porphyro for her St. Agnes Eve lover. He is her dream's unspeakable concrete filling, and she the longed-for repose of all his desire and admiration. The love they make constitutes the most erotic haven of intenseness in all Keats; and here the triumph of art is to disfeature the police-court question "what actually happened?" without compromising

[1] XXXV.   [2] VI.

the haven's dedication to sex. When we speak, ploddingly again, of metasexual orgasm, we are saying that *St. Agnes's* "solution sweet" is nothing but sex and more than the sex our single lives—the only ones we have—can give us. The next stanza reports

> *'Tis dark: quick pattereth the flaw-blown sleet:*

the moment of the lovers' conscious coming apart. All Porphyro says is "This is no dream, my bride, my Madeline!" She replies "No dream, alas!", and beyond her fear that he will leave her lies another pain which his faithful staying can't mend.

St. Agnes gives narrative scope to "the warm Love" of the ode *To Psyche*. The poem is also an extended meditation on the last five words of the *Nightingale*: "Do I wake or sleep?" Again it is touched, very delicately, by the *Nightingale's* sad aftermath, the desolation of the *Urn*, the burst grape of *Melancholy*; while its entrusting of dream to tale, imagination to history, foreshadows the marvellous naturalism of *Autumn*. *St. Agnes* does again the love of Lorenzo and Isabella who

> share
> *The inward fragrance of each other's heart.*

But beautiful as it is, *Isabella* remains content somehow, even at its best, to be minor. *The Eve of St. Agnes* does *Isabella* again after nature as Cézanne proposed to do Poussin again after nature: more truly, and more intensely. That bedroom climax of nature and art includes setting, the room itself as well as what happens there. In its early stanzas the poem has a relatively open and easy texture which allows us to use it as an introduction to the odes. For example, a good way of appraising the "soft-conched ear" of *Psyche* and the "downy owl" of *Melancholy* and the "clammy cells" of *Autumn* is to think of the knights in armour on that bitter evening,

> *To think how they may ache in icy hoods and mails.*[1]

And to remember the limping hare, the sheep huddled "in woolly fold", and the birds:

> *The owl, for all his feathers, was a-cold.*[2]

The owl of *Psyche* is the *St. Agnes* owl more densely conceived; the infeeling of Negative Capability unites them. "Downy" does not come right because it was well observed. Nor is it primarily felt, as one might stroke an owl and proceed to convey the sensation.

[1] II.   [2] I.

"Downy" is infelt, the owl lives as he can within his swaddling case of feathers as surely as the knights freeze in their armour. What lies on the surface in *St. Agnes* gets knitted into the body of the ode and becomes, in the final seamless compression, unobvious.

But when we reach Madeline's bedroom Keats's narrative begins to read more like an ode and less like its own opening. The room itself, "silken, hush'd, and chaste", has the concentration of a sandalwood box; as in the odes, observation moves insistently away from seeing. The window of the room has coloured glass which "blush'd with blood of queens and kings"—the warm bruiselike blushing that is felt from within. The moon shines through the glass. Madeline kneels at her prayers:

> *Rose-bloom fell on her hands, together prest,*[1]

and there is the effect the pre-Raphaelites thought they understood. The same window is

> *diamonded with panes of quaint device,*
> *Innumerable of stains and splendid dyes,*
> *As are the tiger-moth's deep-damask'd wings. . . .*[2]

Of course Keats has taken note of the tiger-moth, and of course his initial thought is to colour. What proclaims him, though, is the incitement lurking within "deep-damask'd": the incitement to draw sensation inward and press the mind's fingertip against that rich powdery nap. His big poems, like his small ones, spring from the hunger which "deep-damask'd" is then called on to appease.

By a thousand such tokens we trace the hunger of the snail-horn back to the creative ardour of the poet, and nowhere more clearly than in *Lamia*, whose heroine "blush'd a live damask", whose wedding guests "felt the cold full sponge to pleasure press'd".[3]

In fact clarity is *Lamia's* leading characteristic. Its peculiar sharpness of definition is an unkind thing, or at least uncomfortable. Before asking why, I want to remark that *The Eve of St. Agnes*, while Keats was in the process of writing it, narrowly escaped being clear too.

Both poems fall within the year—roughly Autumn 1818 to Autumn 1819—in which he was trying to get the Hyperion epic written. Plenty of room for hope and disappointment there. It was

[1] XXV.   [2] XXIV.   [3] I, 116; II, 192.

the year in which his brother died, in which he loved and struggled to hold Fanny Brawne, the year of the odes but also of bad sale and reception for his work. Among the ups and downs of this time it is idle to look for explanation of the fact that *St. Agnes* is the most lavishly confident and affirmative, the happiest of his major poems. Art does not work like that, and in any case the wonderful outcome, his final version and our printed text, was very much an affair of touch and go.

The final version broadly confirms his first draft—the autograph now at Harvard and designated "H" in Garrod's *Apparatus Criticus*. But in between we can discern a radical hesitation; on 11 September 1819 he had a long talk with Richard Woodhouse which Woodhouse describes thus to John Taylor the publisher:

He had the Eve of St. A. copied fair. He has made trifling alterations, inserted an additional stanza early in the poem to make the *legend* more intelligible, and correspondent with what afterwards takes place, particularly with respect to the supper and the playing on the lute. He retains the name of Porphyro—has altered the last 3 lines to leave on the reader a sense of pettish disgust, by bringing Old Angela in dead stiff & ugly. He says he likes that the poem should leave off with this change of sentiment—it was what he aimed at, & was glad to find from my objections to it that he had succeeded. . . . There was another alteration, which I abused for "a full hour by the *Temple* clock". You know if a thing has a decent side, I generally look no further. As the poem was originally written, *we* innocent ones (ladies & myself) might well have supposed that Porphyro, when acquainted with Madeline's love for him, & when "he arose, etherial flush'd" &c. &c (turn to it) set himself at once to persuade her to go off with him, & succeeded & went over the "Dartmoor black" (now changed for some other place) to be married, in right honest chaste & sober wise. But, as it is now altered, as soon as M. has confessed her love, P. winds by degrees his arm round her, presses breast to breast, and acts all the parts of a bona fide husband, while she fancies she is only playing the part of a wife in a dream. This alteration is of about 3 stanzas. . . .[1]

Clarity, our starting point, is Keats's own immediate object in the "additional stanza"[2] inserted between numbers Six and Seven of the first and the final drafts, explaining that it was in accord with the St. Agnes legend that "her future lord" should bring supper to the girl's bedroom and play music there. Reconsidering his poem he will have sensed, as we did just now, a threatened eruption of rationalistic afterthinking in the question, what are the food and music doing?

[1] *Keats Circle*, vol. I, p. 91.   [2] *Poetical Works*, p. 238.

But the much more important clarification centres on his re-handling of "about 3 stanzas". No other record of this survives, and the likelihood is he thought better of his proposal so soon, and excised it so effectively, that neither Woodhouse nor his brother George (the two transcribers of *St. Agnes*) could note it. The general drift is plain, however, from Woodhouse's letter to Taylor; this was not mere tinkering; the alteration aimed a deathblow at the companionship—the shared world—of dream and tale in the poem we now have. Sex is adequate to ripeness in our *St. Agnes* because Keats keeps his back turned on the issue of what actually happened. Not by an effort of will. He is too absorbed to worry. Leigh Hunt once praised his "unmisgiving" genius[1], and Hunt might have added that *St. Agnes* misgave Keats least—except, as we learn from Woodhouse, at this middle stage when he feels a need to justify the food and music, and grits his teeth and plunges into the descriptive shallow clarity of "all the acts of a bona fide husband". Woodhouse's comic wording mustn't obscure the devastation purposed here.

Keats's transient state of mind is refracted through a letter of his own as well as through the honest Woodhouse, and its elements should be held in loose and undogmatic association with each other. He was hurt and angry at public failure. He resolved to be business-like. Ten days after their *St. Agnes* talk he writes to Woodhouse,

Now I am going to be serious. After revolving certain circumstances in my mind, chiefly connected with a late American letter, I have deter-mined to take up my abode in a cheap lodging in Town and get em-ployment in some of our elegant Periodical Works—I will no longer live upon hopes—I shall carry my plan into execution speedily—I shall live in Westminster—from which a walk to the British Museum will be noisy and muddy—but otherwise pleasant enough—I shall enquire of Hazlitt how the figures of the market stand. . . . I will give you a few reasons why I shall persist in not publishing *The Pot of Basil* [*Isabella*]— It is too smokeable—I can get it smok'd at the carpenter's shaving chimney much more cheaply. There is too much inexperience of life, and simplicity of knowledge in it—which might do very well after one's death—but not while one is alive. There are very few would look to the reality. I intend to use more finesse with the Public. It is possible to write fine things which cannot be laugh'd at in any way. *Isabella* is what I should call were I a reviewer "a weak-sided poem" with an amusing sober-sadness about it. Not that I do not think Reynolds and you are quite right about it—it is enough for me. But this will not do to be public. If I may so say, in my dramatic capacity I enter fully into the feeling: but in Propria Persona I should be apt to quiz it myself. There

[1] See Mr John Bayley's "Keats and Reality".

is no objection of this kind to *Lamia*—a good deal to *St. Agnes Eve*—only not so glaring.[1]

His mood is a tangle of determinations to make money, to write poems that can't be laughed at, to silence the reviewers and please the public; to refrain from publishing the "smokeable" *Isabella* and (we already know from Woodhouse) to render *St. Agnes* as unsmokeable as possible.

Lamia, in any case cannot be smoked; it satisfies his present tough and professional criterion for success in the world; people want "sensation of some sort", and *Lamia* will give them "pleasant or unpleasant sensation".[2] The background to this estimate is supplied by Woodhouse and himself: the calling a spade a spade in the sexual climax of *St. Agnes*, the calculated downward thrust of the conclusion into "pettish disgust",[3] and, transforming the whole familiar scene, a worldlywise distrust of the ardent, self-vindicating, smokeable dream: "The imagination may be compared to Adam's dream—he awoke and found it truth". That was nearly two years ago. Now, on the heels of *Lamia*,[4] his letter to Woodhouse affords a sad and sensitive postscript to this "truth", a commentary on the tension between the actual and the real. In facing facts—lodging within reach of a library, going to Hazlitt for advice about commercial journalism—he is being realistic as one calls it; but the valued thing which almost everybody will miss, he says, in *Isabella* with its "inexperience of life", is "the reality". And *Isabella* is real because "in my dramatic capacity" (for "dramatic" understand "negative-capable": a most revealing usage) "I enter fully into the feeling".

Lamia stands at the opposite pole to *Isabella* and the unmutilated version of *St. Agnes* in this matter of Negative Capability; entering *fully* into the feeling is what that poem wittingly avoids. Before he put pen to paper Keats prepared himself for *Lamia*, so his close friend Charles Brown records, by "much studying of Dryden's

---

[1] *Letters*, vol. II, p. 174. The "American letter" contained bad news about money.

[2] *Ibid.*, p. 189.

[3] He was proposing:

> *with face deform*
> *The beadsman stiffen'd, 'twixt a sigh and laugh*
> *Ta'en from his beads by one weak little cough.*

Against this, his first and last thought is

> *The Beadsman, after thousand aves told,*
> *For aye unsought for slept among his ashes cold.*

[4] A letter of 5 September, six days before the meeting with Woodhouse, reports *Lamia* finished (*Letters*, vol. II, p. 157).

versification".[1] The merest glance—the opening couplet—confirms this:

> *Upon a time, before the faery broods*
> *Drove Nymph and Satyr from the prosperous woods.* . . .

But he has his own end in view, he is no sedulous ape, he is after a laconicism and a brio which the master of the middle style can help him into. At once "prosperous woods" reveals his fine selective ear; conceive of prosperous woods in *Isabella* or *St. Agnes*. The occasional line straight out of Dryden,

> *That, while it smote, still guaranteed to save*—[2]

is the exception which proves the *Lamia* rule of a Drydenesque tone adopted for a special purpose.

We bump into this purpose at moments of direct comment from the poet:

> *Love in a hut, with water and a crust,*
> *Is—Love, forgive us!—cinders, ashes, dust;*
> *Love in a palace is perhaps at last*
> *More grievous torment than a hermit's fast:*—[3]

that sort of sentiment sounds best in that sort of style. It recalls the "facts are facts" temper of his letter to Woodhouse. But whereas the letter allows us, as nearly all his letters do, to reach through to the attractive man who wrote it, the verse of *Lamia* is hard, facile, unresonant, and bewildering in its clarity.

Lamia comes very near the end of the story of Keats's efforts to be clear: broadly, that is, to command intellectual purposiveness, to get on top of his own gift. Early on, in *Sleep and Poetry*, he pronounced the distinction which he meant to live his writing life by—and what could be clearer?—between the pleasant realm of Flora and Pan, and the agony of human hearts. Then *Endymion* took the thing he had in him to say and pinched and poked it into the shape of the neo-Platonic tale that required to be told. September of 1819 finds him approaching the end, where everything happens thick and fast. *St. Agnes* is being mauled about, *Isabella* declared unpublishable[4] (another decision which he reverses), a money-making sally into journalism brusquely envisaged. On the twenty-first of the month he writes to tell John Reynolds, "I have given up *Hyperion*".

---

[1] *Life of John Keats*, p. 56. Woodhouse reports to Taylor (*Keats Circle*, vol. I, p. 94), after discussing *Lamia* with Keats, that "the metre is Drydenian heroic".
[2] I, 339.   [3] II, 1.
[4] The "smokeable" of Keats's letter becomes, in Woodhouse's account to Taylor, "It appeared to him mawkish" (*Keats Circle*, vol. I, p. 90).

Hyperion (momentarily to conflate the two versions) is about the defeat of the Titans by the Olympians, and specially Hyperion by Apollo. In prospect Keats named Apollo the hero of his epic, and when he came to write he broke down on the instant of Apollo's becoming "a god". The deification of Apollo is essentially, I said, an attempt to rationalise ripeness. Or to consummate the actual by taking thought. Or to prove Adam's dream. The crux is certitude, and clarity.

So it is with *Lamia*. On the surface there is no observable connection, for the Hyperion fragments are studied out of Milton and Cary's Dante translation, while *Lamia* turns, through Dryden, prevailingly jaunty. Beneath all this a bond of mature but uncreative, indeed deathly, self-knowledge unites them; the standpoint of both is analytic and critical. In the Hyperion venture, having seen the prose truth about his master metaphor, he seeks to confirm ripeness, philosophising it towards and even into certainty ("truth"). In *Lamia* he does not seek to confirm the "what" which the Imagination of his Adam's dream letter seizes, but to place that "what", to nail it down and be tough-minded about it. So *Hyperion* and *The Fall* murder what they mean to save while *Lamia* achieves the cruel deed it sets out to do. Just as Keats told Woodhouse he was delighted to hear him say he felt "pettish disgust" at the end of the altered *St. Agnes*, because this was "what he aimed at", so he would find—or profess to find—satisfaction in the respectful dismay touched by revulsion with which *Lamia* affects posterity.

This reaction can be approached by observing that the story is shared between three characters, Lamia, Lycius, Apollonius, who are so placed in relation to each other that the reader's sympathy has nowhere to lodge. I don't mean that Keats thwarts naïve expectations as to readily distinguishable heroes and villains, but that he throws the entire apparatus of our response into disarray. Lamia is a witch[1] who gets the god Hermes to transform her from her present serpent shape into a beautiful woman so she may pursue her love for a young Corinthian called Lycius. He is overwhelmed by her and takes her to his house where they live in sensual peace for a time. Then he has the idea of making a public show of their love, with bridal feast and friends present. Among these, uninvited, comes Lycius's old master the philosopher Apollonius, who stares across the table at Lamia, pierces her disguise, and calls her by her name. Whereupon she gives a shriek and vanishes; and Lycius dies at once.

[1] Lamia is the Latin name for a witch who sucks children's blood.

On the one hand Keats makes no bones about Lamia being a witch, and on the other he scolds Apollonius for spoiling the party. The whole poem is infected with this teasing duality, it spreads through the spaces between the three protagonists, and later discussion has always (I believe) boiled down to an attempt to address the schizophrenic object convincingly. It may of course be taken as veiled autobiography. Thus Middleton Murry:

Keats is Lycius, Fanny Brawne is the Lamia, and Apollonius is Charles Brown the realist trying to break Fanny's spell over Keats by insisting upon her as the female animal. The identification seems transparent. . . . The truth about the Lamia is that Keats himself did not know whether she was a thing of beauty or a thing of bale.[1]

For this, or any alternative reading from life, the documentation is very, very slender. If something like it be true, and naturally it can't be disproved, we are left with a restatement of our initial question, in terms of sources.

Think of *Lamia* as a triptych. The girl-serpent is the middle panel. On her right Lycius, and on her left Apollonius. And now, assimilate Lycius and the girl to *St. Agnes* and the enactment of Adam's dream, and Apollonius and the serpent to *La Belle Dame sans Merci* and negative ripening (which is otherwise withering or the theme of the lady vanishes). The schizoid personality of *Lamia* embraces the two wings of the triptych. Asking how the poem does this one is brought back to the beginning, that is to Keats's intensive study of Dryden. He wanted clarity, and got it first and foremost, in his own poem, through a very brilliant externality of impression:

> *She was a gordian shape of dazzling hue,*
> *Vermilion-spotted, golden, green, and blue;*
> *Striped like a zebra, freckled like a pard,*
> *Eyed like a peacock, and all crimson barr'd;*
> *And full of silver moons, that, as she breathed,*
> *Dissolv'd, or brighter shone. . . .*[2]

One reason for arguing against visual-pictorial accounts of Keats is to appreciate the singularity of *Lamia*. At last we have a poem whose descriptive progress is wedded to the eye, to light. Its Greek and legendary material seems unearnestly handled because the characteristic Keatsian penetration is absent; and so the spatial and temporal consequences of that penetration do not follow either; the snailhorn has been denied, and the story flows insensi-

---

[1] *Keats and Shakespeare*, pp. 157-9.   [2] I, 47.

tively brisk. This is a work of surfaces: of "frecklings, streaks and bars", of "phosphor glow / Reflected in the slabbed steps below", of "crystal polish". Sight has expelled feel, except where feel can be made to agree with the new Drydenesque hardness:

> *his galley now*
> *Grated the quaystones with her brazen prow—*[1]

where end-stopped feel turns outward and abrasive.

But the snakeskin narrative was devised for a special purpose, to contain the soft amour of Lycius and Lamia. And thus the poem begins to bind the wings of the triptych inward upon its centre—at a fearful price, since precisely here, in this folding of their love within a hard bright envelope, appears the deathly knowledge of the poet who is placing his own dream.

As a snake, Lamia is all surface. As a woman and Lycius's mistress, fund of sensual joy, she is pure inwardness. The erotic ideal, the question of feel as Lycius states it, is

> *How to entangle, trammel up and snare*
> *Your soul in mine, and labyrinth you there*
> *Like the hid scent in an unbudded rose?*[2]

The secret scent and the self-enwrapped flower are entirely familiar. This must be Keats. Whereas the contrast of woman and snake belongs only to *Lamia* and the new knowledge of life which he claims for *Lamia*. The snake is one with the story and the fact; the woman and the ripe love have no reality beyond the tender assumptions of Adam's dream.

The confined dream-status of love in *Lamia* appears quite early, in a short prologue to the main story. Hermes's agreement to change Lamia from snake into woman is secured by a crude *quid pro quo*; the god too is intent on sex ("bent warm on amorous theft"), and in return for his putting love within her reach she undertakes to produce the invisible nymph he is chasing.

> *She breath'd upon his eyes, and swift was seen*
> *Of both the guarded nymph near-smiling on the green.*
> *It was no dream; or say a dream it was,*
> *Real are the dreams of Gods, and smoothly pass*
> *Their pleasures in a long immortal dream.*
> *One warm, flush'd moment, hovering, it might seem*
> *Dash'd by the wood-nymph's beauty, so he burn'd;*
> *Then, lighting on the printless verdure, turn'd*

[1] I, 223.   [2] II, 52.

To the swoon'd serpent, and with languid arm,
Delicate, put to proof the lythe Caducean charm.
So done, upon the nymph his eyes he bent
Full of adoring tears and blandishment,
And towards her stept: she, like a moon in wane,
Faded before him, cower'd, nor could restrain
Her fearful sobs, self-folding like a flower
That faints into itself at evening hour:
But the God fostereth her chilled hand,
She felt the warmth, her eyelids open'd bland,
And, like new flowers at morning song of bees,
Bloom'd, and gave up her honey to the lees.[1]

Once again the elements are familiar. The point is, too familiar. Those last six lines read as if Keats had decided to save his critic trouble and give him infolding, infeeling, temperature contrast, dispersed hand and eyelid, the ripeness metaphor, honey for the mind's palate—the essentials in a nutshell. We flinch, ungratefully, from the taint of something that lies between self-parody and self-prostitution. We are reacting against the new knowledge in *Lamia*; and the key to what Keats knows, and how we react, is this flippant talk about divine dreaming. The love which Hermes enjoys is either "no dream" or it is the "real" dream of a god. Here is the killing analytic touch, so relevant to and so remote from the companionship of actual and real in *St. Agnes*, and from the antiphonal dialectic of the odes. The reality of Hermes's dream is a heartless postulate; therefore his love-experience, the "warm, flush'd moment" and what follows, lacks imaginative body. But it has been lent a rhetorical voice, the bodiless voice of great Keats, which is why those who rejoice in Keats find the voice distressing.

Lycius, unlike Hermes, is no god; the poem does not claim reality for his human dream of love. Because, however, the reality of divine dreaming is schematic and inert, nothing can grow in the poem's human soil either. Real and unreal are both barren categories; the feel-rhetoric undercuts them, and we come to see that Hermes's fainting, "self-folding" flower and Lycius's "hid scent of an unbudded rose" are the same thing. There is no profit in calling them real or unreal. They are the true but the placed thing, and desolating therefore.

The snakeskin narrative is leathery, bright and very visual, whereas the confined dream of love is a sort of imaginative cannibalism. The snailhorn lives off itself, explores and exploits itself,

[1] I, 124

and, as always, snailhorn entails stasis; even here the deep secret taste of Lycius's love is retold in the held picture of the lover

> bending to her open eyes,
> *Where he was mirror'd small in paradise,*[1]

(isn't that fine) while Lamia the loved object, "tiptoe with white arms spread",[2] strikes the classic attitude of Keats's Hyperionic natural sculpture; and the stars looking down on their love-making—

> *While, like held breath, the stars drew in their*
> *panting fires—*[3]

tell us exactly what underlies the hushed and sealed-in tension of such images elsewhere: the much more reticent star in the sonnet, for example, "watching with eternal lids apart". *Lamia's* stars have the slight exaggeration of overexplicitness which betrays this poem's love-rhetoric throughout. For a moment—

> *Now on the moth-time of that evening dim—*[4]

we may suppose everything is as it was in *Isabella* and *St. Agnes*, but not for long.

The price of making *Lamia* unsmokeable turns out, then, to be the surrender of that sovereign quality which had made the other poems unmisgiving. He devises square brackets of the ironical fancy within which he can state his dream and yet not reveal (as he expresses himself in the letter to Woodhouse) "inexperience of life and simplicity of knowledge". Clarity remains the fundamental issue, deeper than *Lamia's* cynicism. His notional brackets warn the reader, simultaneously, that dreams are dreams and facts are facts. And this contrast becomes an active presence in the poem's cross-reference between Lycius and Apollonius. Lycius feels his dream—which means his woman and his overexplicit love-rhetoric. Apollonius, who occupies the left panel of the *Lamia* triptych, sees the fact:

> *The bald-head philosopher*
> *Had fix'd his eye, without a twinkle or stir*
> *Full on the alarmed beauty of the bride,*[5]

and his eye apprehends the snake she is. Sees means sees; Keats places enormous stress on this philosophical, observing eye. As

---

[1] II, 46.   [2] I, 287.   [3] I, 300.
[4] I, 220.   [5] II, 245.

Lamia turns "deadly white" under its gaze Lycius urges Apollonius:

> *Shut, shut those juggling eyes, thou ruthless man!*
> *Turn them aside, wretch!*[1]

appealing to the wedding guests,

> *Mark how, possess'd, his lashless eyelids stretch*
> *Around his demon eyes! Corinthians, see!*
> *My sweet bride withers at their potency.*[2]

But "his eyes still / Relented not, nor mov'd";[3] until

> *Lamia breath'd death's breath; the sophist's eye,*
> *Like a sharp spear, went through her utterly,*
> *Keen, cruel, perceant, stinging:*[4]

the very opposite of the snailhorn-eye "shut softly up alive".

Apollonius's eye is the organ of fact. Fact and dream collide when Lycius conceives the plan to publicise his love which was hitherto "shut from the busy world"[5] and drive his mistress in open triumph round Corinth,

> *While through the thronged streets your bridal car*
> *Wheels round its dazzling spokes.*[6]

The shock of change from the "purple-lined palace"[7]—a dark tactile purple—which had housed Lycius's love to those dazzling spokes in the open streets summarises the clash of fact and dream. Afterwards, the world enters the palace and the dream vanishes, pierced and destroyed by Apollonius's seeing eye. In Apollonius the daylight of public Corinth and the outward Drydenesque narrative meet. And so the poem completes the binding to itself of the two triptych-wings.

Keats did not intend us to dismiss Lycius as a fool for making his disastrous public plan. Rather, the poem lets drift free for our contemplation the question whether Lycius was able to help himself. He and Lamia are reclining side by side, a coarser version of Cupid and Psyche,

> *with eyelids closed,*
> *Saving a tythe which love still open kept,*
> *That they might see each other while they almost slept;*
> *When from the slope side of a suburb hill,*
> *Deafening the swallow's twitter, came a thrill*

II, 277.   [2] II, 288.   [3] II, 295.   [4] II, 299.
     [5] I, 397.   [6] II, 63.   [7] II, 31.

> *Of trumpets—Lycius started—the sounds fled,*
> *But left a thought a-buzzing in his head.*
> *For the first time, since first he harbour'd in*
> *That purple-lined palace of sweet sin,*
> *His spirit pass'd beyond its golden bourn*
> *Into the noisy world almost forsworn.*[1]

We cannot be sure that Lycius had any means of keeping the trumpets out, and with the trumpets "the noisy world", and with trumpets and world, "a thought". These things seem to assert themselves, though "almost forsworn" recalls that he had once been Apollonius's pupil in philosophy—that is in the life of thought—and had ears to hear the trumpets. When Lamia understood what was happening,

> *she began to moan and sigh,*
> *Because he mused beyond her, knowing well*
> *That but a moment's thought is passion's passing bell.*[2]

She knew that the clash of fact and dream could not now be averted.

> *"Why do you sigh, fair creature?" whisper'd he:*
> *"Why do you think?" return'd she tenderly:*
> *"You have deserted me;—where am I now?"*[3]

At once he protests; but she is right. For he continues,

> *"My thoughts! shall I unveil them? Listen then!"*[4]

And his thoughts prove to be his public plan, the bridal progress and feast, nothing else.

Lamia's very special sharpness of definition declares itself chiefly in this intruding of thought upon passion. The incident is a rounding-off operation, a clean dismissal of a subject first raised in the Adam's-dream letter, nearly two years before:

I am the more zealous in this affair, because I have never yet been able to perceive how any thing can be known for truth by consequitive reasoning—and yet it must be. Can it be that even the greatest philosopher ever arrived at his goal without putting aside numerous objections? However it may be, O for a Life of Sensations rather than of Thoughts!

Lamia nails this issue with incisive, murderous neatness: clarity once more and finally. The technical brio of the verse supports a theme of thought's intrusion upon passion, which is to say fact's clash with dream. The poem reads most effective as cruel comedy.

> *"Why do you think?" retur'd she tenderly. . . .*

[1] II, 23.   [2] II, 37.   [3] II, 40.   [4] II, 56.

And in equating thought with fact one remembers that the air Keats breathed was soaked in the British empirical tradition— Locke's "clear and distinct ideas", the range of things Hazlitt will have talked to him about[1]—and one regards *Lamia* itself, in its clear and distinct visuality, as fact's narrative likeness, or thought's sharpness of feature mirrored in the outward event.

Just as the reader is not meant to call Lycius a fool, so he should not conclude, with Lamia vanished and Lycius dead, that Keats has written a poem about the folly, still less the wickedness, of dreaming. His energies are bent upon the sheer incompatibility of fact and dream; this has to be expressed with all possible conviction, and Drydenesque brilliance. Apollonius cried "'Fool!'"— and "'Fool! Fool!' repeated he"[2]—to Lycius while his eyes were running through the woman to the snake; but when Lycius first met Lamia, Apollonius, hitherto his "good instructor", now seemed "the ghost of folly haunting my sweet dreams".[3] The right wing of the triptych can claim as much authority as the left. If—a big "if"—the trumpets, the world of fact and thought, can be kept out, dreaming is and remains fine. Keats still longs for the truth at the end of Adam's dream. Nor does he need to arrive at *Lamia* to discover that dreams are fragile. In this poem, the separation of dream and fact which had been so natural and tender and (within the story) beautiful at the moment of Madeline's waking in *St. Agnes*, and so very artistic—therefore rescued while confessed —in the tragic lyricism of the odes, is allowed to harden into incompatibility.

The result is that dream and fact both suffer, and the force which lifted them, in the other poems, into a rapt dialogue between the actual and the real, cannot be summoned in *Lamia*. Nothing could be more suggestive than the two occurrences of "real" in the poem. The first we have just met: Hermes's sight of his nymph was no dream; or if it was a dream, then "real are the dreams of Gods". The second is provoked by Lamia's successful efforts to persuade Lycius that she is entirely human, without "any more subtle fluid in her veins / Than throbbing blood".

---

[1] They saw a good deal of each other in London, and it is not surprising that only a slender written record survives. Keats's letter telling John Reynolds he is preparing "to ask Hazlitt in about a year's time the best metaphysical road I can take" (*Letters*, vol. I, p. 274) faintly reflects their intellectual companionship. Hazlitt's *Essay on the Principles of Human Action* is in the list of books belonging to Keats which Woodhouse drew up after his death.

[2] II, 291-6.   [3] I, 376-7.

> *Let the mad poets say whate'er they please*
> *Of the sweets of Fairies, Peris, Goddesses,*
> *There is not such a treat among them all,*
> *Haunters of cavern, lake, and waterfall,*
> *As a real woman. . . .*[1]

In both places he is appealing to the criterion of flesh and blood. Facts are facts. Real means actual. One can corner his reality here as is never possible in his greatest work. Poising fact against dream, contriving their fatal encounter, *Lamia* is a big poem but not a great one; it covers the ground of his maturest interests, and yet when we ask what it has to say for itself we find it has given up the heroic part of the 1819 enterprise.

To see that real now means actual is to understand how dreaming gets confined and placed in *Lamia,* and why the eloquent tension between dream and fact has been diminished to a stony dogmatism of inevitable discord. The supremely clear poem ends up, ironically, in chaos. Keats does not intend Apollonius to refute Lycius. Apollonius is the "consequitive reasoning "of the Adam's-dream letter, and Keats still, when he comes to write *Lamia,* cannot "perceive how any thing can be known for truth by consequitive reasoning". Apollonius pierces the dream and asserts the fact against it, but he knows nothing "for truth". This would not emerge from the unaided story, which tells how the seeing philosopher unmasks a witch; therefore Keats has to shore up the dream against the fact. He punishes the fact, unreasonably. He (as well as Lycius) reduces philosopher to "sophist". He asks, in a summing-up vein,

> *What wreath for Lamia? What for Lycius?*
> *What for the sage, old Apollonius?*[2]

And answers,

> *for the sage,*
> *Let spear-grass and the spiteful thistle wage*
> *War on his temples. Do not all charms fly*
> *At the mere touch of cold philosophy?*
> *There was an awful rainbow once in heaven:*
> *We know her woof, her texture; she is given*
> *In the full catalogue of common things.*
> *Philosophy will clip an Angel's wings,*
> *Conquer all mysteries by rule and line,*
> *Empty the haunted air, and gnomed mine—*
> *Unweave a rainbow, as it erewhile made*
> *The tender-person'd Lamia melt into a shade.*[3]

[1] I, 328. [2] II, 221. [3] II, 227.

That sudden gratuitous snap at "cold philosophy" is the most quoted piece of *Lamia*, partly—sinister sign—because it is a detachable Romantic sentiment, and partly because it throws into sharp relief the problem of the schizophrenic poem. I think we should accept that it is unfair to Apollonius and maladjusted to the work of art. Its tone is all wrong. It has the impossible task of injecting, *ab extra*, virtue into the dream; and, failing, it moves us once more to apply Keats's principle against himself and "hate poetry that has a palpable design upon us". The dream must pay its way inside the story, and if it can't, no feeble declamation about heavenly rainbows and angels' wings will help it. Contrast the unappropriated religious rhetoric here with his "clasp'd like a missal" of Madeline asleep. In these *Lamia* lines Keats is gesturing towards an encounter between the real and the actual which never took place.

The confined and placed dream is, inevitably, unactual; this forms the converse of the shrunken meaning of "real" in *Lamia*. Love's "purple-lined palace" is a magic—black magic?—structure of illusion; so is the "glowing banquet-room", and its décor:

> *Fresh carved cedar, mimicking a glade*
> *Of palm and plantain, met from either side,*
> *High in the midst. . . .*[1]

The reading ear pricks up at "mimicking"; surely a *Lamia* word, calculated and unsmokeable. How much depends on the unspectacular gap between this mimicry and the feigning fancy of the odes! Twenty lines later Keats shows his hand:

> *each guest, with busy brain,*
> *Arriving at the portal, gaz'd amain,*
> *And enter'd marveling: for they knew the street,*
> *Remember'd it from childhood all complete*
> *Without a gap, yet ne'er before had seen*
> *That royal porch, that high-built fair demesne;*
> *So in they hurried all, maz'd, curious and keen:*
> *Save one, who looke'd thereon with eye severe. . . .*[2]

Apollonius of course. His seeing eye penetrates building as well as bride; and in the quotation from Burton's *Anatomy of Melancholy* which Keats appended to the poem Burton had suggested to him in the first place, "all her furniture was, like Tantalus' gold, described by Homer, no substance but mere illusions . . . plate, house, and all that was in it, vanished in an instant".

[1] II, 125.   [2] II, 150.

For the incompatibility of fact and dream has to be rendered complete. And in that tight neat disconnection resides *Lamia's* knowingness and tonal flippancy. Everything, it transpires, may be deduced from the shrivelled significance of "real"—the clarity and ultimate chaos, the troubles besetting both fact and dream. Dream suffers more than fact, as we should expect, since fact refers us to *Lamia's* Drydenesque merits while dream abuses feel. Again and for the last time Keats undoes our anti-Arnoldian work on his behalf and puts the "merely" back into the concept of the merely sensual poet. This is the mood of his tampering with *St. Agnes*. Porphyro, he insists, "acts all the acts of a bona fide husband"—which calls for a bona fide wife, a real woman. Lamia (the bride, not the admirable bright snake) exudes a vulgarity which nothing could save. She assumes the Indian Maid's role of erotic virtuoso and dandles it horribly,

> *As though in Cupid's college she had spent*
> *Sweet days a lovely graduate, still unshent,*
> *And kept his rosy terms in idle languishment.*[1]

From this spongy sick centre a demoralising sexuality spreads through the entire dream. She is a sadist:

> *Her soft look growing coy, she saw his chain so sure;*[2]

and, having got Lycius, she tortures him:

> *"Alas! poor youth,*
> *What taste of purer air hast thou to soothe*
> *My essence? What serener palaces,*
> *Where I may all my many senses please,*
> *And by mysterious sleights a hundred thirsts appease?"*[3]

(Alas, too, for the prostituted snailhorn.) Under this treatment Lycius

> *Swoon'd, murmuring of love, and pale with pain.*[4]

So Lamia

> *Put her new lips to his, and gave afresh*
> *The life she had so tangled in her mesh:*[5]

and on with the "sweet sin". But Lycius also can be "perverse" as Keats puts it:

> *in self despite*
> *Against his better self he took delight*
> *Luxurious in her sorrows, soft and new.*[6]

[1] I, 197.   [2] I, 256.   [3] I, 281.
[4] I, 289.   [5] I, 294.   [6] II, 70.

To which dread delicious challenge Lamia proves herself entirely adequate, summoning a masochistic *persona* for the occasion:

> *She burnt, she lov'd the tyranny,*
> *And, all subdued, consented to the hour*
> *When to the bridal he should lead his paramour.*[1]

A distinction emerges, however, between "Cupid's college" which is perhaps the worst thing in all Keats, and the stuff of this dream-love. The latter, "perverse" or not, is apprehended from out of human sex; the claim for *Lamia's* unbookish experience was not lightly made. A strand runs through the poem which then underpasses Arnold's, Tennyson's, the pre-Raphaelites' Keats, and reappears entwined in Swinburne and the Nineties. Many will like *Lamia* none the better for this strand, but they are bound to understand more about the knowing tricks it gets up to. Because sophistication places the dream, and because sex articulates the dream, the poet who has let us see him throw brackets of his own wishful supposing round the dream can go on to claim anything he happens to fancy for sex. Naturally Keats claims what he does fancy. He explains, carefully, as if it were the summit of her erotic accomplishment, and with a solemn lumpish technicality which jogs the reader alert, that Lamia has some special power to unravel pleasure and pain:

> *A virgin purest lipp'd, yet in the lore*
> *Of love deep learned to the red heart's core:*
> *Not one hour old, yet of sciential brain*
> *To unperplex bliss from its neighbour pain;*
> *Define their pettish limits, and estrange*
> *Their points of contact, and swift counterchange;*
> *Intrigue with the specious chaos, and dispart*
> *Its most ambiguous atoms with sure art. . . .*[2]

And sure enough after that prelude, when she breathed love to Lycius,

> *from amaze into delight he fell*
> *To hear her whisper woman's lore so well;*
> *And every word she spake entic'd him on*
> *To unperplex'd delight and pleasure known.*[3]

This unperplexing gift may seem an odd thing to stress. Here is a rare instance of Keats casting back, semi-privately, over his own short writing career. Endymion's unknown goddess grapples in a

[1] II, 81.   [2] I, 189.   [3] I, 324.

long blissful love-throe with him—"Let us entwine hoveringly"—
and suddenly the pleasure has vanished and

> *"I am pain'd,*
> *Endymion: woe! woe! is grief contain'd*
> *In the very deeps of pleasure, my sole life?"*[1]

The problem is again how to unperplex. And similarly in *The Fall*
where the matter is rather obscurely and inconsistently philo-
sophised:

> *Every sole man hath days of joy and pain,*
> *Whether his labours be sublime or low—*
> *The pain alone; the joy alone; distinct:*
> *Only the dreamer venoms all his days,*
> *Bearing more woe than all his sins deserve.*[2]

And in *Hyperion*, when Apollo played his lyre and the universe

> *Listen'd in pain and pleasure at the birth*
> *Of such new tuneful wonder.*[3]

But the centre of the pain-pleasure spectrum, as *Hyperion* suggests, is
that oxymoronic savour which comes with the perplexing of the
mind's palate: the bees of *Isabella*,

> *Even bees, the little almsmen of spring-bowers,*
> *Know there is richest juice in poison-flowers.*

And *Melancholy*,

> *aching Pleasure nigh,*
> *Turning to poison while the bee-mouth sips. . . .*

Or the perplexing motif may be handled lightly, as in the
"Welcome joy, and welcome sorrow" lyric—"Oh the sweetness of
the pain!" Or it may be sharpened towards sex, as in the "breathing human passion" of the *Grecian Urn*

> *That leaves a heart high-sorrowful and cloy'd,*
> *A burning forehead, and a parching tongue.*

Which brings the wheel full circle to Lamia, the new but expert
bride.

For Keats, Lamia is the magical unperplexer, the partner he
tritely dreams of. Pleasure, pain, the entire scope of feel, dictates that
repeated "unperplex", an idiosyncrasy with noble connections

---

[1] II, 822.   [2] I, 172.   [3] III, 66.

though its interest here is diagnostic only. So with "convuls'd" in Lamia's metamorphosis from snake into woman:

> She writh'd about, convuls'd with scarlet pain:[1]

echoing the "fierce convulse" of that other metamorphosis in *Hyperion*, when "young Apollo anguish'd" towards divinity. So too at the withering moment, the negative outcome, when Lycius is watching the effect of Apollonius's eyes upon his dream-partner, the unperplexer:

> *"My sweet bride withers at their potency."*[2]

A verbal and unfeeling "withers", this one, but still an encouragement to put Apollonius, the seeing man of thought and fact, the anti-dreamer, in the left or *Belle Dame* wing of the *Lamia* triptych.[3] Through its half-intended ironies and manipulating of an established vocabulary, *Lamia* builds up a scrapbook of personal memories, snailhorn and other, for the reader who comes after if not for the writing poet.

3 'To Autumn' *Revisited*

The stubble-fields looked warm that Sunday after the manner of "some pictures", and this struck Keats so forcibly that, as he tells John Reynolds, "I composed upon it".[4] There lies the impulse

---

[1] I, 154.   [2] II, 290.

[3] I keep mentioning *La Belle Dame*, but the Tragedy *Otho* which Keats was writing alongside *Lamia* ought to be remembered too. *Otho* is about a prince, Ludolph, who gets himself into a *Lamia* situation by marrying a beautiful enchantress, Auranthe, who is other than she seems. Like Lycius, Ludolph is swept into "soft responses", and the immediate comment of a bystander is "How deep she has bewitch'd him!" (III, 11). This bewitching constitutes *Otho's* tragic axis.

More remotely, the abandoned satire *Cap and Bells* recalls *Lamia* in its illicit mixing of human and non-human loves and its fairy Emperor who "lov'd girls smooth as shades, but hated a mere shade". The satire also has a painful element of self-parody rather like *Lamia's*:

> *Whereat a narrow Flemish glass he took,*
> *That once belong'd to Admiral De Witt,*
> *Admired it with a connoisseuring look,*
> *And with the ripest claret crowned it,*
> *And, ere one lively bead could burst and flit,*
> *He turn'd it quickly, nimbly upside down. . . .* (XLVII)

The ripe claret and bursting beaded bubbles are too close to the *Nightingale Ode* for comfort.

[4] Page 225, above.

behind the Ode; a double impulse, I now add, in that the fields which were warm like some pictures were also warm unlike and better than the green fields of Spring. "Aye better than the chilly green of the Spring" says the letter; and the poem modulates this thought into

> Where are the songs of Spring? Ay, where are they?
> Think not of them. . . .

Why introduce the Spring? Or perhaps, why not? Anyone out walking on a fine autumn day might turn his mind, contrastingly, to the Spring. But in fact Keats had a special reason. He was in the middle of a journal letter to his brother and sister-in-law, and on the Monday—the day after the walk and before the letter to Reynolds—he wrote to them like this:

Some time since I began a Poem call'd *The Eve of St. Mark* quite in the spirit of town quietude. I think it will give you the sensation of walking about an old county town in a coolish evening. I know not yet whether I shall ever finish it—I will give it as far as I have gone. *Ut tibi placent!*

> Upon a Sabbath day it fell;
> Thrice holy was the sabbath bell
> That call'd the folk to evening prayer.
> The City Streets were clean and fair
> From wholesome drench of April rains,
> And on the western window panes
> The chilly sunset faintly told
> Of immatur'd, green vallies cold,
> Of the green, thorny, bloomless hedge,
> Of Rivers new with spring tide sedge,
> Of Primroses by shelter'd rills,
> And Dasies on the aguish hills.[1]

Thus the Spring was helped, if not brought, to mind by *The Eve of St. Mark*. And the impulse springing from unlikeness turns out to be just as close a tangle of art and nature as his musing on pictures and stubble-plains. *St. Mark's* "chilly sunset" stands in the simplest seasonal opposition to the "soft-dying day" of *Autumn*; indeed the whole ode may be spelt, by way of counter-thought, out of the single word "immatur'd" in the fragment he was copying that Monday, and which he never finished.

I want to draw together the record of these three days: the walk, the two letters, the ode. The date is late September. Keats could not know, nor anyone else, that with *Autumn* written his important

---

[1] *Letters*, vol. II, p. 201.

work was almost done. There seemed to be other things ahead, in particular "a few fine plays". He felt well. He was twenty-four.

Hindsight teaches a different lesson, and shows his end plainly demonstrable in his beginning. We expect to go, and have gone, to the 1817 volume for the elementary grammar of end-stopped feel, for temperature contrasts, for the direct, unabashed appeal to pleasure in himself and responsive "sensation" in his reader. But the yield of those three days in 1819 will do as well—or better. For here his "Really, without joking, chaste weather" gives what we should look for in vain in early Keats, the morality of feel. It is the voice of the grown man, the force we apprehend beneath "wholesome" and "clean and fair" in *St. Mark*, the gratitude that moves us so strangely from within the simple verb "bless" in *Autumn's* third line.

On the Tuesday, the last of the three days, he wrote to Woodhouse as well as to Reynolds. He copied *Autumn* fair for Woodhouse, but before he did so he said:

Dear Woodhouse,

If you see what I have said to Reynolds before you come to your own dose you will put it between the bars unread; provided they have begun fires in Bath—I should like a bit of fire to night—one likes a bit of fire. How glorious the Blacksmiths' shops look now—I stood to night before one till I was very near listing for one. Yes I should like a bit of fire. . . .[1]

Keats standing before the blacksmith's fire is an image that bespeaks the deep sanity and peace of his imagination. We should bear that fire in mind when we wonder where the domestic instinct of *St. Agnes* comes from, how Porphyro can announce that he has "a home" for Madeline, not just unabsurdly but with confidence strong enough to cradle the poem's sex. A similar fire, the same warm apprehension, may be at work in the ode itself, for the soundness of "sound asleep" in the middle stanza reverberates like a memory of childhood's safe comfort.[2] The blacksmith was a Winchester blacksmith where Keats was staying. Winchester became happy for him in the central habit of his genius: on one and the same day Woodhouse hears about the blacksmith and Reynolds receives the confession "I never lik'd stubble-fields so much as now", and his brother and sister-in-law are told simply, "Now the time is beautiful". He lodges alone; but he tells the last pair, quoting his *St. Mark* again, "You would scarcely imagine I

---

[1] *Letters*, p. 169.

[2] The association of fire and sleep and domestic peace goes back to the sonnet "Small, busy flames play through the fresh laid coals" of November 1816.

could live alone so comfortably 'Kepen in solitarinesse'". Solitude reappears incidentally in a letter to Haydon the painter:

The view of the high street through the gate of the city in the beautiful September evening light has amused me frequently. The bad singing of the Cathedral I do not care to smoke—being by myself I am not very coy in my taste.[1]

That quaint word "smoke" again. What would he have said now, strolling happy by himself, about *Lamia* and the criterion of smokeability? I expect he would have laughed and turned his back on that stuff and praised the weather, as in a letter to his sister, and described the joy of "fair atmosphere to think in—a clean towel mark'd with the mangle and a basin of clear water to drench one's face with ten times a day.... Still I enjoy the weather, I adore fine weather as the greatest blessing I can have".[2]

The weather and Winchester and solitude are all deeply implicated in the ode *To Autumn*. These are special to itself. Equally, the ode is one of a classical series, the last of the five.

Concern with transience binds the five odes together. Their common basis is the folk-truth of change and decay, of *tout passe, tout casse, tout lasse*; they set off in their different directions from this starting point. The two with the shortest journeys are the saddest and the most serene, *Melancholy* and *Autumn*. Both of these stay within touching and tasting distance of *tout passe* throughout, and, because they set up no eye-catching structure over against sheer transience (*Melancholy* none at all[3] and *Autumn* only the "never cease" dream of its bees), a direct temporal approach to them has fewer initial pitfalls than to the others; we don't entangle ourselves in questions like, what does Keats intend by the immortality of the nightingale or the eternal warmth of the love pictured on the urn?

Deploying my spatial argument, I made mention of the inescapable falsehood and crude hyperbole, and the platitude, attending Keatsian time when it is not received as he conceived it, projected upon the plane of space. *Melancholy* escapes being hit by this consideration since its temporality is satisfying as it stands, especially in the ode's climax: the unburst grape is tasteless and the burst grape is over. Transience is Keats's subject, and the pessimism of that last observation is agreeably pert. But the temporal theme in *Melancholy* satisfies us only because the grape itself is right, in other words because transience has been articulated through taste with the same blind sureness that leads him to

---

[1] *Letters*, vol. II, p. 221.   [2] *Ibid.*, p. 148.
[3] I understand the ode's "temple" and "sovran shrine" in the spirit of Kant's remark that only the permanent can change.

realise the non-transient structure of *Psyche* in its mind-space ("Yes, I will be thy priest, and build a fane / In some untrodden region of my mind"), and of the *Nightingale* in the dream-space of embalmed forest darkness, and of the *Grecian Urn* in the art-space of a painted, mimetic love and sacrifice. *Melancholy* proceeds from the twisting and forehead-kissing and the downy owl of the opening stanza to the first mention of its subject, "the melancholy fit", at the beginning of the second. And now the pattern of taste, the intensifying and drawing inward of sensation, asserts itself tyranically:

> But when the melancholy fit shall fall . . .
> Then glut thy sorrow on a morning rose,
> Or on the rainbow of the salt sand-wave,
> Or on the wealth of globed peonies. . . .

The discretion is admirable with which transience gets silently carried by the morning rose (before the sun has got at it) and by the melting rainbow and sand-wave (between tides), so that the "Beauty that must die" generalisations of the final stanza arrive like a divine confirmation of loss. And it is taste which has been lost and which the last stanza will dilate on, with its burst grape and the pleasure-pain oxymoron of its sipping bee-mouth. The external aspect of the rose yields to the gravitational tug of "glut"; and anyone who supposes there is no way of glutting sorrow on a sand-wave other than ordinary looking at it, should reflect upon the insinuating little palate-adjective "salt" for a moment. Likewise, Keats speaks expressly of Melancholy as "seen of none save him . . ."; but when we emerge the other side of the burst grape at

> His soul shall taste the sadness of her might,

the visual import of "seen" has become almost a figure of speech in a poem whose business is to tell the snailhorn's tragedy.

Autumn too is full of glut, but the season's glut, not the glutting of sorrow. It contemplates transience, for a sunny day is no less a wasting natural joy than a rainbow or flower or grape. Indeed this ode stands only a little further from pure transience than *Melancholy* does, a distance measured by its bees; but while *Melancholy* is the least spatial of the odes, proving transience immediately on the pulse of taste, *Autumn* grasps the spatial dimension at once historically, through the Sunday scene outside Winchester on 19 September 1819, and aesthetically by bringing to birth the poet's premonitory "warm—in the same way that some pictures look warm".

Aesthetic warmth, whatever that may be—the thought brings one near to the *Grecian Urn*—is at any rate not a wasting joy. But Keats was too much a realist to use the warmest-looking picture, or picture-poem, as if it were his blacksmith's fire. Whence, then, the partnership of profound naturalism and equally profound human contentment in the ode? Where is his joy in the dying year?

Those happy letters from Winchester and *To Autumn* itself come close on the heels of *Lamia*, and *Lamia* is the poem where "O for a Life of Sensations rather than Thoughts!" gets dramatised into a tight, bright tale of incompatibility. Keats's inclination had always been to map the self as a place of double lodgment, for Lycius and Apollonius, feeler and thinker. An outburst like

> *Do gently murder half my soul, and I*
> *Shall feel the other half so utterly!*[1]

has their uneasy cohabitation at the bottom of it; but not until and only in *Lamia* does the hardening of tension into incompatibility take place.

During the Spring of 1819, two or three months before *Lamia* and close to all the odes except *Autumn*, Keats wrote an uneven sonnet *On Fame*:

> *How fever'd is the man, who cannot look*
> *Upon his mortal days with temperate blood,*
> *Who vexes all the leaves of his life's book,*
> *And robs his fair name of its maidenhood;*
> *It is as if the rose should pluck herself,*
> *Or the ripe plum finger its misty bloom,*
> *As if a Naiad, like a meddling elf,*
> *Should darken her pure grot with muddy gloom:*
> *But the rose leaves herself upon the briar,*
> *For winds to kiss and grateful bees to feed,*
> *And the ripe plum still wears its dim attire,*
> *The undisturbed lake has crystal space;*
> *Why then should man, teasing the world for grace,*
> *Spoil his salvation for a fierce miscreed?*

The whole thing is very much a sensations-and-thoughts question. Reading, one may strike a *Lamia* attitude and object that men are not roses or plums, and if they are being kissed by the wind or possess a misty bloom, cannot help being self-conscious and "fever'd" about it, cannot help "meddling"; facts are facts, as

---

[1] *Endymion*, IV, 309.

Lamia insists, and self-consciousness is a fact of our humanity; so "the man" of the first line ought to be Everyman.

The sonnet itself reads much less clearcut than this; and, although "the man" has become "man" in the penultimate line, it seems to envisage human roses who leave themselves on the briar of pure feel, and human plums who refrain from fingering their bloom in thought. "Why then should man . . .?" suggests things could be otherwise.

That possibility stays alive, goodness knows how, underneath *Lamia* and becomes *To Autumn's* unspoken prologue. *On Fame* (really, *On Feverishness*) asks to be read in the light of that Tuesday when Keats copied out the ode for Woodhouse and went on to describe his present state:

Quieter in my pulse, improved in my digestion; exerting myself against vexing speculations—scarcely content to write the best verses for the fever they leave behind.

Perhaps "the best verses" means, in his own heart just now, *To Autumn*; anyhow it points the contrast with the sonnet which, while not among his worst verses, opens up the old yawning gulf between characterful roses and plums and grotesquely inept humanity. He is still capable of

> *vexes all the leaves of his life's book,*
> *And robs his fair name of its maidenhood*

in the Spring of 1819, and capable, less surprisingly, of the hollow pretension running through the last two lines (compare the "Death is life's high meed" conclusion of "Why did I laugh tonight?" from the same Spring). The crucial problem persists—crucial for Keats and his critic—of mind's rendering and humanity's credible presence within the poetry of feel. Even now we stand and watch the thing he can do snap clean away from the thing he cannot. And the thing he can do, rose and plum, then turns intense before our eyes, intense towards feeding and kissing, ripeness, bloom, the consummated actual.

The picture of ripeness in *To Autumn* tells the story of rose and plum again, but now there is no thoughtful, feverish mankind standing outside that picture and being ranted at for failing to get inside. The humanity of the ode amounts to the figure of Autumn in its successive poses (which is the poem's Hyperionic natural sculpture), and to the painting poet. Keats puts himself inside his autumn scene by living his own insight,

> *The flower must drink the nature of the soil,*
> *Before it can put forth its blossoming:*

before it can write the ode *To Autumn*. This truth is neighbour to that of the Vale of Soul-Making, the finest passage in all his letters.

The point at which Man may arrive is as far as the parallel state in inanimate nature and no further. For instance, suppose a rose to have sensation, it blooms on a beautiful morning, it enjoys itself—but there comes a cold wind, a hot sun—it cannot escape it, it cannot destroy its annoyances—they are as native to the world as itself: no more can man be happy in spite, the worldly elements will prey upon his nature.

Neighbour in time as well as in spirit, for the Vale is part of a long journal letter to America, and the sonnet *On Fame* follows immediately. Now when Keats wrote out the sonnet for his brother and sister-in-law (this being the only surviving autograph) he put a proverb at the head of it:

You cannot eat your Cake and have it too,

The proverb forms a bridge between the vale and the sonnet. Just because it is transitional, we find the reference to both of them oblique. Applying the proverb to the vale one might reflect: Man cannot enjoy the beautiful fine morning alongside the rose and then opt out of nature when the cold wind comes. Applying it to the sonnet: If you want to be visited by bees like the rose, you must leave yourself on the briar as the rose does. The closeness of sonnet to vale then becomes obvious, since the rose also leaves itself on the briar to endure the "annoyances" which are the suffering, soul-making theme of the vale.

The rose on the briar in all weathers is the very flower which

must drink the nature of the soil
Before it can put forth its blossoming:

and the ode *To Autumn* tells us what the soil tastes like. This poem is not one to flourish its scars; its way of projecting a feel which we now understand to be Keats's final essay in the pleasure-pain oxymoron, is the ripeness metaphor. But scarcely a metaphor any longer, since, extending through the artifact's nature-space, the autumn scene has possessed the poem. And the realised presence of Autumn shares with Keatsian consummation as we meet it everywhere, the double character of fulfilment and death. Such crude impertinencies as the Indian girl's

We might embrace and die: voluptuous thought!

have now been dissolved into the season's soft atmosphere, bound within the poet's inspiration, made beautiful. The Psyche-moth's

Liebestod, also beautiful, has been done again, unhectic, after nature. No less a climax than *Psyche* or *Melancholy*, this last ode carries the antiphonal whisper, the *Nightingale's* "forlorn" and the *Urn's* "cold", across its surface; its stubble-plains record the year's death within the garnering of the year's corn.

But instead of being the greatest of the odes, *To Autumn* would be paltry by comparison if Keats had not made it possible to apprehend him inside his poem, the human rose on the briar. Certainly one must look to that special time at Winchester when he found saying yes to life so simple. That time presents the pure extreme of the pungent selflessness we recognise him by: I am thinking of the figure in the doorway of the blacksmith's shop. It is an impression which runs down to the hidden point where man and artist are one. Even when the sufferings of his last year drew him into a tight ball of misery, and therefore of self-consciousness, we find an embryo poetry, a breaking free into the unknown sensuality of death, in "O! I can feel the cold earth upon me—the daisies growing over me". This feel of his own death falls within a larger anxiety for Severn, his companion and nurse:

Four days previous to his death—the change in him was so great that I passed each moment in dread—not knowing what the next would have—he was calm and firm at its approaches—to a most astonishing degree—he told me not to tremble for he did not think he should be convulsed—he said—"did you ever see any one die"—no—"well then I pity you poor Severn—what trouble and danger you have got into for me—now you must be firm for it will not last long—I shall soon be laid in the quiet grave—thank God for the quiet grave—O! I can feel the cold earth upon me—the daisies growing over me—O for this quiet—it will be my first"—when the morning light came and still found him alive—O how bitterly he grieved—I cannot bear his cries.[1]

The link between such unselfishness and the impersonal effect of the odes, *To Autumn* specially, is not demonstrable any more than it is to be doubted. As things are, the involution which seals off the rest of the series into their own kind of objectivity has disappeared in *Autumn*, except at the level of rhyme-scheme. There is nothing remotely comparable to the syntax of the *Nightingale's* first sentence, or, inside that sentence, to the semantic thickness of "too happy". Another "too" occurs in "shade to shade will come too drowsily" in *Melancholy*. What does that mean? Then why "hungry generations"—hungry and treading—except as a secret token of the snailhorn? It is important not to brush aside the in-

---

[1] *Keats Circle*, vol. I, p. 224.

scrutable element common to all the odes except *Autumn*.[1] Of
course this does not turn them into symbolist poems, but it does
play its part in the autonomous, self-communing effect which
Autumn achieves by other means.

Autumn proceeds descriptively. Being about ripeness it describes
ripeness at length. Without saying so, it is about death as well as
ripeness, which might seem to call for a devious art like that of the
other odes. But, true to its direct nature, *Autumn* introduces death
by naming it—twice, in the "soft-dying day" and the wind which
"lives or dies". This happens in the third stanza, the death stanza,
the stanza of the stubble-plains and the robin who earns the name
"red-breast" more and more with the approach of winter, as his
colour brightens. Autumn being its subject still, the third stanza is
not devoted entirely to death, the "full-grown lambs" appear
there too. At no point does the ode speak the language of *La Belle
Dame* whose brief moment of ripeness—

> *The squirrel's granary is full,*
> *And the harvest's done—*

is immediately borne down by fading and withering. Instead of
the double focus of *Autumn*, *La Belle Dame's* harvest is just a toneless
end—in fact "done"—like Wilfred Owen's "finished fields of
autumns that are old".

So, reconstructing the proverb, the vale, the sonnet: you cannot
have the grown lambs without the exhausted stubble-plains, nor
the robin's extreme of joyful red without the winter. Keats's own
more economical summary is the "gathering swallows" of the ode's
last line. They gather for departure, are another signal of winter
in the death stanza. And yet "gathering" is the last of the poem's
harvesting and perfecting words, and the most grateful of them all
for no other reason than that it brings the ripe and the dying truths
of Autumn (and *Autumn*) together. It exerts its Shakespearean will
over nature and art until there is no knowing, nor is there any
asking, which is which.

---

[1] Distinguish the effect made on contemporaries by the new voice of a
major poet. Thus Byron told Leigh Hunt that he found "O for a beaker full of
the warm South" unintelligible.

POSTSCRIPT ON ROMANTIC FEELING

SAYS mad Lear to blind Gloucester,

Yet you see how this world goes.

Gloucester replies:

I see it feelingly.

Just here, in a college production which was otherwise not memorable, the boy playing Gloucester raised his hands and passed them to and fro, with careful method, as if over the features of a large known face. The tactile pedantry of his gesture was moving to witness. It seemed true to the play's pain and patience and its groping apprehensions.

The first production, the actor-playwright's own *King Lear*, may have rendered this exchange quite differently. It would suit the humour of the age and perhaps of the particular work for Gloucester to move in the direction of the king's voice, and bump into a stage prop, and sit down and rub his shin, exclaiming "I see it feelingly", amid laughter.

Today Shakespeare is still, before all else, a Romantic spirit, the admiration of Goethe and Coleridge. But how far they were discovering the historical Shakespeare and how far they were seeing themselves reflected in what they read, of course cannot be known. The Eighteenth Century thought Caliban a greater feat than Hamlet, not observable and therefore a larger invention; and we can't even be sure it was wrong there.

The hands of that undergraduate Gloucester expressed blindly, "feelingly", a tragic relationship between the man and things outside himself. Lear suffering on the heath, exposed in the storm "to feel what wretches feel", had already tasted a tragic solidarity with other human beings. At the very end of the play Edgar exhorts those who are left:

> *The weight of this sad time we must obey;*
> *Speak what we feel, not what we ought to say.*

And his words admit, perhaps insist on, a tragic divorce between the natural impulse and the voice of duty.

Feeling and nature continue interwoven throughout *Lear*, and the greatness of this theme for our modern selves is in part an immemorial wealth that sets people talking about renaissance humanism, and behind that medieval order, and behind that Greek Stoicism, and behind that. . . . And partly it is a more detectable Romantic inheritance in which Edgar states the tension of heart and head, Gloucester that of self and world, Lear that of one man and all men.

HEART AND HEAD

"When a man begins to think he ceases to feel" wrote Rousseau. His huge international vogue was fostered by such flourishes. Not that there was anything very original about his broad championship of feeling, or his habit of playing feeling against thought: "This world is a comedy to those that think, a tragedy to those that feel" (Horace Walpole, in fact, writing to the Countess of Upper Ossory) is the sort of *mot* that came easily in those days. What marked Rousseau out for acclaim, and down for execration, was the absolute value of the feeling he promoted and wanted everyone to believe in. The perfectibility men (Condorcet, Godwin) may have been comparably optimistic, but theirs was a rationalising tradition and not a sentimental one.

Find the heart's natural way, Rousseau said, and follow it. This is the only knowledge worth having, the only principle to live by, in religion, morals, politics, art, education. Nature was his cry no less than feeling. Nature, though, was invoked by both sides in the Classical-Romantic debate, because it could be made to exemplify system and good sense as well as vital mystery. Vergil resolved in Pope's poem to draw only "from *Nature's Fountains*", but when he set to work,

Nature *and* Homer *were, he found, the same.*

Whereas feeling was appealed to by one side only; so that feeling is the bond between Rousseau and Romanticism, while nature has to be left out of account as unmanageably protean.

Rousseau was a great man but by no means a great philosopher, and he shows at his speculative weakest in the thought-feeling justapositions which occur in his writings everywhere. He must accept blame—the scandals of his life apart—for the popular misconception of a propagandist on behalf of licence, because he tried to have it both ways in this great affair of heart and head. For various polemical purposes, speaking up for the heart, defending it against Voltaire and d'Holbach, irony and science, he made the thought-feeling rift appear as stark as possible. Philosophising, he wanted to heal the breach and establish the reason, the rational form, of his own anti-rationalistic convictions. The second was not his forte. We remember his views on the human phenomenon of

271

conscience—*amour de soi*, *pitié*, their interaction on the ground and in the bone—and forget the abstract moral argument.

The same is true of the Romantic generation. Nobody conceived an interesting philosophy of feeling. Jacobi, J. S. Beck, even Schleiermacher, are not important names here, and the greatest single achievement of Romantic intellect, Hegel's *Phenomenology*, is avowedly anti-Romantic because contemptuous of this part of Rousseau's legacy[1]. Later, as the Nineteenth Century unfolds, metaphysics extricates itself from the dead-end of feeling and prospers in consideration of the will: Schelling hesitantly, and Fichte with his restless probing Ego; then Schopenhauer and Nietzsche.

Morals and conscience provide a clear heart-and-head focus since it was here that Rousseau caught the attention of one very important near-contemporary, Hume, and one even greater successor, Kant. Both these recognised that Rousseau's widely dispersed deliberations broke in two always at the join of conscience and rational morality. Hume took the modest path of accepting (in discipleship to Rousseau[2]) that moral judgments are rooted in feeling, of going on to discriminate nicely between feelings, but of rejecting the possibility of a universal rational morality: his conclusion being that moral conviction is "entirely relative to the sentiment or moral taste of each particular being". Kant was more Rousseauite than Hume in his moral absolutism, and less Rousseauite in everything to do with the moral role of feeling. The best, indeed Kant thought the only, hope for a metaphysic of morals was to keep a man's feelings outside his moral life. So while Hume maintained that to judge something virtuous is to express a special sort of "pleasing sentiment" towards it, and located the impulse to morality in this sentiment, Kant's feeling of respect for the moral law is sealed off both from moral insight and the exercise of directing the will in accordance with that law.

Kant excludes feeling from the substance of morality by establishing its harmless identity with that substance. The feeling of respect (*Achtung*) cannot incite us to determine our will in accordance with the moral law, nor can determining our will produce the feeling, because the feeling *is* the determination of the will—not in accomplishment out there (so to speak) but in awareness that the will is being determined. Consciousness of determination

---

[1] For the "philosophy" of feeling one goes naturally to the creative writers and to a few fringe figures—notably to J. G. Hamann who is still underestimated.

[2] And in the longer British tradition of looking inside one's breast for the truth about morals: Hobbes, Shaftesbury (who found benevolence there in place of Hobbes's selfishness), Hutcheson, Hume.

articulates itself in the feeling. The feeling "is not a motive to morality", he says; "it is morality itself subjectively considered as a motive".

Objectively considered, Kantian morality is the response men make to the law they find within their hearts. This finding is rational, not sentimental, but its rationality is practical merely. Men know a rule; they do not know an object of thought, a thing; and on this distinction between the universally valid principles which practical reason affords us in our living and the things which pure reason (speculation) strives to comprehend in their objective truth, hangs a vast eloquent dualism. We cannot know real things but we cannot help hearing real commands within us. For pure reason fails where practical reason must succeed. Objects of thought reach us under the conditions which govern the mind's receptivity: space, time, and the other facts of mental digestion (the categories); we cannot escape these conditions and know reality (things-in-themselves) face to face. But as moral beings we play host to reality in the form of an importunate "Thou shalt", a voice from outside nature and therefore free of time and space and all finite mental process.

This direct assault by reality upon our one human heart carries Rousseau's imprint, as Kant was quick to say. In a famous acknowledgment he records that it was Rousseau who awakened him to a truth of momentous consequences, namely that a man does not need to be clever or learned or polite in order to know his duty: "I despised the common man who knows nothing. Rousseau set me right".

But then their roads divide, for the disconnection between the moral system and the natural wisdom of the heart in Rousseau could not escape Kant's analytic gift. Kant expelled feeling from morality. *Achtung* accompanies the moral life always, but is no part of it. *Achtung* is at once our human glory and our shame, since we receive and honour the moral law as finite rational beings, and know that our actions ought all to be determined by it; but we also know that we can never fully satisfy its demand. From this situation arises the two-faced feeling of respect. Could we lift our mortal fates clean out of nature, neither the feeling nor the concept of duty would exist for us; life would be one perfect cloudless blue of the holy will's conformity with the moral law.

No such serenity is possible, and in saying so Kant is making a logical and metaphysical, not a psychological and empirical observation; he is stating a necessity of our double existences, phenomenal and noumenal as he calls them, inside nature and outside.

Addressing ourselves to the moral law in assurance of our free-dom—for we know we *can* obey—we leave the natural man behind and enter an infinity of rational self-fulfilment. Doing this or that in our daily affairs we re-enter nature where all is appearance and nothing is free and our most earnest strivings, like everything else that is and happens, are at the mercy of natural causality. *Deciding* to do this or that (determining the will) catches us inside and out-side nature simultaneously. We are here both submitting to the moral law in blank noumenal devotion and referring natural actions (as regards their form only) to the law. Kant did not think hard enough about this simultaneity. But it has one very impor-tant outcome, which is that nothing can take away our moral freedom or mitigate our natural servitude; and in Kant's system, with its underlying dualism of practical and pure reason, our in-vulnerability depends precisely upon our helplessness. The free-and-necessary knot is his gift to Romanticism and one of his gifts to all posterity.

If appearances are things in themselves, freedom cannot be upheld. Nature will then be the complete and sufficient determining cause of every event. The condition of the event will be such as can be found only in the series of appearances: both it and its effect will be necessary in accordance with the law of nature. If, on the other hand, appearances are taken for no more than they actually are; if they are viewed not as things in themselves, but merely as representations connected according to empirical laws, they must themselves have grounds which are not appearances. The effects of such an intelligible cause appear, and accordingly can be determined through other appearances, but its causality is not so determined. . . . Thus the effect may be regarded as free in respect of its intelligible cause, and at the same time in respect of appearances as resulting from them according to the necessity of nature. This distinction, when stated in this quite general and abstract manner, is bound to appear extremely subtle and obscure, but will become clear in the course of its application. My purpose has only been to point out that since the thoroughgoing connection of all appearances, in a con-text of nature, is an inexorable law, the inevitable consequence of obstinately insisting upon the reality of appearances is to destroy all freedom.[1]

Romantic consciousness is Rousseau's conscience expanded from moral heart-certainty into uncategorised feeling and played upon by Kant's philosophy. If people had grasped the interdependence of Kant's metaphysical modesty and his severe ethical splendour, no doubt his immediate influence would have been much more

---

[1] *Critique of Pure Reason*, second edition, p. 564, translated by H. W. Cassirer.

local and technical: common sense never understands philosophy, as Hegel remarked—though philosophy must embrace common sense or stand refuted.

The misinterpretations of Kant were gross and had their funny side. Herder, intending praise, called him the German Shaftesbury.[1] Not merely could he have quelled Shaftesbury with his little finger; the gap between Shaftesbury's "moral sense" and Kant's practical reason, the two things Herder wanted to compare, is where the difference in quality appears most obvious. Shaftesbury worked inside a loose Cambridge-Platonic and empirical tradition (a foredoomed blend) and went in search of a grail called intellectual intuition: intellectual because a true knowing and intuition because immediate like sense-experience. The moral sense belonged with the sixth or inner senses—Rousseau's *sens intérieur* for example—which cropped up all over Europe. Most of it was idle talk and is now forgotten since it is clear that the effective thinking was going on elsewhere; and the point of pausing over Kant's relations with Rousseau and Hume is to suggest where that elsewhere was. Contemporaries and many successors failed to see what was at stake in the double argument for a confining nature in the first *Critique* and a moral law whose service is perfect freedom in the second. They either took the first on its own (like De Quincey) as an anti-metaphysical tract, or blurred and vulgarised the second, again in isolation (like Herder and Hazlitt), into a defence of intellectual intuition.

Both reactions constituted a travesty of Kant. Together they ensured for him the sort of Romantic centrality which understanding of his work would have made impossible. Indeed common sense misconceives Kant, but it is also true that he gives provocation to common sense. He does reawaken the vague Platonic longing for a sight of real things, and his distinction between constitutive and regulative employment of Ideas of Reason cannot prevent the plain man meeting the truth face to face, to his own satisfaction, in the transcendental system. The differences between Kant's practical reason and Rousseau's voice of conscience shrink into triviality when the one turns out to be no less an unprovable yet undeniable presence than the other: for the moral law is simply given, "is given as a fact of pure Reason of which we are *a priori* conscious, and which is apodictically certain"—and Kant himself goes on to appeal to "common sense". Whereupon common sense exacts a just revenge on him. We know that the actual

[1] In "Kritischen Wälder": *Sämmtliche Werke* (1878), IV, p. 175. We shall see that the interesting link is between Shaftesbury and German aestheticism.

human business of trying to be good is not very like his picture. Most of the time we are not listening to commands. His concept of the good will, its neat isolation, is something experience only very partially confirms. The lay imagination responds wholeheartedly to the free-and-necessary knot, but coolly to the rest.

So Romantic Europe became aware, amid general excitement, against a background of fashionable determinisms, that Kant had spoken up for moral freedom. Understanding his argument was a different matter; even the primary distinction between freedom to dispose the will and impotence to know objects was not widely grasped. And in the process of receiving Kant his stress upon *moral* freedom became so slight that the delimitation was often forgotten. And similarly with his stress on *natural* necessity. Why then bother about Kant at all, as they certainly did bother, if his work was going to be assimilated to the tide of illuminism and occultism which, together with more substantial versions of intellectual intuition, swept over the continent in the late eighteenth century? The free-and-necessary knot is the answer. His is a remarkable case of genius highly unpopular in its pedantic strenuousness and difficulty receiving, at once, considerable popular favour—though not of course in England.

Everywhere men held to feeling, talked what Dr. Johnson called "the cant of sensibility", and also wanted—many of them—to see and understand and know for sure. Rousseau had been endlessly resourceful in suggesting how the heart need not be blind, unintelligent, unprincipled. When Kant comes on the scene he is first and foremost "un coeur sensible" for Mme. de Staël, German Romanticism's hugely successful interpreter. Others less ignorant than she could not but be struck by the chill of his mind and the difficulty of getting reassurance from him on any heart-and-head questions. Of all his disciples Coleridge has the most to tell us now. Kant, he says, laid hold of him "with giant hands" and saved him from the confusion of his early allegiances. Against Godwin and the wider British empirical tradition, Kant confirmed him in his reading of Plato, the New Testament, the gnostic writers, Spinoza, and helped him to satisfy his syncretic urge: "My mind feels as if it ached to behold and know someting *great*—something *one and indivisible*." It never became very clear how this was going to happen; but Coleridge said again and again, in different contexts, that a great indivisible something only reveals itself to feeling minds.

Both his syncretism and his conviction that deep thinkers feel purely and strongly, place Coleridge at the centre of intellectual

Romanticism. Moreover he runs through the gamut of contemporary attitudes to Kant in his own shifting interpretations. Sometimes he writes as if he had not the faintest idea what Kant was up
to. Sometimes he scolds him in an informed, rather Hegelian spirit,
for letting his epistemology stand rebuked by the courage of his
ethics. Sometimes he Christianises the practical reason. He even
supposes that German politics prevented Kant from concluding
that the thing-in-itself was, after all, knowable.

Because Coleridge was philosophically literate, and garrulous,
and faint in personality, he gave back to the age its transient,
fragmented voice. So we read his formal prose, and letters, note-
books, table-talk, and find there the metaphysical yearning of a
generation heaped up in a sort of predictable chaos; for although
he is too eclectic and easily blown about for one to guess what he
will say next, his systematic hopes are always being pulled back
into the orbit of feeling. It must not be left to poetry to demonstrate
that feeling is surest knowing.

SELF AND WORLD

One library of books about Romanticism presents the movement
as a discovery or rediscovery of the external world, and a second
even larger library concentrates on the riot of introspection which
spread across Europe at that time. The going outward and the
turning in are equally Romantic, and only on the surface do they
contradict each other. Rousseau's self-scrutiny in the *Confessions*
and *Les Rêveries du promeneur solitaire* stands opposite his loving contemplation of nature; these are two wings of a single sensibility, as
again, less obviously, in *Émile* and in his absurd novel. A passage
from the Second Walk shows Rousseau becoming most himself
when the two wings support between them a vaguely-shaped
central area of feeling. Further, it suggests that Rousseau most
himself is Rousseau most Romantic.

Night was falling. I perceived the sky, a few stars, and a little verdure.
This first sensation was a delicious moment; only through it could I feel
myself. In that instant I was born to life, and it seemed to me that I
filled with my frail existence all the objects I perceived. Entirely
inside the present, I remembered nothing; I had no distinct notion of
my individuality, not the least idea of what had just happened to me;
I did not know who I was or where I was; I felt neither hurt, nor fear,
nor anxiety.

The English reader recognises this state of affairs immediately.
All our Romantic poets write about experiences which are heavy

with meaning (like Rousseau's sense of being "born to life"), and near to silence in their telling; and which are simultaneously experiences of self and world. The differences between individuals are of course all-important: we begin to touch the originality of each when we say that Shelley whips the world up into a bright streaming transcendental froth and spends himself in his own sort of volatile communion, removed yet colourful and urgent, with this wished-away "intense inane"; that Keats draws the world slowly, solidly, sensually, in upon himself, to taste its impossible yet dreamed perfection; that Wordsworth's best early poetry is engaged in an "ennobling interchange / Of action from within and from without" in which self and world are equal partners and self gets called "creator and receiver both, / Working but in alliance with the works / Which it beholds"; that Coleridge, in his wonderful double drama of consciousness and faith, adrift on a rotting sea of nature and eternity, is now repelled by the "slimy things", now moved to bless the watersnakes "unaware" in their newly discovered and grace-imported beauty, the self with the dead accusing lump of world, the albatross, round its neck. None of these is Rousseau's "I filled with my frail existence every object I perceived"—which means that his genius too is its own master, while sharing with all the others a habit of self-definition through recurring patterns of adventure with environment.

Then there is Byron, the greatest enemy of cant in our poetry, who often indulges Romantic cant of the "I can see / Nothing to loathe in nature" sort. He is the exception which proves the English rule. For although he likes to talk as if he too were struggling to find himself in and through external forms, as if the nature-symbol were his imagination's chief instrument, Byron's real strength lies elsewhere: in plain open action and social impress, a creative journalism of posture, easy reflection, public avowal. His version of the self-and-world dialogue is radically unlike those of the other important Englishmen, though it goes back to Rousseau as much as theirs do, and its character is just as Romantic. To this day he ranks second only to Shakespeare among the English poets in popular continental reckoning. They acclaim the action-reverie polarity in Byron, and trace its pedigree from the novelistic and self-dramatising Rousseau, to *Sturm und Drang*, to the new German —especially Goethe's—understanding of *Hamlet* which made the prince quite suddenly the most talked-of figure in world literature.

When these considerations are given due weight it ceases to be surprising that Byron should have more in common with Hugo, say, and the rhetoric of coloured waistcoats, than with our own self-and-world poetry. Also the concept of Romanticism becomes, at a stroke, less parochial. Instead of championing rival Romanticisms on opposite sides of the English Channel, one vivid and contentious, the other subtly quietist, we recognise the same truth everywhere, the one genetic fact. This fact looms larger than Rousseau, certainly, and much more complex; but he is the best man when it comes to directing foreign eyes towards our lyrical and meditative verse, or towards Hazlitt's impressionistic prose for that matter, or *Wuthering Heights*; and turning our English gaze on their literature of revolt and escape, of spectacular Napoleonic fulfilments out in the dust and glare, and noble failure against hopeless illiberal odds.

Nature-poetry and public essay are both concerned to impress the feeling self upon, or test it against, or nourish it with, otherness and externality. Faust's *streben* and Wordsworth's wise passiveness are both voyages of discovery. And if the passive man suffers "blank desertion", and if the other thrusts out in French or German ebullience, then falls back, rebuffed, upon his privacy in French or German despair, his extremes of mood are far-ranging and his own, while our picture of him continues Romanticly fixed.

The humanism of the movement is its indestructible core, as friends and enemies often remark, and Rousseau it was who Romanticised Christianity by naturalising it. Romantic feeling may be intensely religious (anyhow as sensible people understand religion) but not markedly theocentric. *"Il faut que Dieu les touche"* is not a Romantic sentiment, nor are Redemption (remember Keats's vale of soul-making) and Original Sin, Romantic doctrines. The home of the religion of the heart will always be the human heart. When religious orthodoxy begins to bite deep into a man's Romanticism, as happened with Friedrich Schlegel's and Coleridge's theorising and Wordsworth's poetic practice, the scene is becoming one of warring incompatibles.

In this dialogue between self and world one cannot very profitably distinguish between the turning inward for certitude and the turning outward after some confirming voice. These are complementary ways of looking at the Romantic search for total environmental sense. Wordsworth calling himself "creator and receiver both" and Coleridge replying that "we receive but what we give" are occupied with inner and outer values equally and in the same breath. Instinct tells us that their disagreement is taking place as close to the centre of Romanticism as it is possible to get. Education supports instinct here and stresses the poet's absorption in their environmental debate, but it adds the warning that the form in which they are casting the argument, the give and take between poet and wild nature, is an English emphasis. Goethe writes like this sometimes, which is one approach to the fact that Goethe is only sometimes Romantic. Leopardi writes about men in relation to wild nature—seasons, stars, weathers—often and beautifully, and yet we do not comfortably think of him as Romantic at all. His fastidious intellectual conscience holds him back. (I do not mean his pessimism.) His commitment to the environmental debate is never quite wholehearted; so Leopardi's nature retains a classical limitation, is closer to Vergil's in its depths and to English landscape-poetry on its surface, than to the absolute thing *The Prelude* and the *West Wind* and *To Autumn* and *Dejection* are about.

Eighteenth-century Europe grew aware of the environmental debate as a condition peculiar to itself when it studied ancient Greece and saw clear signs there of men living at spiritual peace with their mortality. The Greek sculptor experienced no painful discrepancy between the natural form in front of him, his human model, and the idea in his head. Their religion was anthropomorphic and expressed itself thus without misgiving. Everywhere could be found accord and fittingness, so German Hellenists believed. But this peace was no more, and a sad knowledge of its loss characterised modern men especially.

Hence the close entanglement of Graecomania and Romantic theory. And just as Romantic Heart and Head is Rousseau's conscience played upon critically by Kant, so Self and World is Rousseauite nature subjected to the fierce divisive stress with which Kant conceived his spheres of nature and the supersensible, phenomenon and noumenon. Rousseau's holistic account of the natural state is not destroyed by Kant (of course I am making two men stand for an epoch) but it is strained and tugged at. Rousseauite man lives in one world and at peace with his world, if only civilisation would let him. Kantian man, as our glance at his ethics revealed, lives in two strictly separate worlds. Romantic man makes Rousseauite affirmations but has read Kant and only half believes them—which is why describing Romanticism is so difficult.

Surveying entire the mental history of the west, Hegel proposed "unhappy consciousness" to denote the running sore of man's dissatisfaction with all finite forms. The unhappy consciousness is a larger postulate than the environmental debate between self and world, but may be understood to include it. Hegel blamed the Jewish God, our maker and judge lifted beyond all human comprehending, reason's despair, unrepresentable by art (the Roman conqueror entered the temple at Jerusalem and was amazed to find no image),—Hegel blamed Jehovah for the death of that lucid Greek joy. Judaism was always unhappy. Christianity *knows* itself to be unhappy, for the word became flesh and thus expressed the desolating separateness of the person Jesus who came and changed the world and went away, and our notion of God. The immediate pain of his disciples mindful of a loved, departed presence ("Henceforth I call you not servants but friends") is ours for ever. The intuition of his risen Godhead will always chafe against the memory of his life on earth.

The historical Jesus possessed the world's first unhappy consciousness, and Kant was, for Hegel, its latest human voice of genius. Kant both sharpened and mollified the unhappiness of Descartes, whose method of doubt brought the vision of a metaphysical night sky in which each blazing human star asks, each of itself, "What do I know?", and answers *Cogito ergo sum*. This is the certainty which cannot be undercut, which to deny or to doubt is to reaffirm. In any event, *cogito*; and if a malicious demon is at work here, "let him deceive me as much as he likes; he can never bring it about that I am nothing, so long as I think I am something". Thus Descartes gave men rational certainty of self by an argument which was bound to awaken doubt about everything else; the cost of his clean break with medieval decadence was the surrender of the corporate assumptions which had kept our Christian-Aristotelian family close. From now on we know ourselves as single and thinking energies, and the rest is total potential scepticism.

Descartes, therefore, prompted the outbreak of dualistic systems in which philosophers admitted their Cartesian solitude and also tried, Descartes included, to do something about it. After him the not-self of sticks and stones and other people, and God, was immensely changed for thought. At the end of this process stands Kant, both king of dualists and healer of dualism. He rang down the curtain of nature and placed reality the other side. But this division is not a solitary distress since we all fail in the same way to know real things. And Kant also bound our noumenal selves to each other and to the universe in freedom, under the providence of Reason, by the moral law which commands every human will.

Hegel's earliest work shows him a disciple of Kant, but restless almost at once, and handling with some of this mature resourcefulness and power the distinction between duty which confronts and love which works within. This begins to sound familiar, for ethical conjurings of love will soon become the general policy. Shelley in particular had just one important thought, which was "The great secret of morals is love".

Now, all over Europe, love and morals are joined by aesthetics in a Romantic trinity. In this age of *Einfühlung* art becomes an exercise of love; to imagine is to reach out in sympathetic joy and fill, Keats says, "some other body". But Keats was puzzled about the moral import of his attitude, and assumed that the poet who "has as much delight in conceiving an Iago as an Imogen" must shock "the virtuous philosopher". Whereas Shelley, like Coleridge and some Germans, saw that the imagination which can comprehend an Iago in his free and vicious identity has succeeded in loving its neighbour as itself. Those words of Jesus, Hegel observes in his theological *Jugendschriften*, are not an appeal to the yardstick of self-love. They are God's gesture of respect towards the life he and we share.

Love soon moves to the edge of the Hegelian scene; but not before it has taught him its lesson, has impressed its double character of a yeast active in the heart's stillness and a force impelling the lover outward and towards the precious object of his contemplation. Love as possession and surrender is the spirit informing the technicalities of mediation in the *Phenomenology* and later Hegel. It is the hidden zeal of the dialectic, driving thought on through the shattering of each in turn of thought's limited conclusions. Love, with death, arms Hegel's historical vision in its sweep from Judaism to Kant. The unhappiness of the unhappy consciousness began, and continues, in its loveless relations. The Jewish God was always humanity's master exacting our tribute of blind faith, and always humanity's slave toiling to sustain our theory of the universe. Both these representations, the tyrant and the poor abstract drudge, our metaphysical abasement and our stupid conceit, were brutal in their outwardness, and the west has remained trapped by and in them. It does not matter that with Kant religion has dwindled into an appendage to moral philosophy, because the blank lordship and servility are still perfectly reflected in that imposed command, that demanded formula, which comes to us out of the dark.

Hegel did not propose to illuminate this unhappy Kantian scene with the light of love, but of reason. As his own rationalism grew more assertive and one quarter mad, so he locked himself inside the triadic monism of his logic, the house haunted by love's ghost. His account, in part unfair, of Kant's shortcomings centres on the blind-man's-buff separation of groping subject and undiscoverable object; Hegel's Kant is busy reaffirming an entire Platonic realm of realities ranked one for one behind the appearances which hem us in.

The Kant of our fair appraisal unquestionably split human beings in two, into phenomenal selves and noumenal selves; and it is a fact of the history of ideas that under his influence German philosophy soon found itself suspended, as if forced by him into an anguished choice, between the subject (Fichte's Ego) and the object (Schelling's Absolute). But Kant's things-in-themselves, though he writes carelessly about them (why plural?), are there to indicate what *can't* be known, not *what* can't be known—they place in the reader's lap the *Critique of Pure Reason*, a book which Hegel did not respect sufficiently.[1]

He scolded Kant for failing to trust reason absolutely, and Romantic writers for a complete neglect of their rational duty. Kant lacked the courage to lose himself in order to find himself in his thinking, while they shrank from thought altogether and relapsed into a state which Hegel again and again calls mere feeling.

The task of Hegelian reason is set by his insistence that Kant's curtain of nature conceals no secrets; behind the curtain "there is nothing to be seen unless we ourselves go behind". In prospect the adventure looks like a game with words. Undertaking it, reading Hegel, is a more equivocal experience which shuttles one to and fro between verbalism and a solid mental vigour which only Plato has matched; and nowhere is the oscillation more weird than in his piercing of the Kantian veil, in his attempt to prove that wherever thought ventures to go it has nothing to find or fear but reconstitutions of its growing and intelligible self.

The word-game aspect fades, except for some specialist Hegelians, and the intellectual drama remains. (But is it a verbal or a dialectical fact—of course it is both—that *aufheben* means both to cancel and to save?) In his *History of Philosophy*, and in the *Phenomenology* most of all, Hegel invests the life of thought with a fatefulness, a body and breath, with a voice of pain which transforms ratiocination into a bloody spiritual struggle and entitles us to claim him for Romanticism. It is a superficial objection that he considered himself anti-Romantic and a more exact reasoner than Kant. They meant different things by reason. What Hegel called logic is rampant metaphysics. While Kant proves himself at every turn a child of the Enlightenment—in his deism, his science, his explicit moral maxims in the age of legal code-making, the neat containment of his aesthetics, the pressure of teleology against unhistorical reason, his entire chinese-box cast of mind—Hegel embraces the

---

[1] On the other hand Kant's early *Inaugural Dissertation* (1770) does unquestionably postulate a second world of real objects knowable by reason—a most vulnerable Platonism.

mess and imponderability, the terribleness, of human beings and of history. Hence the exhileration which his sudden appeals to "life itself" are able to arouse. He is committed utterly to the environmental debate, the dialogue between self and world: this constitutes his sense of "life itself".

Sometimes, like Schiller's Fiesco, he longs to take the universe between his jaws. And then he is content to be a tune under an open sky, a morsel of the Absolute. This shift entails no contradiction since all the time he is spinning one self-and-world coin in the air of his rhetoric—a currency which turns up, modified but recognisable, everywhere. Coleridge is half-unwittingly popularising Hegel and the Idealist tradition in his talk of objects which "*as* objects are essentially fixed and dead", in contrast to objects which live and grow in the eye of thought. The Wordsworthian poet "carrying everywhere with him relationship and love" as he walks the world, imagines in the true spirit of the *Jugendschriften*. But the closest links, naturally, are with the dramatic impulse of German Romanticism. They were fascinated, as we were not, by action and the deed; for them, the debate between self and world took place in a tragic, Hamletish twilight where act and actor may be contemplated, and frozen by art, in mid-stride between the soul's dark dreaming and affairs.

ONE AND ALL

"We have all of us one human heart." Wordsworth who detested Rousseau often talked the purest Rousseau—which ought to be no surprise, since the pan-European movement they belonged to was big and characterful enough to drown the strongest personal aversions.

Where more or less everybody had been saying that art imitates nature—external nature or some generic condition of human manners or morals—people began to maintain that art expresses feeling. Latterday critics sometimes react to this change with the judgment that Romanticism encouraged a bad sort of particularity; it was his own feeling that the Romantic artist wanted to express, and herein lay a danger of incomprehensibility (for how could he give access to the unique thing tucked away inside him?) and of an unpleasant exhibitionism in which private sensibilities might be paraded and fondled in the street.

Such hostile observations are half true and very misleading. The poet who wanted to write about "something within which yet is shared by none" also believed in the one human heart beating inside him, and in thus expecting to have it both ways, Wordsworth spoke on behalf of the whole movement.

A very large part of Romantic hopes and claims turns on a mystic interpenetration of universal and particular; and here, once again, German Shakespeare criticism proves a sensitive index. They said, Coleridge elaborated, and we have it in our bones, that the more perfectly Hamlet is himself and grows into his unforgettable singularity, the more fully and movingly does he embody a universal human truth. Never mind what the truth is about. The point is how they, and we still, see Shakespeare's triumph; for seeing it this way makes it difficult to have patience with Johnson's admonition against numbering the streaks of a tulip. Here emerges a crucial anti-neoclassic persuasion, in which the Augustan general is being attacked from both sides and squeezed to extinction by the Romantic particular and universal. The Doctor's allowing of singularity at the level of "diverting individual circumstances" makes us smile. When Blake cries out against Reynolds—it might have been Johnson—"To generalise is to be an idiot. To particularise is the alone distinction of merit", he expresses his own emphatic, very abrupt Romanticism.

For Blake leaves the particular's living connection with the universal unargued; he assumes it, and does not speculate like Coleridge and the Germans—and he lacks the sober practicality that went into the making of the Lyrical Ballads Preface. The Preface is our chief English exposition of Romantic One and All, not direct and purposive, not knowing at all clearly what it is doing, but burrowing down instinctively after a one-and-all poetic diction: a diction which will both carry the poet's unique voice and be "the very language of men"—a human bedrock. This explains the anxious recastings ("the real language of men", "language really used by men") and the reiteration of "permanent" in the essay. It also throws light on its omissions and unwise emphases. The appeal to "humble and rustic life" was primarily meant to further the search for a one-and-all diction, not to put the rich, the smart, the blue-blood, the town-dweller, beyond the poetic pale. The language men "really"—permanently, universally—use is co-extensive with their one human heart, but it can be better studied in the simple, recurring pattern of the fell-farmer's existence than in places where that language and that heart have been overlaid by unnatural surroundings, bad education, borrowed wit, and the shifting trivialities of fashion. The Wordsworthian poet is first and foremost "a man speaking to men".

Henry Crabb Robinson, who was one of a handful of Englishmen familiar with the German scene, called on Herder with the Lyrical Ballads Preface in his pocket. Herder approved what he read, and no doubt (though Robinson doesn't say) he discoursed upon the one-and-all theme he found there. Development, elucidation, were certainly called for. In England we scarcely rationalised the cult of folk-poetry, especially ballad, which we shared with the rest of Europe. We took our Romantic primitivism for granted, while others were giving it historical and metaphysical extension.

Herder dedicated his powers to the organic metaphor. Organicism, hideous word, is much larger than the primitive question, and contains it, and thereby reminds us that Romanticism was not primarily a literary movement. Societies, civilisations, languages, works of art, single human beings, manifest life and ask— at least they asked Herder—to be studied on the analogy of the flower. For antiquity and the Middle Ages, living things carry an assurance of being understood, the soul being at once a vital and intelligible essence; they do not first and foremost and ultimately live. Descartes and Newton, geometry and physics, machine-models of reality, evade life. But life thrusts its omnipresent mystery upon us. The polyp, said Hegel, incarnates the same formless fire as the nightingale and the lion. Each embodiment is particular, though— the organism's own.

Thus Hegel followed Herder, but then so did the whole movement. Everything that intellect and imagination attempted at that time bends back upon the organic metaphor. They all wanted their work to come as naturally as the leaves to a tree. One tree, many leaves: the metaphor embraces the movement's corporate as well as its primitive theorising, and intertwines them. The search for the past, the natural, the feelingful past, the past of simple songs, was also a search for a lost human solidarity; and Romantic medievalism—O for those guilds and corporations and that agrarian commonalty—stated both longings together.

Like Goethe and Coleridge (Herder had been a medical student) Rousseau was a serious botanist, and it points straight at his Romantic potentiality that the primitive and corporate elements of his organicism jostle each other in his writing, incoherently and violently even. The muddle helped to make him a provocation beyond compare. Even in the technical *Du Contrat Social* it remains evident that he cannot liberate the machinery of the contract and its democratic outcome, the General Will, from the sentimental dogmatism of the one human heart. The dogmatism compounds, Romanticly, our shared and timeless humanity with the state of nature from which we once emerged: once as supposed history or once as deliberate myth-making, it is often unclear which. The machinery, on the other hand, belongs to the European Enlightenment.

Kant's rationalism, a far greater monument of the Enlightenment than Rousseau's political theory, proceeds on the assumption that reason is universal whereas feeling is particular. The Romantic conviction was precisely opposite: intellect lies at the mercy of specialised developments and clever *parti-pris* devices; feeling binds us to each other in conscience, grief and joy. Today, in long retrospect, Kant stands at the threshold of ethical individualism, each man attending to his inner voice, not the inner voice as Kant intended. Romanticism's impact on the moral law has had unforeseen consequences.

And so another true likeness emerges, One and All this time, out of the play of Kant against Rousseau. History embalms the crux for our consideration, and makes plain in doing so that its substance is spiritual and therefore answerless. Nobody gets proved right and nobody wrong; the firmest statements gain a questioning lift as we reapprehend the virtue running through them, in copious writings like Herder's and small single documents like the Lyrical Ballads Preface; and the same is true of post-Kantian metaphysics, especially of the *Phenomenology* (Romantic reason's greatest feat, I said) where Hegel sets out to unite One and All before our eyes. In that book we endure our thinking, like our deaths, alone, and are swept by thought into the feast of life, the "Bacchanalian revel where not a soul stays sober". Hegel's purpose in wielding the organic metaphor is to show that the history of philosophy also falls to the lot of single minds.

CONCLUSIONS

The truth of feeling is the one universal persuasion of Romanticism. "No man," said Blake, "can think, write, or speak from his heart, but he must intend truth." Beethoven inscribed his Missa Solemnis "*Von Herzen*"—from the heart. That was its guarantee.

To be greatly bothered about feeling's aboriginal corruptness is to be unRomantic, usually in a Christian cause. To lose interest in feeling because it is personal, vague, soft, and not the essential business of art or thought, or because it has no special immunity from the cheapening pressures of life, is to become post-Romantic.

Therefore the Wordsworthian poet striving to render our feelings "more sane, pure and permanent" has the task of restoring to feeling its pristine Rousseauite glory, of making feeling more itself. Delacroix, who also hated Rousseau (and who admired Voltaire!), nevertheless speaks for the movement when he remarks that works of art would never date "if they contained nothing but genuine feeling"—for "the impulses of the human heart never change".

Ask Blake what truth it is that Romantic man intends from his heart, and the answer cannot be simple. Blake himself intended Desire, his own sort of demonic love; and love indeed became our English intention and largest insight. But Blake's love was very unlike the loves of Shelley, Keats, Coleridge, Wordsworth; and each of these was different from the others.

Outside England even the vastness of love cannot contain Romanticism. Attempts to study the movement through its chosen subject, material or ideal, quickly fail. Likewise with temperament. It is a fact, but not a fundamental one, that most French and some German and Italian historians believe in a defining pessimism; and Croce assumes in his *Estetica* that Romantic feeling was characteristically violent and hectic. Englishmen know this will not do.

But we also cherish our provincial dogmas: that Romanticism was above all a literary and even a poetic—even a lyrical—event; that its expressive core was the nature-image; that everywhere people were talking about the imagination, flourishing it like a master-key.

A thought to the interplay between Rousseau and Kant will correct these distortions, though of course only through a silent enlarging of vision. The imagination provides a neat example. Rousseau often seems, and is, close to English ways of thought, yet not until late in his life, in the *Dialogues*, does imagination come to the fore—and then as a consoling rather than creative power. In Kant's transcendental scheme animals (who cannot form concepts) possess imagination. The dog knows his master, for Kant a very humble sort of knowing. Certainly he is obscure and not always consistent on imagination, and, confusion apart, the third Critique is importantly different from the first. But Coleridge was bound to come to grief when he tried grafting Schelling's *Einbildungskraft* upon Kant's.

And yet Coleridge's failure is full of interest. He hoped to resolve the tension of heart and head by means of the felt knowledge which imagination yields. Also the tension of self and world, and thus to make "the external internal, the internal external, to make Nature thought and thought Nature". Also that of one and all, where most clearly we may observe the Schellingian graft failing to take. Kant's imagination is universal but uncreative (and rather uninteresting), a fact of our mental digestion; while Schelling's imagination is creative but far from universal, a special talent. This expresses the Coleridgean form of the one-and-all dilemma. His primary imagination ("the living Power and prime Agent of all human Perception") is Kantian to the extent of the little word "all", and the rest is a shuffling across to Schelling, the secondary imagination, and the wishful assertion that the secondary is "identical with the primary in the *kind* of its agency", differing "only in *degree*, and in the *mode* of its operation". Coleridge could do no more towards establishing some underlying identity of the artist's symbol-making power with ordinary human perception. He, following Schelling, tried to make imagination bear the full Romantic burden, while the movement as a whole held to feeling.

The Kantian dog, for example, looks different through Romantic eyes, but not because those eyes contradict Kant's view of imagination. What happens is that the dog's manner of knowing his master becomes ennobled. The real centre of interest is heart and head, as grows clear when the Romantic animal joins the little child, the savage, peasant, lunatic, the wild wanderer, the man gripped by dream, hallucination, nightmare, in a genuinely symptomatic, pan-European emphasis on kinds of heart-knowledge that go hand in hand with feeble or non-existent intellect. Compare the Romantic discovery of visionary madness in Shakespeare. Or the new delight in Cervantes. Don Quixote is "not more ridiculous than ourselves" according to Dr. Johnson. Less ridiculous would be the Romantic verdict. They turned to Spinoza who had laid his finger on Descartes's busy care to keep the emotions out of thinking, and had called it vain: who had converted *cogito*, the epistemological core of Cartesian selfhood, into an ethical flame. They endorsed Voltaire's shrewd indentification of Pascal as the enemy within the Enlightenment, not just because "the heart has its reasons", but for his dismissal of human parts except as parts of human wholes: for the holism which Spinoza, Rousseau, Herder, Hegel, and, more diffidently, Coleridge, will persist in.

In full, the Missa Solemnis inscription reads "From the heart— may it reach the heart". The truth of feeling has to be communicated, and communication is the problematic essence of the likeness I called One and All. Talk of art as expression leads Romanticism both to the solitary voice that utters, and to the shared humanity of the utterance. (Again imagination must be subordinated; theories of sympathetic and associative imagination form part of the picture, they do not characterise the painting.) At one extreme, the Herder extreme leading back through Rousseau to the neglected Vico, the speaker becomes the mouthpiece of the

Volksgeist; at the other he stands opposite society, alone with his sensibility, Goethe shouldering and intrigued with the burden of his *Dumpfheit*, Leopardi his *noia*, Keats his indolence.

English individualism finds the corporate part of this story hard to take seriously. We even tend to ignore its clear traces in our own cardinal Romantic essay, the Lyrical Ballads Preface, where the thinly argued continuity of the writer with his public (*via* the language really used by men), of literature with life (feeling will out into words), of morals with aesthetics (good feeling breeds good writing), leans upon broad European sources which its author was largely unaware of.

These are real national differences, as real as the difference between "England expects" and *la gloire*. We often dislike the bravura of French Romanticism and the blatancy of German, and occasionally say so; while they feel just as strongly about the bourgeois mildness of ours. They and we draw opposite conclusions from the agreed fact that of our major poets only Byron is translatable.

A further likeness suggests itself, Doing and Being, because of the obvious force of the action-reverie antithesis. But consider the uneasy status of event in England. Here the Pantisocracy scheme (twelve gentlemen and twelve ladies, already familiar with each other's dispositions, were to embark for America, found a colony, improve their minds, have children, perhaps swop partners) strikes ourselves as an aberration. It belongs across the Channel. Romanticism everywhere was a humourless phenomenon, but Pantisocracy goes with the taint of Wertherish excess in young Southey and Coleridge, and indeed it drove Coleridge into his suicidal marriage. Byron apart, Romantic Doing was not for our imaginations. Poor deceived Mary of Buttermere, the innkeeper's daughter, is a preposterous invasion of *The Prelude*, but she is made to measure for a *Sturm und Drang* heroine.

Mary would also do for cheap romance anywhere, which is another way of indicating national boundaries. Our middle-class genius was fastidiously collected; their Romanticism had a Byronic coarseness and spread which made it capable of assimilating a thousand Marys. They had a direct use for Rousseau's vulgarity: for those titillating antinomical situations in his novel where the girl who is technically unchaste proves herself a moral heroine. Endless were the repercussions of Lord Edouard Bomston's assurance to the lovers: "Your two souls are so extraordinary that they cannot be judged by the ordinary rules."

But over there they also had immediate employment for Kant's patrician speculations. Rousseau said with many inflections but always earnestly, "The whole morality of human life is in man's intention"; and Kant would have agreed with him, while at the same time denouncing Bomston. Everything depends on the will's solitary submission to the moral law, on intention; but the law expresses itself in maxims which hold good for everybody. Without universalisation, no rational morality—this is the one-and-all tension as Kant states it in the second Critique and, more concisely, in the *Grundlegung*.

The "they" who had direct employment for Kant were almost entirely his fellow-countrymen. Many Germans had what Hegel had supremely, the power to sense the impact of original thought, and to infect life with its dire excitement. In and through Kant's dryness and monstrous elaboration they came upon the human theme, our freedom in an unfree world. This was their present tragic impulse, and a light to read the past by; they enjoyed untangling the free and necessary threads in the older drama, especially Calderon's Christian conclusions; Don Quixote's dreamlike inviolability within nature made him a Kantian saint, a hero of reason.

Thus the western world looked and still looks first to Germany for a rationale of the experience we all shared. (Pushkin was far enough away to say "Romanticism" is nonsense—Shakespeare is Romanticism.) The concept itself emerged from German contrasting of Greek and northern civilisations, then from talk between Goethe and Schiller, from the latter's Naïve and Sentimental essay and the journalism of the Schlegels. We all underwent my three tensions, we did not all theorise.

Heart and head evoked everywhere an admission, often a glad acceptance, of vagueness. Language was untethered from the object it had been committed to in a Hobbesian label-like fashion, and from the distinct notions of the understanding, and now expressed feeling. We lose clarity this way, said Burke *On the Sublime and the Beautiful*, but we gain strength. English readers of Burke, Hazlitt and De Quincey, toyed with the distinction between a literature of power and one of knowledge. Coleridge floated the aphorism that "poetry gives most pleasure when only generally understood". But Kant pounced on Burke's remarkable essay and squeezed it for the purposes of his own aesthetics. Then A. W. Schlegel protested against the tightness of Kant's idea, especially his exclusion of the sublime from art, and constructed a theory of tragedy which again has no English counterpart, on the basis of the Burkean-Kantian sublime. Men as unlike each other as Novalis and Schelling were weaving metaphors of balance, equilibrium, harmony—the "musical mood" which for Kant was the conceptless truth about aesthetic experience—and were anticipating Carlyle and Pater, and the French, by half a century. In the case of Schiller's *Gemütsfreiheit* the musical mood was taken beyond art and beyond Romanticism (though the German academic retrospect upon themselves is nearly always too narrow), and made an ideal to live by.

These were all heart-and-head attempts to deal convincingly with emotional and intellectual experience, to draw everything within the presiding gaze of feeling and hold it there. While Hazlitt was observing modishly, "In art, in taste, in life, in speech, you decide from feeling and not from reason", the Germans were doing some hard work. A number of terms like Yearning and Irony earn capital letters because of the extent to which Germans surrounded them with commentary; and this was not just a business of heart and head but of all three tensions.

Feeling itself led us in England to a few gruff distinctions between what deserves the name of feeling and "a taste for rope-dancing, or Frontiniac or Sherry". In common with the rest of Europe we were on the way to feeling's shifts and insincerities and its final uninterestingness, preparing the post-Romantic retreat. Here again the German doubts and probings were articulate beyond our own. They attacked the naïve heart-anchored unity of Rousseau's natural man, in the name of complex human truth and the drama. They gave posterity ideas and characters—Hamletish again—of radical self-alienation, of double and divided soul.

Zwei Seelen wohnen, ach, in meiner Brust

was Faust's cry, and the process did not end there; Goethe assured Eckermann that Mephistopheles had as large a share in his nature as Faust had.

But having created the concept of Romanticism the Germans proceeded to box it in. The French followed suit. What is an Englishman to make of a people who tell themselves that their movement began in 1830 and ended in 1847? Because our own Romanticism was more hazy-edged and absorbent, it discouraged the growth of neighbouring terms. Thus Realism never gets off the ground in England as a literary-historical category; we needed Stendhal to explain to us that Walter Scott was a realist.

The story of Europe's allegiance to feeling is one of failure as well as success, though the whole continent can afford to laugh at

T. S. Eliot when, with trivial adroitness, *Tradition and the Individual Talent* drives a wedge between feeling and emotion. "Poetry is not a turning loose of emotion," he says, with an eye to "an inexact formula" as he calls it, "emotion recollected in tranquility" and similar declarations. But, in the same essay, "the business of the poet is . . . to express feelings". The feeling-emotion distinction is the merest forensic device. Other parts of his argument, the Symbolist stress on the end-product (making objects as opposed to expressing feelings being the crux) and the wider convictions about concreteness which he shared with Marinetti, Pound and Hulme, are worth taking seriously.[1]

The gap between emotion and feeling had been postulated, created, exploited, in decadence betrayed, by Romanticism itself. Many of the criticisms voiced in the Twentieth Century hit a later situation. Hulme's "spilled religion" taunt hurts Rousseau and Romanticism and the religion of the heart, but its real target is Feuerbach (*Das Wesen des Christentums*, 1841) and his admirers who reduced Christianity to human self-projection, "the dream of the human mind", our imagining of what we ourselves might be. The obsessive inwardness which Hegel, waging his private war against "mere" feeling, first imputed to Romanticism, eventually becomes the truth. The fleeting expression called indolence becomes the face of *ennui*. Romanticism's demonic strain works itself out in an often silly satanism. The one-and-all tension lends a surface plausibility to the laying at Romanticism's door of Fascism and everything we don't like about liberalism.

Feeling united Europe, and national differences ran deep. Keats illuminates both conclusions as brightly as, and more warmly than, any writer anywhere. He tells John Reynolds: read *Hyperion* and put a mark beside the lines which speak to you with "the true voice of feeling". That instinct draws him into the middle of the picture, and enables him to express change in its blunt totality as professional men of letters almost never can. Placing his letters next to his contemporary Jane Austen's is a bit like *reading* Goya side by side with Ingres, or Beethoven with Cherubini; for those are the people to go to for the raw international language of Romanticism.

---

[1] But note how Eliot overplays his hand when he says "the poet has, not a 'personality' to express, but a particular medium, which is only a medium and not a personality, in which impressions and experiences combine in particular and unexpected ways". Every work of art is a personality, and a personality bound closely to the artist's personality because he made it and gave it the character, the self-possession, by which we recognise it as a work of art.

The worst educated of our poets at that time, Keats reveals in his two long narratives a European strain less obvious than Byron's but, strange to say, more seriously metropolitan: the transcendental machinery of *Endymion*, with the Platonic dualism and divisions and "triple soul" talk that follow; *Hyperion's* evolutionism and the tragedy of Beauty's worldly fate. These poems do not succeed, but they put him at the opposite pole to Chateaubriand whose life was lived at the centre of affairs and whose imagination was provincial. Keats had the German knack of being abstract and vulgar simultaneously.

Matthew Arnold on English Romanticism reminds me of Disraeli on the Liberal front bench opposite him: a range of extinct volcanoes. Our poets had suddenly been and gone and the show was over. The justice of this view depends on the completeness of the break between the vogue of Sensibility and Romanticism at one end, and between Romantics and Victorians at the other.

Only Keats refuses to fit Arnold's picture. The sensibility-verse of the others simply gets abandoned. "She wept—Life's purple tide began to flow" has no connection with the lasting Wordsworth. Coleridge gets William Bowles out of his system, after doting on him and addressing him "My heart has thanked thee, Bowles, for these soft strains" in the *Morning Chronicle* of December 26, 1794. So with Byron's first volume meant for the public, and with Shelley's odd weepy-gothic blend. But Keats's 1817 Poems declare the true however immature talent. The clean break which is evident elsewhere—Lamb tells Coleridge "I love you for dedicating your poetry to Bowles", but soon decides "I have something more to do than to feel"—not only fails to occur in Keats but is the beginning of wisdom about him.

At the other end, Keats and Keats alone has a formative stake in the Victorian aesthetic milieu. Again this is strangely European since the German overvaluing of Shaftesbury goes back deep into the Eighteenth Century and is prompted by his vamping analogies between the "moral sense" and proportion in architecture and harmony in music. Their aestheticism is both pre- and post-Romantic. And as to their Sensibility, the *Aufklärung* is as tearful and pity-focussed as anything we can show, and also intimate with Romanticism in ways peculiar to themselves. The fact that there was no English Lessing is as important as our failure, a little later, to produce an English Herder.

But of course the links between Keats and Sensibility and Aestheticism are forged by his sensual genius and by nothing else. He is himself alone, and he is very English, and the continental

Keats is an accident in the sense in which Shelley's rapid maturing into a European poet at the time of his death is no accident. It just happens that the separation of dreamer and realist in Keats can be given an "ironical" and "yearning" gloss.

The relation between Beauty and Truth was widely discussed in the Eighteenth Century, not least in Germany. The topic forms the central part of the argument in Schiller's long poem *Die Künstler* of 1789, in which he asserts that man *on earth* cannot apprehend truth except in its sensuous form, that is in the shape of beauty. In the beyond, as disembodied spirits, we shall be able to behold the goddess of Truth Urania with her crown of fire, while on earth she appears to us as the goddess of Beauty Cypria, wearing her girdle of charm. The gist of this portion of Schiller's poem is contained in the lines:

> *Was wir als Schönheit hier empfinden*
> *Wird einst als Wahrheit uns entgegen gehn.*

Is this also the burden of the Urn's advice and the true significance of the last lines of Keats's poem?[1]

Yes in so far as the *Grecian Urn* is a generalised European muddle. Otherwise, emphatically no. The sensible truths people tell round and about Keats are more baneful than lies in their power to deface his truth. And yet he is Shakespearean. And his heir could only be another great English Poet. Tennyson and Arnold are students of Keats, but Hopkins reawakens the very thing: "I am soft sift in an hourglass"—the same but introverted. And Hopkins knows the feel of God: "dost touch me afresh? Over again I feel thy finger". He would have admired the cleansing sea in Keats's sonnet but not the "priestlike task", not the silent reversal in which sacrament becomes subordinate to nature. And Hopkins uses his eyes for seeing with. He too is himself alone. His sensual spirituality is as unique and as English as Keats's sensual humanism.

[1] Professor E. L. Stahl, writing in the *Times Literary Supplement* of 19 March, 1964.

INDEX OF PERSONS

Alcibiades, 3, 10
Aristotle, 19, 281
Arnold, Matthew, 32-41, 44-7, 99, 103, 120-1, 134-5, 141, 185, 257, 294-5

Bailey, Benjamin, 2, 50-1, 77, 115, 117, 169, 177, 198
Barrie, J. M., 204
Bate, W. J., 150
Bayley, John, 11, 244
Beattie, James, 166
Beaumont, George, 17
Beck, J. S., 272
Beckett, Samuel, 23
Beerbohm, Max, 173
Beethoven, Ludwig van, 287, 289, 293
Blake, William, 285, 287-8
Blunden, Edmund, 137
Boccaccio, Giovanni, 14, 30-1, 236
Bowles, William, 294
Brawne, Fanny, 40, 54, 72, 76, 97, 116, 166-7, 177, 191, 203, 243
Bridges, Robert, 135, 197, 199
Brontë, Emily, 30
Brown, Charles, 71, 73, 77, 122, 128
Burke, Edmund, 291
Burton, Robert, 256
Bushnell, N. S., 205-6
Byron, Lord, 5, 101, 189, 278, 290, 294

Calderon, Pedro, 291
Carlyle, Thomas, 292
Cervantes, Miguel de, 289
Cézanne, Paul, 241
Chateaubriand, Vicomte de, 294

Cherubini, Luigi, 293
Clarke, Charles Cowden, 122
Coleridge, Samuel Taylor, 5-6, 10, 17-18, 32, 65, 147, 165, 167, 170-1, 173, 189-90, 270, 276-9, 282, 284-6, 288-91, 294
Condorcet, Marquis de, 271
Cox, Jane, 193-4
Croce, Benedetto, 288

Darwin, Charles, 90
Delacroix, Eugène, 287-8
De Quincey, Thomas, 275, 291
Descartes, René, 281, 286, 289
D'Holbach, Paul, 271
Dilke, Charles Wentworth, 16-18, 118
Disraeli, Benjamin, 294
Dostoevski, Feodor, 20, 30
Doyle, Arthur Conan, 26
Dryden, John, 245-8, 257

Eckermann, Johann, 292
Eliot, T. S., 160, 293

Feuerbach, Ludwig, 293
Fichte, Johann, 272, 283
Fielding, Henry, 115-16
Fitzgerald, Scott, 1
Forman, H. B., 177
Freud, Sigmund, 13

Garrod, H. W., 1, 8-9, 41, 97, 135, 205-6, 243
Gaulle, Charles de, 191, 194
Godwin, William, 271, 276
Goethe, J. W., 270, 278-80, 286, 290-2
Goya, Francisco, 234, 293

Hardy, Thomas, 60
Haydon, B. R., 3, 9, 41, 70, 78, 113, 118, 162, 214
Hazlitt, William, 32, 35, 119, 165, 169, 189, 245, 254, 275, 278, 291-2
Heath-Stubbs, John, 197
Hegel, G. W. F., 272, 275, 280-4, 286-7, 289, 291, 293
Herder, J. G., 275, 285-6, 289, 294
Herrick, Robert, 148
Hobbes, Thomas, 272, 291
Homer, 169
Hooker, Richard, 193
Hopkins, Gerard Manley, 295
Howard, John, 193
Hugo, Victor, 278
Hulme, T. E., 293
Hume, David, 272
Hunt, Leigh, 12, 41, 131, 166, 235, 244
Hutcheson, Francis, 272

Ibsen, Henrik, 20
Ingres, Jean, 293

Jacobi, Friedrich, 272
James, Henry, 18, 30
Johnson, Samuel, 32, 276, 285, 289
Jowett, Benjamin, 173
Joyce, James, 20

Kant, Immanuel, 32, 272-7, 280-3, 287-92
Keats, Fanny, 33, 181
Keats, George, 70, 86, 115, 128, 169, 178, 189, 244, 261, 267
Keats, Georgiana, 70, 86, 115, 169, 178, 193-4, 261, 267
Keats, Tom, 2, 70-4, 76, 189, 243
Knox, Ronald, 4, 7

Lamb, Charles, 294
Lawrence, D. H., 20, 47
Leopardi, Giacomo, 280, 290
Lessing, G. E., 294
Lovejoy, A. O., 6, 11
Lyell, Charles, 90

Marinetti, F. T., 293
Maxwell, J. C., 17
Milton, John, 83-4, 90, 100, 118, 162-4, 189
Morris, William, 235
Murry, J. M., 248

Newton, Isaac, 286
Nietzsche, F. W., 272
Novalis (F. L. von Hardenberg), 291

Owen, Wilfred, 269

Pascal, Blaise, 289
Pater, Walter, 292
Petrarch, 12
Pirandello, Luigi, 22
Plato, 117-20, 193, 283
Plutarch, 4
Pope, Alexander, 271
Pound, Ezra, 293
Poussin, Gaspard, 241
Proust, Marcel, 20
Pushkin, A. S., 291

Reynolds, Jane, 114-15
Reynolds, John Hamilton, 3, 61, 64-6, 79-81, 90, 100, 103, 166-7, 197, 260
Reynolds, Joshua, 285
Rice, James, 3
Robinson, Henry Crabb, 285-6
Rollins, H. E., 1
Rossetti, D. G., 173
Rousseau, Jean-Jacques, 5, 271-280, 284-93

Schelling, Friedrich, 32, 272, 283, 288-9, 292
Schiller, J. C. F., 284, 291-2, 295
Schlegel, A. W., 291
Schlegel, Friedrich, 279, 291
Schleiermacher, Friedrich, 272
Schopenhauer, Arthur, 272
Scott, Walter, 292
Severn, Joseph, 35, 268
Shaftesbury, third earl of, 272, 275, 294
Shakespeare, William, 4, 9-10, 16-20, 32, 52-3, 75-6, 81, 113, 151, 162, 197-9, 270-1, 278-9, 285, 289, 291
Shelley, Percy Bysshe, 5, 26, 35, 47, 52, 189-90, 192, 278, 282, 294-5
Sophocles, 160
Southey, Robert, 290
Spencer, Herbert, 90
Spenser, Edmund, 52, 140, 150
Spinoza, Benedict, 276, 289
Staël, Mme. de, 276
Stendhal (Henri Beyle), 292
Swinburne, Algernon Charles, 258

Taylor, John, 2, 28, 48-9, 137, 166, 243-4
Tennyson, Lord, 90, 215, 295
Tighe, Mary, 166
Tolstoi, Leo, 19-20

Van Gogh, Vincent, 209
Vergil, 224, 271, 280
Vico, Gambattista, 289
Voltaire, François, 271, 287, 289

Walpole, Horace, 271
Wellek, René, 6, 11
Whitley, Alvin, 9
Wilde, Oscar, 35, 232
Wittgenstein, Ludwig, 170
Woodhouse, P. G., 30
Woodhouse, Richard, 8-9, 20, 35, 38, 60, 70, 96, 98, 107, 134, 167, 197, 243-5, 262, 266
Wordsworth, William, 5-6, 10-11, 17-18, 32, 58, 66, 89-90, 100-1, 118, 131, 159, 162, 190, 278-9, 284-8, 290, 294

Young, Edward, 232

INDEX OF KEATS'S POEMS

Autumn, To, 16, 33, 53, 57, 71, 85, 124, 135, 150, 154, 168, 172, 201, 204, 216, 221, 224-8, 230-1, 260

Bright star! 40, 43, 135, 203, 230-2

Calidore, 7, 13, 54, 124, 153, 194

Cap and Bells, The, 71, 122, 151, 260

Dear Reynolds . . . , 64-7, 79-81, 90, 172, 207-10

Endymion, 2, 8, 11, 13-14, 15, 28, 33, 41, 48-57, 61-4, 67-70, 73, 75, 79, 85-90, 99, 103, 127-52, 162, 166-71, 173-93, 196, 198-204, 207, 211-12, 217-18, 224, 226-7, 246, 259, 294

Eve of St. Agnes, 1, 16, 29, 33, 38-40, 53-4, 61, 73, 126, 150-2, 155-6, 180, 183, 186-7, 220-1, 226, 229, 232-48, 250, 257, 262

Eve of St. Mark, 13, 16, 73, 115-16, 261-3

Ever let the Fancy roam . . . , 217

Fairy's Song, 25

Fanny, Ode to, 40

Grecian Urn, Ode on a, 13, 66, 84-5, 154-5, 164, 172, 176, 216, 219-26, 230-1, 237, 259, 264-5, 268, 295

Had I a man's fair form . . . , 127

Hadst thou liv'd . . . , 21

How fever'd is the man . . . , 265-7

Hyperion, 47, 57-8, 69-91, 95, 97, 100, 102, 105-12, 114-16, 121, 131-2, 137, 142, 144-5, 151, 159-64, 170, 209-14, 226, 247, 259, 294

Hyperion, The Fall of, 14, 21, 33, 91-105, 107-14, 121, 125, 131-2, 137, 142, 145, 151, 159-64, 170, 209-10, 214, 216, 218, 247, 259

I stood tip-toe . . . , 12, 75, 123-6, 146, 153, 195

In a drear-nighted December . . . , 8-9, 35-41, 219

Isabella, 13-31, 38, 73, 132, 152, 229-30, 235-7, 244-6, 259

King Stephen, 151

La Belle Dame sans Merci, 175-7, 178, 182-3, 194, 230, 248, 260, 269

Lamia, 13, 33, 73, 115-16, 148, 171-2, 178, 180, 188, 224, 228-9, 242-60, 263, 265-6

Light feet . . . , 126

Melancholy, Ode on, 13, 21, 27-30, 85, 103, 116, 124, 133, 149, 204, 206, 209, 216, 221, 228, 231, 234, 259, 263-4, 268

Much have I travell'd . . . , 71, 156-9, 161, 214, 230

Nightingale, Ode to a, 1, 16, 33, 43, 55, 100, 112, 124, 133, 143, 166-8, 172, 176-7, 204, 210, 215-16, 218-19, 221-3, 225, 230, 237, 268

Nymph of the downward smile . . . , 152-3

On Receiving a Curious Shell, 125

On Seeing the Elgin Marbles, 162

Otho the Great, 73, 126, 151, 206, 227-8, 260

Poems, 1817, 11, 122-7, 129-31, 134, 152-8, 194-6, 225

Psyche, Ode to, 21, 141, 143, 150, 154, 165-8, 171, 204-8, 210, 216, 221, 237-8, 240-1, 264, 268

Sleep and Poetry, 21, 40-8, 53, 55-6, 64-7, 79, 84, 90-1, 98, 101-2, 119, 123-5, 130-1, 147, 154, 171, 194-5, 202, 216, 246

Song of Four Fairies, 13

Specimen of an Induction to a Poem, 12, 124

Spenser! a jealous honourer . . . , 195

Standing aloof . . . , 135

Time's sea . . . , 197-9, 230

To B. R. Haydon, 162

To Charles Cowden Clarke, 14, 125, 154, 195

To George Felton Mathew, 122, 124, 136

To Lord Byron, 147

To My Brother George, 13, 123, 125

To Sleep, 42, 61, 230

To Some Ladies, 154

What can I do . . . ? 177-8

What is there . . . ? 202

When I have fears . . . , 75

Why did I laugh tonight? 202, 266